Architectural Representation and the Perspective Hinge

Architectural Representation and the Perspective Hinge

Alberto Pérez-Gómez
Louise Pelletier

The MIT Press Cambridge, Massachusetts London, England

First MIT Press paperback edition, 2000

© 1997 Massachusetts Institute of Technology

This book was set in Meta and Bembo by Graphic Composition, Inc., and was printed and bound in the United States of America.

Library of Congress Cataloging-in-Publication Data
Pérez Gómez, Alberto, 1949–
    Architectural representation and the perspective hinge / Alberto
Pérez-Gómez, Louise Pelletier.
      p.   cm.
    ISBN 978-0-262-16169-5 (hc. : alk. paper)—978-0-262-66113-3 (pb. : alk. paper)
    1. Architectural drawing.   2. Perspective.   I. Pelletier, Louise,
1963– . II. Title.
NA2700.P4   1997
720′.22′2—dc21   97-11186
                                                      CIP

10 9 8 7 6 5 4 3

For Beatriz

C o n t e n t s

pages vi–xi

Prelude

pages 2–87

Mapping the Question: The Perspective Hinge

Variation One

pages 88–175

Architectural Representation and the Distorted Image

89 ~ **Against a progressive history of the image.** The use of projections in antiquity: Ptolemy. 97 ~ *Scenographia* **and optical correction from Vitruvius to Perrault.** Euclid's *Optics* and the priority of embodied experience. 105 ~ **Model and scenography.** From mode and module to scale model. 111 ~ *Sciographia* **and projected shadows.** Barbaro and Scamozzi: the architectural section as shadow or imprint. The objectification and systematization of shadows in perspective. 125 ~ **The extent of infinity.** Girard Desargues's projective geometry and Juan Caramuel de Lobkowitz's theories: two frameworks for the use of projection in architecture. 138 ~ **Relocating anamorphosis.** The initial disjunction of undistorted presence and distorted appearance: from magical manipulation to innocuous game. 149 ~ **Constructing a distorted order.** Desargues's projection as totalizing vision. Caramuel de Lobkowitz's *architectura oblicua:* a "strange" symbolic order. 158 ~ **When the center becomes peripheral.** Distorted appearance as a denial of perspective depth. 161 ~ **The confrontation between theory and practice.** Guarino Guarini's critique of Caramuel.

Variation Two

Cosmological Perspectives

---

177 ~ **Setting the world in motion.** The implications of a Copernican world-view. 185 ~ **Redefining a hierarchical universe.** Johann Heinrich Lambert's cosmological theory. 195 ~ **Recentering the world.** Lambert's reversible perspective theory and his perspectograph. 205 ~ **The eccentric point of view.** Lambert's perspective and its relationship to *quadratura* and *scena per angolo*. 214 ~ **Perspective *fantaisies*.** Jean-Laurent Legeay's disrupted perspective space. 227 ~ **A world of scientific light and objective shadows.** The beginning of scientific photometry. 230 ~ **Framing the Earth.** From mythical maps of temporalized space to Lambert's modern cartography. 243 ~ **Cosmological volumes.** The (Platonic) architectural structure of the cosmos: a theme for early parallel projection in Renaissance and Baroque perspective treatises. 266 ~ **Truth as measurement: fortifications and isometry.** Representation in Renaissance and baroque treatises on fortification. Filarete, Simon Stevin, Vauban, and others. Perspective as a military discipline in the eighteenth century. Back to natural perspective: the fusion of perspective and mechanistic optics. Different consequences of the "naturalization" of perspective.

Variation Three

The Image without an Observer in a Scopophilic World

Coda

371 ~ **Projection revisited: the reversibility of optics.** Projection revisited in art and cinematography. The chiasm of light and shadow as the site of truth. 377 ~ **Digital space.** The potential of absolute fluidity and the pitfalls of increasing fixation and reduction. 383 ~ **Philosophical corollary.** The world as technology. *De architectura* in ten notes.

Illustrations

Variation One

Architectural Representation and the Distorted Image

Variation Two

Cosmological Perspectives

Variation Three

The Image without an Observer in a Scopophilic World

Coda

Acknowledgments

A long project such as this accumulates innumerable debts. We have been fortunate to be able to work in the challenging academic context of the History and Theory of Architecture Graduate Program at McGill University in Montreal. We are grateful to our colleagues and students, both locally and internationally, for many conversations and discussions on the topic of architectural representation. Deserving special mention are Professor Dalibor Vesely of Cambridge University, for his Socratic introduction to the subject; Professor Juhani Pallasmaa of Helsinki University, for his insights into modern art and its relationships to architecture; and Professors Marco Frascari, Joseph Rykwert, and David Leatherbarrow from the University of Pennsylvania, Professor Detlef Mertins from the University of Toronto, and Professor Karsten Harries from Yale University, for their specific suggestions. We have learned much about what is actually possible in contemporary architecture from distinguished practitioners, artists, and thinkers, such as John Hejduk, Daniel Libeskind, Steven Holl, Yasuo Yoshida, Katsuhiko Muramoto, Richard and Gregory Henriquez, Peter Eisenman, Sverre Fehn, Dan Hoffman, and Svein Tønsager. Conversations with David M. Levin, Philippe Nys, Kurt Forster, and Donald Kunze have also informed this work. Phyllis Lambert's and Roger Conover's life-long commitment to raise the level of architectural discourse has been a great encouragement for the completion of our book. Professor Stephen Parcell from the Technical University of Nova Scotia was our first reader and critic. His rigorous comments were particularly helpful.

A number of research assistants collaborated on the project, particularly in the compilation and annotation of bibliographical sources and graphic material. Our special thanks go to James Aitken, Andrea MacElwee, Joanna Merwood, Stephen Pack, and Tracey Eve Winton.

The resources of both the Blackader-Lauterman Art and Architecture Library at McGill University and the library and special collections of the Canadian Centre for Architecture were crucial for the realization of this project. We would like to thank the staff in both institutions for making our work easier. Deserving of special mention for specific research assistance are Paul Chénier and Gerald Beasley at the CCA. Renata Goodman, also at the CCA, was extremely helpful with translation, as was Martina Kögl, an undergraduate exchange student at McGill. Our appreciation also goes to Susie Spurdens, secretary of the History and Theory Program at the university, for her help with the final version of the bibliography.

We owe a special debt of gratitude to the Social Sciences and Humanities Research Council of Canada, which awarded us a three-year grant to pursue this project. Preliminary bibliographical work was made possible through seed money granted by the Institut de Recherche en Histoire de l'Architecture, an interdisciplinary institute co-funded by the Canadian Centre for Architecture, the Université de Montréal, and McGill University. A sabbatical leave from McGill University made it possible to complete this project in reasonable time.

Architectural Representation and the Perspective Hinge

Prelude

Mapping the Question:
The Perspective Hinge

Only when man becomes like a god and projects
light (and Music) can he truly see clearly and attend
to the disclosure of being.

* * *

Frances C. Lonna, after soloing in a military fighter jet, 1987

Translation vs. Transcription

Experimental video, computer graphics, and virtual images have radically transformed the late-twentieth-century understanding of reality and continue to challenge the complex discourse surrounding visual representation. The fragmentation and temporalization of space initiated by film montage and modernist collage have opened up a truly infinite realm of poetic places for the human imagination, which await their translation into architecture. During the last two decades, the seductive potential of virtual space has expanded beyond all expectations, through both technological breakthroughs and artistic endeavors, yet the architectural profession is still reluctant to question the transparency and homogeneity of its means of representation.

Architectural conception and realization usually assume a one-to-one correspondence between the represented idea and the final building. Absolute control is essential in our technological world. Although drawings, prints, models, photographs, and computer graphics play diverse roles in the design process, they are regarded most often as necessary surrogate or automatic transcriptions of the built work. However, an invisible *perspectival hinge* is always at work between these common forms of representation and the world to which they refer. To disclose appropriate alternatives to the ideological stagnation plaguing most architectural creation at the end of the second millennium, the first crucial step is to acknowledge that value-laden tools of representation underlie the conception and realization of architecture.

The process of creation prevalent in architecture today assumes that a conventional set of projections, at various scales from site to detail, adds up to a complete, objective *idea* of a building. Whether or not the architect is effectively or legally responsible for the production of construction documents (working drawings), the assumption remains. These projective representations rely on reductive syntactic connections; each projection constitutes part of a dissected whole. They are expected to be absolutely unambiguous to avoid possible (mis)interpretations, as well as functioning as efficient neutral instruments devoid of inherent value other than their capacity

0.1a

| 0.1a | 0.1b |

Two computer-generated images from an experimental studio directed by Professor Kent Hubbell at the Department of Architecture, Cornell University (1994–1995). The students, David Nam and Emily Chang, used "Form Z" software to generate work that challenges more conventional applications of similar tools to design.

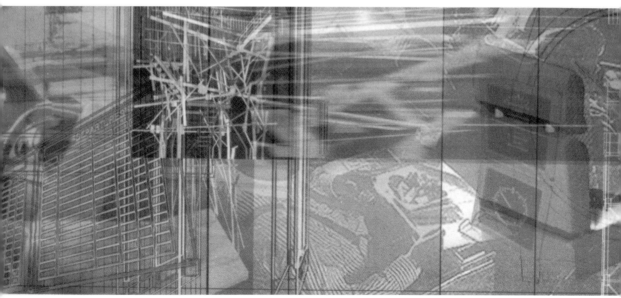

0.1b

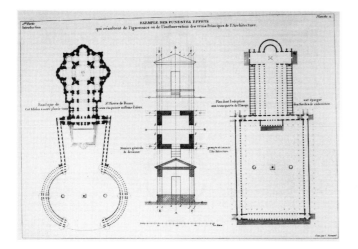

A plate from J.-N.-L. Durand's *Précis des Leçons d'Architecture* (1819). Durand's demonstration of the "correct and effective way to design," illustrated in the center of the plate, shows the precise coordination of plan, section, and elevation, the "set" that constitutes the "objective idea" of a whole building. The comparison between the plans of the pre-Renaissance Basilica of St. Peter in Rome and the modern building from the sixteenth century purports to show the "calamitous effects" evident in the modern example, resulting from the lack of observation of the "true principles of architecture," ultimately epitomized by descriptive geometry.

for accurate transcription. Professional architects generally see architectural drawing in this light.

The descriptive sets of projections that we take for granted operate in a geometrized, homogeneous space that was construed as the "real" space of human action during the nineteenth century. Our implicit trust in the application of a scientific methodology to architecture derives from techniques prescribed by Jacques-Nicolas-Louis Durand in his *Précis des Leçons d'Architecture* (1802 and 1813).[1] Durand's *Mécanisme de la composition* was the first design method to be thoroughly dependent on the predictive capacity of these projections. For him, descriptive geometry was the modus operandi of the architect. Although descriptive geometry promoted simplistic objectification, this projective tool is a complex product of a philosophical tradition and technological worldview that defines the European nineteenth century and leads to our own "world order." It is, therefore, not something we can simply reject or pretend to leave behind. As Hubert Damisch has pointed out recently in his tour de force on the origins of perspective, the destructuring of perspectival depth by the avant-garde in twentieth-century art has not prompted our culture of television and cinema to make the projective distance "a thing of the past."[2] In architecture, as we hope to demonstrate, the focus is rather on defining the nature of a "depth" that the work must engage in order to resist the collapse of the world into cyberspace, a depth that concerns both the spatial or formal character of the work and its programmatic, temporal, or experiential dimension.

Functionalist motivations of our technological world have promoted the pragmatic capacity of architectural drawing over its potential to construe a symbolic order. For architects it is important to remember that a symbol is neither a contrivance nor an invention—nor is it necessarily a representation of absolute truths or transcendental theological values. Symbols embody specific historical and cultural values.[3] While it may be easy to recognize that buildings possess experiential dimensions that cannot be reproduced in a conventional representation, the task of constructing a meaningful built environment for contemporary human action is *not* a simple proposition. Expecting architectural representations to embody a symbolic order—indeed, expecting them to function like any other work of art—will seem controversial unless we revise the common assumptions about art and its relationship to human life that have been with us since the eighteenth century, assumptions that will be examined throughout this book. For architecture the difficulty of manifesting a symbolic order is necessarily double, since it concerns both the project and its "translation"—an unfolding that is seldom present in other arts.

Projective drawing need not be a reductive device, a tool of prosaic substitution. Projection evokes temporality and boundaries. Defining the space between light and darkness, between the Beginning and the Beyond, it illuminates the space of culture, of our individual and collective existence. Closer to the origins of our philosophical history, projection was identified with the space of representation, the site of ontological continuity between universal ideas and specific things. The labyrinth, that primordial image of architectural endeavor, is a projection linking time and place. Representing architectural space as the time of an event, the disclosure of order between birth and death, in the unpredictable temporality of human life itself, projection is literally the hyphen between idea and experience that is the place of culture, the Platonic *chōra*. Like music, realized in time from a more or less "open" notation and inscribed as an act of divination for a potential order, architecture is itself a projection of architectural ideas, horizontal footprints and vertical effigies, disclosing a symbolic order *in time,* through rituals and programs. The architect's task, beyond the transformation of the world into a comfortable or pragmatic shelter, is the making of a physical, formal order that reflects the depth of our human condition, analogous in vision to the interiority communicated by speech and poetry and to the immeasurable harmony conveyed by music.

Since the inception of Western architecture in classical Greece, the architect has not "made" buildings; rather, he or she has made the mediating artifacts that make *significant* buildings possible. These artifacts—from words, to many kinds of inscriptions and drawings, to full-scale mock-ups—and their relation to buildings, however, have not remained constant throughout history. As late as the Renaissance, for example, the only drawings truly "indispensable" for building (from a technological standpoint) were *modani* or template drawings, though these were considered important enough by their authors to be carefully protected from unscrupulous copying.

For architects concerned with ethics and not merely with aesthetic novelty, who seek the realization of places where a fuller, more compassionate human life might take place, that these mediating artifacts and tools be appropriate is paramount. Fortunately, the traces of our own tradition are rich in potential lessons and alternatives. This book offers a collection of historical narratives of different "scales," ranging from the general to the specific. Although we felt it was important to trace the genealogy of the problem of representation from the early discourse on vision and optics—including the complex development of *perspectiva naturalis*—and to relate it to the tools of the architect in the Western tradition, particularly to optical correction (which appears as an issue in all Western architectural theories and dates back to classical antiquity), this work should not be interpreted as a general history of perspective. The plurality and complexity of perspective theories and practices have been made evident by many recent works on the subject.[4] Rather, we chose deliberately to examine a handful of central and marginal figures, both well-known and exceptional works in the history of architectural theory and perspective, that reveal the complexity and potential contradiction inherent in any linear history of representation. While embracing the illuminating differences that appear through historical analysis, we offer a plot that culminates in the last part of the book in a wider philosophical reflection. Our ultimate aim is to probe the possibilities of building architecture as a poetic translation, not a prosaic transcription, of its representations.

Architectural Meaning and the Tools of the Architect

It is our primary assumption that there is an intimate complicity between architectural meaning and the modus operandi of the architect. It must be granted, however, that the meaning of an architectural work is never simply the result of its author's will. Once the work occupies its place in the public realm, a multitude of factors related to context, use, cultural associations, and so forth have an impact on how it is perceived. Nevertheless, the architect cannot abdicate personal responsibility.[5] The changing relationships between the intentions of architectural drawings and the built objects they describe hold important lessons for architects who wish to exercise ethically the personal imagination and construe a better, richer place for human dwelling.[6]

Prior to the Renaissance, architectural drawings were rare, certainly in the sense that is familiar to us. In the Middle Ages, architects did not conceive of a *whole building* and the very notion of *scale* was unknown. Gothic architecture, the most "theoretical" of all medieval building practices, was fundamentally a *constructive* practice, operating through well-established traditions and geometric rules that could be applied directly on site. From the footprint of a building, construction proceeded by rhetoric and geometry, raising the elevation as discussions about the building's face continued, almost until the end. The master mason was responsible for constructing a model of the city of God on earth; but only the Architect of the Universe possessed a comprehensive foreknowledge of the project and was deemed capable of concluding the work at the end of time. The various expressions of Gothic cathedrals were the result of different generations and diverse methods applied by itinerant bands of stone masons who migrated around Europe to work on various building projects. Multiple styles, as in the Cathedral of Chartres, or compromised geometric systems, as in Milan Cathedral, were regarded not as an inconsistency but as a layering of different responses to structural or symbolic problems that arose during the course of construction.[7]

Starting with the Renaissance, we should examine the relationship between architectural drawings and the buildings they describe with greater care than has been customary. From the most important architectural treatises and their respective contexts, it is evident that the maturation from architectural idea to built work was systematized to a degree far less than we now take for granted. During the early Renaissance, the traditional understanding of architecture as a ritual act of construction had not been lost. The concept of a sympathetic universe, thoroughly alive, was dominant throughout the fifteenth and sixteenth centuries. Different orders of reality—from a stone to God, from a point to a three-dimensional solid—were connected by a chain, by erotic links or *vincoli*. While this concept was based on the old Aristotelian cosmology, it was increasingly open to manipulation by magician-architects interested in ensuring a happy life, emulating the order of the heavens.[8] In this cultural context, the "instrumentality" of the tools or drawings of the architect obviously must be qualified. Projecting the geometric physiognomy of a building or city was a prophetic act, a form of conjuring and divining,[9] not merely the personal will of the author. Architectural drawings, therefore, could not be conceived as neutral artifacts that might be transcribed unambiguously into buildings.

But during the fifteenth century, architecture also came to be understood as a liberal art, and architectural ideas were conceived increasingly as geometric *lineamenti,* as ubiquitous two-dimensional, orthogonal drawings. This transformation marks the beginning of a practice that contemporary architects take for granted, and it was related to a new mathematical and geometric rationalization of the image that radically departed from classical (Greco-Arabic) theories of vision.

Theories of Vision and the Reciprocity between Seeing and Being Seen

In the case of flat surfaces lying
below the level of the eye,
the more remote parts appear higher.
In the case of lines extending forward,
those on the right seem to be
inclined toward the left,
and those on the left seem to be
inclined toward the right.

Euclid, "The Optics"

From antiquity to the Middle Ages, many scientists and philosophers sought to understand the phenomenon of vision. The very notion of *theōria,* which accompanied the birth of Western intellectual disciplines in classical Greece, privileged vision over the other senses as a vehicle of knowledge. The corresponding model for Western art, Greek tragedy, implicitly separated the orchestra or stage from the spectators in the amphitheater, signaling the transformation from a world of fully embodied participation in rituals (where human action, regardless of its reflective ethical value, was assumed to be at one with nature) to a world in which the spectator participated vicariously through vision (and hearing). Despite this separation, the citizen still participated knowingly in the order of culture, just as the philosopher and the scientist contemplated the order of the cosmos from a *distance.*

This distance has marked Western civilization, and continues to affect its science and art. It made reflective thought, authorship, and metaphysics possible. It also opened up in Sappho's poetry the bittersweet space of eros—neither absolute lack nor fulfillment—and coincided with the inception of alphabetic writing and the "objectification" of speech. This distance made it possible for "space" itself to become an object of artistic representation, as in the earliest (erotic) novels of our tradition, in which lovers are kept apart until the last page.[10] Named as *chōra,* it is also a "hyphen": Plato's space of ontological continuity, the ground that makes it possible for

Being and beings to relate and to share a name, in language and in human action. This distance, therefore, is what enables *participation* after the inception of the "reflective" individual. While this distance does not anticipate perspective, it is nevertheless a condition for perspective and perspectival epistemologies, that is, philosophical systems in which the constituting ego reduces the presence of reality. This distance, a primary depth rather than a perspective, made it possible for Greek scientists and philosophers to articulate the discourse of geometry and optics, while maintaining the primacy of a reality that is given to human perception in its primary tactile and synesthetic fullness. While *perspectiva artificialis* arises out of a specific cultural horizon (the Renaissance), the discourse on depth and distancing remains crucial for architecture, particularly in the context of a technological world fueled by an obsession to close (or ignore) the space between the body and the world, fulfilling all desires—the utopia of functionalism—and making a disembodied humanity "whole" with a fully "constructed" environment.[11] The quest might be, as some have argued, to usher in a new "mythical" age in which humans, devoid of ego and reflective preoccupations—indeed, like members of archaic ritualistic cultures regarding "nature"—engage technology (our nature) without resentment, as "pure" action, as play and seduction. The question for postmodern humanity is whether the collapse of this distance, which is not reducible to vision but

11

| 0.3 |

The Greek theater at Epidaurus, a sanctuary dedicated to Asclepius, god of medicine. Psychosomatic healing was associated with *katharsis;* it took place through the space of participation, a "distance" disclosed and bridged by the dancing chorus, located literally between the spectators sitting in the amphitheater and the permanent stage buildings.

Photo by A. Pérez-Gómez.

retains a visual dimension (best characterized as perspectival en-framing—the depth of virtual reality), will not signal a loss of the possibility of acting ethically and compassionately. However difficult it may be to bear, operating in the frustrating bitter-sweet space of desire, the personal imagination is perhaps our finest accomplishment as a species; it is the medium of ethics and our best assurance against self-destruction.

Thus we may start to articulate the complex genealogy of the problem that concerns us. In Western thought, the mysti-cal and scientific imagery of light can be traced back to the myth of the cave in Plato's *Republic,* where he states that a knowledge of eternal forms may be acquired from the imperfect material world by a process analogous to vision. Blaming Plato for our own ocularocentrism would be inaccurate; nevertheless, the belief in the importance of vision was firmly entrenched in the Western tradition during the Middle Ages. Philosophizing within an Aristotelian and Christian framework, Thomas Aqui-nas asserted that the objective basis for beauty was cognition, centered mainly in the senses of sight and hearing: "Good is the object of desire[;] . . . beauty, on the other hand, is the object of cognitive power, for we call beautiful things which give plea-sure when they are seen." For Aquinas, there was no greater pleasure than true knowledge, the discovery of orientation and a sense of purpose in a hostile and disorienting universe. For this reason, he believed that art should imitate not the appearance of nature but rather the very purposefulness of the universe, the "intelligence that moves toward sure goals by definite means." [12]

Ancient and medieval theories of vision did not evolve from a concern with representing an autonomous visual world. Such a concept was simply inconceivable before Kepler's dis-cussion of the retinal image and before post-Cartesian psychol-ogy. Premodern theories, therefore, were never motivated by a concern with formal appearance that we may associate with the post-Renaissance understanding of the fine arts, especially painting, sculpture, and architecture as they are commonly viewed today. *Perspectiva naturalis,* the discipline of optics or the science of sight, was first elaborated fully by Euclid in the third century B.C.E. It was related specifically to mathematics and was often used as a means of grasping the physical and metaphysical structure of reality, whose essence was believed to be similar to light.[13] In *perspectiva naturalis,* things could be conceived as luminous geometric relations that followed the laws of radial diffusion. Later, in the Middle Ages, this would suggest a "clear" understanding of theological truths.

Euclid assumed that light traveled in straight lines and observed the geometric laws governing reflection and refraction. In his *Optica,* he demonstrates how the appearance of objects is a function of their relationship to the observer, a relationship that could be expressed accurately through geometry. In the ever-changing, irregular, and imprecise world of human experience prior to the scientific revolution, this precision was a unique characteristic for a wondrous phenomenon such as vision, and it had a long-lasting impact on European intellectual and practical disciplines. It also revealed that what a person *experienced* did not always coincide with what he or she *saw.* Theories that elaborated on Euclid's demonstrations dealt mainly with three aspects of vision: physical or philosophical questions about the propagation of images toward the soul; mathematical questions about the geometric perception of objects in lived space; and, particularly during the Middle Ages, medical questions about the anatomy of the eye, whose answers would aid in treating disease.[14] For Euclid, the eye was an active participant in the phenomenon of vision rather than a passive receptor. His theory confirmed a popular understanding of perception that did not abstract the senses or conceive of human subjectivity and the world as emancipated, autonomous entities.[15] Tales like the one reporting that Scythian women "have two pupils in each eye and kill people by sight if they happen to look at them when angry" were repeated by Roman writers such as Pliny the Elder and medieval philosophers such as Roger Bacon.[16]

Plato's theory of vision, included in *Timaeus* as part of his geometric cosmology, was relatively undeveloped, yet it was the point of departure for subsequent elaborations in the Western tradition.[17] He thought that a light flows from our eyes, a subtle fire similar to the light of the sun. When exterior light is fused with the inner light flowing from the eyes, luminosity is strengthened and we can perceive the colors of visible objects.[18] This is an insightful metaphor of reality as neither a purely subjective construct nor an objective fact but as something in between, in the *metaxy* that is the realm of ontological continuity and human experience. Plato's theory suggests that humans partake of the light of the heavenly luminaries, which are endowed with eternal (mathematical) motion, and that this communion occurs through vision. Aristotle objected to the theory of visual light emanating from the eye and argued against the corporeal nature of light. He agreed, however, that the transparent nature of light creates a continuous medium between the eye and the object and allows motions (i.e., colors) to be transmitted to the observer's mind. Alexander of Aphrodisias, also concerned with defining the nature of this medium, called this mixture of air and fire *pneuma* (breath, spirit) and explained sight as a "stress of air" at the base of the cone of vision.[19] Despite their differences, all of these theories emphasized the medium between the observer and the visible object as the *reality* of visual experience, regardless of whether substance "flows" in either direction.

Medieval writers engaged in a polemic between extromission theories, inspired mainly by Plato and Euclid, and intromission theories, originating in Democritus's atomism and in Epicurean philosophy. Intromission theories argued that the observer passively receives luminous matter or rays. Al-Kindi's ninth-century optical treatise, *De aspectibus,* was an elaboration of Euclid's *Optics,* while the tenth-century Arab scientists Avicenna and Al-Hazen, more influenced by Aristotle, preferred intromission. Avicenna argued that the crystalline lens in the eye acts like a mirror, receiving the form of things in its anterior flattened surface before transferring them to the soul. Al-Hazen also defended intromission theory in his *Perspectiva,* noting that the eye is hurt by exceedingly bright lights. From Euclid he took the geometry of the visual cone and denied the "physical reality" of the visual rays, but related the phenomenon of vision to a passive observer.[20] In his theory, the act of perception occurs in the human head, and not in the space between the object and the eye.

In the thirteenth century, Roger Bacon and Robert Grosseteste were influenced by Al-Hazen, but they never accepted his intromission theory.[21] Bacon explicitly merged the act of seeing with the act of being seen, arguing that a mirror image of one's face would be inconceivable unless "a species issued from the eye were returned to the eye."[22] John Pecham, Witelo, and Grosseteste, the most important writers on *perspectiva naturalis* in the late Middle Ages, all agreed with Bacon. Coincidentally, they also shared a theological interest in *lumen* and *lux,* the divine light emanating throughout the universe. In the Neoplatonic metaphysics of light, particularly the writings of Pseudo-Dionysius the Areopagite, dioptrics (the science of refraction) and catoptrics (the science of reflection) associated beauty with truth, as the luster of God was manifested through anagogy in the experiential world.[23] St. Augustine (354–430) had reiterated the classical notion that musical harmony is conducive to beauty and had associated it with the works of the Christian Creator: "God is the archetypal light, the sensible light is the imitation."[24] Grosseteste marveled at light as the supreme manifestation of God and held that its luster, color, and mathematical properties culminated in a divine unity. In his commentary on Pseudo-Dionysius's *Divine Names,* Grosseteste defined light as the greatest and best of all proportions, as it is proportionate with itself. This identity was the basis for the indivisible beauty of God, "for God is supremely simple, supremely concordant and appropriate to Himself."[25] Like St. Augustine, Grosseteste extrapolated the notion of visual beauty from the beauty of music derived from simple numerical proportions. He held that the material world first appears as light; its form, therefore, results from the radiation of light. Since light radiates in straight lines, it gives the world a regular, geometrical shape; thus beauty appears through form.[26] St. Bonaventure (Giovanni di Fidanza, 1221–1274), whose writings influenced the program of Franciscan church architecture, expressed it even more poetically: "Light is common by nature to all bodies, celestial and terrestrial. . . . Light is the substantial form of bodies; by their greater or lesser participation in light, bodies acquire the truth and dignity of their being."[27]

We must emphasize that while *perspectiva naturalis* sought to clarify human vision, it was concerned not with representation but with understanding the modes of God's presence; it was part of the quadrivium of liberal arts. In Pseudo-Dionysius's mystical writings, sensible light leads to the contemplation of absolute darkness, the true place of God. The appearance of a painting or a building was not an end in itself.

Significantly, Thomas Aquinas associated *perspectiva naturalis* with harmony in music, never with drawing or any other graphic method. Humanity lived literally *in* the light of God, under God's benevolent gaze. This was the light of the golden heaven of Byzantine frescoes and mosaics, as well as the sublime and vibrantly colored space of Gothic cathedrals, a light whose multiplicity, like voices in a musical composition, was the very condition for the unity of its metaphysical concordance.[28] In both cases, the concordant light reconciled multiple colors into the harmony of the One and contributed to the geometric order of Heavenly Jerusalem on earth. In Hagia Sophia and Chartres Cathedral, for example, light dematerializes the geometric structure of the building and challenges our expectation of gravity. The breath-light of God fills the spaces and miraculously seems to make these immense structures stand. In this context the manifestation of God's presence is not an aesthetic object but an epiphany in *time:* in the time of ritual and the sermon, in the time of speech rather than the written word, in the ordered human temporality epitomized by rhythm, eurythmy, and harmony.

From Natural Perspective to Artificial Construction

The concepts of perspective that emerged in the early Renaissance retained implicit connections with classical optics, particularly with its theological and gnoseological connotations of vision and the symbolism of light. Some contemporary writers have noted a discontinuity between "geometrical optics" and *perspectiva artificialis,* because the latter does not "imitate vision,"[29] but the real issue concerns truth as the ultimate goal of art, at least until the inception of aesthetics in the eighteenth century. Since the Renaissance, writers on perspective and architecture have always tried to reconcile their geometric constructions with traditional optics; their frequent incapacity to do so poignantly revealed potential contradictions inherent in their new forms of hegemonic visual representation. This complex genealogy that characterized the emergence of perspective theories from traditional optics is particularly important as we try, in the present work, to tell the story of perspective as a *hinge* for architectural representation, examining a transforming relationship between practice and theory, between the making of images and the making of buildings, and thus telling a story that is necessarily different from other related accounts whose focus has been restricted to painting.[30]

Nicholas of Cusa's *De Visione Dei* (1453), for example, applied a geometric concept of the visual cone to a theological discussion. The text was intended to accompany an icon of God, elucidating the relationship between geometric vision and sacred representation.[31] After observing how the icon seems to behold everything around it and seems to follow us in a personal way, regardless of our changing location, Cusanus reiterates the Neoplatonic belief that men shall enter the icon's most sacred darkness in order to sense the presence of "Inaccessible Light." The icon enables us to contemplate eternal life as in a mirror, because "eternal life is only [His] blessed gaze," by which He never ceases looking upon us most lovingly, "even to the point of beholding the most intimate recesses of [our] soul" (4, pp. 14ff.). At issue is the substantial difference between human and divine sight. In God, according to Cusanus, "seeing is not other than hearing, tasting, smelling, touching, perceiving, and understanding" (3, pp. 10ff.). The Absolute Gaze of God is a sign of Absolute Love (4, pp. 14ff.). God's sight is infinite and all-encompassing, while human vision is conditioned by the body's location and by its imperfections and passions. Nevertheless, "Absolute Sight is present in all seeing, since all contracted sight exists through Absolute Sight and cannot exist without it." Furthermore, Cusanus asserts that "God's seeing is His being seen by us" (5, pp. 19ff.).

While Cusanus grasped some of the principles of geometric projection that regulate the experience of depth in the world, he emphasized that only God has access to a ubiquitous center of convergence, and therefore only He can possess the vision of truth. For God alone, sight is truly "the eye. . . . For the eye is like a mirror; and a mirror, however small, figuratively receives into itself [all things]" (8, pp. 34ff.). Human beings, of course, do not share this experience, because our sight is imperfect. Aiming at perfection, the sacred representation is not a "construction" of the world as it is presented to the (human) eye; it is rather an all-encompassing mirror image of the world, made accessible by the vision of God. The image "implies" an infinite point, but it is *inaccessible* to the human viewer because it is *antithetical* to the human condition. Cusanus's concept is consistent with his better-known geometric definition of God, in *De Docta Ignorantia,* as a "circle whose center is ubiquitous," implicitly associating God with geometric infinity. Consequently, the Renaissance privileged human works regulated by geometric forms that approximate God's perfection, such as centralized churches, temples, villas, and cities. Cusanus's *scientia* revealed a basic framework for Renaissance art and culture. His declaration of the importance of human knowledge, a geometric *scientia* applied to Christian dogma, was a profound innovation that distinguished this work from previous medieval theology. Cusanus's philosophy reveals both the new position of man poised to transform the world and his renewed humility in the face of a newly found responsibility: man's vision (and knowledge) is reciprocal, but it is not commensurate with God's vision.

From a purely technical point of view, Renaissance linear perspective could be postulated independently of traditional optical theories.[32] While the "continuity" between *perspectiva naturalis* and *perspectiva artificialis* was noticed by some artists, only Lorenzo Ghiberti, in his *Commentaries* (ca. 1445–1450), took the trouble to summarize medieval optical theories as a precedent of linear perspective.[33] Euclid's *Optics* had a greater impact on perspective writers with an interest in mathematics, such as Piero della Francesca in the fifteenth century and Egnatio Danti, Federigo Commandino, Daniele Barbaro, and Guidobaldo del Monte in the sixteenth.[34] Artists, on the other hand, were more interested in empirical rules of perspective. In a manuscript of Euclid's *Optics* found in the library of Federigo da Montefeltro, duke of Urbino, which was probably known to Piero della Francesca and his circle,[35] there is evidence of a literal identification of Euclid's visual cone and the pyramid of Alberti's *costruzione legittima.* Clearly, *perspectiva naturalis* was never absent from the artists' consciousness, and this accounts for the complexity of discussions about perspective in architectural representation.[36] The distinction between an artist's use of perspective to construct a picture and a beholder's perception of the result became more marked after the late fifteenth century.[37] In the early seventeenth century, however, Guidobaldo del Monte was the first to seriously consider the position of the observer, the distance to the object, and the angle of view as points of departure for a perspective construction, which would enable the eye to take in the object in a single glance. This awareness of the embodied observer as an element in perspective construction was absent in earlier writings, in which the observer and the viewing distance remained implicit.[38] During the fifteenth and the sixteenth centuries, optical theories based on the primacy of synesthetic perception (including constant motion, binocular vision, and tactile perception) could not be reconciled with an increasingly reductive geometric representation of the visual world. This could finally happen only when the very assumptions of what constitutes the truth of reality, radically transformed by the philosophers and scientists of the scientific revolution, became a cultural belief in the early nineteenth century, and the modern scientific optics of subjectivity was born.

In the fifteenth century, *perspectiva artificialis* had distanced itself from the tradition of classical optics in order to develop a coherent mathematical discourse in line with the quadrivium. Writers explicitly downplayed philosophical questions concerning the propagation of visual rays and the movement of an image from an object to the mind. In book 1 of *De Pictura,* Alberti writes: "Indeed among the ancients, there was considerable dispute as to whether these rays emerge from the surface of the eye. This truly difficult question, which is quite without value for our purposes, may here be set aside."[39] In accordance with the Renaissance pyramid of vision (inherited from the Euclidean notion of the visual cone), a perspective image was regarded as a window on the world, although many still believed that the eye projects its visual rays onto an object and that perception is a dynamic action of the beholder upon the world.[40] In fact, Filarete imagined the eye as a magnet, attracting images during the day and becoming incapacitated at night. In his architectural treatise (1460–1464), Filarete wrote that darkness acts upon vision like dampness on a lodestone, impeding the perception of visual rays and, with it, our capacity to see in perspective. The order of the built world had to endure the absence of light, literally and metaphorically—this was

0.4

Illustration of optical correction from Jean Martin's first French edition of Vitruvius's *De architectura* (1547). The importance of optical correction is a pervasive discussion in treatises from Vitruvius to the eighteenth century, probably originating in Euclid's *Optics*. Optical correction compensates for the "weakness" of sight, in order for buildings to appear perfectly proportioned as we experience them synesthetically, with all our senses.

never an insignificant problem before the advent of illuminating gas and electricity.

For Renaissance artists and architects, one of the most important sources was *De architectura,* by the Roman architect Vitruvius (first century B.C.E.). Vitruvius had discussed optical correction in architecture as a corollary of the Euclidean cone of vision, demonstrating an awareness of the dimensional distortions brought about by the position of an observer and his visual angle. As evident in great examples of classical architecture, the aim was to *avoid distorted perception* caused by the position of an observer (by increasing the size of lettering placed high on an architrave, for example) and to convey perfectly regular proportions to the observer's synesthetic perception, always primarily tactile. Throughout the Renaissance, perception did not change substantially. When queried about parallel lines, anyone would have answered that in the world of action these lines obviously *never* meet. The hypothesis of a vanishing point at infinity was both unnecessary for the construction of perspective and inconceivable in the perceptual reality of everyday life. The central point (*punto centrico*) of Alberti's perspective construction often is associated wrongly with such a "vanishing point." In fact, the point of convergence in his *costruzione legittima* is defined as a "countereye" on the "window" (or, in contemporary terms, as the central point on the picture plane).

Throughout Alberti's treatise, sight occurs explicitly in a *finite* world. This qualification is crucial for our argument, as we try to demonstrate that Renaissance architects were not ready to accept *perspectiva artificialis* as a means to generate the design of a building, either as a system or as a form of predictive visualization.[41] It has recently been suggested that *perspectiva artificialis* can be explained not as a progressive move toward "pictorial naturalism" but as a form of "architectural representation," which arose as a topographic technique for surveying.[42] During the early Renaissance, measuring the world's physical and cultural features was a crucial, novel activity that interested many architects like Filippo Brunelleschi, Filarete, and Francesco di Giorgio. The constellation of artistic practices, including painting, perspective, architecture, and surveying, was driven by a search for truth and by a desire to reveal the "measured" reality of the world of experience. However, the relationship among these disciplines cannot be reduced to an instrumental matter of cause and effect. The Sienese Francesco di Giorgio Martini, for example, being primarily a painter and designer of fortifications, includes a short section on perspective in a chapter on mensuration in one of his *trattati* on *Architettura, Ingegneria e Arte Militare*. This chapter teaches the measurement of surfaces and volumes, of unknown heights, depths, or distances, through triangulation; and in this context perspective (proportional relationships) is introduced as a technical device rather than as a tool of representation.[43] Indeed, we may surmise that while maintaining the primacy of the world "as given," the Renaissance practitioners insisted on promoting painting to the realm of the liberal arts and giving new dignity to vision as a means of acquiring truth in the sublunar world of human experience. Triangulation methods in surveying obviously link with orthographic representations the observed ruins or topographic accidents that were of interest for architects, surveyors, and military architects. The awareness of the mathematical properties of proportional triangles (gained from Euclid) certainly played an important part in the new perspectival understanding of relative size in relation to distance. This does not mean, however, that a correspondence between orthographic drawings and perspective representations simply can be taken for granted.

In the fifteenth century, the growing fascination of painters with linear perspective did not lead to a geometric systematization of pictorial depth, nor did it instrumentalize the process of architectural creation. The world of everyday experience relied on qualitatively distinct places and poetic narratives that integrated the golden age of antiquity with the current cosmological order. Homogeneous space could exist only in the supralunar realm, where the regular motions of heavenly bodies provided a normative order for auspicious action in the human realm of constant change and corruption. The "windows" of perspective paintings were punctual ontological epiphanies whose degree of geometric abstraction was a considerable innovation. Fifteenth-century painters also used mirrors as flattening devices to present this geometrized depth that was not evident to the naked eye. The technique suggested an underlying complicity between optics and perspective. Brunelleschi, Alberti,

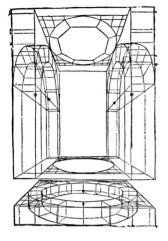

| 0.5 |

A perspective construction of architectural elements, from Serlio's *Five Books of Architecture* (1545).

and Filarete all invoked the use of mirrors to demonstrate the "truth" of perspective.

There were, of course, important connections between the painters' experiments and the architects' concern with creating geometric order in the human domain. The painters' interest in mathematical depth and human events was manifested most clearly in paintings that told a story in an architectural setting. In exceptional cases, such as the well-known "ideal city" panels,[44] painters presented the architecture of public spaces without a *storia,* as if they were scenographic backdrops awaiting inhabitation. Architects often were also painters; boundaries between the liberal arts were fluid, as disciplinary specialization did not exist. Sebastiano Serlio was the first architectural writer to include a full chapter on perspective, and in the opening pages of the second book of his treatise (1545) he insists that the best architects of his time all began as painters and that consequently a knowledge of the *costruzione legittima* was crucial for architects. However, he states clearly that *perspectiva artificialis* was used primarily by painters and by architects who design theatrical stage sets or *tableaux vivants* for urban rituals, and he differentiates between a perspective for painters to be used on "flat walls" and one for architects or scenographers

| 0.6 |

The tragic stage, from Serlio's *Five Books of Architecture.*

| 0.7 |

"to be realized materially and in relief."[45] After Serlio's chapter culminates with his famous presentation of different stages appropriate for the three genres of classical theater, throughout the rest of his treatise no further mention is made of perspective in architectural design.

These complexities have obscured the role of linear perspective techniques in fifteenth-century architecture. The *costruzione legittima,* developed by Brunelleschi and Alberti for the art of painting, was associated with architecture primarily because the regular geometry of architectural subjects enabled perspective depth to appear, and less obviously because of the quasi-magical generative power attributed to mathematics and proportionality in revealing the secret structure of the cosmos. Indeed, perspective shared its geometric nature with the newly defined *lineamenti,* the drawings that effectively turned Renaissance architecture from a medieval construction into a liberal art. According to Alberti, the *lineamenti* enabled the full geometric idea of a future building (specifically the plan and the facade) to be conceived in the mind's eye of the architect. By the mid-sixteenth century the relationship was becoming so complex that Claudius Tolomeis and Pomponio Gauricus insisted on the need to distinguish architectural drawing from sculpture and painting,[46] although it is precisely an unwillingness to accept such a distinction that characterizes Michelangelo's extraordinary production. During the Renaissance, geometry was not a purely formal, abstract discipline, while drawing was always *more* than geometry. Geometric order could appear in art and nature, in the space of ontological continuity increasingly identified with the realm of human action (art and construction), although its essence still belonged to the absolute and precise supralunar realm of the divine. Not surprisingly, Andrea Palladio's treatise included idealized versions of his own villas that reveal harmonic "proportionality" while disregarding

The "Ideal City" attributed to the school of Piero della Francesca (early 16th c.) was conceived as part of the furnishings near the *studiolo* in Urbino's Ducal Palace. This painting located in Urbino is one of three similar existing works (the others are in Baltimore and Berlin) that excludes narrative. The Ideal City certainly evokes silence. Like other Renaissance ornamental works such as *intarsia,* it is *about* that which can be geometrized, the constructive realm of human culture. It seems to exclude the glance that glances back, suspending time or rather dissolving it in space. As a framework for human action, these representations disclose a mystery related to the new liberal arts and their power to transform the world. The emphatic bilateral symmetry of the Ideal City speaks not of a qualitative identity of left and right, construed as a typical characteristic of architectural order, but rather of the bilaterally symmetrical structure of the human body as a privileged site of such order—a structure for which left and right were still, in the context of Renaissance culture, qualitatively distinct. In the Renaissance, human life itself provided a script for the drama they framed. Regardless of their actual status regarding the practice of scenography, these architectural perspectives were site-specific and framed "meaningful action" in everyday life.

Trompe l'oeil at Santa Maria presso San Satiro, by Bramante, Milan (1482). This is perhaps the earliest application of *scenographia* or *perspectiva artificialis* to a building project. While this truly exceptional work can be used to demonstrate the implicit homology of three-dimensional and two-dimensional space since the inception of the *costruzione legittima* in the fifteenth century, one should not simply infer a reductive intention or even its cultural possibility. Given the extreme curvature of the wall, the intention may have been to recreate not the apse of a Latin cross, but rather a radial space corresponding to the original central plan of Santa Maria, an experiment on centralization, one of the crucial debates about the nature of Renaissance sacred space that would culminate in the project of St. Peter's in the Vatican and Bramante's own *Tempietto* of San Pietro in Montorio in Rome.

Photos by A. Pérez-Gómez.

0.8

0.9

precise dimensions, as well as an ideal plan of his Basilica at Vicenza that does not indicate a desire to raze and replace the significant medieval building he in fact carefully "renovated."[47] The architects' interest in *perspectiva artificialis* responded to a concern for revealing the geometric dimensionality of experiential depth. This interest was implicitly founded on a belief in the primacy of embodied order over vision alone, and in the revelatory power of mathematical regularity, capable of demonstrating the presence of the transcendental as it framed human action in the sublunar world. In retrospect, this new form of representation was also a first step toward a rationalized visual image, detached from the theocentric medieval universe.[48]

Filippo Brunelleschi is credited with the earliest example of a systematically "constructed" linear perspective (1420). His founding experience has been "reconstructed" by Hubert Damisch through a careful reading of Manetti's biography of Brunelleschi.[49] On a small, rectangular wooden panel, Brunelleschi painted a symmetrical representation of the octagonal baptistery in Florence's Piazza San Giovanni, as seen from the threshold of the Duomo. He then perforated the panel at the vanishing point and asked observers to verify the "correctness" of the representation by looking through the orifice from the *back* of the panel toward a mirror that the observer held in the other hand. Brunelleschi could have constructed the perspective geometrically, although there is no documentary evidence that he did so; most of the inferences point rather to an "inductive" empirical process.[50] Reporting Brunelleschi's experiment in his treatise on architecture (ca. 1460), Filarete emphasized the importance of using a mirror to perceive the flattened image and thus to "discover" a geometric order in the visual world.[51] Regardless, it is obvious that Brunelleschi thought the mirror was needed to see the effect of the panel, *already* constructed in perspective. Furthermore, according to Manetti, Brunelleschi did not paint the sky on the panel; instead he applied a reflecting surface (*ariento brunito*).[52] Following an argument by Giulio Carlo Argan, Damisch claims that Brunelleschi assumed that the sky simply could not be represented in perspective because it could not be geometrized. For Damisch, this proves that Brunelleschi's interest in perspective stemmed from his architectural concerns rather than from painting. It is certainly possible to construe this experiment as a search for a precise tool of architectural ideation and representation, and to interpret Brunelleschi's architectural production—for example, the rhythmic modulation of the internal space of Santo Spirito—as a demonstration of his awareness of linear perspective. However, such simplistic interpretations not only are inconsistent with other documentary evidence but also distort the history of representation in architectural practice. Brunelleschi himself is said to have worked mostly from models in his building projects.[53]

While the mirror in Brunelleschi's baptistery construction captured changes in daylight and the movement of clouds, introducing the temporality of the *spiritus* of nature into the representation itself, it was also a powerful magical device, not simply a quasi-scientific instrument to simulate the assumed appearance of reality, as argued by Damisch.[54] Pressing our eye against the back of the panel, we witness an apparition, a reflection in which the sky is doubled and luminous, simultaneously immutable and changing, while the realm of true mobility and mortality becomes fixed in a geometric architecture set in proportionally accelerated depth. Like all other artistic productions of the Renaissance, this work sought to reveal the *whole,* a "truth" that is more than a collage of heterogeneous orders. After lamenting the absence of good painters, sculptors, architects, and augurs in his own time, Alberti dedicated his book on painting and perspective to Brunelleschi, who exemplified the very possibility of recovering truth through the works of human creation.[55]

Brunelleschi's experience shows that he could not conceive a building in homogeneous space. Because the panel was meant to be placed in a specific position at a predetermined height, addressing not only the depicted building but also the space between the baptistery and the Duomo, the building clearly would be *nothing* without its context. Furthermore, we see the apparition through the orifice without physically being *in* the space of geometric order. The ambivalent positioning of the point of view (fixed yet not specifically determined) confirms the heterogeneity of Renaissance lived space, which is indeed the space of architecture and its representations. When a century later Giorgio Vasari, the admirer of Michelangelo, suggested that Brunelleschi constructed the perspective of the baptistery from a plan and an elevation, he was consciously or unconsciously presenting a case to undermine a "technique" that he believed did not do justice to true foreshortening.[56] Obviously the relationships among plan, elevation, and perspective soon became evident in the experience of buildings. From the standpoint of architectural design, however, the potential homology among plan, elevation, and perspective as forms of visual projection was not immediately realized. Indeed, it would have been impossible for a Renaissance architect to believe that a building's meaning could be reduced to its visual representation, to a two-dimensional, diaphanous section through the pyramid of vision, and that thus architecture's full presence could be reduced to perspective, using the latter as a "language" to generate a design.

Alberti also emphasized the difference between the drawings of the painter and those of the architect. In *De Re Aedificatoria* II.1, in a discussion on the usefulness of rough, undecorated models in design, he pointed out that the architect and the painter both reveal *depth* (*prominentias/rilievi*), but in very different ways. While the painter "takes pains to emphasize the relief of objects in paintings with shading and diminishing lines and angles" through the methods of linear perspective that Alberti disclosed in his book on painting, *De Pictura,* the architect represents depth (*raffigura i rilievi*) by drawing the footprint or *ichnographia*—literally, an inscription parallel to the plane of the horizon (*mediante il disegno della pianta,* or, in Latin, *ex fundamenti descriptioni*)—and in other drawings represents the shape and dimensions of each face or *orthographia*—an inscription on the vertical plane—"without altering the lines and maintaining the true angles." The architect draws as if his work would be judged "not by the apparent perspective" (James Leoni's translation) or "not by deceptive appearances" (Joseph Rykwert's translation) but "exactly on the basis of controllable measures" (our translation).[57] Alberti advocated the use of simple, unadorned models for generating architectural ideas. We would take issue with recent art historical interpretations that acknowledge only the presentation role of models, claiming that "it was increasingly tempting to take patrons by surprise with enticing views of a project."[58] Elaborated drawings in that case would be more effective than "unadorned models." Nor does Alberti's insistence on the importance of simple models constitute a proof that he could conceive of a systematized triad of plan, elevation, and section, precluding the need for more "finished" or "prescriptive" models.[59] Although art historians still take this systematization for granted, it is not evident in most material from the period. Alberti rather recommended the use of model as a specific design tool to work out the relationship between geometric *lineamenti* and the volumetry of building. The assumed perspectival "hinge" among architectural "ideas" was simply absent from the conceptual operations of fifteenth-century architects.

Filarete's treatise on architecture, rather than Alberti's, was the first to include perspective in the architectural processes of ideation. In his didactic dialogue, Filarete examines the question of drawing and discusses Brunelleschi's discovery, trying to explain to a skeptical prince the effects of foreshortening on a picture plane.[60] These perspectival effects, he insists, are particularly visible in a mirror, to an observer "looking with one eye." It is in this context, evoking a surveying operation, that Filarete stresses the importance of understanding the site for buildings and cities, and determining their plan "rationally" (*con ragione*).[61] From this account it would be possible to infer a projective intention to draw the site in perspective (just as Alberti recommends that painters lay out the floor plan of a space according to the *costruzione legittima*), and then proceed to design the building in volume.[62] Yet Filarete draws his ideal site as a *plan* superimposed on a view of the natural and topographic features of the place chosen for the future city, thus combining

| 0.10 |

The site plan of the city of Sforzinda, from Filarete's *Trattato di architettura* (ca. 1464).

the ideal and the specific. His plan, made "with reason," is centralized and polygonal, reflecting the geometry of the cosmos in the city.

When Filarete speaks about the process of maturing a project by making its drawing "in the mind," it is unlikely that he would be referring to linear perspective. Instead, the traditional *ichnographia* and *orthographia* were generating devices; like the seeds of a plant, they were meant to germinate slowly until the building is born. Elsewhere in his treatise, Filarete discusses four steps to be followed in architectural creation and emphasizes that in each translation—from proportions to lines, to models, and to the building—every artifact embodies a specific state of concept's maturation. He notes that connections between these different states are similar to the changes observed in the living world of nature, analogous to alchemical transmutations and not to mathematical transformations.

Binocular Vision

In Renaissance treatises on perspective drawing, starting with Alberti's *De Pictura,* binocular vision was often reduced to a single point of view: the apex of the pyramid of vision. The fact that we perceive a single image even when looking with both eyes was usually explained with a physiological hypothesis in which both optical nerves would meet in a single point, somewhere in the middle of the head.[63] The perception of depth by an observer reduced to cyclopean vision, however, required the introduction of a device to determine the foreshortening. In Alberti's theory of perspective, this new element became an abstract screen, a template or window frame (known today as the picture plane) intersecting the visual rays at a given distance. But foreshortening (or acceleration) continued to rely on intuition, and contradictions were often remarked as the position of the intersecting screen remained arbitrary. Leonardo da Vinci, for example, questioned the very theory of the visual cone, arguing that "visual power" was not situated at a point: "A small object placed in front of the eye does not prevent us from seeing objects behind it, as it would if the eye perceived from a point."[64] Leonardo's interest in perspective was closer to

A plate from Jacopo Barozzi da Vignola, *Le Due Regole della Prospettiva Pratica* (1583), clearly demonstrates an awareness of problems created for perspective by binocular vision. The lower half of the image shows a version of a hinged plane, the most popular of all perspectival devices.

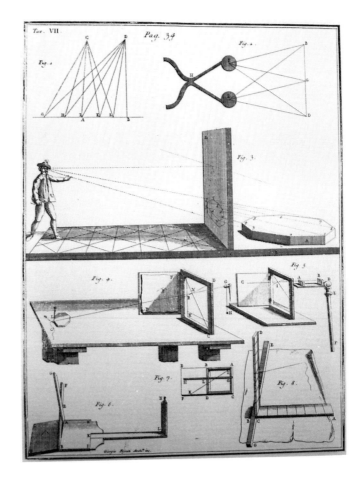

that of the medieval philosophers, marveling at the mathematical properties of light.[65] Analyzing the proportional diminution of objects on the picture plane in relation to the position of the observer, he postulated an analogy between visual systems of proportional diminution and musical harmony, in which a perspectivist determines his "intervals" in the way a musician composes his notes.[66] Thus the musical harmony of the supralunar realm could become manifest by choosing an appropriate acceleration rate for perspective depth.

Although Renaissance writers on perspective, such as Alberti and Piero della Francesca, almost invariably started with Euclid's theorems, in the opening pages of his book Alberti took care to distance himself from medieval mathematicians who "measure the shapes and forms of things in the mind alone and divorced entirely from matter." His interest in perspective was related directly to its application to painting, and he writes: "We, on the other hand, who wish to talk of things that are visible, will express ourselves in cruder terms."[67] Despite the crucial differences between Renaissance perspective and medieval optics, the quest for true knowledge through vision was always present. However, in the new representational interests of Renaissance art, "knowledge" should not be identified with the positivist truths of modern science. For the arts, knowledge involved personal orientation in a specific cultural context, including its metaphysical (mythical) and theological dimensions. It would be false to assume that the artists' interest in perspective after the Renaissance was equivalent to the desire of contemporary empirical science "to study nature directly through vision."[68] Most sixteenth-century treatises on perspective included a chapter on vision and optics that acknowledged irreconcilable differences among experience, physiology, and mathematics. While these texts sought to develop a primarily empirical understanding of perspective depth into a geometric system, they retained a distinction between the constructed *perspectiva artificialis* and the physiology of vision—a distinction

| 0.12 |

A sketch by Leonardo da Vinci shows a draftsman drawing an armillary sphere with the help of a transparent plane (ca. 1510). This is a rare example showing Leonardo's interest in linear perspective, which he called *perspectiva accidentalis*. The choice of the subject matter is not arbitrary. The representation being created is itself of the geometrical order of a harmonious cosmos. Leonardo, Luca Pacioli, Dürer, and Barbaro associated perspective with the representation of cosmic order in the form of geometric solids.

Milan, Biblioteca Ambrosiana, Codice Atlantico Ira (new 5).

Perspective machine, from Vignola's *Le Due Regole*. This curious machine shows two observers creating a perspective, seemingly in order to "corroborate" the mathematical depth of the world, given that monocular vision was evidently inadequate. The perspective representation is emphatically "artificial": it is created from instructions dictated by the operative who views the image. The drawing is made on a gridded page, suggesting that perspective could be used for operations that require precise measurement.

that would endure until the advent of modern scientific optics. Many of these new works, furthermore, remained as theoretical or mathematical elucidations, with no obvious applications in artistic practice.[69]

In Jacopo Barozzi da Vignola's *Due Regole della Prospettiva Pratica* (1583), a "second observer" (or distance point) was introduced as a second element to regulate the foreshortening. Mathematically, this problem was solved in the late 1550s by Federigo Commandino, who first associated cartographic projection (through an analysis of Ptolemy) and *perspectiva artifi-*

cialis. The distance point was projected onto the horizon line, at a distance from the central point equal to the distance between the eye of the observer and the plane of the image. In other words, Vignola's method introduced a second observer who looked perpendicularly at the beholder, at the same distance from the central point, thereby making possible the rationalization of depth. Before the introduction of the distance point, *perspectiva artificialis* had been, strictly speaking, a heterogeneous collection of intuitive monocular constructions based on the apex of the cone of vision as a simplified eye.

Sectioning the Cone of Vision: The Nature of Theory

While an increasing rationalization of visual perception began to influence the geometry of depth in sixteenth-century painting, artists still relied on their predominantly tactile experience of the world to create perspective images. Although perspective theories were more or less mathematical, one should not assume a simplistic division between a "mathematical tradition" and a "practical tradition" in this regard, a division presuming a disciplinary autonomy that appears only in the wake of the Napoleonic university.[70] The relationship between theory and practice that we take for granted, as a result of the scientific revolution, was not truly at work until the late eighteenth century. Modern writers often assume an instrumental relationship between perspective texts and artistic practice, although the very conditions for such instrumentality did not exist before the transformations brought about by Desargues's theory. From the fifteenth century to the late seventeenth century, the disclosure of mathematical truths in discourse was still mostly a contemplative "practice"—a liberal art like painting, architecture, and sculpture—preoccupied with revealing a space of ontological continuity. In that regard, the "metaphysical" speculations about Platonic bodies in perspective in Luca Pacioli's *Divina Proportione* (Venice, 1509) and Wenzel Jamnitzer's *Perspectiva corporum regularum* (Nuremberg, 1568) are not in essence different from the "scientific" mathematical speculations on projection of Commandino, Benedetti, and Guidobaldo del Monte.

| 0.14 |

One of Albrecht Dürer's several illustrations of perspective devices, from his *Unterweysung der Messung* (1525). In this case the machine is in use, with a draftsman employing a net and an eyepiece to draw a nude figure with the correct proportions required by foreshortening. One can only acknowledge the uneasiness produced by the objectification of the model, indeed *not* an architectural space, as well as the inescapable erotic atmosphere of the interaction. The net, potentially the space of enframing, remained a zone of participation in the sixteenth century.

In this connection, we should remember the limited instrumental application of most perspective apparatuses described in treatises. Albrecht Dürer's famous machine (1525), for example, consisting of an eyepiece and a glass panel, was mainly intended to demonstrate a rigid method for copying nature by cutting a section literally through the cone of vision. Significantly, Dürer's machine is still an appropriate metaphor for the scientific objectification of reality. It shows man placing the world in *his* cone of vision, making it difficult to acknowledge the *reciprocity* of perception by the Other (originally God), the intersubjective (erotic) reality that makes us possible as embodied consciousness in the first place. Philosophically, this coincides with the growing occultation of Being in what Heidegger calls "the age of the world picture," the substitution of the world as presence for a fragmentary world of decontextualized objects awaiting our exploitation, a mere re-presented reality that necessarily conceals its ground of truth: that is, the horizon of *things,* now excluded by the frame. In retrospect we can recognize this as a precedent of *our* technological vision, the public reality in and through which the architect's work must "speak."

Although drawings, such as those we find in sixteenth-century treatises by Dürer and Philibert de L'Orme, may reveal an interest in projections coupled with a growing concern for the technical instruments of the architect, they are not simply equivalent to modern projection drawings in their instrumental relationship to a building process. Dürer's practical manuals on geometry and human proportions are particularly challenging. The German artist was evidently fascinated with the possibility that the geometrical proportions of the human body could be understood through projective methods. In his *Unterweysung der*

Messung (1538) there is no explicit consideration of symbolism or metaphysics. Sections of human bodies, vertical and horizontal, are envisioned through operations analogous to the perspectival section through the cone of vision, deployed in geometrical space; they invite a contemporary reading as precedent for electronic imaging operations. These drawings, obviously inspired by Piero della Francesca's earlier work on perspective, include some of the earliest examples of "plans" conceived as systematic horizontal sections through a solid body. Furthermore, in the third book of *Vier Bücher von menschlichen Proportion* (1528), Dürer experiments with a projective device, which he calls alternately "converter" and "falsifier," that transforms human proportions according to age and physical type, ranging from "normal" to monstrous and grotesque. Paradoxically, as Michelangelo would sharply point out, Dürer seemed to have no interest in identifying specific gestures or physiognomic types. He was obviously fascinated with the abstract instrumentality embodied in the mechanism of projective transformation, which suggested the existence of unity in diversity even though the original proportion or perfect archetype might be inaccessible to human reason. To avoid interpreting Dürer's work as a simple precursor of modern reductive techniques, we should place it in its proper theological and philosophical context. For our purposes, it suffices to suggest that this context is not radically different from that made explicit by the early Renaissance writings of Nicholas of Cusa,[71] in which only God has access to the vantage point of absolute truth and can perceive the identity of all human proportions. On the other hand, the artist, a "learned ignorant," must accept relentless change and diversity following the "projective" act of Creation itself, and perhaps must be content with the possibility of understanding the perspectival mechanism of such diversity. When we add to these considerations the traditional understanding of medieval constructive geometrical operations, still present in Nuremberg in the early sixteenth century, the diagnosis of Dürer's interest in instrumentality made by modern art historians must be radically qualified. Indeed, the evidence always shows that Renaissance artists, architects, and builders had not yet developed a mentality that would allow individual projections to be coordinated within the universal, operational

Tracings [0.15] and elevation [0.16] for the *trompe* of the Château d'Anet by Philibert de L'Orme (1648). This small pavilion, cantilevered from one of the corners of the internal courtyard of the palace, was constructed with stones magically floating in midair. The transmutation's traces, the geometrical projections on paper that made possible the reconciliation of the building with the force of gravity, demonstrate the ineffable unity of the *prima materia* through artifacts of human fabrication.

Montreal, Collection Centre Canadien d'Architecture / Canadian Centre for Architecture.

0.15

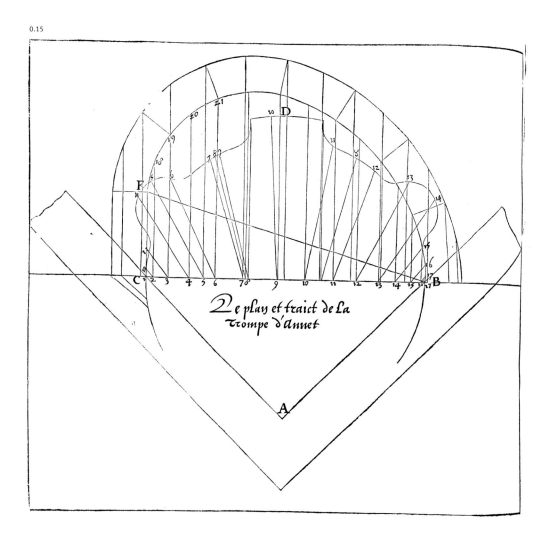

0.16

0.18

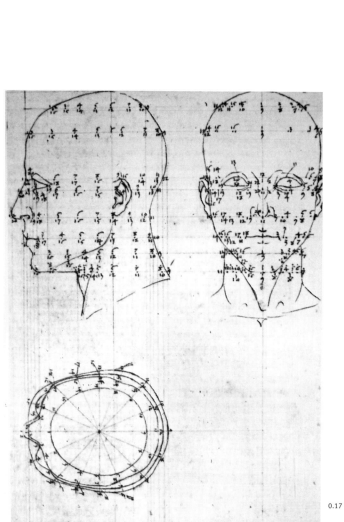

0.17

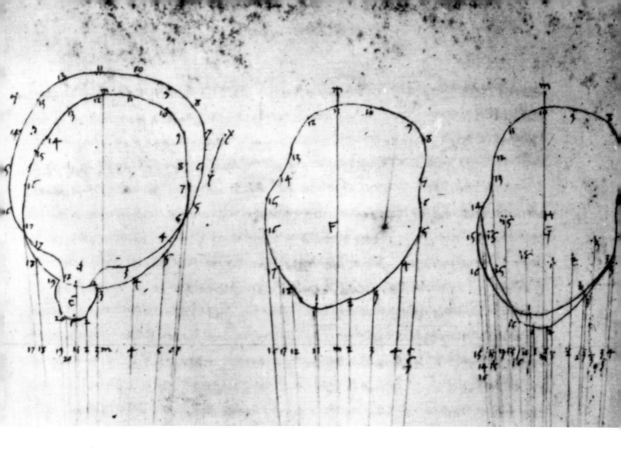

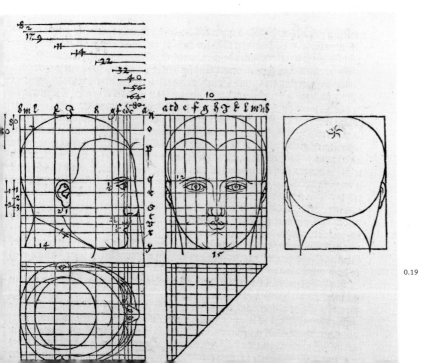

0.19

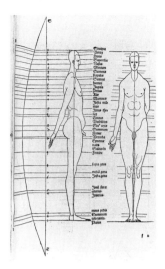

framework of descriptive geometry. Their collective space was not the homogenous, geometric entity that post-Galilean science would postulate as a space of experience, the entity to which we have now grown accustomed.

In the late Middle Ages, a plan generally was conceived as the composite "footprint" of a building, and an elevation as its "face." These architectural "ideas" coincided with the horizontal and vertical dimensions of lived space, yet they often included apparent contradictory information that was nonetheless important in nonhomogeneous space-time; they were not "precise" projections homologous to perspective. Moreover, as we have suggested, the notion of vertical and horizontal "sections" was not common before the sixteenth century, just as anatomy rarely involved the actual dissection of cadavers until the early modern era. When section drawings were introduced into the process of architectural ideation, they were not simply extrapolated from other drawings such as the plan and the elevation; rather, they seem to have originated from a fascination with the role of buildings as gnomons or shadow tracers. There was an overlapping of the notion of section as a cut with that of section as shadow or imprint, revealing the presence of *light* and the order of the day (a propitious time), yet framed by the order of architecture, which was capable of enduring darkness. Vincenzo Scamozzi's treatise *L'Idea dell'Architettura Universale* (1615) contains fascinating examples of this ambiguous concept of section.[72] The coordination of the vertical and horizontal sections of buildings reveals that light and shadow constituted the architecture's symbolic order, very much in the spirit of Vitruvius, who had introduced gnomons—together with *machinae* and buildings—as one of the three artifacts within the province of architecture. Measuring time and space through poetic *mimēsis* was the original task of the architect, and it remained a prime concern for Renaissance architects.[73] The obsession with revealing the inside of bodies—dissecting and magnifying as roads to knowledge—took hold of European epistemology only after the mechanization of physiology in the seventeenth century.[74] The apparent truth of a section cut through the pyramid of vision promoted the use of sections in architectural representation. Eventually, scientific projections (i.e., the modern plan, section, and elevation) would be conceived as homologous *sections* along the *x*, *y*, and *z* axes. Sections became a legitimate embodiment of architectural ideas because they were more precise than composite drawings and therefore were considered more appropriate to embody Platonic truths.

In the sixteenth century, however, Michelangelo still regarded the living human body as the foundation of all art and precociously criticized Dürer, whatever his theological and cosmological motivations, for attempting to define a static image of the human body. Michelangelo's entire work emphasized life and movement—qualities that were often excluded from architectural theory in the Renaissance. Architects had become increasingly concerned with the clarity and fixity of measure and proportions. Michelangelo criticized Dürer's *Vier Bücher* for its articulation of theory to the detriment of the quality of life: "[He] treats only of the measure and kind of bodies, to which a certain rule cannot be given, forming the figures as stiff as stakes; and what matters more, he says not one word concerning human acts and gestures."[75] Unlike a growing number of his contemporaries, Michelangelo resisted making architecture through geometric projections, as he could conceive the human body only in motion. While Leonardo da Vinci and Dürer regarded anatomy as a dissection of cadavers, following Andreas Vesalius's *De humani corporis fabrica* (1543), Michelangelo's anatomy always focused on the live body, associating beauty with health. He acknowledged the life of the whole through the articulation (the hinge) of fragments of the human body. Consequently, Michelangelo rarely expressed depth through geometric perspective. Rather, he understood depth as the primary dimension and disclosed it by capturing the movement of a figure. This movement in Michelangelo's drawings must still be called foreshortening, but here it implies the definition of forms in movement, in length, breadth, and depth, in which their mutual interrelationships are not fixed. The artifact, painting, sculpture, or building captured the motion of purposeful life in a single instant. Profoundly influenced by his belief in the reality of Christ as God incarnated in a mortal body, Michelangelo's work seems intent on dissolving the opposition between life and death; it thus reveals the "flesh" of the world, the primordial substance of a live universe.

Michelangelo's architectural drawings are a form of *disegno* of the live body. The plan study for a Florentine fortified gateway [0.23], imbued with muscular tension, and the sketch investigating the relationship between human figures and architecture in the Sistine Chapel [0.24] are never subjected to the laws of linear perspective. Michelangelo's foreshortening is of a different order. His construction drawings, such as the multiple molding designs (as shown here for the Laurentian Library and its cornice, 0.21) and his diagrams to cut stone (in this case the marble for the tomb of Julius II, 0.22), betray a particular intimacy with the building process. Like his sculptures, these drawings sought to disclose life and motion, and their resolution into the unity of matter, rather than geometrical *lineamenti*.

0.21 | Florence, Casa Buonarroti, 53 A *v.*
0.22 | Florence, Casa Buonarroti, 67 A *v.*
0.23 | Florence, Casa Buonarroti, 21 A.
0.24 | Detroit, Institute of Arts (42).

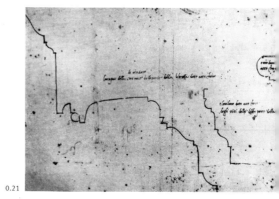

0.21

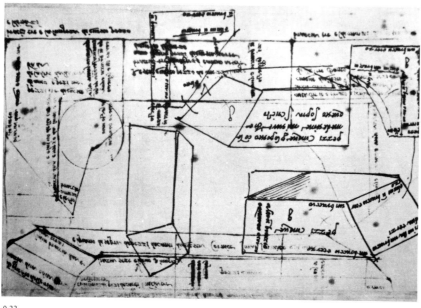

0.22

43

0.24

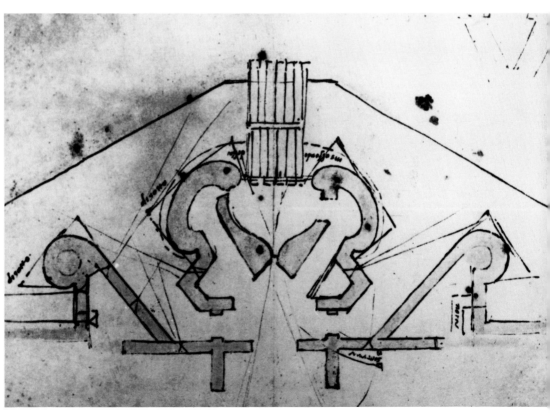

0.23

For Michelangelo this was the most effective manifestation of *phantasia*, the individual artist's imagination that had received legitimacy after Dante's interpretation of Christian reality in the *Divine Comedy*. Properly developed, the imagination was considered superior to philosophy and contemplation (*vita contemplativa*, the liberal arts), as well as to the application of technical knowledge (*vita activa*, the mechanical arts). This *vita voluptuaria*, or erotic knowledge—also selected by Poliphilo in the *Hypnerotomachia Poliphili* (1499) as the right way to seek architecture—offered a powerful capacity to grasp the divine dimension of the world, along with its ultimate poetic truth.[76] Dante had made an association between light, as an attribute of heaven that descends "of itself, or through a will which sends it down," and the imagination that moves the poet and leads him to the truth. Thus *phantasia* enabled the artist to "see clearly" (*perspicere*—also the origin of *perspectiva*), being "like sense in that it perceives the particular, corporeal and present" but also superior to the senses in that "with no external stimulus, it yet produces images, not only present, but also past and future and as such cannot be brought to light by nature."[77]

In Renaissance perspective, foreshortening relied on a visual construct in which depth was articulated within a framed geometric field presented frontally to the observer. Bilateral symmetry was often the compositional choice of painters. The image and proportions of objects were then foreshortened within this undistorted frame. Foreshortening techniques developed by Michelangelo, however, negated this frame to acknowledge peripheral vision and frontal extensions. This quality of vision also defines the conception and the experience of Michelangelo's architecture. In his work our bodily presence seems to haunt the building as the architecture moves with us. Because it includes the peripheral experience, his architecture remains intelligible even when distorted.[78] Michelangelo still could perceive a simple sketch to be the symbol of a whole architectural intention, the seed of the whole work.[79] His *perspectiva* is *phantasia*, the power of metaphor: constructing artifice from bodily fragments, capable of blending together the most distant objects or keeping apart those that are naturally most intimately connected. His buildings, perhaps the most outstanding architecture of his century in Europe, are remarkably original, for they are based on an embodied approach to the task of building that rejects architectural projections and *lineamenti*. If we remain deeply touched by Michelangelo's architecture, it may be precisely because his work, while engaging a modern, productive imagination, is based on a nonperspectival (nonobjectifying) approach to designing places.

In northern Italy, Daniele Barbaro, an eminent humanist and mathematician best known as Palladio's friend and patron, was also very careful to exclude *perspectiva artificialis* from the realm of architectural ideation. Barbaro's decision was particularly significant because all his work was profoundly committed to the relation between mathematics and all artifacts of human fabrication, a commitment that even led him to confer a new dignity onto the traditionally underrated mechanical arts.[80] Indeed, in his profusely annotated edition of Vitruvius's *Ten Books* (1567) he expounds on optics alongside a passage in book I where Vitruvius mentions that the architect must know the science of optics to understand the light of the heavenly bodies and how it affects buildings. Barbaro explains that *prospettiva* (optics) is "the name of the whole and of the part." As a whole, optics studies the properties of natural light, "straight, reflected, and refracted," and its benefits for "the sight and soul of mortals." When it refers to "the part," however, *prospettiva* concerns "practice" and is capable of producing "marvelous things," such as the effects of distance, foreshortening, and relief of objects on flat surfaces. After quoting the passages where Vitruvius discusses optical correction, and after referring to stage-set paintings ("the part of *prospettiva* that is called *scenographia*"), he reiterates that *prospettiva* is necessary for the architect, and that Vitruvius was well aware of it.[81]

This is, however, only the beginning of the story. In his treatise on perspective, Barbaro greatly expanded his commentary on the architectural "ideas" of Vitruvius.[82] We may recall that in Vitruvius's *Ten Books,* the Greek word *idea* referred to three aspects of a mental image that constitutes the germ of a project. These ideas enabled the architect to imagine the disposition of a project's parts. On one hand, *ichnographia* and *orthographia* were straightforward terms and Barbaro simply accepted them. They would be translated eventually as "plan" and "elevation" but did not yet suggest the systematic correspondence of descriptive geometry.[83] On the other hand, he believed that the translation of the third Vitruvian idea as "perspective" resulted from a misreading of *sciographia* as *scenographia* in the original text. The only important application of *scenographia,* according to Barbaro, was the building and painting of stage sets, and this sort of perspective, however important, was recommended mainly for painters and set designers.

Sciagraphy (also written "sciography," meaning etymologically the inscription or description of shadows) was generally understood until the seventeenth century as "the art of drawing shadows." Between the seventeenth and the nineteenth century, it also referred to a cut or section of a building.[84] Yet modern Latin dictionaries translate *scenographia* (or *scaenographia,* as it actually appears in the earliest surviving Vitruvian manuscript) as the drawing of buildings in perspective, and they generally assume that this word is synonymous with *sciagraphia.* As we will elaborate in the next chapter, linear perspective was unknown in ancient Rome, and even when Vitruvius speaks about the three types of stage sets appropriate to tragedy, comedy, and satire (V.6), there is no mention of optics (*perspectiva*) in connection with classical theater. Vitruvius describes the fixed *scaena* as a royal palace facade with *periaktoi,* "triangular pieces of machinery that revolve," placed beyond the doors, whose three faces were decorated to correspond to each dramatic genre. In I.2, Vitruvius describes this *scenographia/ sciographia,* rendered in modern English translations as "perspective." As we will demonstrate, these modern translations fail to do justice to the original text, in which there is no obvious allusion to a geometric construction analogous to the Renaissance *perspectiva artificialis.*[85]

Barbaro argues that *scenographia,* which is "related to the use of perspective," is the design of stages for the three dramatic genres. Appropriate types of buildings must be shown diminishing in size and receding toward the horizon. He does not agree with "those that wish to understand perspective (*perspettiva*) as one of the ideas that generate architectural design (*dispositione*)." To him it is plain that "just as animals belong by nature to a certain species," the *idea* that belongs with plan (*ichnographia*) and elevation (*orthographia*) is the section (*il profilo,*

Elevation [0.25] and plan [0.26] of the classical theater, as interpreted by Barbaro and drawn by Palladio, from Daniele Barbaro's edition of Vitruvius's treatise (1567). The accompanying discussion includes the current debate about musical harmony, analogous to the mathematical order of the universe. The *periaktoi* are conceived as providing surfaces for perspectival painting, appropriate to the three genres of drama.

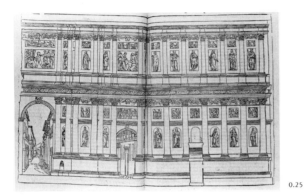

0.25

0.26

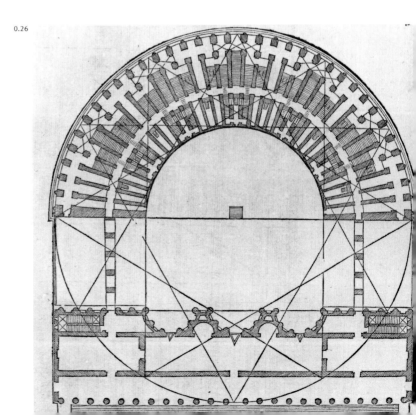

Plan, section, and elevation of a temple appear together in one image
from Barbaro's *Pratica della Perspettiva* (1569). This drawing, unique in
Barbaro's treatise, is meant to demonstrate how *ichnographia, orthographia,* and *sciographia* (section)
belong to the same genre of drawings and constitute the "ideas" to
generate architecture. This composite drawing also includes the presence of the triangular *lineamenti,* the
Platonic first figure of the cosmos,
generating the dome.

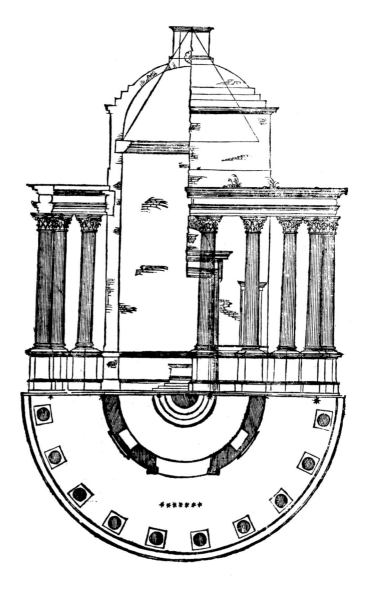

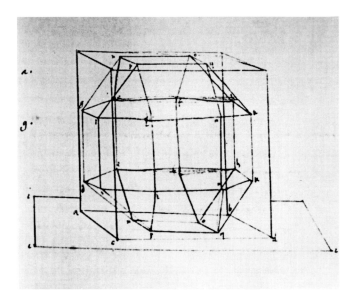

| 0.28 |

Sketch from Barbaro's manuscript on *prospettiva*, showing a space-filling body placed within a cube in perspective.

Venice, Biblioteca Marziana.

detto sciographia), because it is similar to those two other "ideas" that constitute architectural order (*dispositione*). The section "allows for a greater knowledge of the quality and measurement of building, helps with the control of costs and the determination of the thickness of walls," and so on. This is not to be confused with the purpose of a *modello*. The section is useful because it reveals the inside of a building, the architect being "like a doctor" who must know about all of the interior parts. In fact, Barbaro assumes that in antiquity "perspective" referred only to the painted representations on the faces of the *periaktoi*.[86]

Indeed, the *perspectiva artificialis* used in scenography was concerned only with the frontal surface of picture planes framed by a proscenium arch, not with the full three-dimensionality of "lived" space; this explains its restriction to painting and theater. It is in such areas that perspective fulfilled its symbolic function as a means to disclose an ontological depth. A subtle, yet important distinction often was made between *prospettiva* (generally understood as the art of drawing complex three-dimensional volumes from their planimetric projection) and *perspettiva* (which dealt mainly with the surface of the picture plane). Both words come ultimately from the

Palladio's Teatro Olimpico in Vicenza
(1580–1584), with its permanent urban decor in foreshortened perspective.

Photo by A. Pérez-Gómez.

Latin verb *spectare,* "to see." The distinction is subtle: *perspicere,*
meaning "to see clearly or carefully," differs from the more active verb *prospicere,* meaning "to look out at, to look forward or
toward an object." On the other hand, the Italian *perspettiva* and
prospettiva often were used interchangeably to name the new
linear perspective. Barbaro made a distinction between the con-
tents of his published book, *La Pratica della Perspettiva* (Venice,
1569), and an unpublished manuscript with an almost identical
title, *La Pratica della Prospettiva* (Venice, Biblioteca Marziana, MS
IT. IV, 39–5446). In the former he shows how to render buildings in perspective in order to design stage sets, starting from
detailed instructions concerning polygons and polyhedra, while
in the latter he deals mostly with geometric bodies and their
relation to perspective. According to Barbaro, *prospettiva* thus
addressed the practical concerns of artists and architects, since
he assumed that the essence of built architecture was embodied
in the *lineamenti* of these geometric bodies and in the proportional relationships that constituted the "necessary truth" of all
constructive arts. Such distinctions are the norm rather than the
exception during the Renaissance in Europe, and they reveal
some of the difficulties of conceiving a work of architecture
from a set of two-dimensional projections.

These distinctions are further complicated by architects' well-documented interest in the theater, by their remarkably serious commitment to the ephemeral architecture of

urban rituals and celebrations, and by the pervasive metaphor of the *theatrum mundi* as a site for true knowledge, resulting from memory activated by the imagination. We may recall that the *theatrum mundi* was also a privileged metaphor in the design of geometric gardens. Furthermore, there is an obvious continuity between the "tragic stage" and the city of classical architecture, as exemplified by Serlio's engravings of stages and Palladio's Teatro Olimpico. Since its inception in classical Greece, the theater was a paradigmatic site for the revelation of architectural order; moreover, it was an institution particularly conducive to self-understanding in the context of Renaissance humanism, with its new emphasis on existential freedom. This complexity of intentions, rather than being a hindrance for Renaissance architects, became a way to engage the "ungraspable opacity" of *chōra* as the space of architectural representation in the syncretic context of the Renaissance.[87] It is as if the temporal depth of the Greek actor's mask—that is, his ineffable character in the hands of divine destiny—could now be translated by the architect-thaumaturge into the wondrous spatial depth of the Renaissance masques. Spectacle in the elusive boundary between the space of ritual presence and the space of artistic representation was, indeed, a fundamental program of Renaissance architecture.

The Science of the Observer

Beginning in the early Renaissance, the science of classical optics became more autonomous from its medieval theological framework. Already some late medieval philosophers such as Witelo explained cognition through empirical phenomena and associationist models, rather than relying on mystical speculations.[88] It was not until the late sixteenth century, however, that Felix Platter (1536–1614) declared that the retina and the optic nerve were the true organs of vision, and Giovanni Battista della Porta posited the sensitivity of the crystalline humor and compared the eye to a miniature camera obscura, thus radically refuting extromission theories.[89] Both Platter and della Porta greatly influenced Johannes Kepler, who developed the first comprehensive theory of the retinal image. Kepler published a

A recomposed view of Florence by Lancia, for a stage set (1569) [0.30]; stage design by G. Parigi (1586) [0.31]; marble bas-relief by Andrea Sansovino (ca. 1523) [0.32]. Since its inception in classical Greece, the theater was a paradigmatic site for the revelation of architectural order. During the Renaissance, it increasingly borrowed from real urban space and architecture. Real cities often were recomposed to serve as stage sets, showing an awareness of relationships between the city and the theater and, therefore, the common relevance of perspective for architecture and stage design [0.30]. The proscenium arch, however, remained permeable, allowing interactions between the space of action and the space of artistic representation. This ambivalence of the proscenium plane is explicit in the stage design by Parigi for the ballet *La Liberazione di Tirreno* (1586) [0.31]. The depth of the proscenium was not homogeneous with lived space and did not depend on a fixed or predetermined point of view. In this regard, it is analogous to other Renaissance genres, such as the bas-relief, that depicted the mysterious perspectival space of action, as examplified by the marble bas-relief of *The Annunciation*, by Sansovino (ca. 1523) [0.32].

0.30 | Florence, Palazzo degli Uffizi, Gabinetto dei Disegni e Stampe.
0.31 | Florence, Palazzo degli Uffizi, Gabinetto dei Disegni e Stampe.
0.32 | Loreto, Italy, Sanctuary of the Holy House.
    Photo: *Encyclopedia of World Art* (London: McGraw-Hill, 1959).

0.30

0.31

0.32

Cesare Cesariano's theater/labyrinth, from his edition of Vitruvius (1521) [0.33];
Theatrum mundi, from *The Ceremonial Entry of Ernst, Archduke of Austria, into
Antwerp* (1594) [0.34]. The structure of the theater itself came to symbolize architecture as a microcosmic order. In Cesariano's image of a theater/labyrinth, for
example, the archetypal labyrinth, the order of human life translated into architecture, underlies the space of the orchestra, while spectators both contemplate and
act in a centralized monument. Similarly, the central structure or *theatrum mundi*
is an example of ephemeral architecture for urban celebrations, a "stage set" that
makes the political (and cosmic) order visible for all to see and participate.

0.33

0.34

theory of radiation through apertures in his "supplement" to Witelo, *Ad Vitellionem paralipomena* (1604). He demonstrated that the projection created by a source of light passing through an aperture takes the form of the light source rather than the form of the aperture. Thus he resolved an apparent contradiction that had baffled many observers since antiquity: traditionally assumed to travel in a straight line, sunlight, when projected through an irregular orifice into a dark chamber, would invariably appear as a circle and not shaped as the orifice. In the thirteenth century John Pecham had accounted for this mystery by emphasizing that "it is the nature and harmony of light to be circular[;] . . . the spherical shape is associated with light" to be in harmony with itself and with all the bodies of the world.[90] Kepler substituted a simple object (a book) for the source of light and interposed a template perforated with an irregular, multiangled shape between the book and the floor. Then he linked various points on the book to various points on the floor by passing threads straight through the aperture. The result was not a projection of the opening, but rather an outline of the book. Kepler's experimental device, ushering in the mechanization of optics, is in some ways similar to Dürer's perspective machine.[91] Furthermore, Kepler employed the term *pictura* to designate the inverted retinal image. Kepler's theory of vision was the first to postulate a *real* optical image within the eye, a picture that exists independently of the observer, "formed by the focusing of all available rays on a surface."[92]

Within this new mechanical universe of the seventeenth century, perspective became a generative architectural *idea,* in the Vitruvian sense of the term. The inception of the Cartesian modern world and the epistemological revolution brought about by modern science introduced a tension between traditional forms of symbolization and the mechanistic understanding of the world; these transformations precipitated radical changes in the realm of thinking.[93] Galileo assumed the world to be based on fixed essences and mathematical laws deployed in a homogeneous, geometrized space, much like the Platonic model of the heavens. After abandoning the traditional understanding of reality for which position remained an important component of the essence of an object, he thus could posit the far-reaching consequence of his law of inertia; that is, that the essence of an object is not altered by motion. This notion, which for us seems to be an obvious "truth," since our objectifying gaze persists in making abstraction of contexts, was at odds with the experience of the world on which Aristotelian cosmology was founded. In that earlier world, perception, with its double horizon of mortal embodied consciousness and finite qualitative places, was accepted as the primary and legitimate access to reality. The new scientific concept eventually led to a skepticism about the physical presence of the world. With Descartes, man became a subject (a thinking *I* rather than an embodied *self*) who confronts the world as *res extensa,* as an extension of his thinking ego. This dualistic concept of reality made it possible for perspective to become a model of human knowledge and a truthful, scientific representation of the infinite universe. On one hand, the Cartesian mind had to become a geometric "station point" (physiologically, the pineal gland) in order to recognize objective mathematical truths in the world, the only form of knowledge that could thereafter claim legitimacy as intersubjective. On the other hand, the artistic representation of infinity *in* the world, implemented particularly in urbanism and garden design, was a step toward the secularization of power. Giving humanity access to the realm of the infinite, it contributed significantly to the disappearance of limits in nature and to the growth of a technological obsession with the control and domination of external reality through reductive, instrumental means.

Despite this scientific context, baroque perspective in architecture remained a symbolic and rhetorical configuration that enabled the physical, constructed world to retain the qualities that it had always possessed. During the seventeenth century, political space was not yet homogenized, and the primacy of perception as the foundation of truth was hardly affected by this new science and philosophy. Polymaths and philosophers again contemplated the importance of light as a mediation between human and divine spheres, manifested in a broad range of works from the paintings of Dutch mercantile society to the religious architecture of the Counter-Reformation. In the Jesuit tradition of scholarship, Athanasius Kircher, for example, insisted on a hierarchy of lights descending from God, the first *lux,* through angelic *lumen,* to the realm of human experience.

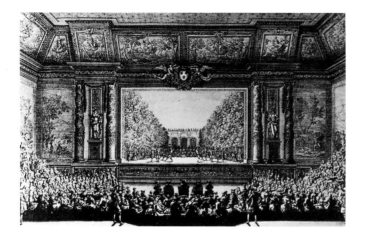

Temporary theater erected by Carlo Vigarani at Versailles (1672), with the king occupying the central point of perspective. Engraving by Jean Le Pautre.

Munich, Theatermuseum.

Slightly earlier, in the context of his monumental reconstruction of the Temple of Solomon in Jerusalem, his colleague Juan Bautista Villalpando insisted on the primary importance of perspective as a Vitruvian architectural idea, associating it with Jesuit practices of visualization that allowed man access to divine truths and demonstrated how God Himself must have designed the temple and presented it as a prophetic vision to Ezekiel. Associating God with an omnipresent light (always near rather than infinitely far) generating parallel projections—that is, the shadows produced by sunlight—Villalpando could praise plans and elevations for their unequaled precision, while understanding them as special "cases" of perspective.[94] Indeed, seemingly unaffected by the earliest experimental observations of diffraction (i.e., the geometrical imprecision along the edges of projected shadows), the prevailing belief in both the rectilinear propagation of light and its "infinite" speed became the foundation for a renewed metaphysics. Even Kepler claimed that the issue was not merely to describe light mathematically but to understand that its *nature* is mathematical, and that it is the ultimate vehicle of the *mathesis universalis,* the link between the corporeal and spiritual worlds.[95] Thus it was possible to perceive a divine order in the scientific study of nature, while in the arts the presence of divine wisdom was conveyed by light (the Holy Ghost), a common allegorical theme during this "new age" following the devastating wars of religion.

Andrea Pozzo's fresco in Sant'Ignazio, Rome (1684–1685). The vault
above the nave is opened to the sky
through the devices of *quadratura*.

Photo by A. Pérez-Gómez.

In this context, perspective was a novel architectural idea, and it became a privileged form of symbolization. The architecture of Versailles, for example, is manifested not only in the plans and sections of the palace; it relies primarily on the implied perspectival order of the garden, the city, and the world, as well as on the ephemeral stage sets and theatrical fireworks that were part of palace life. Similarly, the architecture of the Jesuit church in Vienna by Andrea Pozzo hardly can be reduced to its section or elevation. Rather than remaining on a two-dimensional field of representation as in Renaissance paintings, Pozzo's ceiling fresco is merged inextricably with the three-dimensionality of the architectural space. Projected from a precise point situated at eye level and marked permanently on the pavement of the nave, the illusionistic dome is perfectly incorporated to the built architecture only at the precise moment when a human presence occupies the station point of the *quadratura* fresco.

Although the theory of perspective, as an offspring of the new science, would eventually make possible the control and exploitation of physical reality, seventeenth-century arts, gardening, and architecture were still concerned with revealing a transcendentally ordered cosmos. While post-Cartesian man began to consider himself autonomous from external reality, geometric perspective allowed him to construct and dwell in propitious places by changing the given reality of nature. Another type of perspective projection, anamorphosis, "distorted" the reality it represented by placing the station point in unexpected places, often near the surface of the drawing or painting itself, or by reconstituting previously unintelligible images in conical or cylindrical mirrors. The disjunction of undistorted presence and distorted image had repercussions for art and architecture that can still be felt today and to which we will return at length in Variation One.

Anamorphosis was already familiar to the painters of the Renaissance. Holbein's *Ambassadors* is the best-known example. While references to the art of distorted perspective appear in sixteenth-century treatises, such as Barbaro's *Pratica della Perspettiva* (1569) and Vignola's *Due Regole della Prospettiva Pratica* (1583), it is only in the early seventeenth century that methods of anamorphosis become more precise than the empirical elongation of images along a single axis. It is with Jean-François Nicéron's *Perspective curieuse* (1638) that anamorphosis truly became a method that could be explained and taught through a simple set of geometric rules. In Nicéron's treatise the distortion of appearances still was imbued with theological purpose, but its construction had become systematized as a geometric technique that eventually would be reduced to a method for curious, ultimately inconsequential, optical games.[96]

Perspective as an architectural idea implemented in lived space demonstrates how by geometrizing the world humans could be part of a new social and political order. To gain access to this new transcendental truth was also an aim of philosophical systems throughout the seventeenth century. In his *Studies in a Geometry of Situation* (1679), for example, G. W. Leibniz proposed a science of extension that, unlike Cartesian analytic geometry, would be integral and not reducible to algebraic equations. This project for a "descriptive" geometry more universal than algebra, however, could still magically describe the infinite qualitative variety of natural things. This transcendental geometry was part of Leibniz's lifelong dream to postulate a universal science, which he called at various times *lingua universalis, scientia universalis, calculus philosophicus,* and *calculus universalis.* From all the disciplines of human knowledge, he tried to extrapolate the simplest constitutive elements and their rules of relation, to organize the whole epistemological field into a "calculus of concepts." Although perspective increasingly

Two plates from Johann Jacob Schübler, *Perspectiva Pes Picturae* (1719–1720). The frontispiece [0.37] shows architecture presenting optics (*perspectiva naturalis*) with the instruments of geometry, in order to make it truly useful for artists. As a mathematician and theoretician of architecture, Schübler inextricably linked perspective and architecture, making the practical rules of perspective the foundation of architecture. In the early eighteenth century the connection between perspective (*perspectiva artificialis*) and architecture had become totally explicit, in contrast with the ambivalence present in Renaissance works. The other plate [0.38] demonstrates how clearly the homology of plan, elevation, and perspective was understood. Perspective had become the primary architectural idea, allowing for the conception of architectural space as a geometrized yet transcendental entity.

Montreal, Collection Centre Canadien d'Architecture / Canadian Centre for Architecture.

0.37

0.38

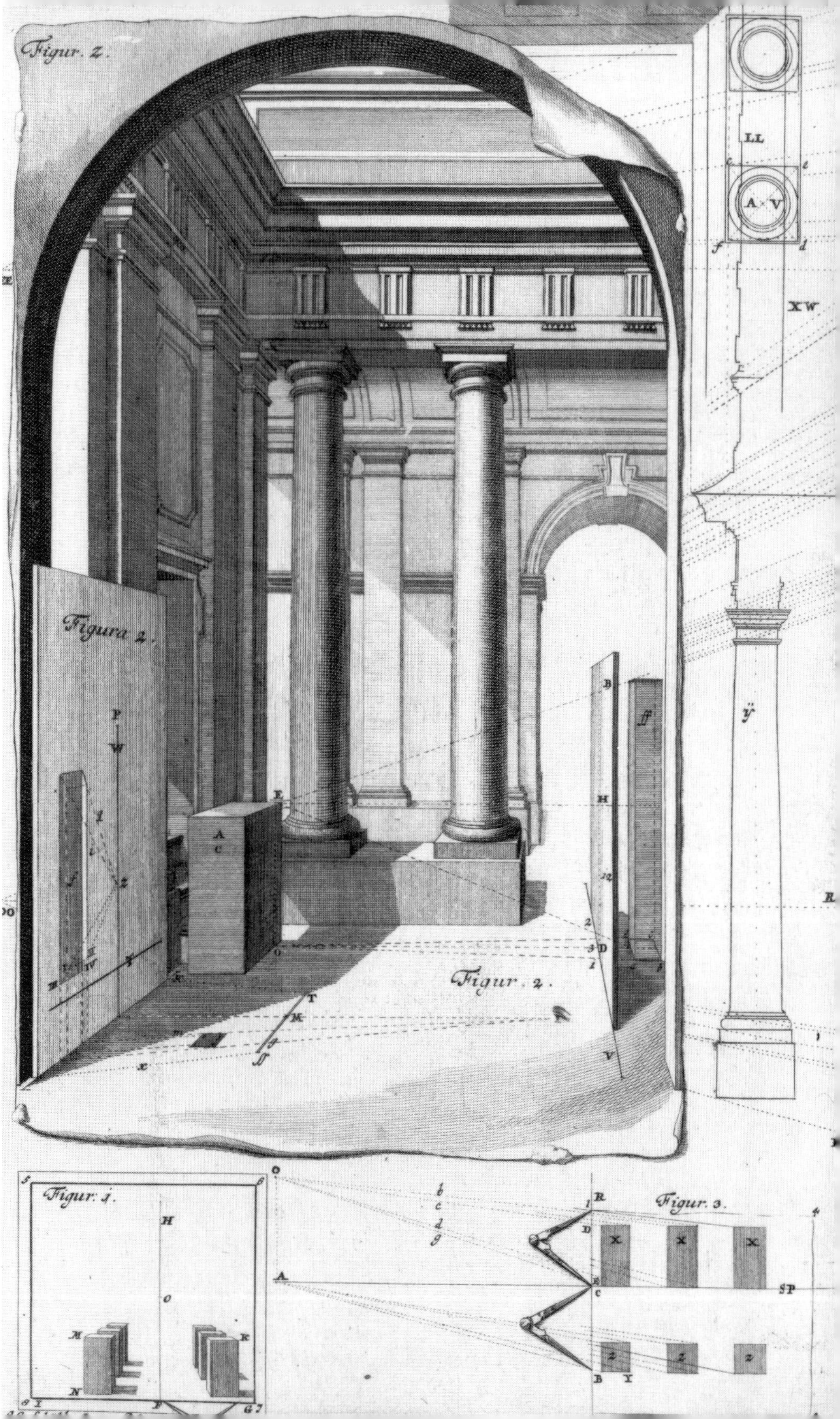
Figur. 2.
Figura 2
Figur. 2.
Figur. 1.
Figur. 3.
LL
A V
XW
A
C
B
H
D
T
M
V
X
SP
z
H
O
M
N
K

Two plates from Jan Vredeman de Vries's *Perspective* (1604–1605), and one plate from Schübler, *Perspectiva Pes Picturae*. Early in the seventeenth century Vredeman de Vries attempted to normalize the representation of geometrical space through centralized perspective. Besides horizontal perspectives that depict garden vistas and room interiors [0.39], he also included vertical views *down into* a space [0.40]. While these latter perspectives appeared at first unnatural and forced, by the early eighteenth century they seemed to be truly systematized, as in the example from Schübler, a "case" that he names *optica longimetrica* [0.41]. The development of this mode of perspective is significant, and clearly related to the use of *perspectiva artificialis* as a vehicle to conceive architectural space.

Montreal, Collection Centre Canadien d'Architecture / Canadian Centre for Architecture.

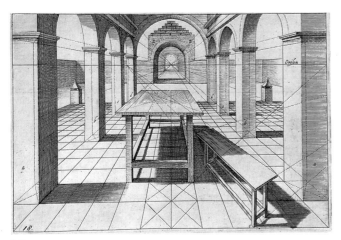

0.39

0.40

TAB.
24.

0.41

| 0.42 | 0.43 |

Two plates from Schübler, *Perspectiva Pes Picturae*. In the first image [0.42], the systematic relationships between *perspectiva verticalis* (normal perspective), *perspectiva horizontalis* (quadratura), *optica lateralis* (flat anamorphosis), and *optica longimetrica* (one-point perspective of internal architectural space from above) are shown in relation to "real" space. The allegoric plate from the same section of his treatise [0.43] shows the relationship between perspective, time, light, and space.

Montreal, Collection Centre Canadien d'Architecture / Canadian Centre for Architecture.

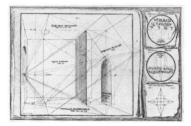

0.42

0.43

became integrated with architecture, it remained limited to the realm of *illusion,* qualitatively distinct from constructed reality. Perspective marked the moment of an epiphany, a revelation of meaning through the God-given geometric order of the world. During a brief period in the European seventeenth century, illusion was a locus of ritual. A revelation of order occurred at the precarious moment when the vanishing point, the geometric center of projection, and the position of the observer coincided, such as in a *quadratura* fresco. While in retrospect this may appear paradoxical, the geometric construction encompassed and sustained the sensuous, and it did not contradict qualitative spatiality. In other words, perceptual truth for the body in action was not contradictory with visual, geometric truth for a passive observer.

The simultaneous emergence of the modern "subject" and of fascination with the camera obscura are therefore not contradictory. Both can be seen as manifestations of the truth inherent in nature's laws. As we have pointed out, in the mechanistic optics of the seventeenth and eighteenth centuries the camera obscura was regarded as a model of the inside of the eye. Within it, images would "constitute themselves" and the observer would witness the laws of vision in operation; this vivid projection was considered a "true" image of the world. The observer in the camera obscura did not occupy the locus of an illusion but rather witnessed an apparition independent of her- or himself. Although this popular device evidenced an external geometric reality, it would be wrong to infer that painters and philosophers believed that it demonstrated a reality in which the subject is absent. The theoretical question of the observer being passive or active was taken up from the tradition of *perspectiva naturalis* and debated by philosophers and scientists, but perspective treatises usually mention the debate without providing an answer. Seventeenth-century perspective methods (with the exception of Desargues's) are based on an embodied viewer whose eye constitutes the center of the perspective construction. Indeed, because geometry was a *scientia universalis* in the seventeenth century, an observer in geometrized spaces such as the camera obscura, gardens, and baroque cities could identify with God's geometric creative will, the only true cause in Nicolas de Malebranche's philosophical system. Whether Des-

0.44

This image, like all others from Hendrick Hondius's *Instruction en la science de Perspective* (1625), rhetorically identifies the "vanishing point" with the eye of the observer.

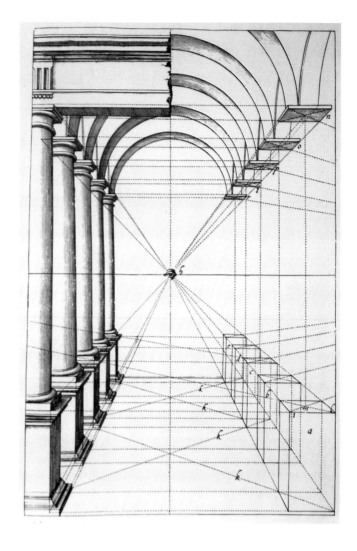

cartes's *res cogitans* (endowed with innate ideas) or Locke's *tabula rasa* (born with an empty mind), the observer of the magical phenomenon of the camera obscura was a passive participant in an essentially Euclidean optical system: an embodied viewer for whom *parallel lines never meet*. We may remember, on the other hand, that some of the greatest European perspectivists, such as the seventeenth-century Dutch artists and theoreticians Samuel Marolois and Samuel van Hoogstraten, were still advocating the extromission theory of vision. The ambivalence permitting the coexistence of the camera obscura and Dürer's perspective machine in a single epistemological model has been mentioned in relation to Kepler's optics. This ambivalence is also particularly striking in Bishop Berkeley's *Theory of Vision Vindicated* (1732). For Berkeley, the truth of reality was disclosed as a projection on a perspectival geometric screen, its grid being an objective universal language, "the language of the Author of nature."[97] This ubiquity of the observer, potentially centered through a transcendental mathematical knowledge and yet decentered from his anthropomorphic cosmos, is indeed the paradigmatic condition of the historical period Michel Foucault has named "the classical age." The observer was already posited as a subject in philosophy, science, and art, while the primacy of embodied perception prevailed in the experience of everyday life.

This argument is at odds with certain conclusions in Jonathan Crary's *Techniques of the Observer,* a provocative study of modern representation.[98] Crary argues that the modern subject and the camera obscura are irreconcilable indexes of different epistemes. Following the insights of Foucault, Crary emphasizes the discontinuity between seventeenth- or eighteenth-century observers and nineteenth-century observers, in relation to shifts in the understanding of vision, rooted in politics and power. While his discussion is most interesting, and on many accounts it diagnoses the rupture between "classical" and "modern" theories of vision in terms similar to ours, Crary overstates the importance of the camera obscura in the seventeenth and eighteenth centuries without discussing its precedents in *perspectiva naturalis.* Though many indeed were fascinated by the camera obscura because of its capacity to represent a resonant, magical image, its application in the arts is a highly speculative question about which there is little factual evidence. Crary's study can be seen, in fact, as a radical antithesis to the "progressive" history of optics and painting that is the premise of Martin Kemp's *Science of Art.* Both of these recent works on problems of representation in the European tradition take extreme positions that appear very problematic. Such complex questions, with great repercussions for our own artistic and architectural practice, demand a different kind of thinking and cannot be reduced to either a simplistic progressive continuity or a radical historicity. In our opinion, the epistemological discontinuities of vision must be acknowledged, but without disregarding a continuity in the history of European science and philosophy. It is our contention that the plot in historical narrative is crucial for discourse to function as a practical philosophy, opening possibilities for ethical action in present-day practice.[99]

Back to Modernity and Beyond

In retrospect, we now can appreciate how architects from the Renaissance to the eighteenth century—such as Francesco Colonna, Michelangelo, Guarino Guarini, and Giambattista Piranesi—questioned the assumed relationship between architecture and perspective and sought other modes of meaningful representation that, particularly after the seventeenth century, *also* involved projection. In his treatise *Architettura Civile* (1737), Guarini proposed an architecture based on "projective" mathematics capable both of precision and of flattering the senses, while he warned architects against abusing perspective and concealing the truth of which architecture is capable. In this connection, he engaged in a fascinating argument with Juan Caramuel de Lobkowitz, whose provocative work we examine in Variation One. Caramuel believed that projective lines should effectively distort architecture and render it oblique, so as to determine a precise vantage point that might reveal its perfect geometry. Guarini's more "scientific" outlook, evident in his comprehensive application of stereotomy (the projective geometry of stonecutting) as the guiding principle for his architectural theory, culminated in his famous Turin churches, where a magical light descends through the evanescent domes and circumscribes the finite human world of experience.[100] In the chapel of the Santissima Sindone, light is far from being an image of rational enlightenment: it is rather an image of darkness—the true attribute of an infinite God, as manifested by the eclipse supposedly witnessed by Dionysius the Areopagite after Christ's crucifixion.[101] Recalling a medieval understanding of divine light, as well as Nicholas of Cusa's description of the attributes of projective vision, this "light of darkness" guides the imagination to the void that is the unity of God and characterizes that unique and moving space containing the most holy

View of the dome of Guarino Guarini's chapel of the Santissima Sindone, Turin.

Photo by A. Pérez-Gómez.

relic, Christ's own funerary shroud, which is itself a negative
projection of God's body.[102]

Amid the work of most seventeenth-century architectural theoreticians and philosophers, who were still striving to
relate the world of appearances and the mathematical truths of
modern science, the work of Girard Desargues was an anom-
aly.[103] He disregarded the transcendental symbolism of geometry, including the power of geometric operations and the
theological implications of infinity. He sought to establish a
general geometric science that could become the basis for diverse technical operations such as perspective drawing, stonecutting, and the design of solar clocks. Until then, theories of
perspective had always associated the point of convergence of
parallel lines with the apex of the cone of vision projected onto
the horizon line. Desargues's *Manière universelle* of 1636 was the
first perspective theory to postulate an abstract observer, whose
position in space could be geometrically projected to infinity.[104]

Kepler had already introduced a point at infinity in a
work on the conic sections, *Ad Vitellionem paralipomena quibus
astronomiae pars optica traditur* (1604). Desargues, however, was
the first to bring this point at infinity to theories of perspective
and stereotomy. Such an accomplishment is difficult to appreciate today, for we now take for granted the effective instrumentality of theories and rely on perspectival representation to
comprehend the world. Desargues maintained that all lines in

Les Perspecteurs, from Abraham Bosse's *Manière universelle de Mr. Desargues* (1648). These images poignantly convey the belief in the power of perspective as a universal method to configure and construct the world — not merely to represent it. Moreover, each and every person inherently possess this power.

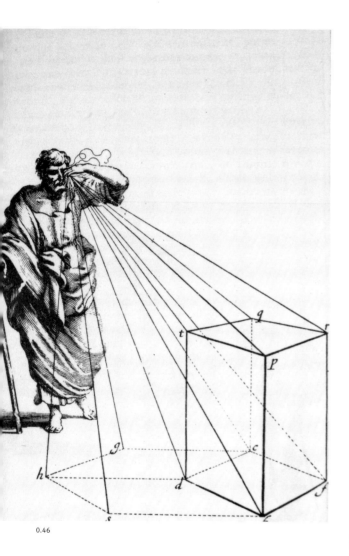

0.46

0.47

our ever-changing, mortal, and limited world actually converge toward a real point. Although this point was infinitely distant, it was present and susceptible to human control and manipulation. Variation One will develop this theme and examine the consequences of Desargues's theory in greater detail. Here we note only that in Desargues's work, perspective became the basic prescriptive science, a new kind of theory anticipating the epistemological shift that would take place during the nineteenth century: a theory purged of philosophical speculation and reduced to a methodology whose sole raison d'être was to control the *practice* of applied sciences in our enframed technological world. Desargues's system was the first attempt to endow representation with an objective autonomy. However, the prevailing philosophical and theological connotations of infinity, as well as the resistance of traditionally minded painters, craftsmen, and architects, made Desargues's system unacceptable to his contemporaries. Nevertheless, his basic aims would be fulfilled near the end of the eighteenth century by Gaspard Monge's descriptive geometry.[105]

Once geometry lost the symbolic attributes it had maintained in Renaissance and seventeenth-century philosophical speculation, perspective ceased to be the preferred cultural form for ordering nature and the built world. Instead, it became a simple re-presentation of reality, an empirical verification of how the external world is presented to human vision. Andrea Pozzo's treatise, *Rules and Examples of Perspective* (1693), occupied an important position in this regard, and it will be examined in greater detail. From a plan and an elevation, his method of projection followed step-by-step instructions to establish the proportions of elements in perspective. By avoiding the geometric theory of perspective, his theoretical discourse amounted to a collection of extremely simple rules and detailed examples of constructions, constituting the first truly practical manual on perspective.[106] However, Pozzo's work may appear to contradict his practice if we compare his systematic teaching of projections to his many famous *quadratura* frescoes, which filled Jesuit churches all over Europe with angels, expressing a religious desire for an epistemological recentering of humanity after the Reformation. The last part of his book developed the method of *quadratura,* in which architectural space is subjected

It is interesting that in the preface of his treatise, Schübler qualifies his *Perspectiva* as a continuation of Andrea Pozzo's work. Brought to an extreme, his position excludes everything in painting and drawing that conflicts with the principles of mathematics. Taken together, two images from Schübler's treatise (1719) offer potentially contradictory readings. The first image [0.48] clearly demonstrates the perspectival hinge at work, appearing in retrospect to anticipate descriptive geometry. *Perspectiva artificialis* could now be employed to conceive architectural spaces, coinciding with the scientific and philosophical geometrization of the world in post-Cartesian epistemology. The second plate, however, illustrating the construction of *quadratura* [0.49], still reveals that the purpose of these methods is primarily to create illusions, a geometric vision of a transcendental infinity, symbolic and yet distinct from lived space.

Montreal, Collection Centre Canadien d'Architecture / Canadian Centre for Architecture.

0.48

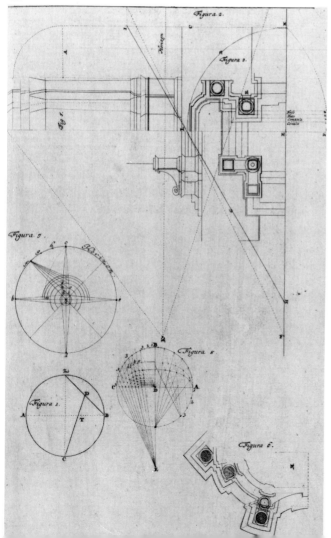

0.49

to the laws of three-dimensional geometry. This operational homology of qualitative lived space and quantitative perspectival space encouraged the architect to believe that a projection could accurately present a proposed architectural creation and, therefore, that one can "design in perspective." This effectively shifted the emphasis of the architectural task away from the traditional construing of symbolic ideas, or poetic making of buildings, to the making of "pictures" of buildings and theatrical backdrops.

After Desargues, further development in perspective theory required accepting the abstraction of the observer as a passive, receptive eye, which contradicted the perceptual origins of *perspectiva artificialis* as a construction in Euclidean geometry. Therefore it is not surprising that eighteenth-century artists, scientists, and philosophers lost interest in the theory of perspective. A significant exception was the cartographer and cosmographer Johann Heinrich Lambert (1728–1777), who was much admired by Immanuel Kant and whose work we discuss in Variation Two. In his treatise *La perspective affranchie de l'embaras du plan géométral* (1759), Lambert suggests returning to the phenomena of the perceived world instead of relying on a set of orthogonal projections. In brief, he sought to return to a "natural" perspective concerned with the visibility of three-dimensional space for an embodied observer. He was also the first to introduce the word "phenomenology" in a philosophy of perception. He believed that perspective is natural to human perception and is crucial for the (scientific) acquisition of knowledge. Unlike Pozzo, however, he argued that perspective should be freed from geometric constructions.

Perspective theory faced a dead end during the eighteenth century. Its predicament would be overcome only after Euclidean geometry itself—the foundation of both perspective construction and its optics—was shown to be inexact and even erroneous by the new functionalized geometry at the beginning of the nineteenth century. Furthermore, the central position of geometry in seventeenth-century epistemology seemed irrelevant for the more empirical, scientific speculations of the eighteenth-century *philosophes*. Despite the rise of "man" as an individualistic, autonomous bourgeois, emancipated from divine justice, and despite the realization of history as a process of human-generated change in which the present is truly *different* from its origins, the world continued to be perceived as an overwhelmingly ordered universe. In this world, presence and representation could coincide, despite an awareness of the impossibility of unmediated natural experience, which emerges in the work of Jean-Jacques Rousseau, and of the conventional character of language and other cultural discourses. Isaac Newton's natural philosophy still was driven by theological and metaphysical concerns; its absolutes—space and time—remained attributes of God.

The process of geometrization introduced by modern science in the seventeenth century was arrested by the empirical emphasis of Newton's work and by a recognition that Euclidean geometry had limited potential for controlling and transforming nature. Euclidean geometry was a science of immediacy whose principles were based on perception; thus it could never become a self-referential theoretical discourse. Seventeenth-century geometricians had reached a limit of abstraction and their achievements were never developed further. A cultural impediment prevented eighteenth-century mathematicians from disproving Euclid's fundamental axiom that parallel lines do not meet. Throughout the eighteenth century, geometry was becoming obsolete as a scientific discipline. Thus, Diderot could state with assurance that "within a hundred years there will be scarcely three geometricians left in Europe."[107]

In this context, architects seemed ready to accept that there was no distinction between a stage set designed with Ferdinando Galli da Bibiena's *per angolo* method (no longer with a privileged point of view) and the permanent tectonic reality of their craft.[108] In a world transformed into a two-point perspective, each individual spectator occupied an equivalent place. Reality was transformed into a universe of re-presentations. In the rococo church, baroque illusion became a potential delusion. Even the privileged vantage points of frescoes became inaccessible to the spectator. These buildings became highly rhetorical, self-referential "theaters," where the traditional religious rituals were no longer unquestionable vehicles for existential orientation.[109] Humanity's *participation* in the symbolic (and divine) order of the world was starting to become a matter of self-conscious faith rather than self-evident embodied

The pilgrimage church of Ottobeuren in southern Germany. Rococo fresco painting preserves illusionism while removing the station point of *quadratura* away from the space of ritual in the nave of the church. Illusionism thus suggests that the distance between the depicted world (of God) and the space of man may be truly insurmountable. This is already the "aesthetic" distance of modern art, potentially excluding the participation of the (passive) spectator from the representation and so running the risk of falling into formalism and cultural irrelevance.

Photo by A. Pérez-Gómez.

knowledge, despite the pervasive (and unquestionably influential) deistic and Masonic affirmation of the coincidence between revealed and scientific truths. The corresponding chasm between the autonomous art object and a passive observer— that is, the potential non-sense of "art for art's sake"—was also first articulated at this time in early discussions on aesthetics (by Alexander Baumgarten), to become a crucial problem for architects and artists ever since.

The concept of theatrical space as the space of architecture coincided with architects' growing realization that meaning itself might be a matter of convention, rather than being guaranteed by nature. For the first time in history, theoretical treatises raised this issue and promoted the notion of *character* as a strategy to generate meaningful buildings. Substituting for the traditional cosmological analogy, the linguistic analogy would eventually become inescapable in modern and postmodern architecture, often leading to extremely dangerous positions such as typological rationalism, self-referential formalism, and pseudo-poetic expressionism. During the eighteenth century, this emerging consciousness resulted in the deliberate application of montage in works by Giambattista Piranesi, Jean-

Laurent Legeay, and Jean-Charles Delafosse—prophetic of surrealist juxtapositions and cubist deconstructions of Euclidean space, already indicative of different attitudes to history and an imagination no longer bound to a firm cosmology. The metaphoric power of the image brought together disparate fragments to reveal something *other;* representations turned into deliberate *presentations* through a critique of the limitations of a poetic *praxis* in the age of reason.

Indeed, Piranesi's vast oeuvre embodies the first deliberate use of montage in architecture to explode and destructure the homogeneous space and linear time implied in perspective. His "history of architecture" is a story reconstituted from frag-

| 0.51 |

Giambattista Piranesi's plate from the *Carceri,* second state (1760). The explosion of perspective into a temporal montage creates a poetic distance that invites participation while suggesting different modes of inhabitation than those expected in the Enlightenment world, where perspective has become the natural, eventually prosaic, depth of experience.

ments of tradition, an "intertextual" construction that nevertheless seeks to legitimate the mythopoetic origins of
architecture. In Piranesi's *Carceri* etchings, meaning is saved at
the expense of perspectival logic. His mysterious projections
involve the beholder in a discontinuous space that invites inhabitation but ultimately awaits the rebuilding of its dislocated
parts.[110] This architecture suggests a potentially different way of
recasting truth into work, a different future "order" for human
life beyond the conventional opposition between the traditional
"fine arts" and technology, an opposition now clearly obsolete.[111] Looking retrospectively at the modern era, we can now
easily identify architectural ideas embodied in critical projects
of many kinds, acknowledging the difficulties of building a
symbolic order in a world preoccupied with production and
pragmatic shelter. Furthermore, this architecture has resisted
absolute, dogmatic truths and, more recently, positivistic science and the pragmatic, demythifying mentality that has under-
scored building practice since the mid-eighteenth century.
Piranesi, we may recall, actually rejected many commissions
while he insisted on calling himself an architect.

Paradoxically, the emergence of "architecture" such as
Piranesi's coincided in the eighteenth century with a greater
objectification of the architectural project through more systematic methods of presentation. The work of Jean-Laurent
Legeay, which we will examine in Variation Two, is significant
in this regard. As a kindred spirit of Piranesi, he was an important teacher of a whole generation of French architects in
the mid-eighteenth century, including Boullée, De Wailly,
Peyre, and Moreau-Desproux. He maintained, as a fundamental premise of his teachings, that a project is not complete without a rendered perspective view of the whole building. Legeay's
totalizing imagination is consistent with early-eighteenth-
century academic attempts to ridicule the secrets of the guilds,
with emerging concepts of the architect as a rational coordina-
tor of craftsmen,[112] and with the ensuing systematization of
construction after 1750. Yet architectural practice during the
eighteenth century was never prescribed by a planner's *devis*—
a comprehensive set of specifications that accompany the project. The builder's experience remained the ultimate criterion
for action, and its lack, in the case of Legeay, led to numerous

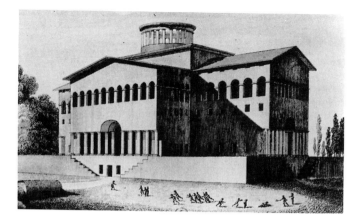

| 0.52 |

A building in perspective shown in its natural context, from Claude-Nicolas Ledoux's *L'Architecture* (1806). Perspective renderings were often used by Ledoux to express a new awareness of architecture as a cultural construction (as opposed to being an absolute, cosmological image) reconciled with its natural setting. This "naturalized" perspective is used as a rhetorical device to reconcile the architect's power of invention (at the end of the classical period) with its intersubjective origin in nature, thus ensuring the role of architecture as an effective social order.

problems.[113] Perspective renderings, however precise, could reveal the character (physiognomy) of the building in its natural site, such as those of Claude-Nicolas Ledoux; yet they could not be conceived merely as predictive tools.

Indeed, the late neoclassical interest in assimilating architecture and painting coincides with the eighteenth-century belief that truth could be attained through representation.[114] Once nature itself was invested with a transcendental power previously reserved for God or a sovereign, both painters and architects sought to represent its infinite immensity. Most painters stopped painting finite settings with symbolic actions and shifted their interest to nature. There is a profound affinity between God's space in Étienne-Louis Boullée's cenotaph for Newton, or in his perspectives for a "metropolitan cathedral," and the infinite space of Turner's landscapes; both present the immense and infinite character of a deistic god, a "natural" character intended to be that of the architectural space itself. Like Piranesi, Boullée emphasized in *Essai sur l'art* that his architecture was exemplified by Newton's cenotaph, not by his constructed buildings. His many theoretical projects are obviously critical works in their own right; they are not formalistic or self-referential games, nor are they merely unbuilt architecture. Ever since the "age of representation," theoretical projects have become a privileged means to question the possibility of a truly poetic architecture in a prosaic world. At the same time, their architecture construes a fiction, a potentially poetic life in the future, best exemplified in Ledoux's original and grandiose nar-

rative *L'architecture considerée sous le rapport de l'art, des moeurs et de
la législation* (1806), an architectural theory radically different
from the Vitruvian and classical scientific tradition.

Casting Light onto Modernity

Toward the end of the eighteenth century, mathematical theories in which infinity was included as a recognizable number
(Leibniz's and Newton's, and particularly infinitesimal calculus)
were finally accepted as mere operational devices devoid of
symbolic connotation. They became instrumentalized and were
applied to various technological endeavors: to mechanics by
J. L. Lagrange, to statics by C. A. Coulomb, and—in architecture and engineering—to structural analysis by L. M. H.
Navier.[115]

This period also saw the development of scientific optics by Augustin Fresnel, who elaborated on earlier speculations
about the nature of light as waves (originated by Christiaan Huygens in 1678) and capitalized on the discovery of light's finite
speed. Before the late sixteenth century, light generally had
been identified with God's presence; it was believed to be everywhere simultaneously, and its speed was believed to be infinite or at least immeasurably great.[116] Indeed, Francis Bacon
(1561–1626) was probably the first modern to be alarmed by

the potential consequences of light having a finite speed. Such a postulate implies a split between "absolute time" and "apparent time," with the frightening consequence that the heavens' luminaries that we contemplate may no longer exist.[117] Nevertheless, it was only in 1676 that the Danish astronomer Ole Roemer, after observing Jupiter's satellites through a telescope, finally proved that light indeed had a finite speed. During the eighteenth century Johann Heinrich Lambert developed the discipline of photometry. Bringing the new scientific understanding of light as a demystified phenomenon to bear upon his theory of perspective had important consequences, which are examined in Variation Two. The most popular optical theory of the Enlightenment, however, was Newton's. He postulated natural light as a compound that could be analyzed into its component colors, abandoning the traditional understanding of color as a substance—associated with the four Aristotelian elements and with musical harmony—which had been present in the Western tradition since antiquity.[118] But Newton's optics is far from being a positivistic science. In his *Optical Lectures,* he adopted a five-color scheme but found it unsatisfying. "In order to divide the image into parts more elegantly proportioned to one another," he identified two additional colors in the rainbow's spectrum, so that "everything appeared just as if the parts of the image occupied by the colors were proportional to a string divided so it would cause the individual degrees [notes] of the octave to sound."[119] In the end, Newton construed light as a phenomenon unlike all other created things in the universe: like sound, it moved through the air in a periodic manner, and was not subject to gravity; it also possessed an inherent mathematical harmony, just as the medieval philosophers had thought, reconciling all colors of the rainbow into white light. These qualities revealed by science were both rational *and* mysterious, and they had a profound impact on the architects and poets of the Enlightenment.

Only after Newton's cosmology was questioned, particularly its theological presuppositions, could optics and *perspectiva artificialis* be thoroughly reconciled on the basis of a "truly scientific" (i.e., projective) geometry. In his *Géométrie Descriptive,* Gaspard Monge emphasizes that artists *must* take into account the laws of optics. Only a synthesis between optics and geometric perspective could become an effective hinge for reductive representation. He writes: "Nothing is arbitrary [in representation]; the appearance of an object depends on the tangents of the planes of the forms in relation to the eye of the spectator, the angle of the incident light and its distance. . . . For each point on the surface, the intensity of light is in direct proportion to the size of the angle of incidence of the ray on the tangent plane at that point and in inverse proportion to the distance from the luminous source."[120] For the first time we hear an invocation of photography—long before its time, of course—as the only scientific, "legitimate" form of representation. Fresnel's experiments with lenses in the early nineteenth century manipulated, magnified, and controlled light sources in a way that led to the modern lighthouse, and eventually to the projector and the laser. Only then did light truly lose its ontological value, and its study was merged with that of other electromagnetic phenomena. Furthermore, Fresnel questioned the need for a medium, such as the "ether" that had been postulated in traditional optics, to transmit light.

Until this juncture, optics had remained a traditional Euclidean science; the world of light—horizon of all that is visible and invisible (and thus true)—remained primarily tactile. The manipulation of light, like the manipulation of infinity, was not a simple matter. Only with the inception of projective optics did light, that most mysterious substance, truly become subject to human will. The projected searchlight beam—metaphor and instrument of panoptic surveillance—eventually would enable the technological transformation of night into day, and the concomitant cultural amnesia enabling humanity to forget that in darkness parallel lines never meet. Nineteenth-century man (and not the baroque prince) finally could assume a dominating gaze capable of controlling the social and natural world through the pure light of reason, supposedly devoid of shadows. We can perceive here (and not in baroque perspective representation) the possibility of truly reductive forms of representation leading to the universe of prosaic forms of simulation (such as journalistic photography, realistic films, and television) that proliferate in our world. Through this consummated synthesis of optics and geometrical perspective, light risked losing its traditional status as the mysterious horizon of things. We may recall how, in Martin Heidegger's diagnosis, the possibility of overcoming technological enframing—the reduction of the world of our experience to a "picture," and of live nature to an inventory of exploitable natural resources supposedly capable of sustaining an ever-growing economy—is related to a potential awareness of the mystery of light. It is significant that twentieth-century scientific theories, such as Einstein's theory of relativity and quantum theory, have reestablished the mysterious nature of light as a substance irreducible to a single scientific explanation. Recent theories in quantum electrodynamics declare that light is made up of corpuscles that travel through different media but do not behave in a "rational" way. In conducting experiments, all we can observe are "probabilities" (notated as little arrows). Though the speed of light seems to remain constant regardless of inertial systems, we cannot define its "essence." Perhaps not surprisingly, the same synthesis of optics and *perspectiva artificialis* led to a new awareness of the temporality of visual perception and made possible the nineteenth- and twentieth-century projective art forms such as photography and cinematography, which have opened for contemporary art and architecture new possibilities for disclosing embodied depth. In the last part of this book, we will outline some of these new possibilities.

From Instrumental Representation to Collective Participation?

The new valuation of visual experience, particularly after 1830, also coincided with the emergence of a reified "subject"—the modern democratic individual—after the French Revolution. The new interest in the physiology of vision had a considerable impact on new art forms whose mass appeal questioned the stifling classification of the fine arts. Architecture was threatened from two sides: by engineers and sociologists, whose disciplines were endowed with greater rational certainty, and by new art forms such as photography and film, which acknowledged better the political "reorganization" of the nineteenth-century observer. Architecture was still partly identified with the secular and religious power structures of the ancien régime.

It is clear that the political and epistemological changes of the early nineteenth century represented a true rupture between *perspectiva artificialis* and modern projective art forms. As we will discuss in the following chapters, however, in articulating the possibilities for architectural representation it is not sufficient to acknowledge such discontinuity. Modernist painting after impressionism, developments in photography, and eventually film cannot be accounted for if the *transformations* implied in geometry and its associated concepts of space and time are not fully considered. The new functionalized *theōria* accounted for a distinct articulation of reality that, in turn, opened up new conditions for human action. Only a thorough grasp of the dialectic between the profound historical roots of the technological project and its specificity during the last two centuries may suggest possible alternatives for contemporary architectural practice.

Indeed, not until the nineteenth century did the systematization of drawing methods enable the process of translation between drawing and building to be reduced to an equation. The key development was the inception of descriptive geometry as the paradigmatic discipline for both architect and engineer. The École Polytechnique, founded in Paris after the French Revolution, trained the new professional class of scientists and engineers. Its fundamental core subject, descriptive geometry, allowed for the first time a systematic reduction of three-dimensional objects to two dimensions and permitted the control and precision demanded by the Industrial Revolution. Without this conceptual tool our technological world could not have come into existence. As we remember, Durand's design method was entirely based on descriptive geometry. His *mécanisme de la composition* and its step-by-step instructions greatly facilitated effective planning by promoting the codification of architectural history into types and styles, the use of grids and axes on transparent paper, and precise decimal measurements. Descriptive geometry became the "assumption" behind all modern architectural endeavors, from the often superficially artistic drawings of the École des Beaux-Arts to the functional projects of the Bauhaus. Indeed, the handsomely rendered drawings in the Beaux-Arts tradition did not provide an authentic alternative to the architecture of the École Polytechnique. Despite sophisticated theoretical formulations based on linguistic analogies concerning the possibilities and limitations of generating meaningful architectural work without theological or metaphysical underpinnings,[121] the architecture of the Beaux-Arts seemed incapable of retrieving a symbolic content through drawings. Rather it tended to formalize appearances with a status of contingent "ornament" or aestheticized art.[122] This made it difficult to question "art for art's sake" and to ponder alternatives for retrieving architectural meaning through genuine symbolization (i.e., intersubjectivity and the spectators' participation) beyond voyeuristic space and linear time.

Axonometry became a preferred architectural tool only after Durand, who was already suspicious of perspective and what he believed were deceptive painterly techniques. Despite their historical origins, it is in the early nineteenth century that the tools taken for granted by twentieth-century architects effectively emerged. While axonometry extended the previous totalizing visions of isometric and aerial perspective a step further into precise objectification, it was also a totally novel instrument of representation, as well as a much more powerful means of control and coordination. The descriptive geometry developed by Gaspard Monge and Jean-Victor Poncelet eventually led to the famous rendition of architectural history by Auguste Choisy at the end of the nineteenth century, with its uncanny axonometric drawings—objectified buildings *truly* without an observer, occupying a homogeneous, infinite space. Axonometric representation became the paradigmatic tool for the architects of high modernity, betraying the same mentality and assumptions that would eventually allow for architectural design through computer graphics. We will develop this complex theme in Variation Three.

Today the obsession with productivity and rationalization that originated in the nineteenth-century has not abated. In conventional architectural practice, the process of maturation from the idea to the built work has been transformed into a systematic representation that leaves no place for the invisible in the process of translation. Even as descriptive geometry sought a precise coincidence between the representation and the object, a different use of projection emerged. Its intention, the model of which is closer to filmic montage, is to transcend the perspectival enframing, to transcend dehumanizing technological values (often concealed in a world that we think we control) through the incorporation of a critical position about the contemporary situation that might regenerate architecture's creative process, thus making possible a truly relevant poetic practice in a postmodern world. Modern art remained fascinated by the enigmatic distance between the reality of the world and its projection. This fascination, with immediate roots in nineteenth-century optical apparatuses such as the photographic camera and the stereoscope, responded to the failure of a modern scientific mentality to acknowledge the unnameable dimension of representation, a poetic wholeness that can be recognized and yet is impossible to reduce to the discursive *logos* of science, while it no longer refers to an intersubjective cosmological picture. Artists since Piranesi and Ingres have explored that distance, the "delay" (in Marcel Duchamp's terms) between reality and the appearance of the world. Defying reductionist assumptions without rejecting the modern power of abstraction, certain twentieth-century architects, including Le Corbusier, Alvar Aalto, Antoni Gaudí, John Hejduk, and Daniel Libeskind, have used projections not as technical devices to manipulate but as tools to discover something at once original and recognizable.

The work of some of these architects will be discussed in the following pages, particularly in Variation Three, where we focus on two examples from the architectural and artistic production of Le Corbusier. Selected images interject conversations around theoretical projects from Piranesi to Marcel Duchamp and Gordon Matta-Clark. These projects, in their own particular ways, establish a space which resists the domination of the enframing vision. In the concluding Coda, we offer some general critical conclusions and discuss how a truly poetic architecture may be seen to exist beyond conventional media and artistic boundaries. Because it is *not* a syntactic set of projections, poetic architecture is singularly difficult to construct, especially in a world where the only "legitimate" modus operandi is an instrumental technology. Theoretical projects have been both experimental, in scientific pursuit of formal discovery, and poetic, in artistic pursuit of an order that might be recognized by the inhabitant as a place for dwelling and personal orientation. Some outstanding buildings by Le Corbusier, for example, fall into this category, constituting a true architecture of resistance, "despite" their full-scale existence and usefulness. These works have subverted the reductive instrumentality of architectural representation and also aimed at transcending the enframing vision, in the process unveiling the true potential of architecture in a postmodern world. Neither intuitive nor irrational, these works are suffused with the *logos* of myth.[123] Their primary mission: to embody the ethical values of the imagining self, and to avoid at all cost the dissolution of the human body into the space of drugs or electronic simulation.

87

Variation One

Architectural Representation
and the Distorted Image

O new marvel of painting!
What might have been nothing comes into being!
Painting, imitating truth and
playing with a *new* art,
turns the shadows of things into reality
and changes all lies into truth.

* * *

Alain de L'Isle

I can see a rose in winter when
there are no roses; therefore the soul has the power
to produce things that don't exist,
like God that creates things out of nothing. . . .
A thing does not come from the outside to the inside,
it arrives at the outside from inside.

* * *

Meister Johann Eckhart

Against a Progressive History of the Image

The debate over the value of representation and the mimetic arts can be traced back to the very origin of Western philosophy in classical Greece, for it addresses the same distancing between humanity and the world. The apparent truthfulness of the mimetic arts was affected by philosophical concepts and theological frameworks. It ranged from the complete skepticism of Plato's *Republic*, which declared that the arts are "twice removed from truth,"[1] to the confident affirmation of medieval theology, which often posited the ability of arts as a model of knowledge to invoke through the visible world a higher truth of invisible beauty. Hugh of St. Victor, who wrote on *ars* (arts, crafts) in the twelfth century, states:

Our mind cannot ascend to the truth of invisible things, unless instructed by the consideration of visible things, that is, so that it will recognize visible forms as notions of invisible beauty. . . . There is, however, a certain similarity between visible and invisible beauty by virtue of the emulation set up between them by the invisible creator, in which, as it were, the glimmers of their diverse proportions form one image. Because of this, the human mind, properly aroused, ascends from visible to invisible beauty. For in visible things, there is form and shape, which gladdens the eye, sweetness of smell, which refreshes the nostrils, goodness of taste, which whets the appetite, and smoothness of body, which excites and attracts the touch. But in invisible things, the form is virtue, the shape justice, the sweetness charity, the fragrance longing, and the song joy and exultation.[2]

In the Eastern Roman Empire, the controversy over the nature of images became an explicit issue in theological debates. The crusade for and against the use of icons in Byzantine rituals provoked a quest for a new pictorial depth, as well as a great awareness of the transcendental character of sacred images.[3] For the iconoclast, the inscription of Christ's face automatically circumscribed and limited divine infinity and the openness of God's word.[4] The iconophiles, on the other hand, believed that iconic *mimēsis* was neither an essential identity nor a realistic reproduction. In his second *Antirrhetic*, Nicephorus the Patriarch defended the practice of icon painting, emphasizing that the icon does not "encircle" Christ's image like an outline of the living son of God. The icon simply guides the gaze of the participant, rather than providing a place of identifica-

The offerings of Abel and Melchizedek, a mosaic from San Vitale, in Ravenna, Italy (6th c.). The mosaic is a clear example of a space of ritual participation being projected "in front" of the image.

Photo: *Encyclopedia of World Art* (London: McGraw-Hill, 1959).

tion. The image of Christ is "empty of his presence and full of his absence."[5] Although the Byzantine world was aware of Euclid's theory of the visual cone, its mosaics and paintings never became windows opening onto a physical space beyond.[6] Instead, the space of Byzantine iconography remained in front of the image, in the space of the church or the room in which it was placed. This merging of the space of the icon and that of its physical context was partly produced by the visual convergence of parallel lines toward the foreground rather than the background. Religious icons were not, strictly speaking, visible ornaments of the church. They were instead manifestations of an otherwise invisible God. Christ, particularly, remained unseen until the icon affirmed and manifested His vision, filling the space of the church with His presence without human architecture ever physically containing Him. Byzantine representation could be integrated within a pictorial system only after the theological concepts that had prevented the objectification of the icon by the human gaze allowed the golden curtain of the icon's backdrop to rise.

There is no depth behind Byzantine icons, because the wall of gold prevents our visual intrusion into the divine space. It reveals and at the same time forbids access to the "beyond."[7] In a theocentric universe, what truly mattered for man was to find himself in God's cone of vision while performing all-

The Dormition, a Russian icon of the early fifteenth century [1.2], and Cimabue's *Madonna of the Angels*, painted in the late thirteenth century [1.3]. These two images, from different cultural contexts and times, both preserve gold backgrounds. They demonstrate medieval spatiality and its theological understanding of projection as the geometric propagation of God's light (His vision), illuminating (and making possible) the ephemeral world of man.

1.2 | St. Petersburg, Russian Museum.

1.3 | Paris, Musée du Louvre.

Two paintings from the early fourteenth century: *City by the Sea,* by the Sienese Ambrogio Lorenzetti [1.4], and Giotto's *Wedding at Cana,* a fresco in the cycle at the Scrovegni Chapel in Padua [1.5]. These images begin to suggest a depth behind the picture plane. This depth is unsystematized and mysteriously layered, yet it relies on a mathematical harmony that governs the supralunar world.

1.4 | Siena, Pinacoteca Nazionale.

1.4

1.5

important religious rituals. Stylistic particularities aside, this was as true in the Western world, for Latin-speaking writers and theologians such as Nicholas of Cusa, as it was in the East. Western philosophers and scientists, however, seemed more curious about the nature of the "curtain" and the possibility of looking beyond. As Jean Paris pointed out in his study on the gaze of the Virgin Mary, the figures in liturgical paintings that had always looked out into human space began to interact with each other within the frame until, in the late Middle Ages, the Virgin mother of Christ adopted a tender demureness toward her child and engaged in a liturgical performance.[8] Eventually the space of "presentation" became a space of action, as the curtain rose to reveal a space for recounting stories—initially religious stories—through gestures and memorable compositions. The thirteenth- and fourteenth-century paintings of Giotto, Duccio, and the brothers Lorenzetti are prime examples. As if on the proscenium of a theater, their scenes were deployed in a hierarchical yet harmonic depth, in layers of variable thickness punctuated by moments of spatial continuity, thus evoking the mathematical order associated with the divine realm. This interest, preceding the inception of the discourses on *perspectiva artificialis,* signaled a momentous shift in the history of representation as it ushered in a concern for the "real" visual depth of a scene represented in a picture.

It is not our intention to engage in a history of painting, but merely to point out the fallacy of a progressive history of the image. Art's traditional quest for truth should not be construed as a search for perfect methods of instrumental representation nor a progressive elaboration of geometric perspective. This is indeed a pervasive and dangerous misunderstanding.[9] Cultural questions of representation cannot be reduced to formal matters. Yet contemporary historians (and architects) often are deceived by an evolutionary history of perspective that seeks early evidence of a perspective "method" in writings on optical correction from Vitruvius onward. In their attempt to demonstrate a progressive use of geometry in representation techniques, some even equate the use of optics in antiquity to the Renaissance *perspectiva artificialis,* or linear perspective. As we have suggested, sources of Renaissance linear perspective obviously can be found in classical optics. In *De Pictura,* Alberti paraphrases Euclid's theorem from *De Optica* to demonstrate that large objects can be represented smaller and in exact proportion: "Let us add the axiom of the mathematicians where it is proved that if a straight line cuts two sides of a triangle, and if this line which forms a triangle is parallel to a side of the first and greater triangle, certainly this lesser triangle will be proportional to the greater. So much say the mathematicians." This theorem on proportional triangles is indeed a fundamental assumption of linear perspective.[10] However, one cannot assume that the organized system of a perspective construction was used to represent or, even less likely, manipulate space before the fifteenth century.

Samuel Y. Edgerton's books on the history of perspective, *The Renaissance Rediscovery of Linear Perspective* (1975) and more recently *The Heritage of Giotto's Geometry: Art and Science in the Eve of the Scientific Revolution* (1991), present a substantial body of scholarship on the subject but regrettably contribute to this "progressive" misunderstanding.[11] Edgerton discusses Vitruvius's use of the term *scenographia,* one of the three *ideae* that Vitruvius considers essential for architectural representation, which is the earliest formulation of this concept in the history of Western architecture (late first century B.C.E.). The meaning of this third *idea,* its association with the science of optics in Vitruvius's work, and Euclid's own potential formulation of a principle for the apparent convergence of parallel lines are hardly obvious or free from ambiguity. Nevertheless, Edgerton claims that *scenographia* describes "a form of linear perspective" developed as a branch of optics and that Greeks and Romans were particularly interested in this "practical" application of optics. He also argues that the system of mapmaking described in Ptolemy's *Geographia* (second century C.E.) is based on a "linear perspective system similar to that of *scenographia.*"[12] In fact, it was the sixteenth-century mathematician Federigo Commandino who, reading Ptolemy's works in light of his own interests, first implied that Ptolemy relied on linear perspective for cartography and orthographic projections for sundials,[13] initiating a potential misunderstanding about the nature of Ptolemy's "science."

This matter demands careful consideration. In his first book, Ptolemy suggests that the reader look at a "motionless

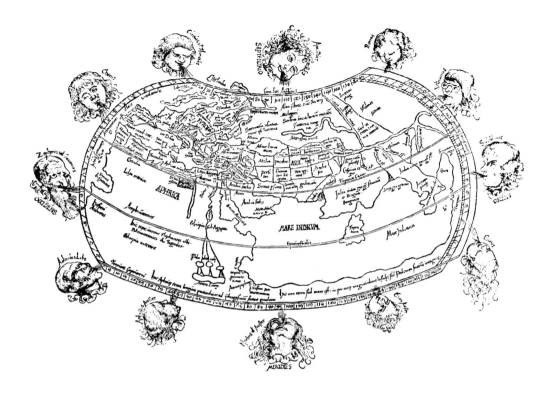

globe through a point before the eyes in which occurs the intersection of that meridian and that parallel which divided respectively the longitude and the latitude of the known earth into two equal parts" in such a way that they "will exhibit the appearance of a straight line" and one can perceive the curvature of the other meridians and parallels on either side of this intersection.[14] Edgerton misinterprets this description as referring to a form of conic section anticipating perspective. In fact, a careful reading makes clear that Ptolemy's text does not describe such a sectioning of the globe through a visual cone, but rather an unfolding of the earth's skin.[15] Ptolemy's reference to cutting in half the length and the breadth of the inhabited world refers to a subdivision of the surface of the globe transposed onto a flat plane, not to any kind of section through the mass of the earth. Moreover, Ptolemy's map itself is not a circle as would be formed by a section through the globe, nor an ellipse as argued later by Edgerton, but an elongated and curved stretch of land—the *oikumēnē*—whose center of curvature lies at the north pole.[16]

Throughout his treatise, Ptolemy favors astronomical phenomena over geographical observations related by travelers. He insists that positions and distances on the earth are best determined by observing the stars. Unlike sixteenth-century treatises on topography and mensuration, which were obsessed with measurement *in* the physical world, Ptolemy maintains that only the sky can be a true reference for understanding the geometry of the earth, and he devises a method for representing the inhabited earth from a description of the "armillary sphere."[17] This last method, characterized by Edgerton as the ultimate "perspective construction" based on the "distance point method," does not identify the observer's position at a given coordinate, as would be expected from a geometric perspective. The points Edgerton identifies as "point of sight" and "viewing point" simply do not exist in Ptolemy's own text. Ptolemaic maps in fact lack a specific viewer, because "they are not representations of the world seen, but of the mathematical essence of the [cosmos]."[18] Indeed, they do not appeal to the eye as an exclusive sense organ of knowledge. Furthermore, the very absence of a predetermined vantage point in Ptolemy's theory invalidates any interpretation that considers the distance between the eye of the spectator and an objectified globe as a measurable or even relevant dimension.

It is obvious that sight is a crucial means of understanding the Ptolemaic world. The gridded globe in Ptolemy's *Geographia,* however, is not a tool for actively transforming the world; it is an object of contemplation. The distance Ptolemy established between the world and its representation is not the geometrized distance of a perspective construction. Instead, it is similar to the distance between the spectator and the stage (*skēnē*) in the classical theater—a space that allows us to recognize the purposefulness of human existence in the plot of the tragedy and in our uncertain destiny. This is also the distance necessary for the philosopher's contemplation of the world. "Such a picture is intended to be a *schēma kat'analogon,* an abstract shape linked with the real world through measurement analogy. The geographical image skips sensorial input to use only the mathematical data collected by geographers and thus to display a superior level of knowledge. The resulting map is a *mimēsis* of a reality not seen."[19]

Scenographia and Optical Correction
from Vitruvius to Perrault

If [painters and sculptors]

reproduced the true proportions of beautiful forms,

the upper parts, you know,

would seem smaller and the lower parts

larger than they ought,

because we see the former from a distance,

the latter from near at hand. . . . [Artists] give their figures

not their actual proportions,

but those which seem to be beautiful.

Plato, Sophist 235, 236a

Propositions about the origin of perspective in antiquity focus on Vitruvius's architectural use of the word *scenographia*. Vitruvius's contemporaries and the early commentators on *De architectura* never would have conceived *scenographia* in terms of linear perspective. According to the first book of Vitruvius's *De architectura*, architecture consists of order, arrangement, proportion or eurythmy, symmetry and decor, and distribution.[20] The *ideae* of arrangement necessitate the use of *ichnographia, orthographia,* and *scenographia.* Here the Greek term *idea* should not be reduced to the concept of drawing, an objectified reading that was introduced into our tradition by Claude Perrault's revised and annotated translation of Vitruvius's *Ten Books* (1684).[21] *Idea* more properly refers to the Aristotelian notion of "image-representation" as *phantasia,* differing from both perception and thought, even though it cannot exist without perception and serves as a precondition to drawing.[22] *Ideae* in the context of *De architectura* are not only physical drawings in the modern sense. Rather, the category still implies the elusive quality of human tools of representation at the inception of our tradition, effectively occupying and revealing a space between Being and becoming. They are mental images kindred to oracular dreams that, as generators of architecture, possessed the fixity that we have come to associate with drawing and writing, without ever abandoning the ephemerality of the lived world and the spoken word.[23]

Since the nineteenth century, however, translations of Vitruvius invariably have rendered the original terms *ichnographia* (horizontal trace or footprint) and *orthographia* (vertical trace or face) by modern concepts such as "plan" and "elevation."[24] They generally also assume *scenographia*—the "semblance or shaded image of the front and the retreating sides, and the correspondence of all lines to the center of a circle"[25]—to be a literal description of perspective drawing. The introduction of these modern concepts implies that Vitruvius's text describes an objective system of coordinates with an absolute correspondence between projections, excluding the temporal unfolding from a graphic representation of space. But the hypothesis of a homogeneous space, with its system of spatial coordinates among plan, section, and elevation, did not appear until the eighteenth century. In *De architectura,* the very notion of order (*taxis*), the ultimate objective of architecture, is simultaneously spatial and temporal. For Vitruvius architecture thus comprises not only buildings but also gnomons (solar clocks), indispensable for interpreting celestial signs, and machines for revealing the spatial and temporal mathematics of the macrocosm.[26] Architecture sought to frame situations to make possible a fortuitous destiny and was thus conceived as the place for appropriate action at the appropriate time. Time thus intervened in manifold ways in the realization of architecture from the *ideae* to the building, as if the horizontal and vertical traces had a status similar to the signs of musical notation, both being subject to temporal actualization. In the experience of architecture, the order is revealed to the inhabitants through their participation in the rituals that the building literally houses.

In antiquity, the notions both of natural place (*topos*) and of space were opposed to the perspective image of the world and to the homogeneous space and time that have become primary assumptions of our instrumental world.[27] In Pythagorean philosophy, space was conceived as *pneuma apeiron,* and only occasionally as *kenon* (void), and it served as the "limiting agent between different bodies." Empty space existed in the Pythagorean geometry of numbers as a notion of limit between natural objects and as a way to ensure their individuality. The dominant notion of *apeiron* still associated the concept of space with that of matter; time and space were not separate mathematical concepts, and air was identified with void. Something similar is true for the Platonic *chōra,* the "third" element of reality (besides Being and becoming), which Plato describes in *Timaeus* as both *prima materia* and as the place and matrix of all things.[28]

The term *scenographia* in Vitruvius's first book may have implied some kind of pictorial depth, as found in Pompeian frescoes and Roman mosaics. Many authors have actually interpreted the "rationality" of these artifacts as evidence of an early manifestation of perspective objectification.[29] Their manifestation of depth, however, seems to indicate a desire to extend lived space and to emphasize the relation between natural places and a geometric, cosmic order, not an intention to subject the whole to a homogeneous geometric construction. This is evidenced by the very subject matter of frescoes in many Pompeian villas. Many depict a window or door that opens onto an exterior setting that is appropriate to the particular ritual associated with that specific room of the house. Whenever human figures are included in the frescoes, they occupy a spatial zone analogous to that of the actors in front of a *skēnē.* In mosaics depicting historical events, such as those from Praeneste (Palestrina), which date back to the time of Vitruvius, we indeed find "shaded images of the front and the retreating sides of buildings." The depicted depth, however, is far from being the homogeneous space of a perspective drawing. Where hori-

1.8

Scene from Euripides' *Iphigenia in Tauris,* a wall painting in the House of Pinarius Cerealis, Pompeii (1st c. C.E.). This painting of a theatrical performance expresses the implicit relationship between painting and the theater as artifacts of representation, both submitted to the laws of optics.

Photo: *Encyclopedia of World Art.*

The Conquest of Egypt by the Romans, a mosaic (1st c. C.E.). These Roman figurative works respond quite literally to some of Euclid's observations in his *Optics:* "In the case of surfaces lying below the level of the eye, the more remote points appear higher[;] . . . in the case of lines extending forward, those on the right seem to be inclined toward the left, and those on the left seem to be inclined toward the right." From these geometric observations it is incorrect to infer a central-point construction, as in Renaissance linear perspective.

Photo: *Encyclopedia of World Art.*

zontal lines converge, these points are *simultaneously* in front of and behind the picture plane within a single image, thus disturbing the expected continuity of geometric space. Furthermore, the narrative nature of the subject matter (the story of the Roman conquest of Egypt, for example)—again reminiscent of a theatrical representation without a defined proscenium, in which the spectator plays a part—manifests a "broken" lived temporality that thoroughly disrupts the spatial coherence of the images, one that would be indispensable for the application of projections as architectural *ideae.*

In another important passage of *De architectura,* again controversial for its potential link to linear perspective, Vitruvius discusses the design of a stage set in a way that may explain the representation of depth in Roman frescoes and mosaics. His description of the painted stage alludes explicitly to the laws of Euclidean optics (i.e., *perspectiva naturalis*) rather than to a geometric construction of depth: "If a fixed center is taken for the outward glance of the eye and the projection of the radii [the apex of the cone of vision], we must follow these lines in accordance with a natural law [the laws of optics] such that from an indistinct object, distinct images may give the appearance of buildings in the scenery of the stage, and so that what is figured upon vertical and plane surfaces placed frontally can either seem to recede toward the back or to project forward."[30] Indeed, the potential foreshortening toward the background and toward the front of the stage, based on the application of optical principles, recalls the spatial hierarchy of the frescoes, which combines a convergence of parallel lines toward the back and what has been identified as some kind of "inverted perspective" in the foreground. Vitruvius describes the "scenery of the stage" as an expanding space that not only creates an illusion of depth beyond the wall of the *periaktoi,* by transforming the permanent stage according to the required genre of theatrical representation, but also projects its illusion forward into the space of the spectator, who is momentarily involved in the space of participation.

The obligatory reference for a discussion on this topic is Erwin Panofsky's *Perspective as Symbolic Form,* a foundational study on the history of perspective that is well known to art historians but was published in English only recently.[31] Panofsky was the first to question common modern misinterpretations of Vitruvius's text, by comprehensively surveying the translations and interpretations of the concept of *scenographia* from antiquity to the early twentieth century. *Scenographia* in antiquity refers to the application of the laws of optics to art in general, including painting and sculpture as well as architecture.[32] In the fifth century C.E., Proclus's commentary on Euclid defined *skēnographia* as the third branch of optics. According to Proclus, it is "the practice which teaches the artist how to ensure that something in his work should not appear distorted by distance or height."[33] This discipline would provide the artist with techniques for regulating the effects of distance between the seer and the seen, and to achieve a desired effect between the background and foreground of an image. His definition of *skēnographia* is in fact a reiteration from Geminus of Rhodes (first century B.C.E.), a contemporary of Vitruvius who defined this branch of optics as "a study of those laws which teach the artist what his finished work will look like so that it will be eurhythmic to the eye of the beholder. . . . Works which are seen from a great distance do not appear as they really are."[34] It is worth reproducing Proclus's quotation of Geminus at length:

Optics and canonics are derived from geometry and arithmetic respectively. The science of optics makes use of lines as visual rays and . . . of the angles formed by these lines. The divisions of optics are: a) the study which is properly called optics and accounts for illusions [errors] in the perception of objects at a distance, for example the apparent convergence of parallel lines or the appearance of square objects at a distance as circular; b) catoptrics, a subject that deals in its entirety with every kind of reflection of light and embraces the theory of images; c) scenography (scene-painting), as it is called, which shows how objects at various distances and of various heights may so be represented in drawings so that they will not appear out of proportion and distorted in shape.[35]

These quotations make it clear that undistorted presence had ontological priority over any sort of distorted appearance, regardless of medium or diverse artistic objectives. Panofsky recognizes that even though the science of optics and the use of optical corrections were remarkably developed and well known in antiquity, the concept of perspective that would be elaborated by painters of the Renaissance as a unified technique for representing space still did not exist. Vitruvius actually refers to the science of optics in terms of optical correction when he describes the proportions of columns and the space between them. In III.3, he describes at length the effect of the density of the air on how the proportions of columns and architraves are perceived. Optical corrections based on *perspectiva naturalis* (i.e., the laws of optics) are "calculated" as a physical compensation to the diameter of columns—or other vertical elements—adjusting their thickness in order to make them appear harmonious to the eye. "The angle columns also must be made thicker by the fiftieth part of their diameter, because they are cut into by the air and appear more slender to the spectators. Therefore what the eye cheats us of, must be made up by calculation."[36] Giving priority to human perception over the absolute proportions of columns clearly postulates that the primacy of architectural meaning relies on the temporal experience of an embodied observer, rather than an objectified projective drawing.

Panofsky, however, fails to grasp the incongruity between homogeneous projective methods and the spatial reality of antiquity. Looking for an explanation of the fragmented vantage point in the complex pictorial organization of Pompeian frescoes, he proposes a rational graphic method according to which parallel lines would converge toward a central, vertical "vanishing axis" construed on the plane of the image. Panofsky's geometric analysis suggests a contradiction (which in fact is not present in antiquity) between the traditional tactile understanding that parallel lines never meet and the visual appearance of parallel lines converging. In fact, in most of these representations the "contradiction" is expressed through individual elements such as ceiling beams or cornices whose two sides are parallel, in a space where the general configuration suggests a foreshortening of the receding ceiling. Panofsky tries to find an "exact perspective" in graphic examples from antiquity, guided by Vitruvius's definition of *circini centrum* as the center of correspondence for all lines. The point or center of a compass—the most accurate translation of Vitruvius's expression—suggests many readings, one of which (Panofsky's) could associate the mark on the page made by the point of the instrument with a hypothetical center of projection representing the eye of the observer.[37] Thus, paradoxically, Panofsky concludes that Vitruvius was indeed describing a sort of linear perspective that was applied by his contemporaries through a homogeneous construction of pictorial depth based on a vanishing axis.[38]

This misreading of Vitruvius had its precedents in early modern architectural theory. In fact, it appears explicitly in Claude Perrault's "revised" translation of *De architectura,* which already offered a reading of the Vitruvian *ideae* that would seem obvious to any twentieth-century practicing architect. Perrault's commentary reveals his desire to understand traditional theory in terms of the epistemology of modern science, and indeed reveals more about his polemical understanding of seventeenth-century architecture and its relationship to perspective than about Vitruvius's original intentions.[39] In the preface, he bluntly confesses that he felt justified to "rectify" the inconsistencies (sometimes attributed to careless copyists) found in the original text, since Vitruvius supposedly was deliberately obscure and malicious in hiding his true ideas so that other architects of his time would not take advantage of them.[40] Perrault assumed that the term *scenographia* referred to a depiction of the entire building, simultaneously presenting the main facade and its sides.[41] Further assuming an objective spatial correspondence between plan (*ichnographia*) and elevation (*orthographia*), he resolved the ambiguity of the word *ideae,* or *species dispositionis,* by substituting for it the notion of "representation," which clearly implies the use of drawings. Perrault most certainly meant to convey the meaning of "perspective" in this passage, since he believed in the importance of perspective as a tool for architects. His translation of *scenographia* is nevertheless faithful to the Latin text and mentions the simultaneous view of the front elevation with the sides converging toward a center.[42]

More significantly, Perrault was the first architect and theoretician in the Western tradition to deny the importance of optical corrections, traditionally invoked to adjust the real dimensions of a building in order to convey, in the primary tactile realm of lived experience, the perfection of a geometric or mathematical order expressed in the discourse of theory and cosmology. Thus he could not have agreed with any of the previous authors and translators who claimed that Vitruvius meant something other than linear perspective in the passage about architectural *ideae.* Indeed, the point seemed so obvious that, unlike his immediate predecessors, he didn't even bother to discuss it. According to him, Vitruvius favored perfect mathematical proportions but recommended optical corrections only to account for the imperfection of craftsmen in the execution of projects. Perrault assumed, in a Cartesian frame of mind, an absolute coincidence between what "is" (the mathematical proportions of a building) and what we see (its phenomenal appearance). Perrault claimed that optical corrections were not important in themselves but served only as remedy for faulty craftsmanship through the ages, and thus they were encouraged by previous writers simply to justify discrepancies between mystifying, imprecise past theories and the practice of architecture. Such optical adjustments should be used only when we want to make certain architectural details appear bigger than they actually are. In short, he believed that perception is not affected by the physical limitations of our vision, since the mind can perceive directly the perfect proportions of a mathematical order. This amounts to a recognition of the absolute hegemony of vision in architectural theory and practice. For Perrault the space of architecture was already homologous with the universal space of Cartesian geometry. Architecture and its representations "existed" in perspective space.[43]

Model and Scenography

While Perrault's denial of the "problem" of optical correction is a radical innovation, providing a justification to postulate in his *Ordonnance des cinq espèces de colonnes* (1683) a rationalized system of proportions for the classical orders driven by the new theory's potentially unequivocal applicability, he was certainly not the first to understand the third Vitruvian *idea* as linear perspective. Already during the Renaissance, once *perspectiva artificialis* started influencing the art of painting, the texts of antiquity often were interpreted in terms of the new drawing techniques. In drawings based on sectioning the cone of vision, the convergence of lines was particularly obvious when the subject of representation was itself architectural, for its angles and straight lines could reinforce the geometric pattern of lines. As we have suggested, this interest of painters in architecture constituted the first basis for an association between perspective and architecture, one that, nevertheless, did not transform the new classical architecture of the Italian Renaissance into a "perspective construction."[44] The long-term impact of the heterogeneous practice of *perspectiva artificialis* on architecture is a complex and fascinating issue.[45]

Vincenzo Scamozzi in *L'Idea della Architettura Universale* (1615) discusses the three Vitruvian *ideae* in a particularly interesting way. Plan, elevation, and *profillo,* he says, enable the architect to translate the essence of the natural and the supernatural world into a copy of the "Modello," meaning a copy of the universe.[46] He translates *scenographia* as *profilo,* which can be either a simple drawing, a perspective, or a model. Scamozzi's definition of *scenographia* does not refer to a precise mode of drawing (such as section or perspective) but rather a manner of representing the relief or depth of a facade, showing the correspondence of all "natural lines" to the eye.[47] For him, it is the mode of natural perception.

The multiple meanings that Scamozzi attributes to the Vitruvian word *scenographia,* and particularly his association of the word *profilo* with *modello,* bear careful consideration. First, we must remember that the word *profilo* often was used as a synonym of *disegno,* the lines expressing the "outline" of an idea formed in the mind of the artist that constitute "the beginning and the end [of the art of architecture]."[48] Similarly, it appears that the modern meaning of "model," referring to an "original" that should be imitated, also acquired currency in the artistic discourse of the sixteenth century, particularly in the Italian context. Before this time, *modello* carried the primary connotations of measurement and proportion, because of its etymological derivation from *modus* and *modulus. Modus* in Latin was properly a measurement for something. It was applied to music, for example, to differentiate the qualitative *ēthos* of the Dorian mode—a virile, sober, and strong modulation—from the character of other modes, such as the Lydian or Phrygian. *Modulus,* the first diminutive of *modus,* was applied to architecture and used by Vitruvius to designate the semidiameter of a column, the indispensable basis for the ratio of good and beautiful proportion. According to Italian, French, and Spanish etymological dictionaries, "model" was used during the Middle Ages as a synonym of "module," and it generated the words "molding" and "mold." It implied a one-to-one relationship between the preexisting order of the universe and human artifacts created as a *mimēsis* of divine purpose. Francesco di Giorgio Martini during the fifteenth century and Vignola during the sixteenth century still used the word *modello* to refer to a quantitative dimension, usually a subdivision of the primary module.[49]

The root of *modello* clearly is present also in the Italian word *modani,* used during the fifteenth and sixteenth centuries interchangeably with *modelli* and *profili* to designate the drawings for cutout templates employed by stonecutters to carve building details.[50] *Modani* not only were the sole "instrumental" drawings absolutely "required" for the construction of a building until the Renaissance, but they were also a fertile ground for displaying the architect's erudition and capacity for invention.[51] Filippo Brunelleschi, for example, is known to have guarded his *modani* with great care, obviously partaking in the medieval craft tradition of secrecy, while Michelangelo displayed his immense virtuosity through innumerable permutations of moldings and profiles. Indeed, it should be remembered that the two Greek terms that have been associated with architectural drawing—and that may have influenced Vitruvius's own definitions—are both related to the execution of architectural details: *anagrapheus,* which probably alludes to template designs for details, and *hypographē,* which likely refers to the full-size drawing of a profile incised on the wall or the floor of a site, such as the tracings that are still visible in some Ionian cities.[52] In addition, the Greek term *paradeigma* probably was associated with three-dimensional forms or models. This tradition remained alive among the cathedral builders of medieval Europe and well into the Renaissance; therefore it must qualify all our retrospective assumptions about architectural representation. While the printed treatises that have come down to us do not discuss *modani,* there is evidence that a book planned by the well-known sixteenth-century architect Bartolomeo Ammanati was to include *modani* among the subjects of interest for theory.[53]

From Italian and French the words *modello* and *modèle* passed to other European languages. According to the *Oxford English Dictionary,* the word "model" was also used as a synonym of "module" in sixteenth- and seventeenth-century English usage. Furthermore, during the same period the word "modell" referred to the whole idea of a building, whether in drawings or in relief (and often implying scale), as opposed to a partial sketch or image of a project. On occasion, it was used to designate the ground plan or *ichnographia* of buildings and cities. In the seventeenth century, "model" often designated full-scale mock-ups of buildings, obviously related to the practice of ephemeral architecture and scenography in the strict sense of the word, that is, the design of stage sets. Eighteenth-century architectural discourse emphasized the modern mean-

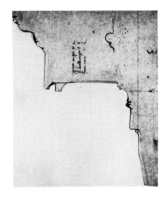

| 1.10 |

A template or *modano* from the sixteenth century. This design by Michelangelo was produced for the cornice of the base of the Medici tombs in Florence.

Florence, Casa Buonarroti, 60A.

ing of "model" as an "original" that should be imitated, under-standing it both as a small-scale representation of a building in relief and as a full-scale mock-up built to judge the appearance of the building "according to the laws of optics."[54] It is signifi-cant that while scenography eventually was assumed to be a perspective representation of a building or a city, during the eighteenth century it also became associated with the represen-tation of a building in relief and was regarded as synonymous with making models.[55] Although dimensions were not stan-dardized until after the French Revolution, permitting the pre-cision we associate today with scale models or *maquettes,* the construction of full-scale models of buildings or details before the Industrial Revolution was much more widespread than one would suspect. Scamozzi's association of *modello* and *scenographia* qualifies Vitruvius's third architectural *idea* with all the etymo-logical richness and ambivalence that the word possesses in the early seventeenth century, and it reveals the prevalence of con-structive over reductive forms of architectural representation and production.

In addition to the scholarly debate over the meaning of *scenographia* in Vitruvius, architects soon began to argue ex-plicitly about the relevance of linear perspective for the practice of architecture. This debate truly became heated during the seventeenth century, amid the early modern fascination with mechanical systems and the new mathematical physics of na-ture. In the following pages we will examine this argument through the works of two exceptional individuals, Juan Cara-muel de Lobkowitz (1606–1682) and Girard Desargues (1591–1661).

Born in Madrid to a noble family, Caramuel belonged to the Cistercian order for most of his life. He was an erudite polymath familiar with over twenty languages; a thinker who corresponded with Père Mersenne, Athanasius Kircher, and René Descartes; a political figure; and the prolific author of about seventy published works.[56] Caramuel's major work on mathematics, his *Cursus mathematicus* (1667–1670), became the basis of his unusual theory concerning architecture as the em-bodiment of theological concepts. Written not in Latin but in Spanish, his *Architectura Civil Recta y Oblicua Considerada y Di-buxada en el Templo de Jerusalem* was published in Vigevano, Italy, in 1678.[57] This meditation on the nature and divine origin of architecture constituted a lifelong endeavor that had started in Spain in 1624 and concluded, late in his life, when as Bishop of Vigevano he applied his theory of oblique architecture in designing the facade of his church.

Like Scamozzi, Caramuel also claimed that the word *scenographia* in Vitruvius meant "model" as opposed to "painting" or "delineation." In his *Architectura Civil,* he defines two kinds of perspective, one of which, he says, is of no use to architects. The Renaissance "artificial" (or "pictorial") perspective described in length by Serlio must be abandoned in favor of a "natural" perspective, because it does not teach how to "make" things that can be painted, but how to draw what already exists as it would appear to the eye if seen from a precise vantage point. On the other hand, he says, "architectural perspective [*Perspectiva Architectonica*] shows how to make things through drawings, . . . so that seen from a specific point, they appear exact to the eyes [*parescan en los ojos puntual*], and exactly as they are represented in drawings."[58] This "architectural perspective" affects the vertical dimensions of drawings or architectural elements placed higher than the eyes, while their horizontal dimensions remain unaffected. Caramuel's "architectural perspective" is indeed a *perspectiva naturalis* that enables the architect to make appropriate corrections to rectify optical illusions.

Girard Desargues, recognized by some of his contemporaries as the most brilliant geometrician of his time, was also a renowned engineer responsible for some unique architectural works.[59] Like Caramuel, he was concerned with the geometric order of the built world, but while Caramuel sought to make an order that would reconstruct the privileged point of view previously reserved for the original Architect—the One who built the world obliquely and gave humanity access to a center of undistorted perception—Desargues's fascination with geometry was of a very different nature. He was interested in finding a purely geometric order devoid of theological implications. His interest in distortions is unquestionably instrumental, as evident in the treatise of his disciple Abraham Bosse, *Traité des Manières de dessiner les Ordres d'architecture Antique* (1664), where his concern for optical corrections is made explicit in a plate

In traditional treatises on architecture, such as the many editions of Vitruvius's *Ten Books*, optical correction was always illustrated by a human being observing a finished building (as in fig. 0.4). It implied that the architect, designing according to proportions, should adjust certain dimensions during the process of construction, according to specific site constraints, in order to convey perfect order and harmony to the inhabitant of his work. Abraham Bosse makes the same recommendation in his book on the architectural orders, *Traité des Manières de dessiner les Ordres d'architecture Antique* (1668), and he insists that everything designed to please our vision must be based on optics. Most significantly, however, he substitutes the "real" building with a "scale" representation resting on the drafting table, implying that the architect could incorporate this awareness into the design process itself. Optical correction thus becomes a "case" of *perspectiva artificialis*, more specifically of Girard Desargues's universal method, ultimately aimed at eliminating the uncertainties of intuition from all technical operations related to the construction of the physical world.

Montreal, Collection Centre Canadien d'Architecture / Canadian Centre for Architecture.

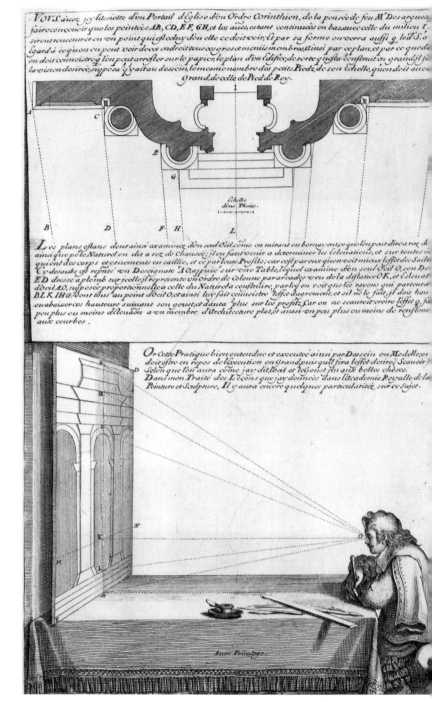

that shows a device for checking the visual effect of a facade by
projecting the vantage point of a real observer in front of a
drawing of the elevation. Using such an instrument, the architect could engage in the traditional operation of making appropriate adjustments to the proportions of his design. However,
Desargues substitutes the "real" building with a "scale" representation resting on the drafting table, implying that the architect could incorporate this awareness into the design process
itself. Optical correction thus becomes a "case" of Desargues's
version of *perspectiva artificialis*. Indeed, Desargues's greatest ambition in geometry was to define a universal method that could
provide a viable scientific and technical framework for controlling the practical aspects of architecture. But despite his hope
for a single, all-encompassing system, his architectural work is
rich and complex, and his precocious projective theory is not
free from ambiguities.

Sciographia and Projected Shadows

In his treatise on perspective (1569), Daniele Barbaro devotes
an entire section to the art of scenography, which he defines as
the perspective illusion necessary to create the three classical
stage sets: tragedy, comedy, and satire. However, he maintains

that while plan (*ichnographia*) and elevation (*orthographia*) inform us about the precise dimensions of the work of the architect, perspective alters the measurements and therefore cannot be included in the same category of Vitruvian *ideae* that define architectural design. Furthermore, he insists that the Latin word used to describe the third species of *dispositio* had been wrongly transcribed. "Many have read *scenographia* in the place of *sciographia,* and have thus inscribed it instead, that is, the description of the stage which wonderfully requires the use of perspective."[60] According to him, the original term was *sciographia*—from *scia-,* which means shadow—and was related to the shaded section or *profilo.* This third species belonged to the same set as plan and elevation, for its precise measurements could inform the entire composition. Even though Barbaro believed in the importance of perspective for the art of painting and stage design, his interpretation of the third Vitruvian *idea* clearly was related to the notions of section and shadows (*adombratione*).[61]

It is important to remember that in the classical tradition, drawing began when a Corinthian maiden outlined the shadow (a profile) of her departing lover on a wall. This story, told by Quintilian and Pliny, is repeated by Alberti in *De Pictura* without his ever associating the projection of shadows with the principles of *perspectiva artificialis.* Significantly, Alberti speaks of shadows in terms of the light of the stars and the heavenly luminaries, following the longstanding theoretical relationship between cast shadows and astronomy, rather than invoking optics.[62] Ptolemy's two works on mapping through celestial observation, *Analemma* and *Planispherium,* sought to represent the heavenly sphere on a plane and most likely depended on shadow projection. This relationship between astronomy (astrology) and "shadow tracers" had been firmly established in the Western architectural tradition since antiquity.

In *De architectura,* Vitruvius emphasized the importance of *both* astronomy and optics for architects. Optics was necessary for formal adjustments and proportional corrections; astronomy, on the other hand, allowed the architect to "find the east, west, south, and north, as well as the theory of the heavens [mathematical and musical harmony], the equinox, solstice, and courses of the stars. If one has no knowledge of these matters, he will not be able to have any comprehension of the theory of sundials."[63] The connection between plan and gnomons (shadow tracers) is further elaborated by Vitruvius in I.6. We may recall that he considered sundials as one of the three products of architecture, together with buildings and machines. Sundials were crucial for determining the orientation of buildings and cities in accordance with the symbolic directions and regions of the heavens.[64] In this way, architecture could be propitious for human life. The relationship between an Etruscan practice in the founding of cities (establishing the main north–south and east–west streets by tracing shadows) and the control of propitious winds is also explicit in Vitruvius's text. The city and the building could thus be healthy, in both a physical and a spiritual sense, in "time" and "space"; we should not forget that *pneuma* itself (spirit or breath) was associated with the winds and with the fire of sunlight, just as temperature (climate) accounted for the inhabitants' "temperament."

During the Middle Ages the science of optics remained generally unconcerned with shadows, its focus instead being the geometric order of light as divine clarity and wisdom.[65] The imprecision and mystery of projected shadows, with their blurred outlines and with their varying color and intensity, were givens in the traditional perception of the world. Yet the tracing of shadows remained a controversial question even after the Renaissance adopted it as part of the problem of representation in painting. According to Graziella Federici Vescovini, Biagio Pelacani da Parma's work on optics (ca. 1390) may have suggested, through his own reading of Ptolemy, that the knowledge of shadow projection could lead to an under-

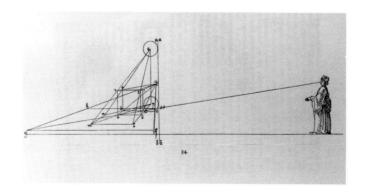

| 1.13 |

Albrecht Dürer's geometric construction for representing projected shadows according to the laws of perspective, from *Unterweysung der Messung* (1525).

Dürer, *St. Jerome in His Study* (1514). In his graphic work, Dürer applied his theoretical understanding of point-source projection of light and shadow. The apparent space in his engraving is a complex layering of heterogeneous zones.

London, copyright British Museum.

standing of the figure of bodies projected onto a plane. Thus, Pelacani seems to have been the first to suggest that "astronomy does nothing without optics" and an understanding of light.[66]

For reasons that should now be obvious, it was not until the Renaissance that a method of shadow projection appeared to Leonardo da Vinci and Albrecht Dürer as an indispensable complement to the new interests of representation in painting.[67] Through his acute, often contradictory observations, Leonardo never could "resolve" the question. It was Dürer who finally demonstrated how to project shadows in paintings according to laws of perspective.[68] The distinction between shadows cast by the sun and those cast by point sources closer to the scene, however, remained unresolved in the Renaissance theory and practice of perspective. This is a crucial issue for architectural representation, one whose importance has not yet been properly understood. In the world of lived experience, light and shadow are inseparable. The ultimate co-presence of light and shadows has been a privileged site for humanity's participation, through vision, in a transcendental order. The concept of shadows as a projection from a higher reality had long been a favorite theological metaphor. In the context of the new ontological epiphanies brought about by *perspectiva artificialis* and its geometric constructions, the projection of shadows was deliberately subjected to the same constructive laws. Sunlight coming into a space through a window was always treated as a "fugal" construction, with lines converging toward a distant vanishing point. The result was not a space homogeneous with lived space, but a space of intensified heterogeneity and mystical presence. Regardless of its nature, the source of light would always be construed as a point analogous to the eye of the painter or observer, *never at infinity.* In seventeenth-century Dutch painting, which is often characterized as the most secular of baroque art forms, we find a combination of extromission theories and an emphatic presence of light, with meticulous perspectival constructions.[69] Both the earthly space of mercantile society and the light that makes it visible are governed by the same projective laws, a layer of geometric illumination upon the clarity of *perspectiva artificialis,* revealing the purpose of human existence in a secular order that might otherwise appear banal.

Well into the seventeenth century, authors such as Salomon de Caus (1576–1626) and Samuel Marolois (1572–1627) remained seemingly unable to postulate a light source at infinity; all light in their perspective constructions still emanated from a point source.[70] Their contemporary François d'Aguilon, however, finally made a clear distinction in his *Opticorum libri sex* (1613) between shadows projected from a point source and those projected from the light of the sun. Although he used Dürer's methods of projection and deemed them appropriate for torchlight, he was the first author to comment on their inadequacy when extended to solar illumination: "Those things which are illuminated by lamps ought thus to be expressed in terms of scenography: as the light is small, the shadows are

spread forth extensively in all directions. Moreover those things which are exposed to the direct rays of the sun are to be represented *orthographice:* from parallel rays the forms that are portrayed share light and shadow."[71] In *Lo Inganno de gl'occhi* (1625), Pietro Accolti furthers Aguilon's criticism of previous shadow projection methods. Moreover, he was the first to introduce this distinction into the literature on perspective.

Although light maintained much of its symbolic power in seventeenth-century architecture, shadows in architectural representation followed very closely the development of perspective drawing. They evolved from representing an irreducible presence in the world of tactile experience to a more restricted meaning, until shadow projection became fully systematized in the work of Desargues, as the typical example of instrumental, projective drawing. This story is best told through some examples. Barbaro, we may recall, preferred to read *sciographia* rather than *scenographia* or perspective in Vitruvius's passage on representation. In a section on light and color in the same treatise on perspective, Barbaro also included a chapter on the projection of shadows.[72] While he adopted his method of shadow projection from Dürer and recognized how shadow projection can make things "marvelously distinct" from one another in painting, he concluded that the correct representation of shadows is more likely to result from experience than from analysis as a problem of geometric construction.[73] Probably influenced by Barbaro, Vincenzo Scamozzi introduced the use of shadows into his practice of architecture as a component of his polysemantic third architectural *idea.* In his architectural treatise, he included a plan and a vertical section of Villa Bardellini as a kind of "inhabited sundial," showing shadows cast onto the ground.[74] The geometric tracings in the plan of Villa Bardellini recall a Rose of the Winds, and with it the Vitruvian tradition. The projected shadows transform the architectural space of Scamozzi's villa into a complex system of relationships that unfolds in a nonlinear temporal sequence. The shadows in Scamozzi's drawings do not acknowledge an ideal position of the sun casting its shadows at a given moment, or even a single source of light that would follow a specific trajectory. The shaded areas in the drawing present more than a realistic representation of space: they disclose the relation between the "soul" and the

Title pages of two Jesuit works on optics and perspective: François d'Aguilon's
Opticorum libri sex (1613), drawn by Peter Paul Rubens [1.16], and Athanasius
Kircher's *Ars magna lucis et umbrae* (1646) [1.17]. Aguilon's treatise was the first
to differentiate clearly between converging shadows produced by local sources,
such as candles and torches, and parallel shadows projected by sunlight, implying
that the sun may indeed be at an infinite distance from the earth. Although this
distinction points toward a greater systematization of shadows, the title page of
his treatise depicting Hermes and Athena speaks of the qualitative difference between light and shadow. Kircher's later work, in contrast, was imbued with traditional hermetic themes and identified sunlight with the illumination of the Holy
Ghost. Its title page reveals a mystical scheme of Neoplatonic inspiration.

1.16

1.17

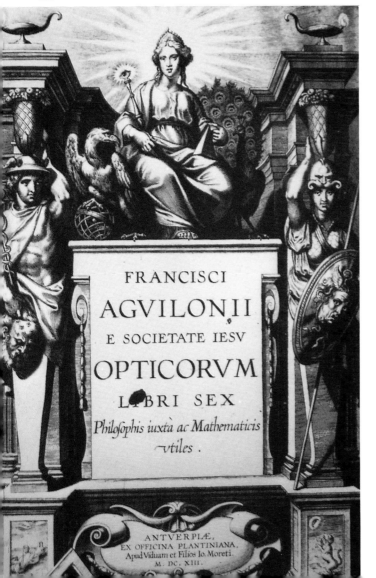

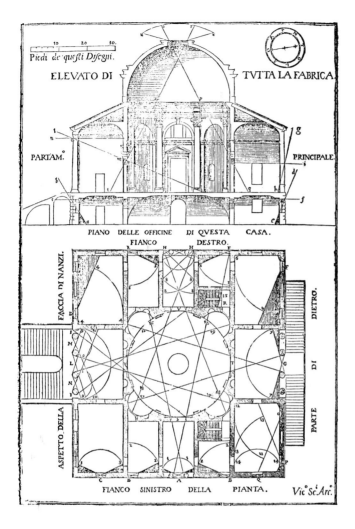

Vincenzo Scamozzi's Villa Bardellini as a shadow tracer, from his treatise *L'Idea dell'Architettura Universale* (1615).

119

"body" of the villa. Scamozzi intentionally denies a complete correspondence among the drawing, the anticipated building, and its shadows, because in his skiagraphy, "shadows reveal the light of architecture—the representation of shadows reveals the idea embodied in the design."[75]

Like Scamozzi, Caramuel also perceived the extended meaning of projected shadows. He shared Barbaro's opinion concerning the "mistake" in Vitruvius's text, which should have read *sciographia* instead of *scenographia,* as well as Barbaro's association between *sciographia* and *adombratione.* Unlike Barbaro, however, Caramuel had no interest in even considering perspective drawing as a tool for architects. In discussing the implications and actual meaning of the third Vitruvian architectural *idea,* Caramuel avoided the historical debate about the confusion between *scenographia* and *sciographia,* and followed Barbaro's path by returning to the Greek terms σκιά (shadow) and σκιαγραφία (translated into Latin as *adumbratio,* and into Spanish as *Arte de dibuxar sombras*). He simply assumed *sciographia* to be the original term intended by Vitruvius. Unlike Barbaro, Caramuel then interpreted *sciographia* as a variation of *ichnographia,* a projection in plan of the contours of a building onto the ground when the sun is at the zenith.[76]

Caramuel claimed that the art of perspective described by Serlio and other Renaissance architects could not be the third Vitruvian architectural *idea,* since it has no application in architecture. "The art of drawing shadows," on the other hand, is essential for both painters and architects. However, he distinguishes pictorial *sciographia* from architectural *sciographia.* The former reveals the volume of objects on canvas by depicting their shadows; this method of representing pictorial depth, he emphasizes, is not associated with perspective projection. Architectural *sciographia,* on the other hand, which Caramuel claimed as his original invention, is also divided into the natural and the artificial. The natural one can be derived from the *ichnographia,* generally understood as the floor of a building. When the sun is at the zenith, it casts the shadow of the opaque stones and delineates all the edges of the building onto the ground. This form of "drawing with shadows," uncannily evoking classical stories about the origin of painting, coincides with *ichnographia,* and for this reason Caramuel uses *sciographia* and *ichnographia* interchangeably in his treatise. Caramuel then asks the reader to imagine these same stones or bases of columns to be made of diaphanous and transparent matter, with the sun directly above them. This time the shadows delineated on the ground would vary in their intensity, revealing the varied thickness of a given profile; in the case of a column, for example, they would indicate the precise dimensions of all elements from the base to the capital, collapsed into a single drawing. The artificial *ichnographia* or *sciographia* is a reduction from full-scale (natural *ichnographia*) to a scale drawing of the plan. Caramuel's

A plate from Juan Caramuel de Lobkowitz's *Architectura Civil Recta y Oblicua* (1678), illustrating the shadow cast by a transparent column and its oblique transformation, illuminated by the sun at its zenith.

Montreal, Collection Centre Canadien d'Architecture / Canadian Centre for Architecture.

121

notion of layering the different sections of a column may seem extremely modern, as it involves the projection of different planes onto a composite drawing. His theory, however, is not without ambiguity, for although his system of projection is formally similar to orthogonal projections, it does not originate from geometric calculations of perspective drawing; nor does it assimilate a vanishing point at infinity to an accessible vantage point, as would be the case with Desargues. For Caramuel, the center of projection remains the sun, *el Sol Cabalístico,* which he believes to be the center of all planetary motions and the ultimate center of undistorted perception, yet inaccessible to man.

As a predecessor to Caramuel's oblique architecture "considered and drawn from the Temple of Jerusalem," Juan Bautista Villalpando's treatise on the Temple of Solomon (1596–1604) also assumed the architectural *ichnographia* or plan to be a projection: not a geometric abstract operation, but literally an image drawn from the light of God that could be realized in human works, revealing to the senses the mystery of Incarnation. Architecture was thus identified as a theoretical discipline in search of truth, analogous to science and philosophy.[77] But in this theological context Villalpando argues against Barbaro and states his belief that Vitruvius should have meant perspective (*scenographia*) in his famous passage about architectural ideas.[78] Perspective, with its precise use of lines and shadows, rather than painterly color (which Villalpando associates with *skiographia*), is the guiding idea of architecture, which Villalpando relates to God's own power to create fully in the mind. In the second part of his treatise, he describes the divine vision of the prophet Ezekiel, who was ordered by God to give the model of the temple (*el modelo*) to those of the house of Israel so that they could measure it. For the ideas of the future building to be measurable, he says, it was necessary to use a "new part of optics, meaning the part that includes all parallel lines that do not converge into a determined point, as in a perspective."[79] While he clearly understood plans and elevations to be "cases" of perspective in which the section of the visual cone is parallel to the plane of projection, he further develops this notion of a "new optics" through an analogy with light and shadows. When a source of light is either larger or smaller than the object that cast the shadow, the shadow itself will be either smaller or larger than the object; if the source of light is equal in size to the object, the resulting shadow will be projected parallel to the object.[80] Similarly, Villalpando describes two forms of vision: the natural one that assumes the eye to be smaller than the seen object; and another form of vision—god-like—that supposes the eye to be equal in size to the seen object. In this second form, vision would be contained either in a cylinder, when the object is a sphere or a circle parallel to the eye, or in any other parallelepiped whose base corresponds to the shape of the object parallel to the eye. While a perspective is conceived as a section through the cone of vision when the eye is assumed to be smaller than the seen object, the plan and the elevation—the "orthogonal" projections—in Villalpando's theory are conceived as sections through the cylinder or the parallelepiped when the eye is assumed to be equal in size to the seen object.[81]

Although Villalpando's understanding of the nature of architectural representation is in some ways very modern, the plan and the elevations of a building were not simply the objective projections that we now take for granted. Their truth depended on the reality of an infinite God, identified with the light of the sun, omnipresent in the world of experience yet casting "precise" parallel shadows. The very notion of an eye (the architect's) that can assume the size of a seen object invoked the all-seeing God who originally dictated the image of the temple, and therefore the orthogonal drawings embody divine "ideas" projected onto the human world as obligatory archetypes for subsequent architectural practice. This understanding of projection bears directly on Caramuel's notion of *sciographia,* in which the plan of a translucent building is drawn from solar shadows. The assimilation of parallel lines to convergent lines, later developed by Desargues as the basis of his universal method to relate perspective drawing to stonecutting principles and sundial calibration, could appear to raise similar issues. Nevertheless, while for Villalpando and Caramuel the whole discussion surrounding parallel and converging lines in architecture either derived from or embodied a theological position, for Desargues the question of projective continuity was devoid

1.20

A projection of "objectified" shadows, first described by Girard Desargues and Abraham Bosse, from John Joshua Kirby's *Perspective of Architecture* (1761).

Montreal, Collection Centre Canadien d'Architecture / Canadian Centre for Architecture.

of metaphysical consequences, being based instead on a demystified understanding of theory as applied science.

Indeed, it should be emphasized that the same universal method that Desargues used for an accurate, scientific calibration of sundials (real shadows) in his treatise on the subject[82] was also applied to the representation of projected shadows in painting and drawing. In short, Desargues devised the *first* "correct" demonstration of the projection of shadows by the sun, understanding that while they *were* parallel—for all intents and purposes, the sun was at an infinite distance—and remained parallel when represented in a painting or drawing parallel to the picture plane, they still had to respond to a vanishing point if they ran oblique to the picture plane, either into or out of the picture. By finally presupposing infinity to be *in* the world, the representation at last could be construed as a true scientific copy of our embodied, visual experience.[83] Abraham Bosse, Desargues's disciple and collaborator, taught this method to the painters at the academy. Despite the artists' reticence to accept the new abstract methods, it seems that at least on this issue Desargues's teaching had a lasting impact on artistic practice, as the painters became capable, though not always willing (for other cultural reasons), of representing homogeneous space as the space of human action. In any case, eighteenth-century writers on perspective, such as Brook Taylor and Joshua Kirby, would state without ambiguity that "the Perspective of shadows upon the Picture is to be determined after the same manner as the Perspective of objects. . . . It is therefore very surprising, that almost every author who has handled this part of Perspective, should have committed such egregious Mistakes."[84]

The Extent of Infinity

The Sun occupies a prominent position throughout Caramuel's treatise on architecture. The Sun is a beneficial planet, he claims, at the center of all planetary motions, and provides light to the entire universe.[85] It is the absolute center of the projection of light, as evidenced by his concept of natural *sciographia*. Yet the earth remains the stable center around which all stars and the whole solar system gravitate. In his theory of planetary motion, Caramuel favors Tycho Brahe's model of the sky as a fluid substance, in which the Moon and the Sun orbit the Earth, while all the other planets orbit the Sun. None of these orbits is elliptical.[86] The Sun's orbit, according to Caramuel, is not centered strictly on the earth but varies according to the changing seasons, describing various *circular,* nonconcentric motions. The eccentric movement of the Sun around the Earth is an important aspect of Caramuel's theory of obliquity,[87] but the centrality of the Earth is crucial and could not be replaced by the two foci of an ellipse.

Caramuel's oblique architecture (*architectura oblicua*), which he believed to be superior to "straight" or traditional architecture (*architectura recta*), was conceived as a distortion responding to a fixed and strategic center, the position from which perfection is made accessible through vision. His unorthodox thesis was discounted as madness by some contemporaries, while others, such as the highly respected Guarino Guarini, disagreed with Caramuel but took him very seriously. It is important to consider carefully the intellectual filiation of Cara-

Caramuel's model of the sky in which the sun orbits the earth following a path that varies according to the seasons, from *Architectura Civil*.

Montreal, Collection Centre Canadien d'Architecture / Canadian Centre for Architecture.

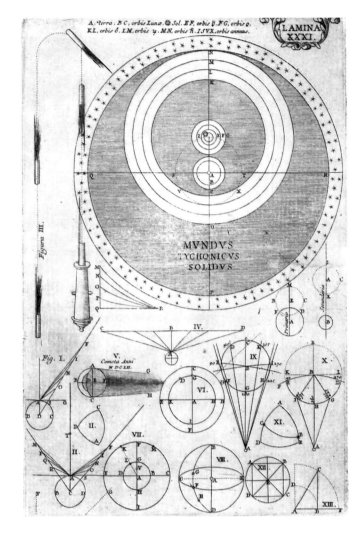

muel's cosmology, particularly in relation to the work of Johannes Kepler (1571–1630). Kepler's law of the elliptical orbits of the planets is itself not explained in terms of double foci. It is presented rather as a deformation of a circle, with the Sun remaining at the center of planetary motions. Since Kepler was trying to provide a "dynamic explanation for planetary motion, . . . the generation of the ellipse is conceived in terms of the *species immateriata,* of attraction and repulsion, not in terms of the geometry of the ellipse with its two foci." [88]

Kepler often has been associated with baroque art because of his law of the elliptical orbits of the planets, formulated in his *Astronomia nova* (1609). Even though he begins the first chapter of his treatise by recalling the suitability of the circle for astronomy because it is "the most perfect of all figures," he is forced to abandon circularity by the end of the third book.[89] In Kepler's mind, God expresses Himself indirectly, forcing man to traverse labyrinths of meaning, but nature remains the means by which God "signifies and communicates to man."[90] There is an obvious connection with Caramuel, who assumed the world to have been built obliquely, and for whom the ideal of a recovered perfection had to be mediated by an intellectual reconstruction. Kepler's first law postulates the orbit of the planets to be a "regular ellipse." His second law postulates that

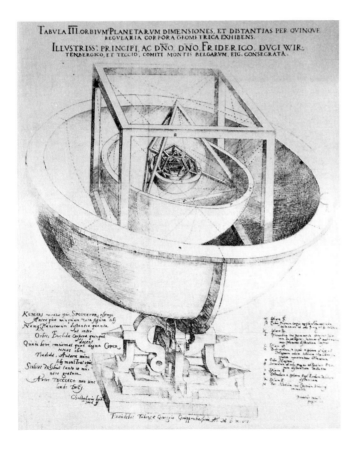

1.22

Johannes Kepler's proposed model of the cosmos, from *Mysterium Cosmographicum* (1597). The structure, based on the proportions of the concentric Platonic polyhedrons, was intended to demonstrate "the arrangement of the members" of the universe. It is worth remembering that this *compositio membrorum* coincides with the definition of eurythmy, which Vitruvius and his Renaissance commentators proclaimed as one of the crucial qualities of architecture.

Caramuel's cabalistic interests are illustrated in a table from his *Primus Calamus ob oculos ponens Methametricam* (1663).

Montreal, Collection Centre Canadien d'Architecture / Canadian Centre for Architecture.

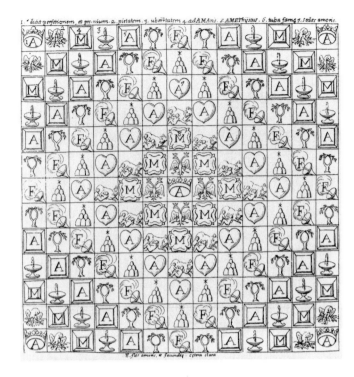

"in equal times, a planet sweeps through arcs of equal areas." In his third law, he says that "it is absolutely sure and exact that the proportion between the periods of any two planets is precisely related by a ratio of 1.5 to 1 to the proportion of their average distance."[91] For Kepler, this precise proportional relationship is due to harmonious proportions in the creation of the universe. Since the solar system comprised six planets revolving around the Sun, separated by five intervals, he also saw in the order of creation the inscription of the five regular (Platonic) polyhedrons.[92]

In Caramuel's system of knowledge, the Sun was also related to the art of *esteganographia* (the art of writing with numbers) in a cabalistic framework, as the light of the intellect that allows one to reveal or conceal secrets.[93] He claimed that *esteganographia* was necessary to the "perfect" architect so that he could communicate a higher and more precise order through his architecture. Moreover, the art of writing with numbers could preserve scientific knowledge from distortion and human forgetfulness. He speculated that the method for describing an Ionic volute, for example, probably did not exist at the time of Vitruvius. His new mathematical language could ensure that such geometrical knowledge could be preserved through time.

Caramuel's intellectual endeavors were driven by a desire for unity. Echoing the theories of a kindred mind, the Jesuit Athanasius Kircher, he believed in a universal science that would be the point of departure for all arts and disciplines. His fascination with mathematics was closely tied to the seventeenth-century interest in a universal language, itself prompted by a desire to reconcile the diverging interpretations of truth and, in a more general sense, to account for the gap introduced between words and things by the new philosophies.[94] Mathematics was to be this universal language understood by all, and architecture the potential embodiment of mathematics. Unlike Descartes, who inaugurated the modern dualistic concept of reality divided into *res cogitans* and *res extensa,* Caramuel simply could not separate mathematics from the sensuous world.

Girard Desargues was also interested in the universality of mathematics and geometry, and indeed all of his treatises make a claim to universality in their titles. Even his short essay, "Easy Method to Learn and Teach How to Read and Write Music," published in Mersenne's *Harmonie universelle* (1636), stresses his general interest in universal theories. Desargues's application of a universal method, however, could not have differed more from Caramuel's idea of universality.[95] While Caramuel's search for a universal language was profoundly theological, Desargues sought a method that would unify and simplify the graphic rules used by various techniques of representation, from perspective drawing to stereotomy and sundial calibration, enabling architects and craftsmen to control the practice of their art by means of a geometric theory. Desargues's first essay on perspective, *Example de l'une des manières universelles du S.G.D.L. touchant la pratique de la perspective sans employer aucun tiers point de distance ny d'autre nature qui soit hors du champ de l'ouvrage* (1636), was certainly an innovation in the history of geometry. Desargues's methods aimed at universality by reducing all possible cases of one specific problem to a single set of rules. In the case of his perspective method, for example, all one- and two-point perspectives could be drawn by following the same set of rules involving one point of convergence and one "vanishing scale" (*échelle fuyante*). His method of stereotomy could be applied to the design and construction of all kinds of vaults, regardless of shape and orientation. Likewise, a single system could resolve all sundial calibrations. Moreover, every method was based on a geometric understanding of conic sections. Desargues's new geometry led him to establish that orthogonal projections were simply a specific case of his perspective method. The notion of continuity among the conic sections, unifying the line and the circle through a coherent succession of parabolas, hyperbolas, and ellipses, was the basis of his universal method.[96]

Gottfried Wilhelm von Leibniz (1646–1716) was also concerned with the question of continuity. For him, the revelation of truth did not occur at the objectified point of perspective projection, as was usually believed in the seventeenth century, but in the temporal unfolding, the transformations connecting all the conic sections. The perspective metaphor was an important concept for Leibniz. In his *Monadology* (1714), he compares the universe to a city whose appearance varies with its observer's point of view, yet remains the same city. These partial perspectives on the world, specific to each observer, did not question the "unity of the universe from a divine point of view,"[97] but rather confirmed its complexity and the mediation needed for man to understand his position in the world. "Just as the same city regarded from different sides offers quite different aspects," he says, "and thus appears multiplied by the perspective, so it also happens that the infinite multitude of simple substances creates the appearance of as many different universes. Yet they are but perspectives of a single universe, varied according to the points of view, which differ in each monad." Leibniz compares the "apparent deformities of our little world" to perspective inventions that appear as confusion "until one finds their true point of view or sees them by means of a certain glass or mirror."[98] While individual points of view provide only partial perspectives on a complex and unified world and all points of view cannot be experienced, they could be described by equations that assert the multiplicity in unity of the monad.

Allee B qui aboutit d'une part à la tour C et de l'autre part au Berceau A

1.24

Solutions to several intersection problems, following Desargues's method, from Bosse's treatise on stonecutting in architecture, *La Pratique du Trait a Preuve de Mr. Desargues Lyonnais, Pour la Coupe des Pierres en l'Architecture* (1643).

Montreal, Collection Centre Canadien d'Architecture / Canadian Centre for Architecture.

131

Desargues apparently was the first to associate the continuity of the conic sections with a universal method of perspective. To unify various perspective methods, he needed an algebraic link among the conic sections that would reduce parallel lines to a special case of converging lines with their point of convergence postulated at an infinite distance. Following in the footsteps of Kepler, who had previously introduced the notion of infinity into the conic sections in order to link the parabola with the hyperbola and the ellipse in an unbroken continuous sequence, Desargues also postulated the notion of a point at infinity in his *Brouillon Projet d'une atteinte aux événements des Rencontres du cone avec un plan* (1639).[99] The greatest difference, however, was that the notion of infinity was brought into the tactile, "relative" world of humanity for the very first time. His unification of all equations relating the conic sections would eventually end the necessity for an initial visual intuition of form.[100] In this regard it is significant that Descartes responded to the publication of the *Brouillon projet* by commenting on the "danger" of assimilating parallel lines to converging ones. This reaction was echoed by a number of scientists and philosophers who were Desargues's contemporaries.[101]

While Descartes claimed in his *Geometry* that conic sections could be explained more clearly and easily with algebra than any other way, Kepler distrusted algebraic calculations. He saw a contradiction in the desire to "analyze" a continuous geometric form with discrete (discontinuous) numbers.[102] Kepler was also opposed to an instrumental use of the conic sections that would question the implicit hierarchy that related them. He believed in a continuum throughout the conic sections in which the circle and the line not only were different but were two extremes of a spectrum that also included other forms. Between these two endpoints, the ellipse tended toward circularity. "Between these lines . . . there is an order that depends on their properties, which is the passage from the straight line to the Parabola through an infinite sequence of Hyperbolas, and from there to the circle through an infinite sequence of Ellipses."[103] In this context, Kepler came to regard the point at infinity as a special case of finite points. As a counterpoint to circular motion in the conic system, elliptical motion could also validate the perfection of the universe.

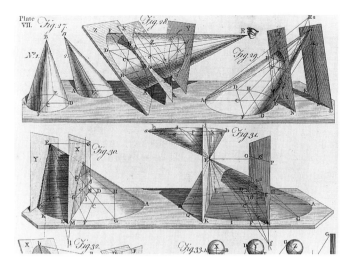

| 1.25 |

The principle of continuity in conic sections, from a late-eighteenth-century Scottish treatise on perspective by Thomas Malton, reiterating the principles of Brook Taylor. Significantly, and unlike Desargues's and Kepler's understanding of the principle of continuity, the cone in Malton's example is still literally identified with the cone of vision, and its apex is still a physical eye, rather than a vanishing point at infinity.

Montreal, Collection Centre Canadien d'Architecture / Canadian Centre for Architecture.

Even though Kepler's theory often is regarded as a precursor to Desargues's because it introduced the notion of infinity within the geometric definition of the conic sections, his cosmological concept of a progression toward perfection was in fact closer to the thinking of Caramuel. The ultimate goal of an *architectura obliqua* was to build an ellipse in the world of man that could be perceived as a circle from the appropriate vantage point. In his *Questions in Genesis,* Père Mersenne (1588–1648) claims that "geometry is useful for expressing more fully God's qualities and works."[104] While Kepler saw the ellipse as a metaphor of motion tending toward perfection— toward the circle—for Mersenne, the parabola and the hyperbola were equally valid for expressing different attributes of God. Even though the cone remained the fundamental figure that generated all others, it was precisely the absence of hierarchy among figures expressed by Mersenne, which is the fundamental characteristic of Desargues's geometric space, that enabled the unified conic sections to become a projective model and the basis of seventeenth-century perspective, making it possible to postulate the notion of an infinite point *in* the world of man.[105] The role of geometry became linked increasingly to representation: "re-presenting" religious concepts rather than revealing the transcendent order of God and His creation.[106]

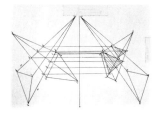

| 1.26 |

A graphic demonstration of Desargues's theorem showing the radical geometric consequences of imagining two triangles in three-dimensional perspective space. Once it is assumed that parallel lines meet in this "real" geometric space, the three-dimensional space is rotated about a hinge and transformed into a unified, homologous, two-dimensional plane. The two seemingly distinct triangles then appear as "mere" projective transformations of a single geometric entity.

M. Schneider, "Girard Desargues, the Architectural and Perspective Geometry" (Ph.D. diss., 1983).

In his *Second Brouillon Projet d'exemple d'une manière universelle du S.G.D.L. touchant la pratique du trait à preuves pour la coupe des pierres en l'architecture* (1640), Desargues clarified some aspects of his perspective method first developed in 1636 and included a new graphic method. He aimed to unify his method of linear perspective with stonecutting, using the same notions about the conic sections. In his theorem of projective geometry, Desargues proposed a method by which "triangles that are in perspective in three dimensions may be brought into a single plane" (that of the paper) for comparison. This principle of rotating planes about hinges in order to create a unified two-dimensional plane—also called the principle of *rabattement*—has become fundamental to modern descriptive geometry. To achieve such an unfolding onto a single plane, Desargues assumed that parallel lines meet at infinity. If they do meet at infinity, he says, a cone and a cylinder are but two species of the same kind, and thus "any cylinder of finite length may be regarded as a segment of a cone with its apex at infinity."[107] He could then conclude that orthogonal—or parallel—projections were merely an instance of perspective projection in which the point of projection lies at an infinite distance from the plane on which the projection occurs. His *manière universelle* was designed to handle all cases of perspective projection by applying a single set of rules and relying on a single vanishing point—postulated at infinity for the first time in the arts—and a scale or ladder. His method did not require the use of any point located beyond the frame of the image, nor did it need to use an "eye point" or a distance point that, in previous methods, could never be placed beyond the edge of the picture.[108] His method of perspective no longer needed to define the position of the observer (unlike baroque perspective and anamorphosis), and by postulating the principal point at infinity, the *manière universelle* could lead directly to descriptive geometry.

Desargues's new theories were always received with reserved interest. His innovations in the field of pure geometry, particularly his discussion of the conic sections, provoked violent reactions from a group of conservative scientists and mathematicians.[109] Descartes was among those who complained about the difficulty of understanding Desargues's scientific terms. In fact, Desargues had introduced a whole new vocabulary in an attempt to clarify some complex geometric concepts related to the conic sections. He was hoping to render his theories more accessible to the uninitiated. As a result, his theoretical improvement of techniques for stereotomy and stonecutting aroused the hostility of both theoreticians and practitioners.[110] By 1640 Desargues already had written most of his work on geometry, but he had to devote much time and energy to defending it in pamphlets and public notices. He also took the offensive when his method of perspective was included without his approval (with "erroneous comments" and no credits) in an anonymous treatise on perspective, whose author was later identified as Père Jean Dubreuil. Desargues was incensed and wrote two violent public notices, "Erreur incroyable . . ." and "Faute et fussetés énormes," that were pasted all over Paris. The controversy degenerated into a nasty exchange of pamphlets and public notices in which was criticized not only Desargues's perspective method but also his entire work and personality.[111] Distressed by these events and by the seeming incapacity of his contemporaries to understand his theories, Desargues withdrew from the debate and let his disciple, Abraham Bosse, carry on his teachings. Despite the partial appropriation of some of his insights by eighteenth-century authors, it is clear in retrospect that not until the early nineteenth century did anyone fully comprehend Desargues's theories, particularly the far-ranging consequences of his radical transformation of the very *nature* of representation, theory, practice, and the assumed relationships among them. The systematization of descriptive geometry by Gaspard Monge (1746–1818) probably constituted the most important turning point in accepting the premises of Desargues's theories. This discipline, taught by Monge at the École Polytechnique after 1795, became a crucial tool for modern engineering and architecture.[112]

While modern descriptive geometry is based on a three-dimensional system of orthogonal coordinates, the Cartesian coordinate system on which Desargues's projective geometry was based is either orthogonal or angular (oblique), depending on the object to be depicted. Desargues's seventeenth-century theory could not be removed as radically as modern geometry from the primacy of embodied, tactile experience. This points to a fundamental difference between Des-

Desargues's principle of unfolding (*rabattement*), from Bosse, *La Pratique du Trait* [1.27], and Gaspard Monge's universal spatial matrix of descriptive geometry (1790s), from R. G. Robertson, *Descriptive Geometry* [1.28]. While Desargues's system of reference retained a concrete initial position in relation to the volume being described, Monge's spatial matrix was construed as an a priori entity where all concrete phenomena could be objectively described by means of mathematical coordinates in three orthogonal dimensions.

1.27 | Montreal, Collection Centre Canadien d'Architecture / Canadian Centre for Architecture.

1.28 | Courtesy of Sir Isaac Pitman and Sons Ltd.

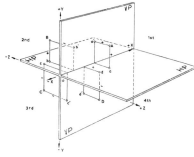

1.28

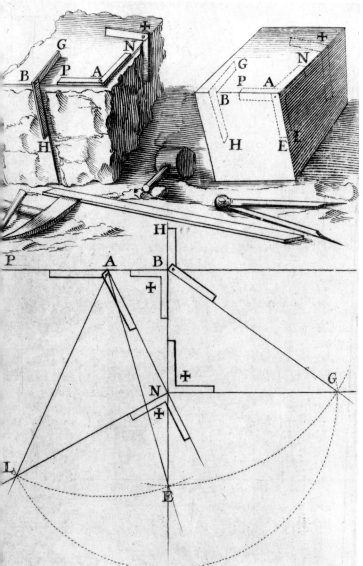

1.27

argues's system and Monge's descriptive geometry: while Desargues's method defined its system of reference according to the actual volume being described, unfolding a geometry that was essentially latent within the volume itself, Monge's orthogonal system remained independent of the object being represented. The system of reference in Monge's descriptive geometry existed as a three-dimensional matrix, extended indefinitely in space, in which any object could be situated and described.[113] Dissociating the descriptive geometric system from the material reality of the described object was a prerequisite to dislocating abstract, homogeneous space from concrete, qualitative place. In other words, while Desargues's system still required an initial form to be visualized, and started with the planes or parallel "facades" of the actual volume, Monge's descriptive geometry began with an abstract cube inside which an object projects its image onto the planes of the cube, regardless of the orientation and inclination of its own planes. Descriptive geometry further removed an object from its planar representation.

Whereas Desargues was already working with infinity, Monge's system relied on limits theory, analogous to the late-eighteenth-century calculus that always shied away from the manipulation of the number ∞. Unlike Monge, however, Jean-Victor Poncelet (1788–1867) understood Desargues's perspective method completely, casting his perspective geometry into a projective geometry of transformations.[114] Like Desargues, Poncelet sought to unfold three-dimensional space onto a single plane of projection, but this time the exercise was driven by an exclusively theoretical interest in emancipating the intellect (mathematical logic) from the concrete imagination and by a progressive desire to improve previous geometric theories. Thus, starting from the assumptions of descriptive geometry, Poncelet's objective was to reduce the world (identified with its geometry) to the single picture plane of perspective. Instead of resorting to a limited artificial construction—the cube of descriptive geometry—he advocated that all geometric operations should take place in the "true" plane of our assumed "natural" vision: the infinite plane of projective geometry. In other words, Poncelet deliberately set out to establish a geometry that could operate without the "hindrance" of images (or optics), establishing the epistemological ground for a true revolution in the realm of representation.

Relocating Anamorphosis

As is well known, the epistemological conditions for modern thought and architecture were established in the seventeenth century. While Desargues and his followers sought to unify representation by assuming a direct correspondence between an object and its image, other forms of representation emerging from the same worldview implicitly questioned this assumed correspondence. Anamorphosis, for example, revealed the potential discontinuity between an object present to perception and its visual appearance.[115] It is a specific form of perspective "distortion" whose technique was developed as the ultimate visual wit during the baroque period. Typically, anamorphosis fixes the observer's point of view in an unusual location and only from this geometric point is the distorted image magically "revealed," as it appears to float on a mirrored cylinder or cone,

| 1.29 |

Hans Holbein, *The Ambassadors* (1533). The anamorphic skull hidden in the image is symbolic of the dangers associated with the liberal arts, particularly the mathematical quadrivium, including architecture and perspective.

London, The National Gallery.

or to "lift off" the wall on which it is painted. In Hans Holbein's *Ambassadors* (1533), for example, an enigmatic skull, whose vantage point remains inaccessible to the normal viewer, floats on the surface of the painting. The vantage point has in fact been expelled intentionally from the frame, somewhere off the upper right corner of the canvas. Seen from the front, the concealed skull dissolves into an elongated patch of color in the lower half of the image, hidden in a different pictorial system than that of the two protagonists. The anamorphosis in this case projects the image of the skull beyond its visual limit, implicitly questioning the status of appearances. The anamorphic component of *The Ambassadors* introduces onto the primary pictorial dimension a second and concealed depth that forces the spectator to leave his or her central position in order to catch a glimpse of another world, which is beyond immediate appearances. The mystery of depth, protected from an instantaneous reading of the totality, needs to be deciphered through a successive inhabitation of the painting.[116]

Like the technique of optical correction mentioned by architectural writers since Vitruvius, anamorphosis was concerned with transforming visible objects so that they would recover correct proportions when viewed from a particular vantage point. A major distinction, however, must be emphasized: while optical corrections modify slightly the physical reality of a work to make it appear perfectly proportioned according to a given angle of vision, anamorphic projections completely dissolve the subject of representation, enabling the viewer to witness the magical reappearance of a hidden image from a geometric construction. Anamorphosis was developed initially as an empirical method to stretch single images such as portraits along a given axis. These images were often situated in a rectangular box with a peephole to behold the projection. Later, geometric anamorphoses were hidden or camouflaged in a landscape that would disappear when the anamorphic subject reappeared. Indeed, many writers strongly recommended that the artist camouflage the distorted images, to prevent the eye from being shocked by disharmony and to emphasize the revelatory capacity of the painting.[117]

Evolving from the same peep box tradition, but impelled by different motivations, the Dutch masters of the peep-

Examples of flat anamorphosis, from
Grégoire Huret's treatise *Optique de
portraiture et peinture* (1672).

Montreal, Collection Centre Canadien
d'Architecture / Canadian Centre for
Architecture.

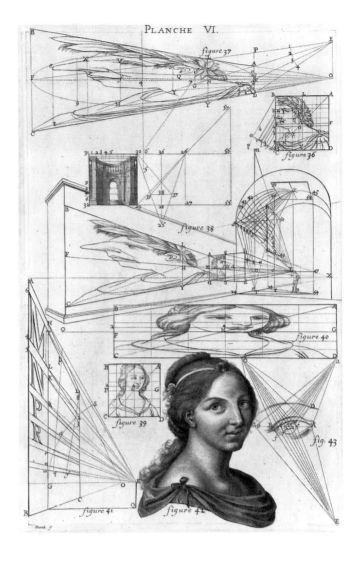

PLANCHE VI.

show boxes in the seventeenth century perfected the art of the
trompe l'oeil. Samuel van Hoogstraten, the great master of the
peep-show box genre, stated explicitly that although the art of
distorted projection was an "artifice" rather than an "essential
art" (particularly when it utilized reflecting globes, angled mirrors, cylinders, and other anamorphic tricks), "a painter must
know about them if he wishes to paint an oblique-angled
round." Moreover, "one can almost paint the corners and

angled walls away," precisely the effect desired in peep boxes. Like Vredeman de Vries before him, Hoogstraten adopted a circular concept of vision from the tradition of *perspectiva naturalis*. He writes: "We see with our eyes, and for that reason no straight line can be drawn that is equally near to our eyes in all places; but well a curve." [118] When one sees a building, it often appears foreshortened, appearing to slope or recede, but this does not mean, he adds, that a painter should portray this unless the painting will be seen from an unnatural position. Here Hoogstraten is merely restating the argument for optical correction, in sharp contrast with nineteenth-century theories of curvilinear perspective that were obsessed with the precise reproduction of retinal appearance. [119]

Indeed, it is the coincidence of the geometric conceptual frameworks and sensuous experience that enabled the European Baroque to be the art of illusion par excellence. As with anamorphic paintings, in Dutch peep-show boxes the spectator must occupy a specific point, and the representation is distorted to convey the double clarity of geometric depth and the geometric projection of light; the result is a remarkably magical depth, where the space of everyday life, miniaturized, acquires a glow and significance. The interest in depicting the world "as is," which is related to the belief in the didactic power of images and the new scientific empiricism such as expressed by Francis Bacon, is also "symbolic" of Protestant ethics and the valorization of mercantile life, revealing a *different* theater of significant experience, yet one equally dramatic as that of the *quadratura* frescoes that we will discuss later. The objects here vibrate with an internalized temporality that is far from the dissection and objectification to which the world is subjected by nineteenth- and twentieth-century scientific imaging techniques. The space of Vermeer or Hoogstraeten remains a medium for extromission theories of light that, contrary to positing a "passive" scientific observer, seem to imply the active involvement of the spectator, affirming in a profoundly original way the new status of humans and human society that is nevertheless intimately related to the order of creation.

Throughout the sixteenth century, numerous treatises alluded to strange, distorted paintings from which dragons and lions emerge when viewed through a peephole, and to ordinary

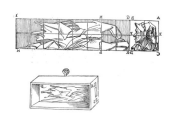

| 1.31 |

Demonstration of primitive anamorphosis, from Jacopo Barozzi da Vignola's *Due Regole della Prospettiva Pratica* (1583).

landscapes transmuting into effigies of a prince when seen from the appropriate vantage point.[120] Early examples of "primitive anamorphosis"—from the child's face found in Leonardo da Vinci's *Notebooks* to those included in Vignola's *Due Regole* and Barbaro's *La Pratica della Perspettiva*—imply or describe a purely empirical technique. Only in the early seventeenth century did a fascination emerge regarding the geometric theory of anamorphosis and its philosophical consequences. Salomon de Caus is the first to describe a geometric technique for anamorphosis based on the laws of visual rays in his treatise *La Perspective avec la Raison des ombres et miroirs* (1612). Until then, anamorphosis had remained an intellectual "secret," with its revelation of images regarded as an act of magic. Tampering with the a priori order of the world through distorted appearances was not taken lightly, even well into the seventeenth century. The marvelous effects of floating images reconstituted in a mirror were attributed to a magical combination of mechanics and geometry. This quasi-divine operation was considered analogous to a "projective" act of creation. Anamorphosis epitomized the dual nature of baroque perspective, which both revealed the truth of reality and demonstrated man's power to modify it.

In his book *La Perspective Curieuse,* Jean-François Nicéron also emphasizes the magical power of geometrically distorted appearances, praising them as one of the most wonderful discoveries in mathematics and geometry since antiquity. He expresses his admiration for "artificial magic," particularly automata, and describes some of the most notorious examples: Posidonius's sphere showing the movements of the planets, Architas's flying wooden dove, Daedalus's automaton, and Albertus Magnus's bronze head speaking "as if by nature." As the automata hide the mechanism that animates them, perspective, according to Nicéron, belonged to a similar kind of artificial miracle. In the preface to his book he refers to Philo the Jew's *De specialibus legibus,* concluding that the real magic or "the perfection of sciences consists in Perspective, which enables us to know and discern more perfectly the beautiful works of Nature and Art and which has been at all time in high esteem not only among the common people but among the most powerful monarchs of the world." Nicéron also posited that the supremacy of vision over other senses was equivalent to the superiority of optics over other sciences. He acknowledges all of his predecessors in the art of perspective and praises equally Villalpando's insight and Desargues's general method.[121]

The technique of flat anamorphosis is based directly on the notion of linear perspective as well as the traditional understanding of optics and the laws of visual rays.[122] In his book, Nicéron discusses an anamorphic device, using Dürer's perspective apparatus as a point of departure: while the picture plane in linear perspective is always placed perpendicularly between the object and the eye (through the cone of vision), he says, the window in an anamorphosis must be displaced and rotated as if on a hinge.[123] Nicéron provides a detailed practical method to construct all sorts of figures that must be seen from a specific off-center position to appear nondeformed. In the last part of his book he also includes a series of demonstrations that deal with catoptrics and mirrors, and specifically with flat, cylindrical, and conical anamorphoses. Nicéron taught the systematic process for distorting forms through reflection as a geometric

| 1.32 |

Jean-François Nicéron's own fresco *St. John the Apostle Writing the Apocalypse*, Rome (1642), from *La Perspective Curieuse* (1663).

Montreal, Collection Centre Canadien d'Architecture / Canadian Centre for Architecture.

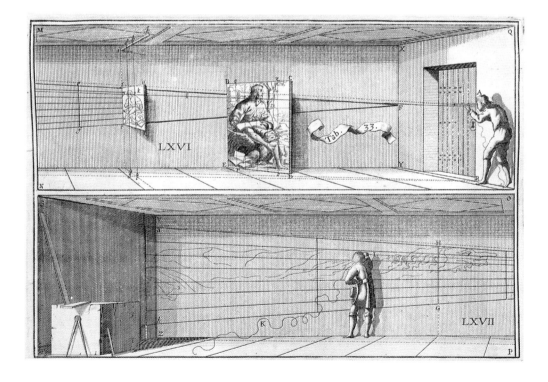

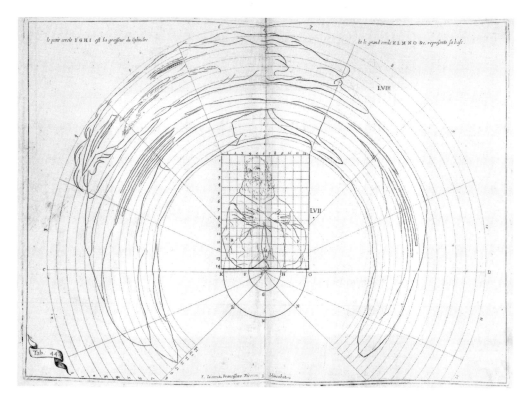

1.33

A cylindrical anamorphosis of *St. Francis of Paola,* from Nicéron's treatise.

Montreal, Collection Centre Canadien d'Architecture / Canadian Centre for Architecture.

operation that requires precise calculations based on Euclidean optics. All these mirror anamorphoses invoke the precise position of the observer as part of the geometric composition; once the images appear in a mirror, they seem to float in a virtual space and fluctuate with the blinking of the observer's eye.

As we have suggested, the wondrous mathematical ordering of seventeenth-century anamorphosis obviously fulfilled more than a need for precision or a desire to manipulate the order of things. In parallel with the development of anamorphic theory, though, geometry and mathematics soon began to present examples of anamorphic projection as scientific "recreations" and treated them as a special category of optical and mathematical diversions. Thinkers such as Descartes, who acknowledged that the distance between mental images and physical objects could potentially become a problem for scientific certainty, provided a philosophical justification to anamorphic distortions, arguing that they provided a concrete reference for meditating on the potential deceptions of sensory experience.

The prolonged correspondence between Galileo and the Roman fresco painter Lodovico Cigoli also reveals their common interest in the nature of appearances and the impact of scientific discoveries on artistic developments. Galileo discussed the famous phenomena of the apparent distortion of sunspots near the outer edge of the sun in the same way he discussed anamorphic images. In a letter to Cigoli, however, he was explicit about his dislike of anamorphosis. He criticized them violently because they distort and hide the truth of appearances, threatening the good faith that an empirical scientist must have in the phenomena of nature.[124] Galileo pointed out that spots near the edge of the sun are "in scorcio" (foreshortened), while near the center they appear "in facia" (head on). He understood that the sun's rays can be assumed to be parallel, given the distance between the earth and the sun, and that the projections through the telescope are orthographic in nature. Galileo recorded the sunspots from the telescope by placing a sheet of paper "four or five *palmi* from the end of the instru-

| 1.34 |

A perspective machine from Lodovico Cigoli's *Prospettiva pratica.* The device enabled images painted on irregular surfaces to appear as "normal" perspectives projected onto a flat section of the visual cone.

ment." [125] Therefore, the projections of sunlight are useful to demonstrate this controversial phenomenon. Cigoli, for his part, was interested in perspective distortions as a means to "correct" the geometry of vaults and other irregular surfaces so that frescoes would appear to be in "normal" perspective on flat surfaces. Although this quest seems similar to the concerns of traditional optical correction, it was in fact very different. In optical correction, visual appearances were altered to match the expectation of perfect regularity in a synesthetic, primarily tactile world. Cigoli presumed that normal perspective—that is, *perspectiva artificialis*—was reality, and that painting should be based on a scientific model. The principles of anamorphosis were therefore a means to overcome distortion inflicted upon visual representation by an irregular support, allowing the image to appear as if projected onto a flat plane. Cigoli thus seems to have been the first artist to understand the geometric construction inherent in true *quadratura,* in distinction to earlier Italian frescoes on vaults and domes.

Geometric order gave humanity the power to modify the world; implicitly it also bore the potential to create a world without shadows, such as the Cartesian *res extensa,* a world where only the pure light of mathematical precision could reveal absolute truth. In his discourse on the *Dioptrics,* Descartes discusses the phenomena of perspective representation and the false appearance of the physical world. Describing the inconsistencies of an image in a copperplate engraving, Descartes justifies the need to transform the image of a physical object to represent it in the most truthful way, and thus confers the ultimate priority to the image over the experiential reality of the world: "On a totally flat surface, they show us bodies raised and sunk at different levels . . . [following] the rules of perspective, they often represent circles more effectively by ovals than by other circles and squares more effectively by rhombus, and similarly with all the other figures: so that often, in order to be more perfect as images and the better to represent an object, they must not resemble it." [126] Once scientists and philosophers assumed that perspective representations reflect the reality of the world (*res extensa*), the limit cases of anamorphosis appeared simultaneously to challenge and promote this belief. [127] In the Cartesian system, God's good faith was indeed necessary to ensure that man was occupying "the right point" from which nature would not appear distorted.

Interestingly, in seventeenth-century treatises on perspective, anamorphosis usually was discussed together with the projection of shadows.[128] The Sun, casting the anamorphic outline of objects on the Earth, appeared to raise similar ambiguities about the borders between reality and the projected world. The perception of shadows, undeniably part of our common visual experience, became objectified, while shadows in perspective became the symbol of an increasingly geometrized space governed by a predetermined vantage point. While the ultimate nonshaded viewpoint remained in the domain of God, who potentially occupied the center of a new heliocentric universe, the shadows cast by the Sun, which were usually "incorrectly" represented as converging projections, seemed to confer a godly power onto man for understanding the structure of a world of pure light. In philosophy and theology, even though

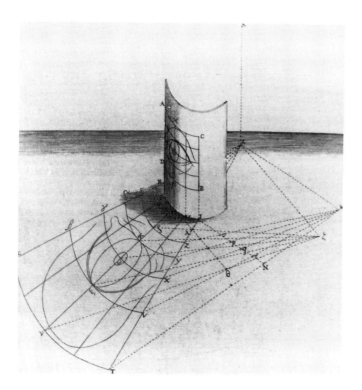

The Eye of God, from Mario Bettini's mathematical treatise, *Apiaria Universæ Philosophiæ Mathematicæ* (1642–1645), projected as an "anamorphic" shadow in the world of man.

Desargues's method of shadow tracing, demonstrated by the deceptively simple "Cubes in perspective," from Bosse, *Manière universelle de Mr. Desargues* (1648). It postulates a point at infinity *in* the world and thus truly systematizes representation of shadows in perspective space. Shadows could thereafter lose their special quality as traces of a transcendent world.

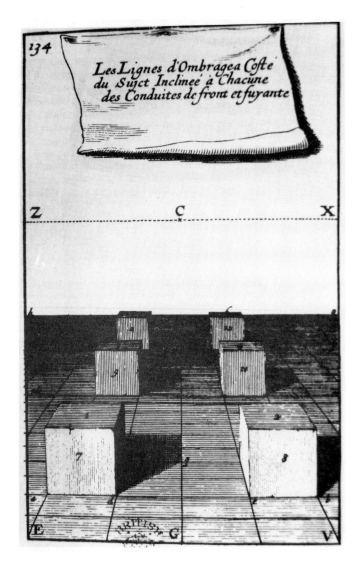

the stability of the earth had been shattered by scientific theories, and the distance between the Universe of God and the world of man had become explicit, this distance was not an unbridgeable gap: man still occupied a place that was geometrically ordered by God for his benefit; he also remained the link between these two distant, yet united worlds.

Shadows became rationalized once the outlines of their projections were determined geometrically. We have shown the difficulties involved in systematizing projected shadows in perspective representation and have examined how they were fully resolved only by Desargues. Eventually, the human experience of a world given, literally, *by virtue* of shadows—vibrant, imprecise, colorful, and complex, resistant to geometric reductions because of diffraction—was relegated to the doubtful realm of subjectivity. Our understanding of the world was profoundly marked by Descartes's objectification of reality and his obsession with pure clarity. This influence has been evident in architectural representation, which since the early systematization of perspective has aspired to evacuate traces of embodied perception.[129] Amid this growing objectification, anamorphoses attempted to relocate their focal point in embodied experience, thus involving the observer in the shadowy realm of *creation* and *participation,* defining the place for any "modern" epiphany and therefore anticipating the conditions for artistic meaning in the centuries to come.

Constructing a Distorted Order

In his treatise on oblique architecture, Caramuel describes the origins of architecture from the Temple of Jerusalem built by Hiram, the master or second architect who followed the plan (*Orthographia*) delineated by the hand of God, the Supreme Architect. The first architecture known to man, however, was military, for when Adam and Eve were expelled from paradise, they passed through the gate of the Garden of Eden, which was guarded by angels armed with flaming weapons. But, Caramuel says, "before there were cities in the world, there were temples. The one that Adam built was enclosed by walls, so that smoke from the sacrifices could exit freely."[130] Caramuel was not the first architect to trace the genealogy of architecture from the temple in order to provide a theological justification for theory, particularly concerning the question of divine geometry and proportions.[131] However, Caramuel's treatise on architecture was the first to include a graphic reconstruction of the Temple of Jerusalem to serve as a model for a polemical theoretical argument. Previous authors, such as Juan Bautista Villalpando or Benito Arias Montano, presented a reconstruction as part of a hermeneutic project guided mainly by theological interests. In contrast, Caramuel, invoked the temple as a historical origin and justification, while the reconstruction itself almost became subsidiary to his theories. Moreover, Caramuel's reconstruction was not based on Villalpando's iconography. The only complete view of the temple in Caramuel's treatise is a copy of an engrav-

| 1.37 |

Juan Bautista Villalpando, *El Templo a vista de pajaro* (1604). The general view of the Temple of Jerusalem is presented as a "parallel projection" kindred to God's own vision.

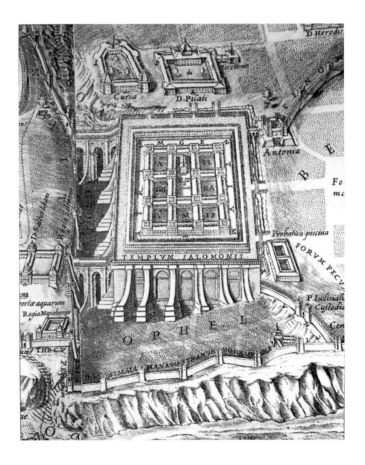

TEMPLI HIEROSOLYMITANI ACCVRATA DESCRIPTIO

| 1.38 |

Caramuel's "accurate description" of
the Temple of Jerusalem in perspective view, from *Architectura Civil
Recta y Oblicua* (1678). The image,
based on Jacob Juda León's reconstruction of the temple, shows the
off-center sanctuary on the right.

151

ing by Jacob Juda León, an asymmetrical variation of Villalpando's, interpreted as part of the Jewish tradition.[132] While
most reconstructions of the Temple of Jerusalem showed more
concern for representing the sanctuary in the current style than
for any kind of archaeological objectivity, Caramuel distanced
himself from the Cistercian tradition and rejected the Jesuit
model proposed by Villalpando in favor of a more "probable"
or "realistic" solution.[133]

In Caramuel's treatise, there is no general plan of the
temple, only fragmentary views and an "aerial perspective
view." According to the engraving and the explanations in the
text, the sanctuary was not located in the center of the espla-
nade, but on one side.[134] For Caramuel, this distortion of symmetry certainly accorded with his oblique architecture.
Moreover, he believed that the entire temple was built on these
principles. Citing Ezekiel's own words, he gives the windows
as an explicit instance of oblique architecture. Caramuel claims
that according to the Holy Scriptures, the windows would have
been wider outside than inside, even though, as he says, this
would be difficult to acknowledge, since all temples and palaces, both modern and ancient, were built in the opposite manner.[135] The building that most faithfully resembles Villalpando's
Temple of Jerusalem is the Escorial built by Philip II, and Caramuel claims that is a "book" containing many ideas about
straight and oblique works.[136] To the question of whether archi-

tects of his time should imitate biblical constructions, he denies that the antique drawings of the temple, the Tabernacle, or Noah's Ark could ever be put into practice. He insists, however, that much can be learned from them: that architecture is embodied in the concept of these archetypal buildings, not in their actual construction.[137]

After making a genealogy of first builders from Vulcan to Daedalus and enumerating the first cities, such as Enochia erected by Cain, and the antique temples, such as the tower of Babel, Caramuel concludes that the first architects (*los Primeros Maestros de obras*) built an oblique architecture to compensate for the weakness of the eyes that causes one to perceive the optical convergence of parallel lines (what he calls "parallaxes"). Indeed, Caramuel considered the convergence of parallel lines a defect of sight, and not a vehicle for reducing reality to an image. This defect had to be rectified by constructing obliquely so that visual perception would not contradict the tactile reality of parallel lines. But it was God, the very first architect, who traced the first lines obliquely: the tropic of Cancer and the tropic of Capricorn; the Arctic and Antarctic Circles parallel to the equator, which the annual solar path (the ecliptic) cuts obliquely at the zodiac; the inclined plane of mountains erected obliquely; and even the rivers that run obliquely.[138] Caramuel's "modern" openness to invention and his questioning of Vitruvius's authority were legitimized by a genealogical understanding of architecture originating with the temple. According to Caramuel, if "oblique" architecture was arguably superior to "straight" (Vitruvian) architecture, this was because God had created the world obliquely.

While Caramuel's oblique architecture was based partially on optical distortions in human vision, the theological impact of God's original oblique lines was far more important. Caramuel believed that since God had built the world obliquely, architects should emulate the given order by maintaining the obliqueness of the tactile (and ultimately mathematical) structure of the world, while revealing the perfect heavenly order from a central given point (the perception of a perfect circle). In other words, using Caramuel's own prime example, the colonnade built around St. Peter's Square in Rome had to be distorted in order to reveal a perfect geometry from the center of the circle. This attitude may seem closely related to the principle of anamorphosis that locates its place of epiphany in the built world; but while seventeenth-century anamorphic paintings started with perspective projections and self-consciously manipulated the rules of geometric construction to create extreme situations that would dissociate presence and appearance, Caramuel's *architectura obliqua* did not go through the process of sectioning the cone of vision. Caramuel, we must remember, discounted perspective as being unimportant for architects. Thus, his *architectura obliqua* seems closer to some kind of "primitive" anamorphosis based on optical correction.

Furthermore, in a section of his treatise devoted to "the lines that are used in architecture," Caramuel introduces a new type of line "unknown to Vitruvius and most moderns" that he calls "Conchil(is)," which he uses to show "an ingenious and beautiful way to diminish columns that should be wider on top and narrower at their base." Caramuel directly criticizes authors such as Vitruvius and Palladio who claimed that columns should be thinner at the top and wider at the bottom. He demonstrates the "falseness" of their theories with two extraordinary arguments. First, he claims that only vertical dimensions are affected by optical angle and therefore, in principle, the diameter of columns should remain constant. Second, even if it were true that horizontal dimensions diminish with distance, if we then wanted the size of a column to look equal at the top and the bottom, it would have to be physically wider on top to compensate for optical distortions.[139] Caramuel gives an example of a tower which "must be wider on top in order to be *a plomo* . . . as any other building." Thus, he states, the projection of its walls would then converge toward the center of the earth.[140] Caramuel's peculiar understanding of architectural stability, disregarded by all of his modern commentators, illuminates the true consequences of his cosmology for his architectural theory. For him, the center of the Earth was the ultimate fixed point in the universe, and the walls of every construction converged toward it. This geometric point was occupied by God and was construed as the cosmological center of absolute vision. Caramuel's *architectura obliqua,* therefore, can be associated with optical distortion only as a kind of "cosmological" anamorphosis. This sharply contradicts the current inter-

Caramuel's counterproposals for the colonnade of St. Peter's Square in Rome, designed according to the principles of oblique architecture, from *Architectura Civil*. From the center of the composition, the oval would be perceived as a perfect circle [1.39a] or, alternatively, four rows of columns would be perceived as one, also producing the appearance of a perfectly circular colonnade [1.39b].

Montreal, Collection Centre Canadien d'Architecture / Canadian Centre for Architecture.

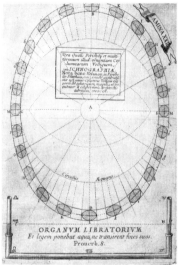

1.39a

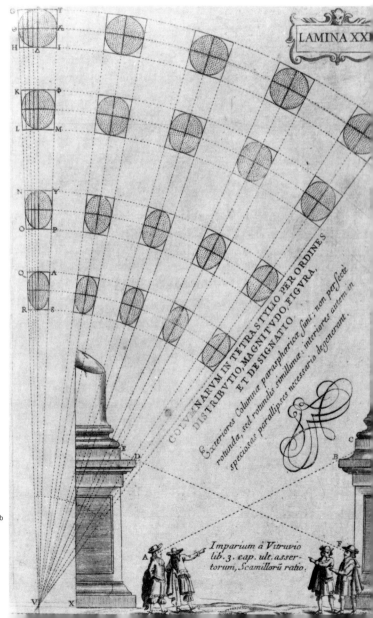

1.39b

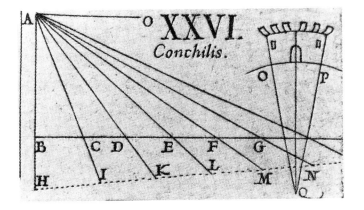

| 1.40 |

This detail from Caramuel's treatise shows how the walls of a tower should be splayed for structural stability: wider at the top to follow their "natural" projection toward the center of the earth.

Montreal, Collection Centre Canadien d'Architecture / Canadian Centre for Architecture.

155

pretation of his work as a variation of seventeenth-century perspective anamorphosis or, worse still, as a deconstruction of classical architecture anticipating postmodern attitudes.[141]

The most important principles of Caramuel's oblique architecture are embodied in his theoretical project proposed for the colonnade of St. Peter's Square, framing the actual physical and political center of the Catholic world. In 1655, he was called by the new Pope Alexander VII to serve as Consultor de la Congregación del Santo Oficio y Rito and to take care of aesthetic matters. His stay in Rome coincided with the erection of the colonnade of St. Peter's Square by Bernini. Not surprisingly, Caramuel expressed strong opinions about the project, as its oval configuration provided an excellent opportunity for implementing his theory on obliquity.[142] A sharp and intransigent polemicist, he started a debate that eventually turned against him, preventing his promotion to the rank of cardinal. He was instead sent south to occupy the bishopric of Campagna. In his treatise, a theoretical project for the square is presented as a critique of Bernini's work. After describing the development of St. Peter's Basilica, including the additions made by every pope, Caramuel severely criticizes the piazza built under Alexander VII. "This oval or elliptical place is quite sumptuous," he says. "It appears beautiful to the eyes of the general public who, ignorant of the principles of architecture, are taken by its impact on the senses; . . . but those who know the art look at it with anger in view of so many mistakes."[143]

In his introduction to the reprint of Caramuel's treatise, Bonet Correa emphasizes the "practical concerns" in Cara-

The colonnade of St. Peter's Square in Rome by Bernini.

Photo by A. Pérez-Gómez.

muel's opposition to Bernini's project.[144] He claims that the oblique architecture of Caramuel was more than an eccentric or whimsical curiosity; instead, it derived from "a new branch of mathematics which, applied to architecture, could resolve all incoherences that plagued the master masons who had to work with inclined planes." Because Bernini's colonnade had "as many errors as stones," Caramuel submitted his counterproject in order to resolve all deformations due to inappropriate uses of perspective. Bonet Correa concludes that thanks to the *virtuoso taller romano* who worked under Bernini, the finished piazza was "almost an application of oblique architecture."[145]

Caramuel may have been concerned with some practical aspects of construction, but it would be fallacious to describe his theory as "instrumental" and his geometry as a "new branch of mathematics." Caramuel was opposed primarily to Bernini's desire to reveal the space of the three successive aisles of the colonnade by adjusting the positions of the receding rows of columns. In Caramuel's view, the correct procedure would have been to increase the diameter of the columns in each receding row according to their distance from a predetermined center, so that from that privileged point a spectator would be presented with a view of a single row of columns hiding the successive ones. His alternative design for the square exaggerated the distortion to emphasize the variations between the different rows of columns. He specified that, in reality, these distortions should be less perceptible in a large building. Unlike anamorphosis, his objective was not to create a deformed architecture—this was merely a by-product—but rather to create the appearance of a perfectly ordered geometric space with an unambiguous center. As a possible metaphor for the theological mystery of the Trinity, an observer at the predetermined vantage point would see a unified row of columns as the space between them collapses: from elsewhere, one would perceive multiplicity.[146]

Caramuel emphasizes that the "most appropriate" perspective tool for architects is not what was taught by Serlio; instead, "there are two lines, a perpendicular and a horizontal one, and visually only the vertical one diminishes with distance."[147] His description clearly suggests optical correction. But even though Caramuel claims that only the vertical dimension is affected, it was the horizontal dimension that was modified in his examples of primitive anamorphosis, especially in his proposed colonnade for St. Peter's Square. Therefore, Caramuel's *architectura oblicua* cannot be reduced to a simple application of optical correction.[148] The complex geometry that regulates the plan of his proposed piazza is not developed into a buildable three-dimensional design. He gives no indications about the facade of his distorted architectural order, and the height and vertical proportions of the columns apparently were not considered.

The collapse of depth created by the negation of foreshortening in Caramuel's oblique colonnade could be seen as a result of Platonic or Cartesian "shadowless" idealism.[149] The absolute clarity of Caramuel's created order, however, was not that of perspective (or of a positivistic world), but rather the absolute clarity of God's presence momentarily revealed in the human realm. This is the "truth" that his project sought to disclose. Through a geometric schema, Caramuel attempted to reconcile a tactile experience of the world with contradictory visual phenomena. He lived in a profoundly Aristotelian, hierarchical world, where the tactility of a constructed order could not be replaced by a purely visual order. In that sense, his *architectura oblicua* was almost diametrically opposed to perspective anamorphosis.

When the Center Becomes Peripheral

In his criticism of Bernini's colonnade, Caramuel also deplored the excesses incurred in the construction of the second fountain in St. Peter's Square, the "Gran Fuente . . . vomitando un Oceano." Once again, his criticism was not based on practical considerations. He was opposed to the concept of two centers or foci for the square. A single central fountain placed in front of the obelisk would have been more appropriate to his oblique architecture. Indeed, as we have suggested, his whole concept revolved around a single constructed center from which an undistorted order would be revealed. Thus, the colonnade could be set up as an oval, understood as a distorted circle with a single center, closely following the geometry he assumed for the sun's orbit around the earth.

Kepler, we may remember, believed that the perfect harmony of the cosmos could be perceived only from an ideal position, from the sun's point of view. Similarly, Caramuel relocated this place of epiphany within the world of man, thus compensating for the new instability of man's position in the universe, brought about by recent scientific and astronomic discoveries. In contrast, when Kepler was faced with the apparent contradiction challenging his belief that man had been placed at the best possible position in the universe, he relocated the Earth within another geometric center: "This globe seems to have been allotted to man with a supreme wisdom, so that he can contemplate all planets."[150] It occupies the central orbit of the celestial bodies—Mars, Jupiter, and Saturn on the outside; Venus, Mercury, and the Sun on the inside. In addition, the proportions of the planets and the distances among all the celestial bodies revealed a perfect mathematical relationship when calculated from the perspective of a terrestrial spectator: "In what manner then were the earth's dimensions adapted to the size of the solar globe?—In terms of vision. For the earth would be home to the contemplative creature, and it was for him that the entire universe had been created."[151]

Kepler went even further, insisting that man's vantage point simply could not have been at the center of the universe. Like Vignola's distance point (or second observer), which determines the true foreshortening of perspective depth by objectifying the geometric organization of pictorial space, the eccentric position of the Earth was in fact the only acceptable location in the universe that could allow man to grasp the true order of the world: "If the earth, our home, did not measure the annual orbit of the other planets—changing from place to place and station to station—human reason would never have arrived at knowledge of the precise intervals of the planets, and other things that depend on those intervals; it would never have instituted astronomy."[152] Fernand Hallyn describes the harmony of elliptical movement in Kepler's theory with a musical metaphor: "If the musical beauty of the universe is the result of *motion,* it is because motion characterizes the *living,* and God wanted the cosmos to be made in the image of living beings." But for Kepler, the perfect harmony of celestial music eluded direct perception by Earth's inhabitants. The celestial symphony was harmonious from the Sun's position only, while man was condemned to a purely intellectual reconstruction. The best man could do was to "know the score; he can never attend the performance."[153] In addition to being able to reconstruct the plan of the universe using the exact distances among the planets, man was also able to understand the harmony of celestial motions from the point of view of the Sun. Such projection of man's mind to the Sun's position was indeed similar to the eccentric positioning of the viewpoint in an anamorphic construction. This new understanding of a cosmic order justified man's desire to create distorted perspectives and constructions that he would overcome by restoring himself to the center.

The issue of symbolic recentering was even more explicit for the other form of distorted perspective perfected in the seventeenth century: the technique of *quadratura* frescoes painted on ceilings, such as the many produced by Andrea Pozzo (1642–1709) for Jesuit churches all over Catholic Europe.[154] Indeed, like anamorphosis, the technique of *quadratura* painting relies on a precise viewpoint to reveal the order of its composition. Like Caramuel's oblique architecture, however, *quadratura* does not dissolve the subject of its representation as do anamorphic distortions. While earlier painters such as Lomazzo and Mantegna had produced "illusionist" ceiling frescoes intended to produce astounding effects, these works were devised through empirical methods involving mirrors and mod-

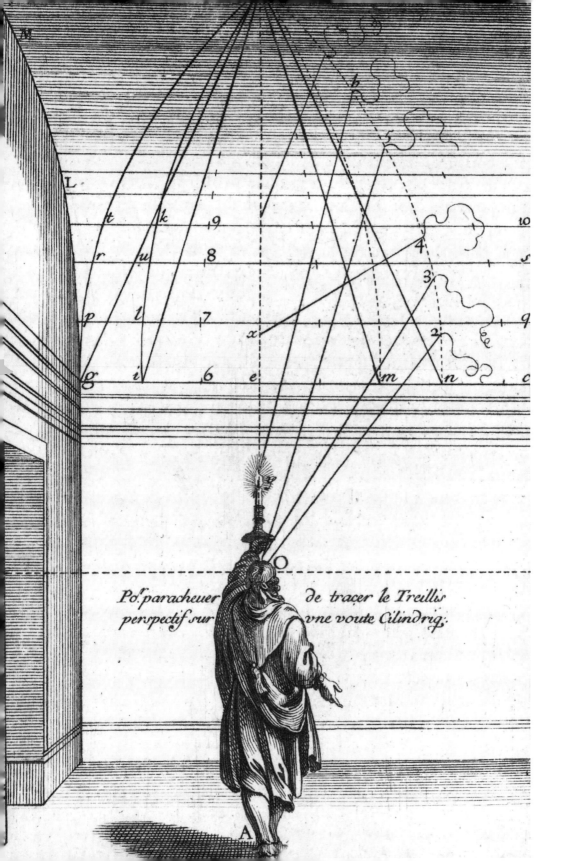

Po.ᵗ paracheuer   de traçer le Treillis
perspectif sur   vne voute Cilindriq.

els (*modellini*), and they often were constructed to be perceived from various vantage points, in an explicitly heterogeneous composition.[155] Pozzo's method of *quadratura*, which was based on geometric perspective, unified the composition according to a single vantage point and introduced it as a third geometric point in the construction. In addition to the principal point and the distance point described by Vignola, a precise vantage point was thus located in the three-dimensional space of the building. From this fixed position in space, a grid was projected onto the complex geometry of the vault and was used to transfer a sketch of the trompe l'oeil into its new architectural context. We will elaborate on the implications of Pozzo's method in Variation Two; for the moment it suffices to recognize that *quadratura*, like anamorphic projections, precisely relocates the position of the observer in order to present that observer with a geometric disclosure of truth. Unlike anamorphosis, however, it no longer questions the ambiguous distance between appearance and reality. Thus, it anticipates the coincidence between visual coherence in an a priori geometric space and the truth of reality that would become the most pervasive precondition for effective knowledge in the modern, scientific world.

| 1.42 |

Method for tracing a perspective grid (*treillis*) onto a cylindrical vault as a point of departure for the geometric construction of a *quadratura* fresco, from Bosse's *Moyen universel de pratiquer la perspective sur les tableaux ou surfaces irrégulières* (1653).

Montreal, Collection Centre Canadien d'Architecture / Canadian Centre for Architecture.

161

The Confrontation between Theory and Practice

The baroque world's interest in allegories such as anamorphoses and oblique architecture characterized early modern man's apprehension about naming the truth "directly," particularly after the traumatic impact of the Reformation, the wars of religion, and the scientific revolution.[156] Baroque art and architecture assumed that it was possible to reveal the essence of a message by "taking an angle." This assumption underlay the theory of Pietro Accolti (active 1625–1642) in his *Lo Inganno de gl'occhi, Prospettiva Pratica* (1625), in which he regards anamorphic drawings as "pictorial secret codes" that turn an image into an enigma that must be solved. The distorted image partakes of the marvelous: "This enigmatic appearance—a shapeless swirl which is nonetheless constructed with the nicest geometrical precision—is no longer Alberti's open window but a riddling, opaque surface which in a flash reveals the truth hidden in it."[157]

Similarly, Emanuele Tesauro (1591–1675) praised the changing appearances of reality. In *Il Cannocchiale aristotelico* (1670), he emphasizes the importance of variation in perception, whether through the eye or an instrument such as a looking glass. Instead of denigrating the impermanence of perception—as is common in some Protestant and Jansenist writings, for example— he praises the human imagination that, with the aid of rhetoric, goes beyond natural limitations and discovers what was "hidden by God." Tesauro was fascinated not only by glasses that enhance vision but also by optical illusions mediated through mirrors, perspective illusions, and other such devices.[158]

To some extent, Girard Desargues was also interested in the possibility of constructing a distorted order that would then be mediated by the rules of geometry. Referring to a perspective drawing executed by Desargues for the painter Philippe de Champaigne, Pigniol described what could be either a *quadratura* drawing or an anamorphosis: "The curious and the connoisseurs observed with particular attention this fragment of a perspective sketch provided to Champaigne by the skilled mathematician Desargues; it is a crucifix surrounded by the Holy Virgin and Saint John. The group appears to be on a vertical plane, while it is in fact on a horizontal surface."[159] Desargues's most devoted disciple, Abraham Bosse (1602–1676), after publishing his *Manière universelle de Mr. Desargues, pour pratiquer la perspective: par petit-pied, comme le géométral* (1648) with the approval of his master, published a second part: entitled *Moyen universel de pratiquer la perspective sur les tableaux ou surfaces irrégulières* (1653), it was devoted entirely to various forms of distortion. It includes a technique for projecting images onto irregular surfaces following optical principles such as the angle of vision. His projection of a grid onto a vault, for example, recalls the technique of *quadratura*.[160] The deformations proposed by Desargues and Bosse were intended to correct visual perception by making the image resemble a "normal" perspective—much as Galileo's friend, Lodovico Cigoli, had intended. In other words, their method assumed that the object must be drawn with distorted proportions in order to appear "real," and that the correctly proportioned image would be revealed only from a specific point. Even though the method was not intended explicitly to create anamorphosis, the projection system

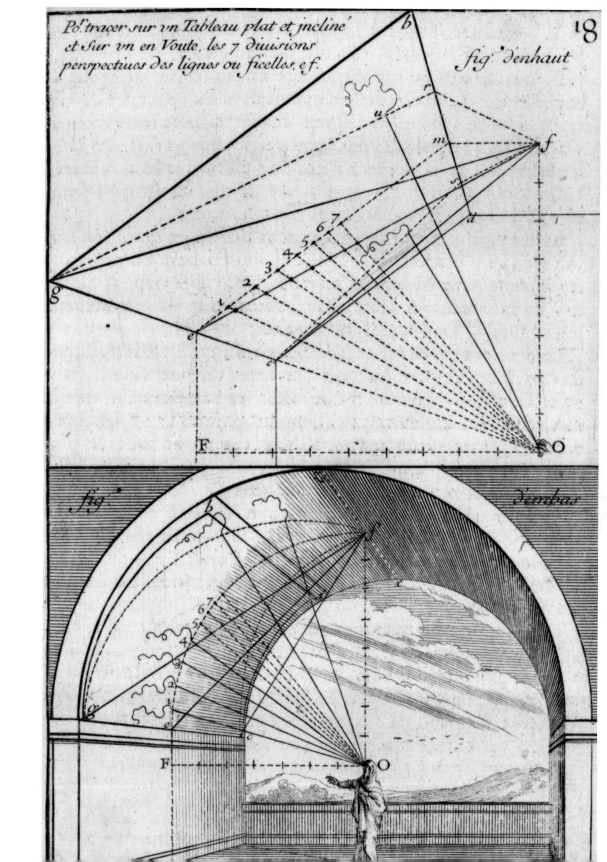

Por tracer sur un Tableau plat et incliné
et Sur un en Voute, les 7 divisions
perspectiues des lignes ou ficelles. e f.

fig. d'enhaut

fig. d'embas

presented in Bosse's second treatise was based on the principle that Barbaro recommended for anamorphosis. The book aroused immense interest but was immediately attacked strongly. This time, the controversy involved the French Royal Academy of Painting, where Bosse once taught. In his book on perspective, Grégoire Huret (1610–1760), the director of the academy, criticized such distortions because they would appear to be very unpleasant when seen from a different viewpoint. Instead he favored anamorphic distortions that completely annihilated the subject matter of the painting, and thus did not shock the eye.[161]

Little is known about Desargues's life, both before and after the publication of his two *Brouillon Projets* and his treatise on stereotomy. During this period, however, he corresponded frequently with leading philosophers, artists, and scientists, such as Descartes, Père Mersenne, and Jean de Beaugrand, as well as Blaise Pascal, who was probably one of his first disciples.[162] Pascal's fascination with Desargues's work is significant in view of the former's association with Port Royal. Although Desargues never was explicitly interested in Jansenism, his intellectual concerns coincided with the Jansenist belief that logic is the most precious discipline in the human quest for truth. Of course this intellectual filiation differs from that of other baroque architects and authors such as Caramuel and Athanasius Kircher, who believed the world was a *rhetorical* construction,

| 1.44 |

Detail of the staircase built by Desargues for the northern facade of the Château de Vizille, Dauphiné, France.

Photo by L. Pelletier.

with mathematics as a universal language and projective operations as a vehicle for the actualization of God's word.

After withdrawing from the intellectual debates surrounding his theories, Desargues seems to have spent the rest of his life applying his ideas to built projects. Even though he claimed not to be a craftsman, he declared explicitly that the best demonstration of his theories' relevance would be to apply them unequivocally to building tasks. Most of his projects were small-scale interventions such as staircases involving complex stonecutting work, or designs of *hôtels particuliers* in Paris and Lyon.[163] Information about Desargues's practical work remains fragmentary, yet there is evidence that complexity of details and a virtuosity of execution characterized his entire production.

In his treatise on the architectural orders, Bosse includes some precious information about Desargues's work.[164] In addition to emphasizing the importance of a clear geometry that must be revealed in the built work, and opposing any compromise, either theoretical or practical, that could jeopardize this geometric purity, Bosse recounts many examples of staircases and other architectural details where geometry was used to resolve formal inconsistencies. In the stair of the Château de Vizille, built in Dauphiné in 1653, Desargues eliminates the abrupt change in the level of the handrail by means of a clever beveling, in order to keep the line of the balustrade continuous around the turning stair. The complex detailing of the handrail made it possible to construct a volume that could hardly be imagined in three dimensions, and that prior to Desargues's system could have been drawn only from an existing model. As Bosse pointed out, before Desargues's stonecutting method, the quality of a built detail was determined partially by on-site adjustments made by the builders themselves. Complex, distorted forms now could be dictated by the architect, demonstrating the virtuosity of his imagination. Even as the architect progressively acquired the tools to describe (and thus prescribe) any buildable form in drawing, theory became an increasingly utilitarian discipline for controlling practice while leaving aside traditional speculations about meaning and appropriateness.

Desargues often was criticized by practitioners for the complexity and inaccessibility of his theories, and by other theoreticians for his claim to universality. Yet his ambition clearly

| 1.45 |

Plate describing the correct and incorrect ways of making a handrail, using an example built by Desargues in the Quartier Mont-marthe [sic], rue Clery, from Bosse, *Les Ordres de l'Architecture*. In the commentary accompanying the three diagrams, Bosse explains the importance of rectifying "the unpleasant effect of breaks or ruptures [in handrails]. For several years, many have tried to correct these breaks in the base and rail (a) and (b), but they have only succeeded at the expense of making the pilasters (ic) and (ba) unequal in height, or else by making the rail and the balusters unequal and by transferring the irregularity to the landings or the steps, making them unequal in height and width as in figure 1."

Montreal, Collection Centre Canadien d'Architecture / Canadian Centre for Architecture.

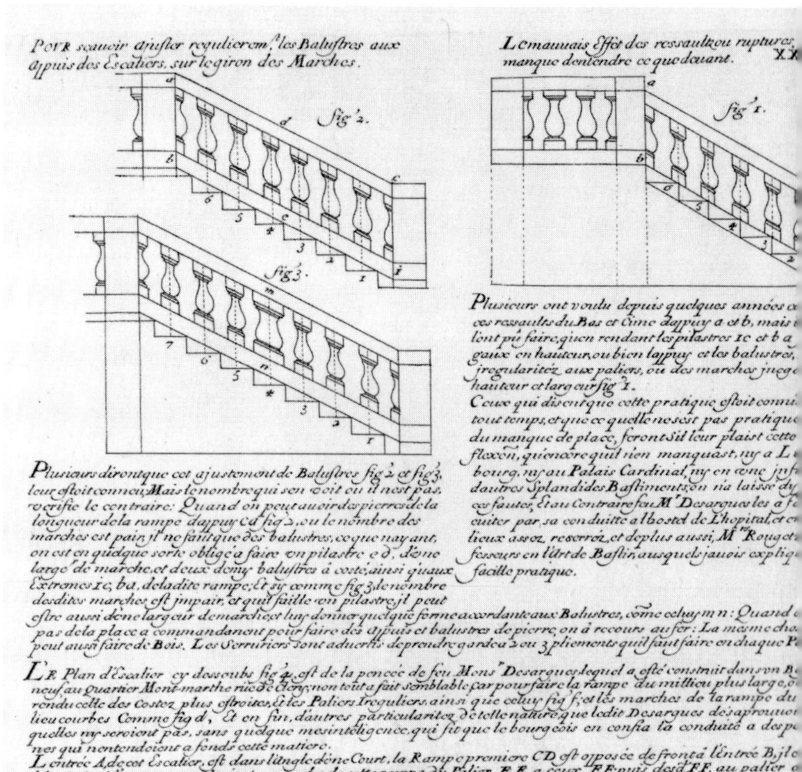

POVR sçauoir aiuster regulierem.ᵗ les Balustres aux appuis des Escaliers, sur le giron des Marches.

fig. 2.

fig. 3.

Le mauuais Effet des ressaults ou ruptures manque de ntendre ce que deuant. X.I

fig. 1.

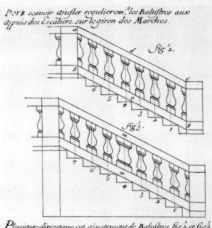

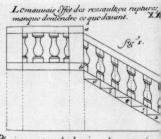

fig. 4.

fig. 5.

fig. d.

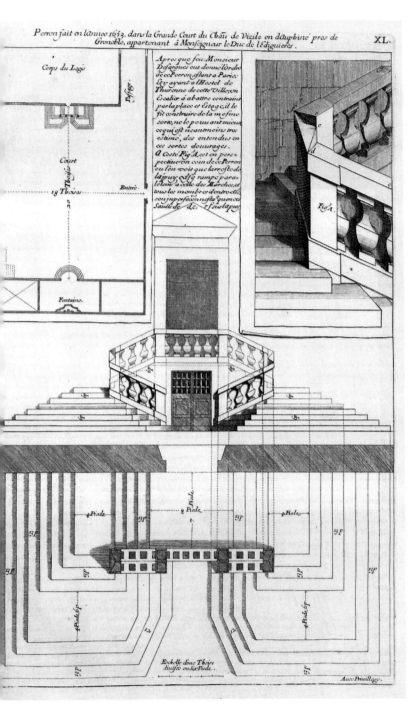

| 1.46 |

Stairway with an "oblique" balustrade, in the Château de Vizille, near Grenoble, from Bosse's treatise on the architectural orders (1688).

Montreal, Collection Centre Canadien d'Architecture / Canadian Centre for Architecture.

167

was motivated by an ethical concern to enhance practice through theoretical tools of conceptualization.[165] At a time when masons were still conscious of the seriousness of spoiling a stone, Desargues sought to provide a general stonecutting method that could replace the imprecise conventional procedures involving trial and error.[166] His method led specific stonecutting problems to be assimilated into a single, generic system. In fact, his system of stereotomy considered the vault and the tower to be essentially identical because the problem of stonecutting is the same. Desargues's method of stereotomy aimed to eliminate the traditional case-by-case resolution of specific problems. Although Desargues was looking for a geometric theory that would enhance and eventually control practice, the very complexity of the method tended to make it counterintuitive.

While most of his contemporaries regarded theory as a means of understanding and explaining a transcendent order present in human works, Desargues seems to have been an anachronism, a modern mind ahead of his time in dissociating theory from its philosophical content so that it could become a tool for practice. His understanding of mathematics and geometry was truly exceptional. Caramuel, for example, regarded geometry as an ordering structure that could be superimposed onto any architecture; practical questions of applicability seemed totally unimportant to him.[167] In contrast, the sole purpose of geometry for Desargues was its application to practice, ushering in its new role as a predictive tool of architectural ideation. Unlike Caramuel, whose "oblique architecture" was intended to re-create a place of "undistorted" perception and to give man access to a "thick" geometric order previously restricted to the vision of God, Desargues believed that the formal issues associated with a straight or oblique architecture were already devoid of theological consequences. Desargues's projections onto irregular surfaces, like the complex constructions and oblique staircases that he designed, were merely demonstrations of a unified "universal method." His general perspective theory was intended to regulate all forms of making in the modern "infinite" world, including *perspectiva artificialis* for drawing and accurate representation, stereotomic projections for precise stonecutting and building, and the calibration of sundials for the accurate measurement of time.

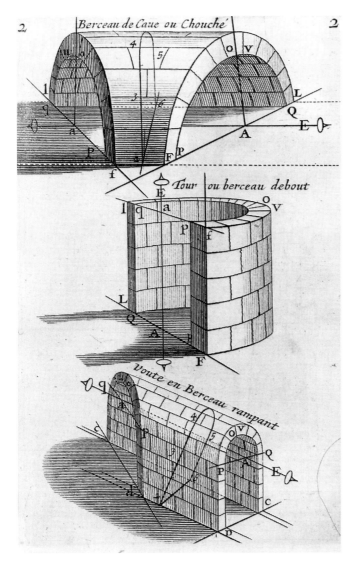

Berceau de Caue ou Chouché

Tour ou berceau debout

Voute en Berceau rampant

In his treatise on stonecutting
(1643), Bosse describes various
vaults and towers as specific examples of the same stonecutting
problem, disregarding the effect of
gravity on their structure. He introduces three specific kinds of "vault":
Berceau de Caue or *Chouche, Tour* or
Berceau debout, and *Voute en Berceau rampant.*

Montreal, Collection Centre Canadien
d'Architecture / Canadian Centre for
Architecture.

Caramuel was severely criticized by practitioners for the whimsical and experimental nature of his oblique architecture. Guarino Guarini, for example, questioned his neglect of essential rules dictated by experience. While acknowledging that Caramuel was the first to write about principles of obliquity, and sharing his fascination with geometry as a fundamental "universal science," Guarini still condemned Caramuel's advocacy of deformation as excessive.[168] Like Caramuel, he acknowledged the importance of optical corrections, but he maintained that perspective perfection should never be achieved at the expense of the true geometry of built architecture. Guarini also criticized Caramuel's geometric inconsistencies in his use of a single center in the design of his elliptical spaces (it was already well known in geometry that an ellipse requires two foci).[169] Some writers have argued that their opposition was only apparent, for Guarini adopted similar kinds of

| 1.48 |

Guarino Guarini's proposal for St. Peter's Square, from his *Architettura civile* (1737).

Montreal, Collection Centre Canadien d'Architecture / Canadian Centre for Architecture.

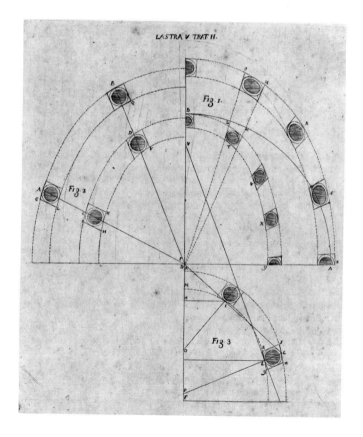

1.49

An oblique balustrade, from Caramuel's *Architectura Civil.*

Montreal, Collection Centre Canadien
d'Architecture / Canadian Centre for
Architecture.

171

deformations in some of his projects, such as the atrium of the
Palazzo Carignano.[170] It is clear, however, that the only practical
deformation on which Guarini agreed explicitly with Caramuel
involved the design of stairs.[171]

Philosophically, both men believed that the role of architecture was to reveal the order of creation through geometry—an active, projective principle for mediating between
mind and body. But Guarini's philosophy was close to the "oc-
casionalism" of Nicolas de Malebranche.[172] Guarini's treatise,
Architettura Civile (1737), was based on a projective, Euclidean
geometry applied to stonecutting and all aspects of construction, while the products of architecture were conceived as geometric figures and volumes. For him, the architect's *modus
operandi,* a geometric art of combination analogous to the creative divine *mens,* resulted in a complex, magical, innovative
work that should never be intentionally distorted as a result
of optical considerations. Distorted architectural proportions
could never reveal the true intention of God. The center of the
chapel of the Santissima Sindone, Guarini's most important
work in Turin, is occupied by the Holy Shroud, one of Christianity's most precious relics—a physical trace of the absent yet
present body of Christ. Here mere human "eccentricity" was
not a justification for distortion. The divine trace contained by
the centralized plan of the chapel is "real," and divine order is
presented for human experience. In his cosmological writings,

Guarini argued that humans could understand fully the regularity and purpose of the cosmos from a traditional, anthropocentric position. Only imagination and a thorough knowledge of geometry were needed to "demonstrate" the apparently irregular motions of the heavenly bodies as complex, regular movements around a fixed center.

In his philosophical work, *Placita Philosophica* (1665), Guarini deliberately rejected the identification of optics and geometry that was becoming prevalent in the painting and architecture of his own time, in works ranging from those of Desargues and Caramuel to the theories of anamorphosis and *quadratura*. He argued that geometry and optics were ontologically distinct. Geometry (*ortografia*) operates with parallel lines and is the basis of architecture, while optics (*perspectiva*) must deal with converging lines. Guarini was profoundly disturbed by the fact that perspective deceives us about the truth of orthogonal constructions. Furthermore, he understood that perspectival images suggest that parallel lines converge at a point at infinity, and this was the greatest lie. A moral question was at stake for him, as he could simply not accept the truth of this infinite point, nor the notion that projection (for architecture and all its constructive operations) is born from convergence to that point.[173] "*Ortografia* does not come from an infinite distance from the eye[;] . . . the idea [is] frustrating and the supposition absurd," because an image at infinity would be so minuscule that it would become invisible.[174] If perspective were true, capable of a total epiphany as implied by *quadratura* painting, this would paradoxically mean the end of appearance. Perspective accelerated the "appearance of the surface of things" and thus distorted the temporal nature of vision in normal, synesthetic perception, creating what for Guarini was a disturbing delusion. Discussing how objects are ultimately perceived in the eye, he concludes that images are like reflections in marble, in which the tactile world loses its "opacity."[175] The tactile world, for Guarini, is never fully assimilated to the optical. The flaw of perspective, in Guarini's cryptic words, is "to make the surface of the body appear," indeed, as a ghostly, insubstantial apparition that reveals too much, too quickly.[176] Caramuel's architecture, subjected to a fugal law of obliquity, was associated with this fault; according to Guarini the aim of architecture instead should be an enduring vision that, in contrast to optical tricks, is a characteristic of things that are *true*.

After his tenure as bishop of Campagna, and due to the intercession of Carlos II, king of Spain, Caramuel was appointed to his last mission as Bishop of Vigevano in 1673. During the last nine years of his life in this city in Lombardy, he produced some of his most ambitious projects, including the writing of his *Architectura Civil Recta y Oblicua,* and his only building, the facade of the Cathedral of Vigevano. This was indeed the only oblique architecture realized by Caramuel. The concave facade fills the east end of the square and stands in front of the church and its adjacent street. However, neither the long axis of the square nor the center of the facade are aligned with the central axis of the church. Of the four "portals," three lead into the church, while the fourth bridges the opening of the street.[177] Caramuel's intervention made the cathedral the most important building of the square and visually regularized the square by making its end facade continuous and by transforming its plan into a rectangle. Unlike anamorphic distortions, in which a decentered viewpoint would distort and obscure a recognizable image, Caramuel's uniform facade makes the off-center cathedral appear perfectly symmetrical. Although Caramuel's oblique architecture was based on the assumption that God made the world obliquely, it implied that the architect had to build not an architecture that *looked* oblique

| 1.50 |

View of Caramuel's church at Vigevano, closing the east of the public square with its striking concave facade. While three of the portals lead into the church, the fourth one (the northern portal) frames the entrance to the city behind.

Photo by A. Pérez-Gómez.

but an architecture that was itself built obliquely (or in this case incorporating the obliquity of the world), so that from a predetermined center it could be visually perceived as a perfect geometry. A stunningly innovative aspect of Caramuel's project was the visibility of the street beyond one of the openings. We walk out of the square, through the facade, "into" the city. Although we have inherited from the eighteenth century the tendency to read such a facade as a gimmicky "stage set," the "collision" with the urban and architectural programs of this work is one more rhetorical figure to express the order that architecture represents, rather than that which it is not.

Desargues, preceding Perrault, already considered geometry as an applied science whose ultimate goal was to control practice. Caramuel, on the other hand, like Villalpando before him and Guarini after him, considered geometry to be important for architects because of its theological and transcendental implications. Interestingly, Villalpando, Desargues, and Caramuel all disregarded tradition by claiming that architecture was an intellectual, explicitly impractical discipline, and that the architect *need not* be a craftsman. The *Maestro de obras* in Caramuel's terminology is also *el Ingeniero*. He takes his name from the fact that while others work with their hands, he first *ordena con su ingenio* (establishes order with his ingenuity).[178] Treatises on architecture from Vitruvius to the Renaissance had advocated a "balance" between *fabrica* and *ratiocinatio*. This plea for a new status of the architect, a prefiguration of the contemporary situation with all its potential problems, was based on two very different sets of values and assumptions. In the case of Desargues, perspective theory was postulated as an effective instrument to control the transition between the concept and the built work. The expertise of the hand, the wisdom of the craftsman, could be discounted and eventually would become irrelevant to the architect. In the case of Villalpando and Caramuel, the role of the architect stemmed from a medieval, Augustinian tradition. Architecture resided not in the built space but in the conceptual order that it defined, opening experience to the contemplation of truth. As a creator, the architect was a generator of ideas, not a mason or craftsman; his works, analogous to God's own vision, were "projective visions" that appeared in the form of plans and elevations.[179] Eventually, however, with the secularization of culture and the transformation of the future-oriented quest for salvation into technological progress, these two antagonistic precedents contributed to the radical, qualitative transformation of the very nature of architectural theory and practice, as well as their traditional relationship.

Variation Two

Cosmological Perspectives

The basis of science is not the definition,
but what is necessary to know beforehand
to constitute the definition.

* * *

Johann Heinrich Lambert, letter to Immanuel Kant,
November 1765

"The philosophers could by no means agree on any certain theory of the mechanism of the universe, which was constructed on our behalf by the best and most orderly Maker of everything."[1] Thus reads Copernicus's justification for his controversial demonstration that a moving Earth can explain more appropriately the celestial phenomena. Copernicus was not the first astronomer to put forward this idea, as we probably owe to Aristarchus of Samos (ca. 310–230 B.C.E.) the first formulation of the revolution of the Earth around the Sun.[2] The provocative status of this theory as *truth,* however, rather than as a traditional astronomical construct aimed at "saving the phenomena," had its paradoxical origins in medieval Nominalist theology, which questioned Aristotelian cosmology to affirm the omnipotence of a Christian God, imagining Him capable of creating the universe in ways that were not immediately accessible to visual contemplation (the traditional sense of classical *theōria*).[3] Taken up by Renaissance humanism, this critique of Aristotle fueled an aspiration to understand the rationality and perfection of God's creation through our intellectual capacity alone, eventually leading to a recognition that even our Earth (and its life forms) might not be unique. Initially assimilated to the Hermetic solar theology of the Renaissance, Copernicus's theory remained polemical during the seventeenth century. Despite a declared intention to better account for a universe "made by God for man," the potential of Copernican theory to disrupt the traditional associations between human purpose and a geocentric universe was acutely observed and dreaded. Modern science and philosophy were already prepared to accept the superior status of conceptual constructs over sense experience, yet, as we have suggested, the world of sensory experience, with its qualitative (Aristotelian) distinctions and orientation, was not given up easily as the ultimate basis of truth.

While the concept of a moving Earth remained theologically suspect for more than a century after being demonstrated by Copernicus, it became increasingly difficult to deny its validity in the observation of natural phenomena such as gravitational acceleration. Like Guarini, Caramuel believed that Earth was the stable center of the universe. He included in his treatise a *Discurso Mathematico* by an admirer of his work, the military engineer Ioseph Chafrion.[4] This text is a commentary on one of Caramuel's major works, *Mathesis Biceps* (Campagna, 1667). In assessing a set of experiments on gravitational acceleration performed by Caramuel, Chafrion entertained the possibility of the Earth's rotation—with the sole intention, he claimed, to "exercise the mind" and to follow the debate between Pythagoreans and Copernicans (led by Galileo). Nevertheless, Chafrion's (and Caramuel's) theological assumption remained unshaken: the rotation of the Earth was unacceptable.[5] Chafrion examined a traditional theory of gravity in which falling bodies do not accelerate with time and compared it to Galileo's theory of exponential acceleration. Common experience, writes Chafrion, invalidates the first theory: an object dropped from a tower accelerates visibly as it falls. This phenomenon could be explained if we make two assumptions: first, that the Earth rotates on its axis and completes one rotation every twenty-four hours; second, that gravitational acceleration is a mathematical constant, independent of the location of the experiment. These two propositions, however, are absolutely false, he emphasized, and any conclusion assuming them can bear no truth.[6] Facing this dilemma, Chafrion embraced a compromise proposed by Caramuel: he acknowledged that acceleration occurs in direct proportion to time, resulting in a lesser rate than Galileo's calculations suggest.

Caramuel's cosmology was based on Aristotelian physics, which distinguishes between supralunary and sublunary motions. While celestial matter moved in a circle around the center of the universe, lighter elements of the sublunary world, such as air and fire, would tend to move upward from the center, and heavy elements such as water and earth would tend to move (and even accelerate) downward. Gravity was understood as the tendency of matter to move toward the center of the universe, assumed to be the center of the Earth. Copernicus's theory, with its moving Earth and central Sun, radically questioned this traditional understanding of the universe. Some of his most notorious opponents such as Tycho Brahe claimed that if the Earth was postulated to move, the effects would then create "violent" motion that would cause the Earth to explode. Moreover, a cannonball "shot toward the West would strike a more distant target than one shot toward the East," since the Earth's motion would influence its speed and trajectory.[7]

In response to these criticisms, Copernicus first postulated the motion of the Earth to be "natural." Therefore, it could not produce "violent" effects. He then defined gravity as "the tendency of the parts of a whole to maintain their unity in a spherical shape," rather than as a natural tendency of matter to move toward the absolute center of the universe.[8] Copernicus replaced the unique center of the Aristotelian universe with a multiplicity of "centers" that tended to take on spherical shapes. Aristotelian physics then could no longer explain the global functioning of the universe, a task that would be taken up by mathematicians. The superiority of Copernicus's system over geocentricism was due to the greater coherence and regularity it introduced to the system of planetary motions. One of its great advantages was to eliminate the equant point, an eccentric point that regulated the movement of planets around the Earth. This was more than a scientific discovery; Copernicus emphasized the aesthetic and symbolic aspect of his system, declaring that "heaven itself is so linked together that in no portion of it can anything be shifted without disrupting the remaining parts and the universe as a whole.[9]

Within the Copernican system, physical laws no longer would permit qualitatively different spaces, since all differences between the sublunary and supralunary worlds were leveled. The Copernican universe eventually would become a homogeneous space, instead of the traditional hierarchy of places, but not before its incorporation into seventeenth-century science.[10] Twentieth-century writers have misleadingly associated this homogeneous and geometrized space with the perspective space of Renaissance painting.[11] But the debate about the infinity of space that led to the definition of modern space could not have occurred before the seventeenth century, since the notion of infinity during the Renaissance was theologically impossible to postulate *in* the world of man. Copernicus's cosmos, indeed, was not infinite space, for each motion had its own center, and the universe itself also possessed an absolute center—the Sun.

The seventeenth-century debate about the order of the universe was concerned particularly with the *geometry* of the cosmos, and connections between architectural theories and cosmology were predicated on this geometric interest. In the eighteenth century, on the other hand, this absolute "picture" of the heavens was replaced by a cosmology based on the relative motions of the universe. Connections between architectural theories and cosmology then began to focus on the *working* of the cosmos, or were increasingly abandoned in favor of ideas concerning architecture's cultural origins and its analogy to language, emphasizing *nomos* rather than *physis*. By the middle of the eighteenth century, space had long ago been postulated by Newton to be infinite and homogeneous, and this had become a basic assumption of the new sciences. Johann Heinrich Lambert (1728–1777), however, one of the century's most distinguished mathematicians—also a precocious geographer, forward-looking cosmographer, and author of a most unusual work on perspective[12]—held a significantly different conception of space. Lambert remained influenced by Copernican cosmology, which led him to describe a hierarchical universe as the basic framework for human action. As both a scientist and a philosopher, Lambert embodied the very complexity of the eighteenth century. He touched upon scientific disciplines as varied as hygrometry (the science of measuring the degree of humidity in the atmosphere), phyrometry (he was interested in finding the absolute zero of temperature), meteorology, and photometry, to name only a few, in addition to his general interest in mathematics and astronomy. We will concentrate on one of his wide-ranging accomplishments, his theory of perspective and representation, in conjunction with his most fundamental epistemological assumptions. We will therefore consider his cosmological studies, but only insofar as they relate to his general understanding of visual appearances and perspective theory.

Lambert was an eccentric character, often introduced with an anecdote about his first encounter with King Frederick the Great. While aspiring to become a member of the Academy of Sciences in Berlin, Lambert was summoned by the royal patron and was introduced to him in a most unusual manner. In a room intentionally darkened so that the king would not be offended by his unorthodox appearance, the prospective member was asked in what sciences he specialized. His answer was

"All of them." "Are you also a skillful mathematician?" continued the king, intrigued. "Yes," replied Lambert. "Which professor taught you mathematics?" the king inquired again. "I myself," was the response. An ironic tone was evident in the king's last question: "Are you therefore another Pascal?" Following Lambert's answer, "Yes, your Majesty," the king dismissed him, and later remarked that the greatest fool in the world had just been presented to him for membership in the academy. A few months later, however, the king changed his mind and appointed Lambert to the Berlin academy. He explained his reversal of opinion by saying that "with this man, one has to look at the immensity of his insights, not at trifling matters."[13]

Lambert was usually depicted by his contemporaries as a rather odd-looking person, not only for his blockhead physiognomy—his large forehead and broad, protruding jaw repulsed many—but also for his colorful character, his unmatched clothes, and his general disregard of etiquette. In his obituary, the perpetual secretary of the academy described Lambert as "an individual to whom the Eye and the Ear could hardly get accustomed." Jean Bernoulli (1744–1807), himself a translator and great admirer of Lambert's work, in *Précis de la vie de Mr Lambert* described his master's appearance as that of a strange being who would have "fallen from the moon."[14] Lambert was forgetful of conventions, and it was said that while commencing his studies on the laws of the reflection of light, he once walked into the finest café in Berlin, drew his sword, and began to make all kinds of movements in front of a large mirror to test some of his ideas, without considering the public around him. In the context of the eighteenth century, when rules and conventions were dictated so strictly, Lambert's loud laughter, his lack of refinement in food and wines, and his general appearance would always betray him as a self-taught man of humble origin.[15] But as soon as he was established in Berlin, he became respected for his scientific achievements and for his personal integrity. He worked in the Prussian Academy of Sciences with Leonhard Euler (1707–1783), who was director of the mathematics department until 1766, and then with his successor, Joseph-Louis Lagrange (1736–1813). Both men respected Lambert greatly. In a letter to D'Alembert, Lagrange

Profile of Johann Heinrich Lambert,
lithographed in 1828 by G.
Engelman.

Montreal, Collection Centre Canadien
d'Architecture / Canadian Centre for
Architecture.

praised Lambert's accomplishments in the fields of mathematics, physics, and mechanics: "He possessed the rare ability to apply calculations to experiments and observations, and to extract from them, in some way, all that was regular."[16] Euler also considered Lambert one of the great minds of his time. He promoted Lambert's candidacy for the chair in astronomy at the Academy of Sciences in St. Petersburg and for a position in mechanics, but political considerations blocked Lambert's appointment.[17] His accomplishments in astronomy prompted scientists to give his name to one of the craters on the Moon.[18]

Lambert's absence from twentieth-century studies on the history of sciences or the philosophy of the Enlightenment,[19] despite his direct and widely diversified contributions, can be attributed partly to the scope of his original thought in an age of incipient specialization. As a contemporary of Euler, Lagrange, and other eminent scientists, his theories in the fields of mathematics, physics, and mechanics often advanced the general knowledge in those fields, but his ideas were often surpassed by the same scientists whom they had initially impressed. Lambert's enduring fame as a scientist rests on his achievements in pure mathematics and geometry. He proved the irrationality of e, the number that is the basis of natural logarithms. Perhaps more significant for architecture and its inveterate quest for symbolic order and unity through geometry, he was also the first to demonstrate the irrationality of π, the ratio between the circumference of a circle and its diameter. For that reason, many claim that he came very close to proving the impossibility of squaring the circle and even to formulating a non-Euclidean geometry.[20]

Lambert was also a respected philosopher. Kant was greatly impressed by his early philosophical writings, so much so that he considered dedicating his *Critique der reinen Vernunft* to Lambert. But their initial "congeniality" remained superficial, for their fundamental ideologies would prove to be almost completely opposite.[21] Lambert's writings on philosophy—particularly his cosmological writings—were directly influenced by Leibniz and the notion of a centered universe. Lambert's model of the universe consisted of a multiplicity of beings, and therefore a multiplicity of viewpoints and perspectives. This multiplicity, however, never contradicted his firm belief that the

Lambert's monument on the cathedral square, Mulhouse, France [2.2], with an inscription [2.3] praising his accomplishments in astronomy: "His ashes rest in Berlin, his name is written in the commemorative calendar of the sky."

Photos by L. Pelletier.

2.2

universe has an absolute center and a hierarchical organization. While Leibniz considered the monad as the absolute center that prevented relativism, Lambert was a good "Copernican" who believed that the center of the world was occupied by an immense and stable core around which other subsystems gravitated. At every scale, the center of a system was occupied by a "regent" whose gravitational influence would dominate the whole system, but would itself be subjected to the attraction of a regent of a superior order.[22] Yet unlike Leibniz and the scientists of his time, Lambert believed in a *finite* universe, and he insisted on assigning boundaries to the creation.[23] Moreover, he could not consider time and space independently, because cosmic order involved not only place but also movement. Lambert's cosmology was in fact defined in terms of movement and a relative temporality instead of an absolute image.

It might be important to recall that in the second half of the eighteenth century, Newton's *Mathematical Principles of Natural Philosophy* dominated scientific thought. His work was indeed the basis of a new natural science that sought to establish all of the laws and consequences of natural phenomena from observation and mathematical analysis, without using any a priori hypotheses. Leibniz's theological metaphysics had been very influential throughout Europe at the beginning of the century, but soon became distrusted by scientists. In that context, Lambert's cosmology, which was based on teleological principles and unverifiable hypotheses, also went against the current Newtonian trend.[24]

Redefining a Hierarchical Universe

The new science always tried to avoid speculation, but throughout the eighteenth century, questions concerning the nature of the universe were never considered an exclusive matter for theologians, philosophers, or polymaths. It is undeniable that scientists such as Newton remained profoundly interested in matters of theology, alchemy, and metaphysics, for example. Nevertheless, in the first edition of his *Principia,* Newton said next to nothing about the stars, except that they do not interfere with the internal arrangements of the solar system, because

SA CENDRE
REPOSE A BERLIN
SON NOM EST ECRIT
DANS LES
FASTES D'URANIE

2.3

185

of their distance.[25] On the other hand, William Herschel—to whom the beginning of scientific cosmology is usually credited, because of the observations and theoretical investigations made with his great telescopes—scrutinized the nebulae and the Milky Way in the early 1780s and concluded that nebulae were star clusters gradually compressed by forces of gravitational attraction. Earlier post-Galilean astronomers had always stopped at the edge of our solar system; it was only after the mid-eighteenth century that scientists sought to penetrate the starry heavens and speculate about the "real" movement of the stars. Between Newton's investigations in the late seventeenth century and Herschel's observations in the late eighteenth century, three major figures contributed to shape the image of the heavens: Immanuel Kant, Thomas Wright, and Johann Heinrich Lambert.[26]

| 2.4 |

William Herschel's model of the Milky Way, from *Philosophical Transactions of the Royal Society of London* 74 (1784), part 2.

Montreal, Department of Rare Books and Special Collections of the McGill University Libraries.

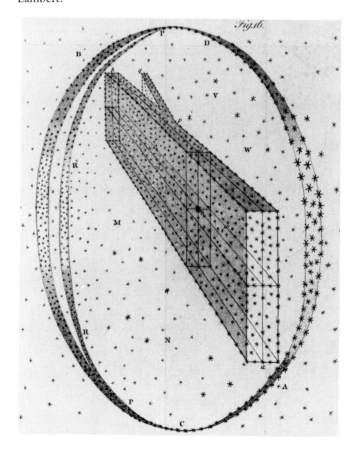

Kant believed, like Herschel, that gravity was the force that transformed chaos into order in a kind of evolutionary way. Their concept of the universe was opposed to that of Newton, who could not abandon the notion of a stable and permanent divine order even though he developed the laws of gravity. Beyond some apparent similarities in their explanations of the Milky Way, Kant's *Allgemeine Naturgeschichte* also is radically different from Lambert's *Cosmological Letters*. Both works advocate a hierarchical concept of the universe and the idea of star systems gravitating around a massive body. However, Kant's viewpoint was evolutionary while Lambert's was static. Kant defended the idea of an infinite universe of galaxies, stars, comets, and planets with their systems subjected to cyclical birth and decay, while Lambert firmly advocated a finite universe of stable shape and structure where comets never would be considered as embryonic planets.[27]

Like Newton and Lambert, Thomas Wright believed in the stability of the universe. He seems to have been the first to suggest that the elongated mass of stars identified as the Milky Way could in fact be a cluster of stars shaped as a flat disk whose foreshortened diameter we observe from an oblique viewpoint. His model of the galaxy acknowledged the off-center position of human observers, while recognizing the divine Creator as the absolute center. In a lecture given in 1734, Wright developed a hypothesis that extended the model of the solar system, assuming that the Sun revolves around an absolute center just as the planets gravitate around the Sun. The only motion allowed to the absolute center was of a supernatural order. Wright extrapolated the basic model of the solar system at a larger scale without really questioning the notion of center. More than fifteen years later, in his book *An Original Theory or New Hypothesis of the Universe* (1750),[28] he developed a more complex cosmology composed of many star systems; each has its own Divine Center and our galaxy is one such system. He also conceived the universe as a spherical shell and sought once more to relocate God at the center.

Lambert devised a similar concept of the universe in 1749, long before his ideas were finally crystallized in his *Cosmological Letters on the Arrangement of the World-Edifice* (1761),[29] and before he had come across any of Kant's or Wright's work.

Two plates from Thomas Wright's *An Original Theory or New Hypothesis of the Universe* (1750), illustrating his concept of the Milky Way. Wright was the first to describe this agglomeration of stars confined "between two parallel planes" as a flat disk [2.5]. Wright describes the second image [2.6] as a section of "an artificial Horizon of a Globe."

Opposite page: Section through the universe showing "the divine omnipresence in each Milky Way," from Wright's treatise.

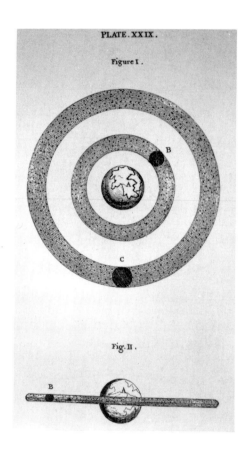

2.6

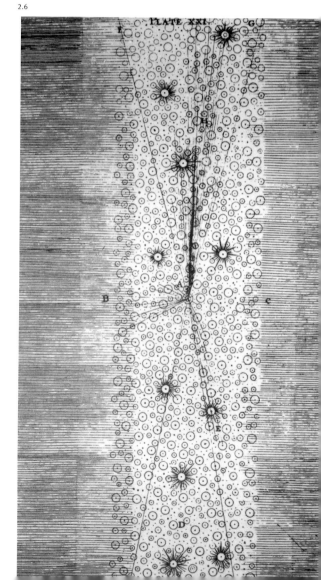

2.7

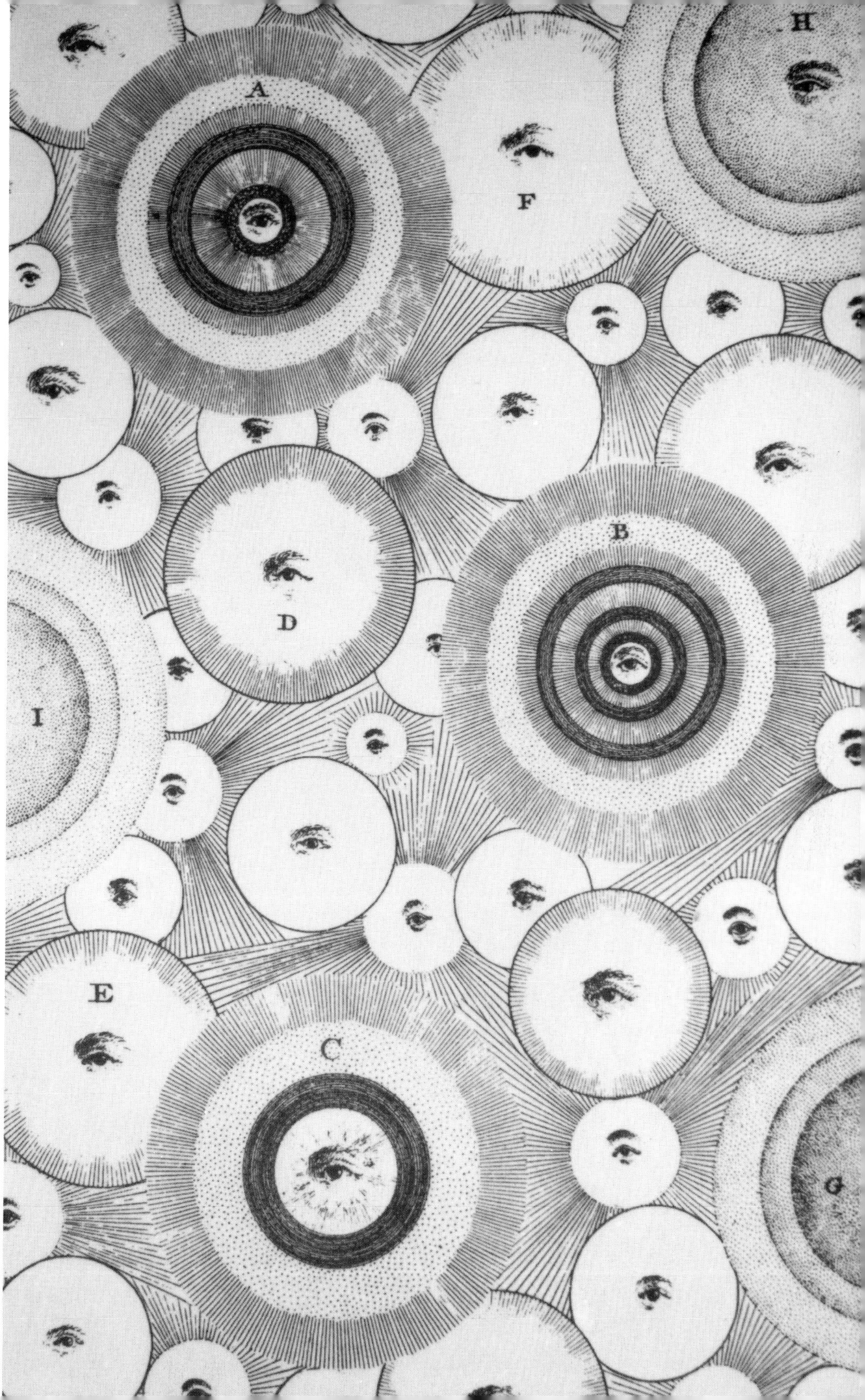

In a letter to Kant dated November 1765, Lambert reveals that his concept of the Milky Way as an "ecliptic of stars" occurred to him as he was observing the sky, some fifteen years earlier. "Contrary to my habits, then, I went into my room after the evening meal, and looked through the window at the stellar sky and especially at the Milky Way. The insight, which I had then, to see it as an ecliptic of the fixed stars, I wrote down on a quarto page and that was all that I had as a written note before me, in much the same way as I am writing this letter."[30] This sketch was the first and only image he recorded to explain the visual phenomenon of the Milky Way, and it summarizes his understanding of the structure of the universe. Like Wright, he believed that the irregular distribution of stars in the Milky Way was due to our eccentric position in the galaxy.

According to an entry in his diary (*Monatsbuch*), Lambert started working on the text of his series of twenty letters on the system of the world in June 1760. Written as a correspondence between two friends, Lambert alternates between posing the questions and later providing the answers. For example, in his First Letter, Lambert expresses a fear common at the time that Copernicus's discovery had made the world a more dangerous place to live, by putting the Earth in motion and subjecting it to potential collisions with comets. Lambert's response in the Second Letter is based on his belief in the "perfection of the arrangement of the world-edifice," according to which the purposefulness of the universe would prevent such a possibility.[31] Lambert's thesis on the motion of the stars around a center was based on two teleological postulates: that celestial bodies are in motion and that they tend toward the self-preservation of the whole.

During 1761, the year when the *Cosmological Letters* appeared, Lambert also published a book on the properties of cometary orbits. This was a notoriously difficult question, which challenged the regularity of cosmological laws. Lambert's pervasive interest in comets—a theme present throughout his *Letters*—was consistent with the teleological assumptions of his cosmology and his basic hypothesis concerning life in the universe. Lambert's cosmology rejected the evolutionary system put forward by Kant and others, in which comets were postulated as embryonic planets. An evolutionary system would have

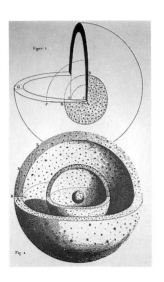

| 2.8 |

The earth within a sphere of stars, from Wright's treatise. Wright imagined the universe to be shaped as a spherical shell with God occupying the center.

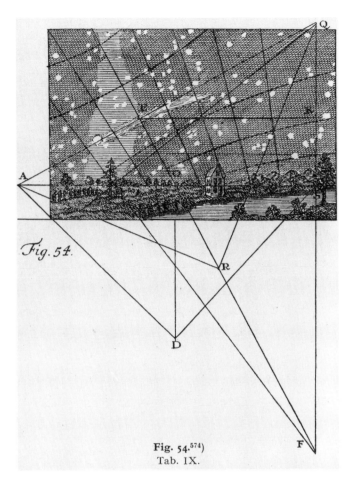

Fig. 54.

Fig. 54.[574])
Tab. IX.

2.9

Illustration of the sky with a comet in perspective, from Johann Heinrich Lambert's *Freye Perspektive, oder Unweisung* (1774). Lambert's fascination with the potential inhabitants of comets was evident throughout his work.

Montreal, Collection Centre Canadien d'Architecture / Canadian Centre for Architecture.

191

implied the possibility of a celestial catastrophe in which Earth could be obliterated. This alternative was simply inconceivable in Lambert's mind, since the universe's purpose was to sustain life and preserve its stable shape and order. Consequently, Lambert also defended the idea that every celestial body, including comets and satellites, must be inhabited by living beings, whose existence should not be ruled out simply because we cannot see them. He supported his argument through an analogy with microscopic worlds whose innumerable "inhabitants" were revealed under a magnifying glass. This belief that the whole universe may be inhabited was not uncommon during the Enlightenment, and it was clearly expressed by Hermann

Samuel Reimarus's rhetorical question: "Why should we alone be worthy of reality?"[32]

In his Fourth Letter, Lambert speculates further on the relative position of the comet's inhabitants and on their possible status as wanderers who view "the edifice of the heavens, the position of each Sun, the plane and course of their planets, satellites, and comets in all their whole interconnectedness."[33] They must all be astronomers, he claims, since they were created with the purpose of viewing the structure of the universe. Lambert speculates that temporality for these inhabitants traveling on a comet must vary with scale and movement. The observation of the heavens "would take place during that long period which allows their habitat to go from one Sun to another, and [the understanding of their own position] would happen when their habitat was on the point of seeking a new path around a Sun to observe that sky from a new angle. They would need centuries, just as single hours go past us, and immortality ought to be their heritage because time is allotted to them according to their performances, just as on our Earth there are insects whose life begins and ends in the course of a few hours because their activity demands no more time."[34] This passage clearly characterizes a worldview in which the observer's vantage point is subject to changes and to relativity, a worldview that presumes the inhabitants of a specific world have been given the means to understand their own position and to make sense of the universe. Considered as a model for the acquisition of true knowledge, perspective enabled Lambert to imagine what living beings on other celestial bodies might perceive in the universe. This ability to reflect on one's own position and to extrapolate one's standpoint from a given perspective is precisely what defined Lambert's cosmological investigation as an "inversion" of perspective, thoroughly connected to his perspective theory and described explicitly in the last section of his *Perspective affranchie* (1759), his main treatise on the subject, published only two years before his cosmological speculations.[35] Like Wright, Lambert had conceived the geometry of the Milky Way as an oblique perspective view from within our own galaxy. Wright had similarly claimed that the stars are "continually crowding behind one another, as all other objects do toward the horizon point of their perspective which ends but with infinity."[36] While Lambert regarded perspective as a form of "natural" perception, his cosmology used the knowledge of the very mechanism that produces appearances—namely, foreshortening—to deduce from it the awareness of our own position. The decentralized point of view in Lambert's perspective was applied theoretically to his cosmology, which reversed the mechanism for creating illusions and instead made the visual appearance of the world into the site of investigation. Indeed, the perspective mechanism enabled humans to disclose the potential illusion to which we could be submitted, as a consequence of our relative standpoint in the universe.

Lambert's *Cosmological Letters* are similar in style to Bernard le Bovier de Fontenelle's *Entretiens sur la pluralité des mondes* (1686), a literary work that popularized astronomical concepts. His writing in the *Letters* is far from being strictly scientific, and in many ways he invokes the imagination of the reader. In his Seventh Letter, Lambert attempts to describe in more detail the strange inhabitants of other planets and celestial bodies. The imagination tends to picture them as better than us, he says, so "we add some wings because we feel that we lack the ability to fly. We would even add fins, if swimming were impossible to man and if death were not the result of drowning!" We also imagine them to be almost immortal, since they need to travel immense distances through the universe. Lambert insists, however, that they must have eyes, even if different from ours, since these are the organs by which we know the world: "The nature of light, its effects, the partnership between soul and body either are not known to us as yet, or are known only insofar as we receive the impressions which the light makes on us, and we seek to fill in the rest through conclusions to which we have as yet no other bases than the ones which we postulate through seeing."[37]

In his article "Vom Trabanten der Venus" (On Venus's satellite) published in the *Astronomisches Jahrbuch für das Jahr 1777* (Berlin, 1775), Lambert speculated about a satellite revolving around Venus and predicted that it would become visible on June 1, 1777, when Venus would pass close to the Sun. How could a great planet such as Venus do without a moon and thus break the universe's hierarchical system of similarity postulated by Lambert? Such was the reasoning that guided his hypothesis, directly in line with his earlier *Cosmological Letters*. The day of the predicted apparition arrived but no satellite was to be seen.[38] Lambert's misfortune with Venus's satellite in many ways is symptomatic of the hypothetical nature of his cosmological work. His *Cosmological Letters* were at odds with the scientific theories of his time, for they were based primarily on speculation. Thus, they remained forgotten throughout most of the late eighteenth and the nineteenth centuries. Even after Herschel confirmed some of Lambert's hypotheses by observing the sky through his large telescopes, Lambert's work still appeared too speculative for the taste of his time. Among other things, Herschel demonstrated the motion of the assumed fixed stars and discovered Uranus, the first new planet of our solar system, thus confirming Lambert's postulate about the fullness of the universe, which implied more planets and satellites. Yet Herschel's discoveries seemed rather to precipitate the general disinterest in Lambert's cosmology. In an age dominated by Newtonian physics, when observation was the mandatory basis for any scientific theory, Lambert's *Letters* could be read at best as an imaginative "cosmological novel."

In short, Lambert's cosmology was based on a priori principles. It presupposed the perfection of God's creation, and such perfection denied the possibility of cosmic cataclysms such as the collision of comets, promoted the fullness of life everywhere in the cosmos, and arranged the universe purposefully into a hierarchical organization. Lambert nonetheless contributed to the very important expansion of scientific astronomy, by considering the structure and motions of the solar system and by investigating the starry universe as a whole. In his system, stars were postulated in motion in free space and at unequal distances from us, shattering the Ptolemaic sphere of fixed stars.[39] In his preface to the *Cosmological Letters,* Lambert himself noted this important turning point in the history of modern astronomy: "While more recent astronomers are very anxious to put in order the sphere of our solar system and to assign each comet its orbit, and to determine in advance its eventual return, hardly any attempt has been made to find out something probable on the arrangement and position of the fixed stars."[40] In discussing his concept that the universe revolves around a central body, however, Lambert always emphasized his indebtedness to Copernicus: "Insofar as Copernicus made the first step, there remains for us and for our descendants still a thousand other steps to take and even then we shall not be perfectly Copernican by a long shot. Inasmuch, however, as we know that the last step will end at the body which directs the whole creation around itself, I think that we are thinking Copernican enough." [41]

Copernicus's cosmology had relegated humanity from the center of the universe to a peripheral position that gravitated around the Sun—the new center of the system. Yet, man still occupied a privileged position in a universe created *for* him. Lambert's model, while never finally questioning this assumption, shattered the remaining geocentrism and went much further in preventing the Earth's inhabitants from occupying anything more than one of many life systems. While the task of artists and architects in a Copernican world had consisted in relocating man at a privileged geometric point (as exemplified by Caramuel's oblique architecture and seventeenth-century anamorphic projections), the "decentralizing" of the Enlightenment's point of view (to use Hans Blumenberg's term) would find its concrete vehicle in Lambert's theory of perspective, a "natural" perspective that defined only a relative image of the world, one of many possible points of view.

Recentering the World

Kant described Copernicus's greatness as having "dared in a manner contradictory of the senses, but yet true, to seek the observed movement, not in the heavenly bodies, but in the spectator." [42] For Copernicus, the origin of the apparent planetary and solar motions was to be found in man himself, in his ability to observe the changing sky and to deduce from it the laws of astronomy. Radicalizing this insight, Lambert sought the explanation of the apparent heavenly motions in the mechanism of perception itself. His intention was to deduce the geometry implicit in the visual world from the laws of vision. His cosmological speculations, as we have suggested, were related directly to his several studies on perspective. This "mechanism," indeed, provided the basis for his wide-ranging scientific and philosophical research.

Lambert's earliest writing on perspective, *Anlage zur Perspektive* (1752), was his first attempt to explain visual phenomena.[43] He began by establishing the foundation for his perspective theory, drawing on the distinction between the tactile reality of the world and a potential visual delusion: "Visible things often appear very different from what they really are." This early text was in many ways an outline of his major work on perspective, *Die Freye Perspektive,* which was published simultaneously in French as *La Perspective affranchie de l'embaras du Plan géometral* (1759).[44] In that book, the fundamental difference between the visual appearance of the world and its physical reality led to a distinction between two different "Arts" or methods of representation, later described as perspective and parallel projection. The first one, he says, "is concerned with drawing an object as it is presented to the eye, placed at a certain height and a certain distance; the other teaches us how to trace its truthful figure in a geometric plan. The latter uses the relationships that really exist between all the parts of an object, while the former borrows its rules from the phenomena of vision, determined by optics, and is interested only in appearances."[45]

The greater "truthfulness" of parallel projection, however, did not make it a more desirable form of representation. Lambert maintained that the two kinds of projection must be considered for their different purposes. In the *Anlage,* he emphasized the implicit connection between them by devoting the core of the manuscript to a strange apparatus, a kind of distorting pantograph or "perspectograph," that allowed a draftsman to construct a perspective projection from the orthogonal drawing (plan) of any given object, starting from the outline of the plan and the relative position of the observer.[46] Useless as a practical drawing tool—the perspectograph could project only the plan of an object, with no regard for its elevation—it demonstrated nonetheless an explicit relationship between the visual reality and the tactile experience of the world by projecting the orthogonal plan into the converging appearance of a perspective view. This "archetypal" device was actually a model that enabled Lambert to understand the phenomena of perception: since the tactile world in which parallel lines never meet is accessible to us through visual appearances where parallel lines are seen to converge, the perspectograph similarly projects in

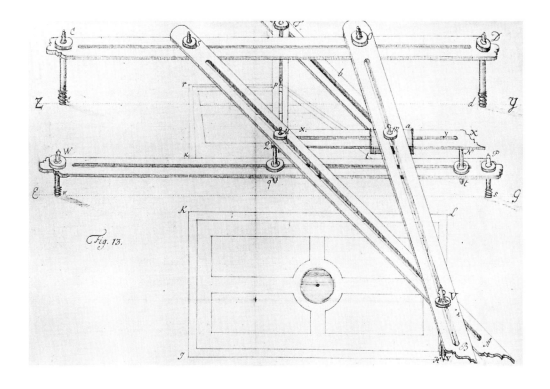

Fig. 13.

perspective the coordinates of our physical world, offering it to our visual perception. This device was also conceptually reversible. Knowing the relationship between the vantage point and the relative angle of parallel lines in a perspective view, the observer could infer his true position in a quantitative, measurable reality, as if in a plan. Even though the perspectograph is not included in Lambert's major work on perspective, its fundamental principle—using the perspective mechanism to deduce one's "true," metric position in relation to the image (the empirical reality of the world)—remains a very important part of *La Perspective affranchie,* especially in the last section, where Lambert defines the principles of "inverted perspective."

We must emphasize that Lambert's fascination with the mechanism of perspective cannot be dissociated from his cosmological convictions, which he believed it demonstrated. His decentralized viewer may have represented only one of many points of view, yet that viewer was never subjected to

| 2.10 |

Lambert's modified pantograph, or perspectograph, used to transfer the orthographic plan of a garden into a perspective plan, from *Anlage zur Perspektive* (1752).

Montreal, Collection Centre Canadien d'Architecture / Canadian Centre for Architecture.

absolute relativism. Even though the universe had been created not for man alone but with the implicit purpose of sustaining life in all its parts, Lambert firmly believed that man possessed nonetheless the crucial ability to grasp his position in an ordered universe and thus to perceive the very purpose of the universe by understanding the mechanism of perception. Therefore, Lambert's intention was not so distant from baroque perspective and *quadratura* frescoes that attempted to relocate man in the world. For example, like Lambert's perspective, Andrea Pozzo's *quadratura* held the potential to identify the preset position where the visual illusion was to be perceived. While Pozzo's perspective theory sought to reveal transcendental, mostly theological truths, he also aspired to represent the world objectively and assumed that his created illusion would be perceived identically by all who stood at the predetermined vantage point. His frescoes were not merely a culmination of previous "illusionism"; their geometric and cosmological implications were dictated by his religious beliefs. The Jesuit Pozzo never ac-

| 2.11 |

Andrea Pozzo's diagram for drawing the false dome in the church of Sant'Ignazio in Rome, from his treatise *Rules and Examples of Perspective* (1700). The image was meant to be placed in a specific position in space: "This figure ought to be placed as much above the eye as the height DO."

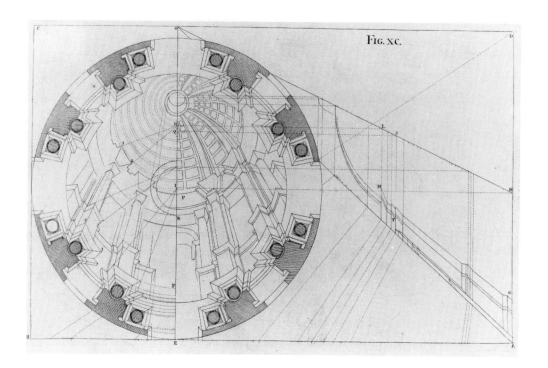

cepted Galileo's theories, and he always assumed the Earth to be at the center of the universe. Consequently, Pozzo's *quadratura* can be seen in many respects as a late model of the geocentric world.

Pozzo's first known work as a painter was a *machina* for the *quarantore,* or forty hours' devotion. From 1671 to 1697, he executed a number of altar paintings and frescoes on the ceilings of Jesuit churches.[47] His best-known works, however, are the frescoes on the ceiling of the nave in Sant'Ignazio in Rome—begun in 1688 with the first segment of the *Triumph of Sant'Ignazio,* for which he was commissioned to correct the proportions of the apse using a perspective illusion—and the false dome for the same church, which was greatly admired by his contemporaries.[48] This work was also reproduced in his perspective treatise as an example of a practical application of perspective extension of space. Pozzo also designed several altars for Sant'Ignazio in the church of the Gesù, various illusionistic theatrical stages for Jesuit dramas—many of them were also reproduced in his treatise—two facades for St. John Lateran, and plans for Jesuit churches throughout Europe. He left Rome for Vienna in 1702, where he painted many more frescoes, notably a depiction of the labors of Hercules on the ceiling of the main reception hall of the Liechtenstein Palace.

Pozzo came to architecture while already active as a painter, and his definition of a good architect was inseparably connected to the knowledge of painting and perspective: "È buon pittore, è buon prospettico, dunque sarà buon architetto."[49] In his designs for theatrical stages for the *theatrum sacrum,* it seemed more crucial than ever for the observer to be placed on the central axis of the composition in order to perceive the effect of a perfect illusion. The decorations for the *quarantore* performances apparently were designed to compete with coinciding carnival celebrations. As part of the *theatrum sacrum,* these performances were "a kind of spectacular biblical pageant in which the church served as both auditorium and scenic setting."[50] Soon, the church of the Gesù became a center for this kind of performance. The architecture of the Gesù seemed particularly appropriate for this kind of scenographic setting because of its sequential progression of elements from one bay to the next. Pozzo incorporated the architectural con-

Pozzo's stage design for the church of the Gesù in Rome, representing the Marriage of Cana in Galilee, from *Rules and Examples of Perspective.* He used a succession of planes and lit the space between them with candlelight in order to emphasize the optical effect of solidity.

Montreal, Collection Centre Canadien d'Architecture / Canadian Centre for Architecture.

text of the church into the composition to a much greater extent than any of his predecessors. He emphasized the continuity between the choir (the stage) and the nave (the auditorium), using lighting effects and his false perspective to extend the apparent space of the church.[51]

Pozzo's stage designs did not involve any real technical innovations. The oblique panels used to promote the illusion of depth were known already to Giulio Troili and had been used in Venetian theaters.[52] His greatest contribution was instead his very method of perspective, with its important implications for architecture. Pozzo's perspective method clearly postulated the homology between a two-dimensional drawing and its projection in three-dimensional space, and it implied a complete and "objective" correspondence among plan, elevation, and perspective. From the beginning of the seventeenth century, this homology between lived space and represented

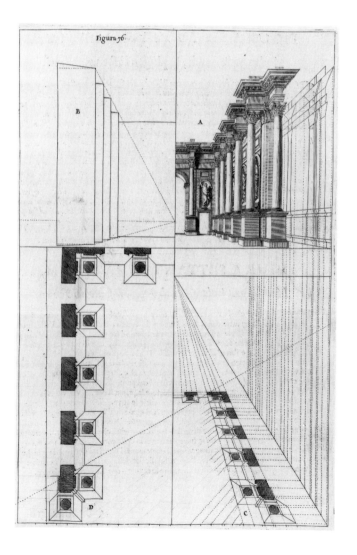

Figura 76.

2.13

Pozzo's drawing method, demonstrated in his treatise, was based on a correspondence among plan, elevation, and perspective.

Montreal, Collection Centre Canadien d'Architecture / Canadian Centre for Architecture.

space was latent in baroque perspective, as the determination of the vantage point in real space became understood as a crucial aspect of perspective constructions.[53] Only with Pozzo, however, would the geometrized space be explained in architectural terms and reduced to a simple method for painters and architects rather than for mathematicians. Consequently, Pozzo's *Rules and Examples of Perspective Proper for Painters and Architects* (1707) became one of the most influential treatises of its kind. During the first century following its publication, more than twenty-five editions and translations were produced.[54] It simplified previous methods and provided step-by-step lessons which assumed that any artist who followed this precise procedure would arrive at exactly the same drawing. Although not explicitly discounted, the talent and personal experience of the artist were no longer an issue. Pozzo believed there was no need for a philosophical discussion of the implications of perspective, since it was self-evidently an objective tool. The treatise simply begins with a technical demonstration of how to draw squares and rectangles in perspective, then continues with more com-

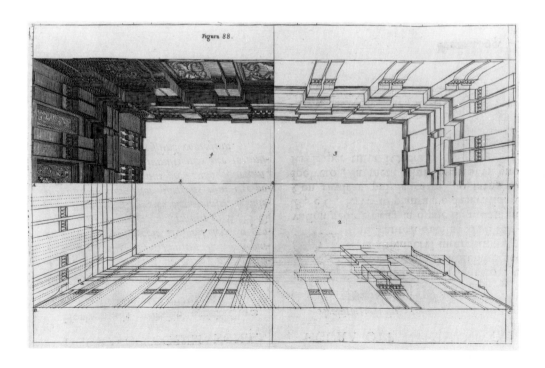

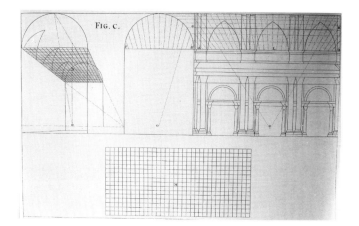

Diagram explaining how to project a perspective drawing onto a vault according to the *quadratura* method, from Pozzo's treatise.

plex figures and concrete architectural examples. The book is heavily illustrated, for every page of text is accompanied with an engraved plate. All of these examples start from a plan and an elevation of a given scene. The second step consists in demonstrating how to increase the visual space of a room and make painted architecture appear solid by projecting it in perspective. Many examples include a detailed method of superimposing several frames and canvas, as in his theater stages.

The last section of Pozzo's treatise is devoted specifically to the technique of *quadratura*. A few drawings describe his method of projecting a perspective image, originally generated from a plan and an elevation, onto a vault or an irregular surface. Once the perspective is drawn in the conventional manner, he projects it through the *quadratura* method: a grided matrix of threads is fixed at the base of the vault, and a candle is placed at the position in space where the illusion of the fresco will be witnessed, at a height corresponding to the eye of the observer. The distorted shadow of the grid projected on the ceiling is drawn in place and used as a transfer grid for the perspective image. Consequently, the *quadratura* projection not only fixes the position of the spectator by involving him physically in the overall composition,[55] it also introduces to the geometric construction a third point in space. In addition to the "principal point" and the "distance point" of Vignola's perspective method, which restricted the representation to the two-dimensional surface of projection, Pozzo's *quadratura* method occupies the volume of the projective space itself; it actualizes the potential correspondence between architectural space and perspective space that will eventually lead to a homology between lived space and perspective space, as with Ferdinando Galli da Bibiena's *scena per angolo*.

If one considers his perspective treatise alone, apart from his lifelong practice as a *quadratura* painter, Pozzo may seem like a thoroughly modern figure in the history of representation, since his perspective method already assumed a homology between perspective and architectural space. But his practice must not be ignored. Although he wrote what is perhaps the first systematic and truly practical treatise on perspective, he paradoxically used this method to produce symbolic compositions whose very program could never admit the premise of homogeneous space. In the preface of his treatise, Pozzo describes the point where all of the lines converge as the "true point, the Glory of God." In the specific case of the fresco of Sant'Ignazio, he refers to that point as the son of God who "sends forth a ray of light into the heart of Ignatius, which is then transmitted by him to the most distant regions of the four parts of the world."[56] Pozzo's *quadratura* frescoes rest upon the foundation of Jesuit theology with its visualization practices, and operate within the sacred space of the church, relocating the human observer at this place of epiphany, as the ultimate participant in the ritual.

Like Pozzo, Lambert sought to understand man's position in the creation through his perspective theory, but while Pozzo identified man's place with the absolute center of Jesuit Catholic truth, Lambert's cosmology could only lead him to acknowledge the inevitable eccentricity and multiplicity of man's point of view. Unlike Pozzo, Lambert was interested in the geometric properties of perspective construction only insofar as they enabled him to understand the mechanism of visual illusions, and to deduce from them a position already assigned to man. Lambert relied on vision itself to develop his theory of perspective, a perspective that was not absolute and systematically rendered like that of Pozzo; but he assumed nonetheless that its basic principles were natural and coincided with those of optics, and therefore that its rules were universal.

Lambert's anthropocentrism, therefore, was very different from Pozzo's. It was based on his absolute belief in the purposefulness of the universe: even though the Earth was no longer at the center, and man was only a part in one of many life systems, the very fact that he was given the means to understand his own position implied a fundamental purpose in the world. Not until the nineteenth century would the notion of a purposeful universe be questioned, when Pierre Simon de Laplace (1749–1827) declared God to be an "unnecessary hypothesis."[57] Later, in the early twentieth century, Lambert's purposeful and ordered universe would be replaced by the notion of absolute disordered and purposeless evolution, in a kind of Darwinism of the universe. Karl Schwarzschild commented on Lambert's *Cosmological Letters* in an address to the Göttingen Academy in 1907: "The planetary system was not originally constructed in such a way that no collisions come about; instead the collisions themselves have produced an arrangement in which they are excluded."[58] In many respects Schwarzschild was a successor to Lambert. An important astronomer, he also advanced the principles of photometry—a discipline founded by Lambert—"by exactly determining the laws governing the darkening of photographic plates."[59] Incidentally, this became the point of departure for astronomers to determine the distribution of stars in space and thus to estimate the relative emptiness of the universe. Ultimately, in place of the teleological order of Lambert's cosmological system (implying an immutable ordered universe), Schwarzschild substituted the opposite concept of an aging *chaos*.[60]

The Eccentric Point of View

A few years after Pozzo produced his last perspective illusions, and almost half a century before Lambert's perspective treatise was published, Ferdinando Galli da Bibiena's *Architettura Civile* (1711) introduced a new mode of perspective that transformed the whole tradition of stage design in Italy and implicitly changed the very nature of perspective representation and its relation to reality. His *scena* or *vedute per angolo,* later adopted by Filippo Juvarra and other stage designers, displaced the focal

Ferdinando Galli da Bibiena's *scena per angolo*, from his *Architettura Civile* (1711).

point of the composition out of the audience's sight by replacing the primary vanishing point—traditionally on the central axis of the baroque stage—by a two-point perspective, so as to create a greater illusion of reality. This illusion was also achieved by adjusting the scale, distance, and perspective acceleration to draw the spectators into the scene more effectively. The diminution of scale was so important to the created illusion that every detail of the painted scenery had to be drawn in perfect proportion, and the actors constantly had to be aware of their location on the stage. In order to give an accurate reading of scale to the whole set, the actors were requested not to approach the slanted floor nor to cast their shadows on the backdrop, since these transgressions of the established distance between the action and the painted background would make them seem like giants and ruin the illusion of depth. In fact, three generations of the Bibiena family so perfected the art of stage scenery that they were declared true "magicians of immensity" who could extend the boundaries of imaginary spaces to their limit.[61]

The basic pattern of the *scena per angolo* was based either on a V-shaped plan, with its acute angle pointing toward the audience, or on an X-shaped distribution of intersecting arcades that spread simultaneously forward toward the proscenium arch and backward through receding rows of columns.[62] Thus, the audience literally was embraced by the architecture of the theater, both permanent and ephemeral, and was drawn into the perspective illusion of scenery that appeared real from every seat in the auditorium. Prior to the eighteenth century, baroque theaters had been built primarily for the symbolic gaze of the king, whose box was always on axis with the focal point of the perspective on stage. From any other seat, one could witness only a partial illusion. The Bibienas' intertwining alleys of arcades and their urban streets running diagonally offstage revolutionized stage design in the eighteenth century. The *scena per angolo,* indeed, established a theatrical space that was more "democratic" than the former central perspective, providing everyone with a better illusion of apparent depth.

The *scena per angolo* identified the space of the stage with that of the city. The interior architecture of the theater was also conceived as an urban facade, with its successive balconies and superimposed architectural orders. The aim was to enable the general public to inhabit a perfect illusion of a perspective space. Once lived space could be equated with its representation, it would be little more than a formality to postulate perspective as being the natural way we see the world. This was indeed the premise of Lambert's perspective treatise: the laws governing representation are dictated directly by the laws deduced from our perception of the world. It is not a coincidence that in the middle of the eighteenth century, while the tradition of the Bibienas' stage design was still flourishing, very few new perspective theories were put forward (Lambert's being the most important exception). Scientists and philosophers generally no longer believed that their interests could be served

The interior of Giuseppe Galli da Bibiena's Opera House in Bayreuth (1748). The Bibienas' designs for theaters and opera houses emphasized the continuity between the space of the performance and that of the city by reproducing the urban facade inside the auditorium.

Photo by A. Pérez-Gómez.

by a further elucidation of geometric perspective, while artists relied more on the possibilities of empirical vision.

In the opening pages of his study on perspective, Lambert expresses his concern about deceptive visual appearances. He notes that distance and viewing angle affect our perception of an object. Later he distinguishes between optics, or the visual science, and perspective. The distinction is one of intentions rather than principles: while optical laws enable us to differentiate between the appearance of things and their true shape, he says, perspective disregards reality by depicting only apparent shapes. But the level of perfection in painting remains determined by the painter's ability to recreate this illusion of appearances, and the greatest possible achievement is attained when the painting deceives the eye. "When birds prey on painted grapes and try to devour them, when a painter himself reaches out to open a painted curtain or to shoo away a painted fly, that is the utmost one can expect of art."[63]

Previous methods of perspective construction, such as Pozzo's, began by locating the horizontal coordinates of the subject in plan, to prevent inappropriate perspective distortions. For Lambert, perspective derived its principles from optics and was therefore natural. Thus, he maintained that the image should be generated from the object itself, its position in plan being deduced only *later,* according to a given angle of perception. It is important, however, to clarify Lambert's definition of optics. More than being a simple system of visual rules, "optics proscribes appearances, and insists instead on truth so as to disclose the mistakes that could deceive the eyes."[64] For Lambert, optics was already a geometric discipline whose purpose was not to regulate visual appearances, but to infer from them the true "tactile" shape of things. The first premise of his perspective method was to eliminate the need to start from the *plan géométral*. Lambert distinguished between these two modes of representation—between an optical perspective generated from the object itself and a geometric perspective generated from the plan. He favored the first mode, which already provides the necessary rules of representation and can show all the different views of an object as if seen directly in front of us, even if it is restricted to the appearances and can sometimes suggest an image unfaithful to the actual object. The second mode of representation, he explained, uses the exact coordinates of a given object, but the method of drawing a perspective starting from the plan is far too complex and involves too many unnecessary lines and points. Consequently, all the problems that illustrate his theory of perspective assume that the plan of any object can be put directly in perspective without starting from an orthogonal plan. One needs to know only one side of a figure and the angle that it makes, he says, to draw the plan directly in perspective.[65] Not coincidentally, this procedure corresponds with the operation of his perspective pantograph, which assumed a direct connection between the orthogonal plan and the plan in perspective.

Lambert also used other kinds of graphic instruments to simplify the geometric operations involved in his perspective method. The instrument he favored was a perspective "protractor" that enabled the artist to divide the horizon line according to a varying scale that increases with distance from the "principal point." Knowing the angle and position of any side of a given object, the artist could trace its plan directly in perspective without initially drawing it orthogonally, using this horizontal scale to reduce the number of geometric operations. Devices such as the perspective pantograph and the protractor lacked geometric rigor, but Lambert maintained that this weakness was unimportant, since only the apparent results mattered. Truth was evident in the geometry implicit in the appearance. To be sure, Lambert did not invent the perspectograph or the protractor. There are numerous examples of such devices being used during the Renaissance and the seventeenth century. His originality rather lies of the use he made of them. Some have argued that Lambert's protractor is in some way similar to Desargues's *échelle fuyante,* thus constituting the missing link in the genealogy of projective geometry that led to Monge and Poncelet.[66] It should be clear by now, however, that in sharp distinction to Desargues, for whom the appearance of the object needed to be reduced to proportional measurement (plan and elevation) before being projected in perspective, Lambert insisted on the importance of starting from the "phenomena," that is, the appearance of objects.

During the 1640s, in the middle of the controversy surrounding the publication of Desargues's *Manières universelles,* the publishers of his rival Père Dubreuil—Tavernier and Langlois—had published another treatise that helped fuel the debate: a book by the French engineer Jacques Alleaume, originally written around 1628, which had been approved for publication earlier under the title *Introduction à la perspective, ensemble, L'Usage du Compas optique et perspectif.* The project was abandoned for unknown reasons, until some fifteen years later when Étienne Mignon decided to publish an augmented version of it under the title *La Perspective speculative et Pratique où sont demonstrez les fondemens de cet Art, & de tout ce qui en a esté enseigné jusqu'à present. Ensemble la maniere universelle de la pratiquer, non seulement sans Plan Geometral, & sans Tiers poinct, dedans ni dehors le champ du Tableau. Mais encores par le moyen de la Ligne, communément appellée Horizontale.*[67] This treatise also made direct use of graphic devices that reduced the sequence of geometric operations. The work, though apparently inconsequential for the history of perspective, is usually recognized for its role in the controversy involving two publishing houses. As we may remember, the debate that had broken out between Desargues and Dubreuil and their respective publishers concerned the originality of the former's *Universal Method* of perspective and the latter's plagiarism of Desargues in his *Practical Perspective.*

In his additions to Alleaume's treatise, Mignon apparently made some genuine contributions. However, it seems that one of Tavernier and Langlois's oblique intentions in publishing

Alleaume's treatise with the subtitle *Manière universelle* was to discredit Desargues and deny the originality of his claim.[68] Yet, if one pays close attention, it is clear that the vertical scale in Alleaume's theory was not equivalent to Desargues's vanishing scale. On the contrary, Alleaume's vertical scale was divided into equidistant intervals, unaffected by perspective foreshortening. The gradation of depth was instead acknowledged by the variation of horizontal intervals. Strangely, Alleaume's method was almost identical to Lambert's own protractor method, which it preceded by almost 150 years. Like Lambert, Alleaume used a protractor to divide the horizon line into unequal intervals, and to transfer coordinates directly from the object to the perspective plan. However, while Lambert clearly described perspective as a natural way to depict the world, Alleaume's first definition qualified theoretical perspective as a construction of the mind, a method to be learned and understood through geometry. In the context of the seventeenth century, perspective could be grasped only as a tool for revealing the geometric, ultimately divine order of things. Lambert's refusal to rely on the *plan géométral* and his insistence on starting directly from the object are characteristic of a novel identification of optics and perspective that could take place only after perspective became accepted as the objective way we see the world, and only after the Enlightenment expressed radical skepticism about the presence of supernatural phenomena in the human world. Lambert went even further in associating geometry and optics: he claimed that his horizontal scale governing the perspective construction of an image could simultaneously measure the real angles of an object, as well as its coordinates. He declared that "all that Geometry teaches us concerning the orthogonal plan can be applied in similar terms to the picture plane . . . with some perspective operations; the image of an object can be drawn in perspective as quickly as the orthogonal plan itself, if we had wanted to start by drawing it according to the ordinary rules."[69] Undoubtedly, for Lambert the whole world was *already* perspectival.

Lambert's concept of perspective as natural perception was implicit in the Bibienas' *scena per angolo,* which was already applying the idea to architecture and theater. The Bibienas' oblique focal points also prefigured Lambert's off-center point

Two plates from Jacques Alleaume's perspective treatise *La Perspective speculative et Pratique* (1643). Alleaume's perspective method used a "protractor" to divide the horizon line into unequal lengths.

Montreal, Collection Centre Canadien d'Architecture / Canadian Centre for Architecture.

2.18

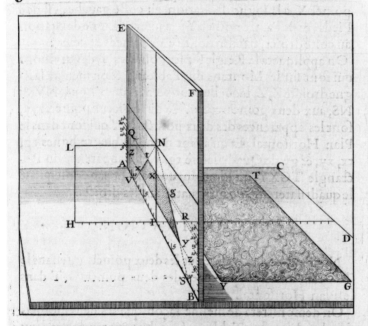

ET PRATIQVE. 93

DEMONSTRATION.

Dans la ligne Q R, fe trouvent tous les poincts efloignez de 20 Pieds, de la Ligne Horifontale; Et dans la li-

gne N V, fe trouvent tous les poincts efloignez, à gau-
che, de la ligne de Station de 19 Pieds; Tellement qu'à l'in-
terfection de ces deux lignes dans le Tableau, fe trouve
l'apparence d'vn poinct efloigné de 20 Pieds, de la Ligne
Horifontale; & de 9 Pieds de la Ligne de Station, tel
M iij

2.19

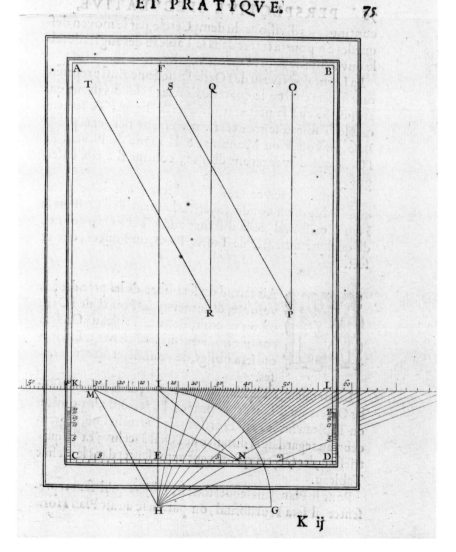

of view. In the last and probably most influential section of his treatise, "Of the Inverse Rules of Perspective," Lambert describes how to find the vantage point of the painter once a painting is complete, and how to find the horizon line in a painting of architectural subjects from the points of convergence of its parallel lines. As with his perspective pantograph, reversibility was a crucial aspect of his theory of perspective drawing; the potential to transform the plan of an object into a perspective view or, conversely, to deduce its plan from a perspective image, assumed the complete naturalization of geometric space. For Lambert, "natural perspective" was more than a set of phenomena that explains vision and the representation of objects: it was a metaphor for explaining the structure of the universe. As in his cosmology, the observer in his perspective theory occupied a relative position that was not assumed to be at the center—a position that would vary with each observer. By understanding the geometric rules that regulate vision, man could reflect upon and grasp his own relative position in the universe. Just as one can locate a painter's viewpoint because reality *is* perspective, epistemologically this implies that man's "place" in the world can be discovered by disclosing its implicit perspectival geometry. As Hans Blumenberg explains, "While in the theory of perspective the thing is to grasp the mechanism of illusions so that one can produce them, cosmology has to reverse the process by using this knowledge for the purpose of discovering illusions to which we could be subjected as a result of our standpoint and our motions in the universe."[70] This conviction that humanity has a place in the order of the cosmos, even if the cosmos itself was not explicitly *propter nos* (made for us, for our purpose), was ultimately the stable ground that prevented eighteenth-century culture from drifting into relativism. Indeed, this ability to reflect on one's own position, the perspectivism that became a way of life in the eighteenth century, would become a basic characteristic of the modern age.

Perspective *Fantaisies*

Lambert's treatise was one of the last original theoretical works on perspective, yet it did not provide a practical method for painters or architects. Written mainly as a theoretical explanation of perspective appearances, Lambert's theory nonetheless acknowledged the imminent assimilation of lived space to geometric space, a necessary condition for artists' eventual self-conscious manipulation of perspective for expressive purposes. The consequences of living in a perspectival world were twofold. Perspective was poised to become an instrument of reduction and predictive visualization, based on a precise correspondence between image and reality. In the hands of artists operating in a *finite* world of qualitative places, however, it could also become a formal tool for the poetic imagination.

In the eighteenth century, geometric perspective lost its privileged status as a "symbolic form" describing the order of the world, yet it would be misleading to assume that perspective was abandoned entirely. The Newtonianism that dominated the scientific world at the time, which meant that any theory not deduced explicitly from observation was disregarded, had a simultaneous impact on geometry and all of its ramifications. Nature was believed to be ruled by coherent laws revealed through observation, and since perspective itself had become natural, there was no need for any theoretician to impose geometric laws onto the perceived image of the world. Nature itself came to be understood as completely rational. Unlike baroque thinkers, who saw geometric perspective as mediating between man and the world by revealing God's order through mathematical proportions, those in the eighteenth century believed that God was present in the order of nature and that this rational order could be understood by man without need for geometric mediation. As geometry became "obsolete," natural philosophy offered a way to explain the world through empirical observation.

The assumption that humanity lives in a perspectival world in fact was consistent with the beliefs that the natural universe is infinite and that we can understand its laws and purpose. However, infinity itself was not part of the realm of human action; it remained the ineffable, "sublime" space of God, a realm that could be fully revealed only through representation. *Physis* (nature) had not yet become the inexhaustible realm of natural resources to which we became accustomed after the Industrial Revolution, a homogenous space awaiting exploitation. In the eighteenth century, disclosing the implicit mechanisms of perception and image making was the only relevant task for any acceptable theory of perspective, and Lambert seemed to have given the final word on the matter. Although no other theory attempted to extend this theoretical discourse, many artists and scientists remained fascinated with perspective as a practical device to reveal the appearance of reality, often disclosing through its representations a superior truth that the experience of reality itself could conceal.

The *vedutista* painters, for example, while often claiming that one-point perspective was the appropriate way to represent the world, were at least in intention close to the modes of depiction identified with the camera obscura and with surveying. Other artists, however, who accepted the premise that we live in a perspective world, took the license to explode perspective itself in the hope of discovering a new poetic depth. Painters and architects such as Giambattista Piranesi (1720–1778) and Jean-Laurent Legeay (ca. 1710–ca. 1786), for example, explored the crumbling boundaries of a traditional world that was already shifting toward an infinite and homogeneous extension; in the process, they developed new ways of fragmenting the linearity of perspective representation that might reveal a depth of human experience now being lost in the systematized rendering of surfaces identified with scientific vision. At issue was the true temporality of vision, embedded in synesthetic perception. Perspective distorted this temporality, assumed the hegemony of an autonomous sense of sight, and consequently presented space emancipated from time—falsifying its character by freezing it or accelerating it. Lambert, only a few years younger than Piranesi and Legeay, also understood the universe to be composed of heterogeneous space-time intervals. We may recall that in his *Cosmological Letters* he claimed that time could not be separated from space because the cosmic order includes not only positions but also movement. The temporal scale of movements in the cosmic system must be proportional to spatial distances. If different systems of temporality rule various areas of our world, then only a nonlinear system of representation could depict its image appropriately. In their architectural fantasies and numerous engravings, Legeay and Piranesi brought together heterogeneous compositions of perspective

spaces guided by multiple points of view, self-consciously engaging the issue of experiential space-time, while working
through perspective as a convention assumed to be the truthful
presentation of reality to human vision.

Like Lambert, Legeay was closely acquainted with
King Frederick II, although this association ended dramatically,
following a dispute in which Legeay was said to have threatened
the king with his sword while arguing about his design for the
Palace of the New Sanssouci. That he worked only briefly as
an architect may partly explain his marginality in the general
history of eighteenth-century architecture. Earlier, however,
Legeay had seemed destined for a more promising career when
he won the Grand Prix in Architecture; in 1737 he was sent to
the Académie de France in Rome, where he stayed for four
years. He returned to Paris with some impressive work, according to Jean-François de Troy, director of the academy at
that time: "He brings back a number of very beautiful drawings,
both studies made from public buildings, and from his own
composition; in his sketchbooks, there is fire and genius."[71]
Since Legeay was only ten years older than Piranesi and both
were in Rome in the early 1740s, some writers have argued
that they could have met there and that each influenced the
other's work. There is a great deal of literature debating the
direction of the assumed "flow of influence" between Legeay
and Piranesi.[72] Parallels can obviously be established, since their
work demonstrates some explicit resemblances. Both were accomplished etchers who favored speculative architecture over
built projects, and their respective graphic experimentations led
them to challenge the linearity of perspective depth. Regardless
of the direction of influence, each initiated a revolution in the
presentation of architectural ideas by questioning the traditional
relationship between architecture and its representation, as well
as between architecture and building.

An outstanding teacher, Legeay was associated for
some time with Jacques-François Blondel's École des Arts.[73]
More important, he taught a whole generation of architects,
including Étienne-Louis Boullée, Jean-Charles Delafosse, Antoine Vaudoyer, Marie-Joseph Peyre, and Charles de Wailly.
Charles-Nicolas Cochin describes Legeay's influence on the
younger generation: "since Legeay's taste was excellent, he

Giambattista Piranesi's *Ponte Trionfale*, from *Le Antichità Romane* (1758) [2.20], and Jean-Laurent Legeay's *Landscape with Flight into Egypt* (1767) [2.21]. While embracing the ocular celebration of the *veduta*, both Piranesi and Legeay self-consciously attempted to subvert the homogeneity of perspective space in their engravings.

2.21 | New York, Cooper-Hewitt, National Design Museum, Smithsonian Institution / Courtesy of Art Resource, NY, inv. 1958-136-1-D.

opened the eyes of many people. The young architects followed his taste as much as they could, maybe as much because of his novelty as from a real understanding of the beauty of his work. It coincided with significant changes in the school of architecture, to the astonishment of all the older architects of the academy."[74] Legeay's experience in Rome left a visible imprint on his teaching. In addition to teaching the classical orders and some exercises on symmetry and simple forms, he introduced a new way of presenting architectural ideas by instructing his pupils to use brushes instead of the ruler and the compass. He also insisted that no design was complete until it included a general view, or an aerial perspective of the project; that is, an atmospheric representation in which depth was conveyed through intensity of color and sharpness of outline, not simply through geometry.[75] Many architects praised the qualities of Legeay's work and his influence on the young architects from the academy in Paris. François-Joseph Bélanger, for example, said that it was because of Legeay and some others that "Devailly [*sic*] was one of the first to abandon the ruler and the compass, and to compose architecture more freely with his brushes." Joseph Lavallée added that "it is only with the architect Lejay [*sic*] that [de Wailly] finally discovered, through the bizarre exaggerations of this new master, the true point of perfection in architecture."[76] Legeay not only taught them a new way to present their ideas but implicitly questioned the very nature of architectural representation. He advocated the virtuosity of an idea over its buildable potential. Perspective drawing became not merely a tool but an aim in itself. This new attitude toward architectural ideation was expressed explicitly in Boullée's epigraph to his *Essai sur l'Art,* where he claims, quoting Caravaggio: "Ed io anche son pittore" (I am also a painter). A few years later, Claude-Nicolas Ledoux would also emphasize the importance of painterly imagination for architecture: "If you want to become an architect, start first by being a painter."[77]

Legeay had consciously redefined the nature of architectural drawing in terms *other* than the geometric *lineamenti* of the Renaissance. This new form of drawing was to become a vehicle for architectural meaning at a time when—as Blondel argued—few important projects were being built, and those that were constructed appeared increasingly prosaic and lacking in "character." Perspective carried the potential to fulfill the dream of clarity and order that comes from complete control of an entire work, as well as the capacity to construe the appropriate *charactère* of buildings in their urban or natural contexts. These representations, drawing from the Enlightenment myth of a rational nature, could still demonstrate the coherence between the "conventional" order of architecture and its "natural" site, revealing an invisible wholeness increasingly difficult to translate into practice. The potential autonomy of architectural drawing would be passionately debated in the following generations. Charles-François Viel, in his book *Décadence de l'Architecture à la Fin du 18ème Siècle* (1800), criticized in one sweeping remark Boullée's excessive imagination, which led to unrealizable theoretical projects, and Soufflot's excessive rationality, which resulted in his reductive design for Ste.-Geneviève—both cases illustrating the consequence of disregarding the practical dimension of construction.

Indeed, while perspective permitted a comprehensive communication of the idea, it suggested implicitly that knowledge of construction was not the responsibility of the architect. We might note that while in the service of the duke of Schwerin, Legeay was commissioned to design and supervise the construction of a castle at Rühn, one of the very few projects for which he had complete control, and that indeed, the new building was torn down shortly after its construction because it was badly built and in danger of collapsing.[78] While Pozzo marked a turning point in the history of representation by establishing a systematic correspondence between building and drawing, in its wake Legeay marked a change that was no less significant: by promoting a split between building and architecture, he inaugurated a tradition that would lead to critical works of modernism in the form of theoretical projects.[79]

Legeay's most significant work was therefore to be found in his architectural *fantaisies* and speculative projects, produced mostly as etchings. Fifty years after Pozzo, for example, he entered a competition for the decoration of a Jesuit theater. The design described in his twelve drawings (unfortunately lost) probably was destined to be built in the courtyard of the Grands Jesuites, on Rue St.-Jacques in Paris.[80] Legeay's proposal for the

Legeay, architectural *fantaisie*.

Berlin-Dahlem, Kupferstichkabinett, inv. 14865.

theatrum sacrum could not have been more different from that of his predecessor. While Pozzo's altarpieces for the Jesuit drama sought to recreate an appropriate religious setting in which man could find his place, Legeay's ambitious architectural project took over the entire composition, conveying instead an impression of immensity in which man would have been reduced to near insignificance, swallowed by cavernous spaces, and dwarfed by extravagant flights of stairs. In his *Mémoires,* Cochin emphasizes the gigantic scale of the project and describes how the actors would have come out from under these monumental stairs.[81] The monumentality of Legeay's ideas had a direct impact on the work of his students, yet it remained emphatically within the boundaries of a contained (finite) world.[82]

Legeay's architectural *fantaisies* were unified by the overwhelming presence of wild nature. The conventional rules and preestablished harmonies of perspectival depth were disrupted intentionally by irrational connections among architectonic elements and by incongruous details. Within a single image, a viewer would be presented with a multitude of fragmentary worlds governed by different perspective systems and thus would be invited to explore every corner of the image. The possibility of a "natural perspective" in a world that maintained its hierarchical structure as a finite constellation of qualitative topoi during the early eighteenth century is in fact a precondition for the outstanding works of Legeay and Piranesi. Their etchings anticipated the temporalization of perspective that avant-garde artists and filmmakers would celebrate in the early twentieth century. Like Piranesi's *Carceri* and *Capricci*, however, Legeay's speculative architecture remained contained within the boundaries of a finite world. Even when his perspective system was fragmented and disrupted, the entire image was always constituted within a frame. Nevertheless, his students became more obsessed with representing a sublime, immense space associated with the infinite realm of a deistic God. Newton's vast, homogeneous sky presented in Boullée's Cenotaph, for example, approximates the experience of infinity in the built realm—the absolute empty space that *is* God's extension *and* the site of universal gravitation. Boullée recreates a new, artificial nature and provides the spectators with a novel access to the notion of "center," while revealing the infinity of Newton's Divine Void.[83] This difference is also obvious if one compares Legeay's project for a city gate, presented in an urban context with an obelisk beyond the opening that marks the spatial boundaries of his intervention, with Boullée's similar project, sited on a boundless flat ground and shown in a frontal perspective whose composition suggests the continuous extension of an elevation drawing.

Legeay was known to his contemporaries mainly for his drawings and engravings, yet he did have a brief career as a

| 2.23 |

Étienne-Louis Boullée, Cenotaph for Newton, night effect. The sublime "infinity" in the work of late-eighteenth-century painters and architects such as Boullée is still a residue of a divine, otherworldly infinity, even if this appears as a representation in Nature.

Paris, Bibliothèque Nationale, Cabinet des Estampes.

| 2.24 | 2.25 |

Comparing a city gate by Legeay [2.24] to a project on a similar theme by Boullée [2.25] makes plain a subtle yet significant shift in the treatment of the horizon. Legeay's gate clearly occupies a worldly site contained by the horizon, whereas Boullée's gate is situated on a ground plane collapsed with the horizon that suggests no site beyond the drawing.

2.24 | École Nationale Supérieure des Beaux-Arts.
2.25 | Paris, Bibliothèque Nationale.

2.24

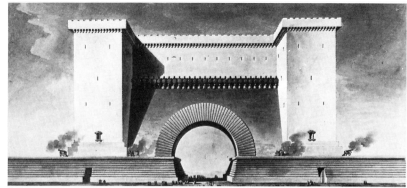

2.25

practicing architect. Toward the end of the 1740s, when he was enjoying a certain popularity with his students, he left for Berlin with an ambition to become the First Architect to the king of Prussia. His long journey led him first to Mecklenburg, where he became, in 1748, the "Architect of the Court" for the duke of Schwerin. His responsibilities included parks, gardens, fountains, and all architectural matters from urban regulations (including the heights of new buildings and the dimensions of streets) to water supply and the planning of all new domestic architecture. He was also commissioned to build the castle at Rühn, where, as we have mentioned, his limitations as a builder became evident.[84] Legeay left the service of the duke in October 1755 and was called to Berlin by the king in December of the same year. He received the title of First Architect and Head of Public Works on January 1, 1756, for a wage less than what he had received working for the duke. There he was commissioned to design the plans for the castle at Potsdam: the "New Sanssouci." Because this year marked the beginning of the Seven Years' War, all construction stopped in Berlin and Potsdam, including the project of the New Sanssouci. It is a strange paradox that this French architect who finally had attained his ambition to become First Architect to the Prussian king was kept out of work in a country that was openly at war with the king of France.[85]

| **2.26** |

Legeay, *Landscape with Architecture and Ruins Viewed under an Arch.*

New York, Cooper-Hewitt, National Design Museum, Smithsonian Institution / Courtesy of Art Resource, NY, inv. 1958-136-1-Y.

Toward the end of the decade, the war had reduced Legeay to inactivity, but he devoted much of his time to drawing. During this prolific period he produced his most fascinating architectural *fantaisies,* deliberately challenging the logic of construction to explore the potential character of architectural space. Legeay spent fifteen years in northern Germany, leaving Berlin after his abrupt dismissal by the king. His return to France was marked by disillusion, for he had been completely forgotten in his own country. This master, so successful in an earlier time, could find no new students. Even his former disciples seemed to have abandoned him. Charles-François Viel de Saint-Maux, in his *Lettres sur l'architecture* (1787), describes the unbridged gap between Legeay and his former students after his return to Paris. Legeay was surprised, Viel says, that his students had put columns everywhere.[86] Legeay could find no work in Paris and was offered a job teaching drawing at a Benedictine school in the provinces. He was literally shunned in his own city for reasons that have been attributed to his eccentricity, his quarrelsome attitude—exemplified by the way he left the services of the king of Prussia—and even his political association with Germany.[87] One should not forget, however, that the early second half of the eighteenth century in France marked the height of Laugier's neoclassicism, with its taste for simplicity and "natural" structural coherence, polemically identified with Greek architecture. In that context, Legeay's eclectic taste for complex geometric manipulations and obscure "Roman" compositions simply may have fallen out of fashion.

227

A World of Scientific Light and Objective Shadows

As we have suggested, Legeay's subversion of homogeneous space presumed a geometric correspondence between orthogonal drawings and perspective projections. However, his experimentations appeared at a time when the very foundation of geometric perspective was being replaced by a greater conviction in the rationality of nature itself, and a more definitive synthesis of vision and perspective. Artists and scientists no longer were interested in perspective theories, or at least in geometric theories that reduced the world to its plan, preferring instead to let nature suggest its own implicit rules. Studies of light and shadow were also affected by this new attitude toward geometry and observation. On one hand, light in art became the qualitative emanation of natural phenomena, diffused and often co-substantial with immensity. It appeared as a mysterious luminosity on the canvas, without geometric constraints, such as in Turner's sublime nature, or as glowing presence captured by the receptive eye of the artist, such as in the interior of Boullée's sacred spaces. On the other hand, the quantifiable aspect of light became an autonomous scientific discipline known as "photometry."

It is no mere coincidence that Lambert, the author of the last original treatise on perspective, was also the founder of photometry. In 1758, the year before the publication of his treatise on perspective, he published his first study on the path of light: *Les propriétés remarquables de la route de la lumière*. In it, he described the new discipline in terms of the brightness of light, its density, and its modification with colors and shadows.[88]

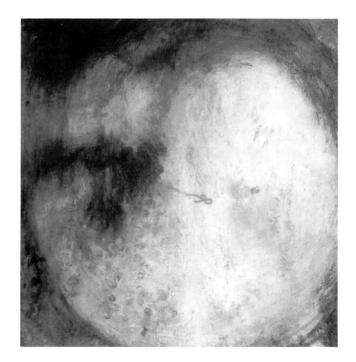

| 2.27 |

William Turner, *Light and Colour — the Morning after the Deluge* (1843). Turner's paintings are filled with "natural" light free from geometric constraints.

London, Tate Gallery.

The following year, he wrote his most important treatise on the subject, *La Photometria sive se Mensura et Gradibus Luminis, colorum et umbrae* (1760), in which he established the fundamental law of the discipline: he determined the relationship among luminosity, angle of incidence, and distance.[89] In the same work, Lambert also discussed physiological as well as astrophysical questions. In quantitative terms he described atmospheric phenomena such as twilight—the first truly novel scientific contribution in this area since Al-Hazen. His interest in photometry and the path of light led him to determine the relation between the angle of refraction and the density of the medium. This theory also had an impact on astronomy, since the changes in the direction of light passing through different media alter the apparent position of stars observed through the atmosphere.[90] He determined the proportion of light lost through reflection, and in honor of his work his name was given to an absolute unit of surface illumination, a "Lambert."[91] Lambert explained the phenomena of light and shadow in quantifiable terms. Yet his intention, however scientific, was not positivistic, for it cannot be dissociated from his broad cosmological interest. It is perhaps significant that like his contemporaries who were interested in this problem, he remained unable to distinguish clearly between the color of things and the color of light. His fundamental objective was always to grasp the greater order that generates these phenomena. His attitude toward photometry was similar in many ways to his interest in the mechanism of perspective: both contributed to his explanation of man's vantage point on the universe.

Lambert's interest in color and aerial perspective also echoed the concerns of Legeay. Lambert wished to apply the scientific principles of photometry to the notion of aerial perspective, and apparently he was the first to demonstrate scientifically that the perception of color is influenced by atmospheric depth. Thus he had to imagine how the quantitative order of light and color might be integrated with his natural perspective. Amid recurring controversies over the nature of light, he tended to favor a wave theory, probably because it was consistent with his photometric observations. His *Farbenpyramide* of 1772, in contrast, attempted to demonstrate that color and tone must be considered together, using two tetrahedrons

| 2.28 |

Lambert's color pyramid, from his *Farbenpyramid* (1772).

to show how various colors—from the saturated primaries to white and black—could express depth.[92]

Framing the Earth

The last section of Lambert's treatise on perspective describes several cases in which the position of the painter's eye can be deduced from a perspective image by noting the position of the horizon, the points of convergence of parallel lines, and the angles of intersection of key construction lines. Lambert claims that this inversion of perspective not only is helpful in finding out the position where the painter stood in front of the scene, in order to occupy an analogous position to contemplate the painting, but also can be very useful in constructing an orthographic plan from a given perspective view, or even in comparing the real view of an object or a city to its image or its plan.[93] Although one of his basic assumptions was that orthogonal plans were unnecessary for tracing appearances, he never believed that orthographic plans were altogether useless, as could be implied from the title of his treatise: a free perspective "affranchie de l'embaras du plan géométral."[94] Instead, the plan must be deduced from the natural perspective itself—from the phenomena.

An equivalence between plan and perspective plan was already implied in his early writings on perspective and in his experiments with the perspectograph. While traditional pantographs used for proportional diminution and enlargement always remained parallel and in the same plane of projection, Lambert's version automatically transferred the plan into perspective, assuming the implicit equivalence between views in two and three dimensions. As we have previously explained, his own device could only be used horizontally, since it operated exclusively with plans. This may be interpreted as a residue of a traditional worldview in which horizontal extensions could only be finite, and therefore were qualitatively distinct from indefinite vertical dimensions. Moreover, it is also in "plan" that we orient ourselves. While traditional pantographs were also used as extensions of Renaissance perspective machines, faithfully transcribing an image perceived through the window frame or the eyepiece, Lambert's perspectograph paid little attention to the appearance of the object to be depicted. The position of the observer, so crucial in Lambert's discourse, became little more than an objectified anchoring point for the process of transcription. Lambert declared that perspective is natural, but also that the order ultimately is given in plan.

Lambert's obsession to find the plan of any given perspective view, the theme with which he concludes his treatise, led him to make major contributions to geography and cartography. Indeed, while his work in other scientific areas is often disregarded, his contribution in the field of mapping generally is considered as "the beginning of the modern period in mathematical cartography." He initiated a new era of research in theoretical cartography by considering "the conformal mapping of the sphere on the plane in full generality."[95] In fact, in his major work on the subject, *Anmerkungen und Zusätze zur Entwerfung der Land und Himmelscharten* (1772), Lambert sought the closest possible correspondence between the spherical shape of the Earth and its geometric representation on a flat surface. The calculations involved in the various methods he proposed were connected directly to his wider interest in the geometry of the circle; these calculations almost led him to posit a non-Euclidean geometry. Many authors have suggested that Lambert, like the Jesuit Father Girolamo Saccheri and the mathematician Adrien Marie Le Gendre speculating on the parallels, stopped at the very threshold of non-Euclidean geometry, more than half a century before it was finally postulated by Nikolai I. Lobachevsky, J. Bolyai, and Carl Friedrich Gauss in the early nineteenth century.[96] According to tradition, Euclid's principal contribution to geometry was his postulate that clearly established the existence of parallel lines and the conditions of the angles produced when a third line intersects them. The equality of corresponding angles is in fact the cornerstone of Euclidean geometry. In his *Euclides ab omni naevo vindicatus* (1733), Saccheri was "the first to discuss the consequences of denying the parallel axiom and to suggest the construction of a geometry independent of it."[97] Similarly, Lambert questioned the primacy of the axiom of the parallels, introducing instead a "spherical geometry." On a large spherical surface such as the Earth, parallel lines eventually would converge. His major dis-

2.29 │ 2.30 │

Lodovico Cigoli's perspectograph, illustrated in Nicéron, *Thaumaturgus Opticus*
(1646) [2.29], and the perspectograph in use, illustrated on the frontispiece of
Christopher Scheiner, *Pantographice seu ars delineandi* (1631) [2.30]. During the
seventeenth century, perspective machines appear to become more efficient,
while evidence of their use in the arts is always scarce. Cigoli, a painter and friend
of Galileo, invented an automated device that could be made to work with some
practice. Cigoli evidently believed that perspective was capable of revealing the
truth of reality, a truthful picture that could be generated mechanically. Scheiner,
on the other hand, was a Jesuit who debated against Galileo concerning the existence of the sun spots that the latter had observed through the telescope.
Scheiner championed the use of the pantograph for painting. Used vertically, this
instrument provided a way to "see" the perspectival diminution of dimensions,
without presupposing a projective method or a section through the cone of vision.

2.29

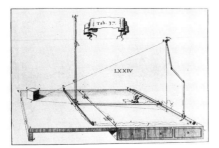

2.30

covery was to demonstrate that the sum of the internal angles of a triangle does not total 180 degrees, assuming that its surface is spherical. This proposition, however, also involved the primacy of a center—and consequently the notion that space itself was not homogeneous.[98] Moreover, Lambert demonstrated that no proportional figures of different size can exist on the surface of a sphere, and that the surface of a triangle cannot increase indefinitely. In other words, Lambert foresaw that if our three-dimensional space is ruled by spherical, non-Euclidean laws, it must be *finite* and must close upon itself. This was the basis of one of the most crucial theses of his *Cosmological Letters,* where he postulated that even though the universe is immense, it must be finite. It is also important to remember that while Lambert demonstrated the irrationality of π in 1769, it was not until 1882 that Lindemann proved explicitly the impossibility of squaring the circle. Unlike the nineteenth century, the Enlightenment could not easily reject the primary evidence of lived experience, including tactile intuition, or the fleeting possibility of unity represented by that famous emblematic problem of philosophy, geometry, alchemy, and architecture in the Western tradition; the squaring of the circle proposed the possibility of reconciling the duality of opposites such as male and female, Earth and Sky, in a primordial unity. Not surprisingly, the eighteenth century would always uphold the coherence and simplicity of natural laws.

Lambert's mapmaking methods can be divided into three major categories based on three extreme theoretical positions of a hypothetical viewer observing the terrestrial globe perspectively. The assimilation of the plan to the perspective view is here all the more obvious. "It is possible to choose innumerable points as the position of the eye from which to view the Earth perspectively," he says, emphasizing the relativity of the vantage point. Three particular "advantageous points," however, are developed. "In one instance the eye is placed infinitely far from the globe, and this yields the aforementioned orthographic projection [similar to a plan]. In a second instance the point is taken somewhere on the surface of the Earth, and this method of projection is called stereographic. . . . Finally, the eye is taken at the midpoint of the Earth, and this method of projection . . . will be called the central projection." Lambert then gives a brief description of the instances in which these three methods of projection are most appropriate.[99]

Lambert's methods of cartography include both parallel and converging projections. Given his understanding of geometry, he could reconcile his belief in a finite universe with the assumption of a point of convergence at an almost infinite distance. In his projective system, the primacy of the plan assumed an automatic correspondence between coordinates in two dimensions and their projection in perspective. But this did not imply an equivalence of vertical and horizontal dimensions. Lambert's space was defined ultimately by experience and thus could not deny the specificity of orientation: while vertical dimensions can seem to be limitless, horizontal extension is definitely finite and stops at the horizon. His theory was primarily empirical and based on observation. He differed with Newton, however, who assumed that there is no difference between the supralunary and sublunary worlds, and therefore that directions in space are not qualitatively distinct. Lambert could not accept this concept of spatial uniformity and rejected the principle of an absolute time. Thus, his space was distinct from what would become the generalized space of modernity in the nineteenth century, following Kant and Hegel. Yet his cartography still is used widely today, and some of his cosmological assumptions are being proven long after Newton's physics has been superseded by Einstein's relativity—because, one could speculate, his theories were based on experience and because they accepted as a premise the relative and finite nature of time and space.

In the very first section of his treatise on cartography, Lambert emphasizes that an adequate map should avoid distorting the size and proportions of the countries and places it depicts. The correspondence between physical places and their representation on a map should be as precise as an engineer's drawing of a house. Lambert was aware of the impossibility of avoiding all the distortions involved in flattening the spherical surface of the Earth onto a plane, and he engaged in a long discussion of the advantages and limitations of his various methods. Some preserved the angles of parallels and meridians as they were transferred from the surface of the sphere to the flat plane, while others gave priority to the relative sizes of countries.

The problem of transcribing the image of a spherical Earth onto a flat surface did not emerge suddenly in the eighteenth century. Ptolemy's *Geographia* (second century C.E.) had already posed the question of an appropriate mode of representation. Two options were possible for "making a portrait of the world": geographers could either use a globe or transcribe the map onto a flat surface. Ptolemy openly criticized his predecessors, such as Marinus of Tyre (active 120 C.E.), for using an equidistant grid of straight lines for both the parallels of latitude and the meridians of longitude. This method was unfaithful to both reality and appearance, and it produced unacceptable distortions of distance and direction: as Lloyd Brown explains, "if the eye is fixed on the center of the quadrant of the sphere which we take to be our inhabited world, it is readily seen that the meridians curve toward the North Pole and that the parallels, though they are equally spaced on the sphere, give the impression of being closer together near the poles." [100] For Ptolemy, the visual aspect of a spherical world already prevailed over the order of an equidistant gridded map. Desiring to retain the spherical proportions on the flat map, he suggested a compromise that he called a "conic projection," in which only the meridians, equidistant at the equator, would be drawn as straight lines converging toward the North Pole, while the parallels would be traced as arcs of circle whose common center would also be at the North Pole. Concerned with finding the greatest resemblance possible, he also suggested a variation on this projection, in which the meridians themselves could become curvilinear, "in that shape in which meridian lines appear on a globe." [101]

As we saw earlier, it is tempting to interpret Ptolemy's concern with representing the appearance of the terrestrial globe as an instance of objectification, and to infer a correspondence between his mapmaking methods and modern perspective theories. However, it was not until the second half of the sixteenth century that the Italian mathematician Federigo Commandino (1509–1575) made an explicit connection between these two disciplines in his *Ptolomaei Planisphaerium* (1558). He associated them through a notion of projection that geometrically linked the circle to the other conic sections. Unlike Ptolemy, who had considered only the projection of circles

Ptolemy's "conic projection" of the inhabited world, from the Codex Ebnerianus.

into circles and had assumed no continuity among the conic sections, Commandino went a step further by proposing that every cone contains a circle in addition to one other conic section. But his theory of conic sections, inherited from Apollonius, was not yet the systematic association between the circle and the parabola into a continuous flow of transforming ellipses and hyperbola that would be formulated by Kepler more than half a century later and then used by Desargues as the basis of his own universal method of perspective. Instead Commandino assumed every transformation of a circle projected in perspective to be a special case of a conic section, very much in the classical tradition of Apollonius. Yet according to Egnatio Danti, Commandino was the first writer to propose a mathematical association between conic sections and perspective theory in his commentary on Ptolemy's cartography. Danti, also a sixteenth-century mathematician, as well as an astronomer, translator of Euclid's work on optics, and commentator on Vignola's *Due Regole della Prospettiva,* believed that Commandino was responsible for solving mathematically the determination of arbitrary points in foreshortening,[102] and thus that he freed perspective construction from its empirical uncertainty. Indeed, Commandino was also the first writer to dismiss the notion that a section through the visual pyramid was a necessary point of departure for perspective. Commandino's theory, motivated by the humanist desire to understand the "truth" in Ptolemy's cartography, led to an association between planispheric astrolabes and perspective through the general concept of *projectio*. Addressed to mathematicians and astronomers rather than artists, Commandino's mathematical constructions—except for his generalized principles of shadow projection—had little impact on art. Only in Lambert's cartography would the parallel between maps and perspective be applied successfully as a practical method of scientifically accurate mapmaking.

Associations between perspective methods and mapping, including a general interest in surveying and the design of military fortifications, had been present since the early Renaissance and became obvious by the second half of the sixteenth century.[103] In his commentary on Vignola's treatise, Danti brought together cartography, cosmology, solar clocks, and perspective. By including in his treatise Baldassare Lanci's "universal instrument," a surveying device also used for panoramic tracing, he was clearly attempting to combine surveying and perspective. Yet it should be pointed out that Danti's endorsement of Lanci's device was not unconditional. He disapproved of the pictorial results produced by using such a device, arguing that it did not accurately reproduce the effect of a section through the visual pyramid. The unfolding of the tracing generated on a cylindrical surface would require additional optical correction. Lanci's remarkable instrument, invented around the mid-sixteenth century, seemed prophetic of nineteenth-century developments in perspective. Yet one could argue that only after lived space was thoroughly identified with a geometrical a priori in science and philosophy, and graphic methods in the arts became systematized, would it become possible to perceive the "truthfulness" of a panoramic representation.

Cosimo Bartoli's *Del modo di misurare* (1564), another important work on surveying, also established an explicit connection between the art of depicting and the art of measuring.[104] The first book of his treatise shows a surveying instrument based on the astrolabe and describes how to survey the land by means of the horizon. This was consistent with early surveying instruments that were based on astronomical measurements. The Earth was measured never directly but always indirectly through reference to the heavens, since preci-

2.32

Baldassare Lanci's "universal instrument" for perspective and surveying (1557) [2.32]; Gemma Frisius's *radio astronomico* for measuring the width of a facade, from *De Radio astronomico* (1545) [2.33]; Jean Dubreuil's perspective devices, using either a veil or a grid to draw a figure in perspective, from *La perspective pratique* (1642–1649) [2.34]. Unlike traditional mapping, which involved the contemplation of heavenly bodies, the desire to survey and measure directly the human world — particularly in relation to constructive (architecture) or destructive (military) operations — coincided with the inception of *perspectiva artificialis* in the Renaissance. The perceived importance of revealing a mathematical structure present in the reality of experience, ultimately an ontological interest, fueled both surveying and the arts. While both surveying instruments and perspective machines relied on the law of proportional triangles, important differences should be noted. Surveying instruments (e.g., astrolabes, compasses, measuring rods, and the *radio astronomico*) aimed at precise measurements, but perspective "machines" did not aspire to become useful machines in the modern sense (i.e., producing "scientific" reproductions of reality). They merely "demonstrated" a conceptual relationship between instrumentality and perspective.

2.32 | Florence, Museo di Storia della Scienza.

2.34 | Montreal, McGill University Libraries Collection.

2.33

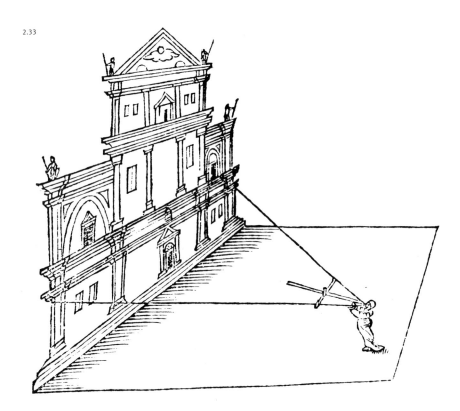

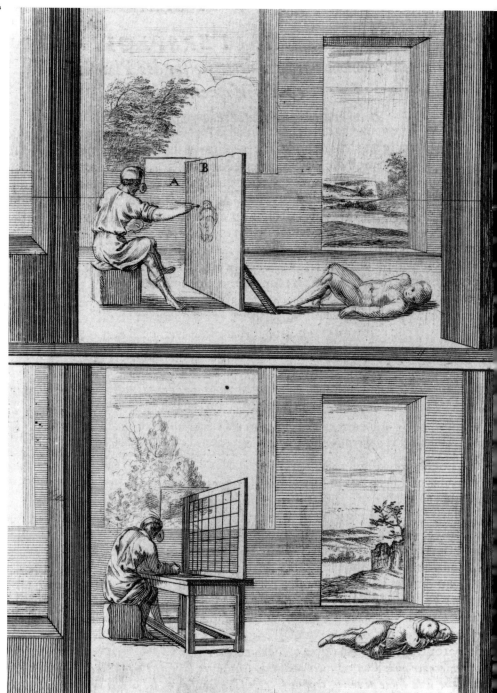

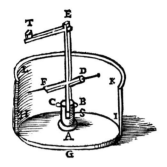

Lanci's surveying device for tracing a view onto a cylindrical surface, from Jacopo Barozzi da Vignola, *Le Due Regole della Prospettiva Pratica* (1583).

sion was associated with the higher realm. Devoted mostly to surveying, Bartoli's treatise did not deal only with the mapping of horizontal surfaces. The third book of his treatise was about measuring volumes, while the fifth book, "Del modo di misurare le prospettive," was devoted entirely to Euclidean geometry and proportional triangles. Bartoli's fifth book is a very good example of the ambiguous meaning of the word *prospettiva* at the end of the sixteenth century: in this context it refers not to an artistic perspective, but rather to the study of geometry and proportional triangles from Euclid. The association between surveying and perspective was all the more natural because both were based on the same principles of proportional triangles. In fact, throughout the sixteenth century, treatises on perspective and treatises on surveying both included an introductory chapter on Euclidean geometry. Giovanni Pomodoro's *Geometria Prattica Trattata dagl'Elementi d'Euclide* (1599) is no exception. Besides the standard introduction to Euclidean geometry, this surveying treatise included a section on geometry applied to the drawing and measuring of areas and volumes of regular and irregular figures, and it established connections with fortification. Such pervasive associations among military architecture, solar clocks, surveying, and the perspective representation of geometric volumes is highly significant. As the next section will make clear, these various disciplines and their products, obviously related to architecture, share a mode of projection related to a desire for precision and the implementation of mathematical proportions in human works, capable of representing the harmony of the macrocosm.

Mapmaking in the late Middle Ages and early Renaissance, however, was very different from the scientific cartography initiated by Lambert. Apart from the Portolano maps, which were produced explicitly for navigation, most Renaissance maps can be considered as cosmological representations. Quite unlike the conception of Lambert, for whom no single map could represent precisely the actual reality of the entire globe, earlier representations indeed strove to render in one complex but single image—often compounded with mythical narratives—the full reality of God's entire creation. The connection between Renaissance cartography and perspective representation was established not through a mathematical equation, as it would be in scientific cartography, but rather at an ontological level. Maps, of course, were often analogous to paintings, enjoying a symbolic function in the political realm. They also fulfilled a role similar to that of fortifications through the proportional association of their parts. In fact, as we will demonstrate shortly, both maps and polygonal fortifications prior to the late seventeenth century were more symbolic than strictly practical devices. The geometry of both revealed the order of the universe.

Even though Lambert's theory of mapmaking may seem extremely objective and precise when compared to the tradition of Renaissance maps, it is interesting that concerning the distorted shape of the Earth—it was already well known that the planet is flattened at its poles—Lambert was not hesitant to suggest a simple approximation and to assume a spherical

| 2.36 |

Left: Surveying device, from Cosimo Bartoli's *Del Modo di Misurare* (1564).

Montreal, Department of Rare Books and Special Collections of the McGill University Libraries.

| 2.37 |

Above: Sundial on an irregular cosmological solid (17th c.).

Florence, Museo di Storia della Scienza.

| 2.38 | 2.39 |

The "Psalter" world map, Anonymous (13th c.) [2.38]; Jodocus Hondius, map of
the world (Amsterdam, 1617) [2.39]. These two maps, four centuries apart, represent two very different visions of the totality of the world. While Hondius's map
expresses a greater concern with precision of measurements, however, both maps
include a very important narrative component.

2.38

2.39

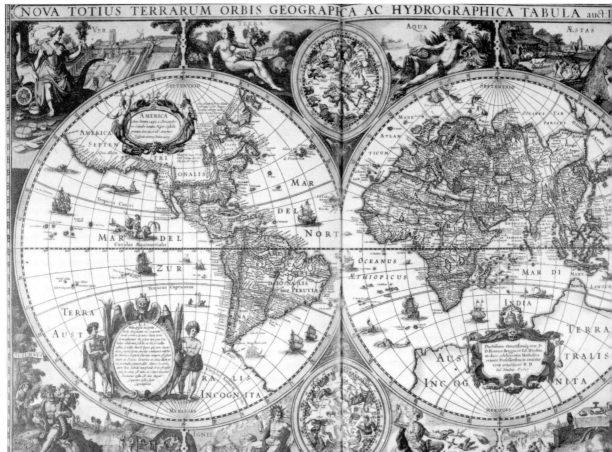

shape for all his maps. Lambert claimed that the shape "is hardly sufficiently different from that of a sphere that one must take note of it in the composition of maps." Moreover, since the coordinates on a map are still far from being exactly determined, he said, a greater precision remains secondary. Lambert concluded that the shape of the Earth on the printed map "becomes more elliptical than the Earth anyway with the press of the copper, and differentially because paper shrinks, and by different amounts in length and width, during the drying process."[105] This passage illustrates that Lambert gave priority to appearance over mathematical exactness, and to experience over reason; but it also shows that he was unwilling to abandon his principles of finite spherical geometry as the absolute ideal of perfection for the terrestrial globe.

Cosmological Volumes

Lambert's experiments with parallel (orthographic) projections in cartography were related to his perspective theory. Section 7 of *La Perspective affranchie,* "About Orthographic Projection, Where One Uses a Vantage Point Infinitely Distant," originally was assumed to be the most important part of his treatise, possibly because of its practical application to military architecture.[106] In it, Lambert developed the common central perspective into a particular kind of projection in which the theoretical viewpoint has been moved away to an infinite distance, causing parallel lines to be represented as parallel. This use of infinity, however, implied not a limitless extension but an extended proportional relationship between the size of an object and its distance from the eye. There are many circumstances, Lambert says, in which one must use a vantage point infinitely distant in order to put an object in perspective. The most ordinary of these cases arises when an object is very small in proportion to its distance from the eye, so that the visual rays seem almost parallel. By assuming that they are, he concludes, we infer the vantage point to be at an infinite distance. Lambert adds that we also use this method when all the parts of an object must be presented to the eye without foreshortening, as in the case of cities and fortifications. It is particularly relevant to mili-

Large sundial, built in 1673 in the Jesuit college, now Lycée Stendhal, Grenoble, France. This solar clock uses the reflection of the sun in a small mirror on the window to indicate solar time, the month, and the zodiac sign.

Photos by L. Pelletier.

2.40a

2.40b

Geometric fortifications from Jacques Perret's treatise *Des fortifications* (1601).
These astounding utopic visions, rendered in very precise isometric projection,
are surrounded by excerpts from the Bible. The spire of the building [2.41b]
touches, at its highest point, the luminosity of God.

Montreal, McGill University Libraries Collection.

2.41a

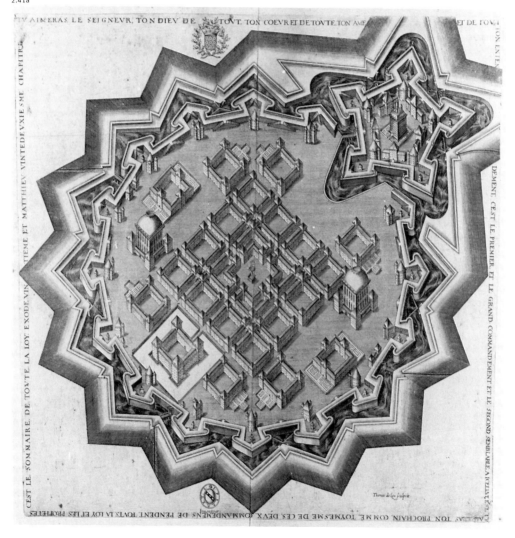

2.41b

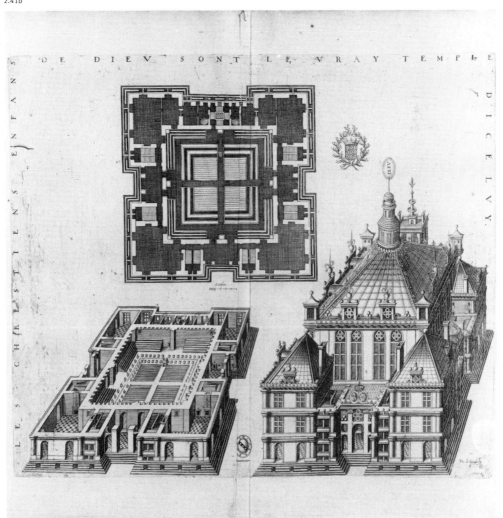

LES CHRESTIENS ENFANS DE DIEV SONT LE VRAY TEMPLE D'ICELVY

tary architecture because it reveals the precise measurements in all dimensions: hence its name of military or "cavalier" perspective.[107]

It is clear that the desire to represent volumes orthogonally was not new to the eighteenth century; it existed long before the introduction of infinity in perspective—before Desargues's *Universal Method.* Whether one thinks about Pompeian frescoes, Byzantine mosaics, the Renaissance representation of fortifications and geometric bodies, or the more recurrent question of shadows projected from the Sun, the mode of representing depth that preserves the parallel quality of lines—based either on a literal and tactile orthogonality, on the ubiquitous nearness of divine light, or on the notion of a viewpoint at infinity—must be considered in relation to particular worldviews.[108] In the Renaissance tradition, its application to fortifications can be traced back to Dürer's *Etliche Underricht, zur Befestigung* (1527). Even before being applied to the tracing of cities and fortifications, however, this kind of representation was introduced in treatises on perspective as the appropriate way to depict regular and irregular "space-filling" bodies, the cosmological volumes of the Platonic tradition. Orthographic projection in that context, whether in the representation of geometric solids, in mapmaking, or in military architecture, was

| 2.42 |

Geometric volume drawn with pen, from Piero della Francesca's *Trattato d'abaco* (after 1480).

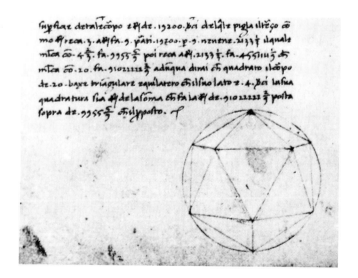

implicitly concerned with representing the wholeness of an object—to render its tactile quality accessible at hand and leave its measurable dimensions unaffected by foreshortening.

One of the first writers to use orthographic projection to represent complex geometric volumes was Piero della Francesca. Piero explicitly pursued significant connections between his mathematical treatises, *Trattato d'abaco* and *Libellus de quinque corporibus regularibus* (after 1480), and his important perspective treatise *De prospectiva pingendi* (before 1482). In *Trattato d'abaco,* he drew with fine pen the regular bodies, inscribing them into a circle to emphasize their proportional qualities, and demonstrated the mathematical rules that regulate their construction and measurement. He considered these rules to be a necessary prerequisite to a thorough understanding of *De prospectiva pingendi,* writing, "a painter need[s] to know the significance of lines and angles in order to understand perspective."[109] Similarly, Luca Pacioli, also a mathematician and a disciple of Piero, depicted models of solid and hollow geometric bodies (possibly drawn by Leonardo da Vinci) in his *Divina proportione* (1509). In the part of his treatise dedicated to architecture, Pacioli insists on the importance of this solid geometry and of stereometry (the practical rules to calculate volumes) as a key to the precise cutting of stone for all architectural elements, and therefore as crucial for the success of building. In this connection, he alludes to the Temple of Solomon described by Ezekiel and includes an image of its gateway. Although he provides no further commentary, Pacioli maintains that this Christian architectural archetype incorporates his concerns with geometry. The image of the temple itself, however, is far from geometrical. Pacioli explains that the craftsman can never implement precise proportions and geometry, because points, lines, and geometric surfaces are not of this world; they exist only in the mind. The point one makes with a pen or a compass is not a real point; there is a "gap" between the ideal and the real world, and mathematics is a bridge across it, an ontological instrument.[110] In a section on proportions in which he adds the equilateral triangle to the Vitruvian square and circle as the basis for the proportions of the human head, Pacioli describes a "perspective frame" with a grid of silk threads, useful to the architect for understanding proportion and proportional relationships. This

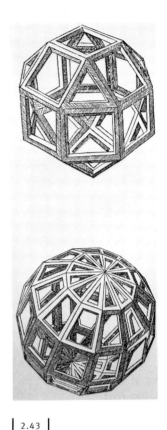

| 2.43 |

Geometric volume drawn as a hollow body, from Luca Pacioli's *Divina proportione* (1509).

proportional grid, nevertheless, is not identical to Alberti's "veil" for the painter. Pacioli's grid for architects is meant to convey concrete, volumetric proportions, rather than to systematize projection. Significantly, both Pacioli and Piero depicted their cosmological volumes in a form of drawing that seems to resist perspective forshortening. The parallel sides of orthogonal planes do not seem to converge as would be the case in linear perspective, since this kind of *prospettiva* does not include a construction point corresponding to the eye of the painter or the to frame of a perspective window. Instead, every volume appears to be self-contained, as if copied from a preexistent solid. All this must be understood in the context of the general connection established between mathematics and the arts of perspective and architecture. Pacioli emphasized this

| 2.44 |

The gateway of the Temple of Solomon, from Pacioli's *Divina proportione.*

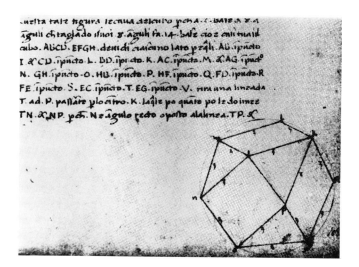

connection by dedicating his own treatise to the students of "philosophia, prospectiva, pictura, sculptura, architectura, musica, e altre mathematice." The association between mathematics and architecture was based on the musical, harmonic, or proportional variations of the five Platonic bodies—the geometric structure of the cosmos. Proportional relationships, or *proportionalità* (a:b::c:d), the ontological basis for all human creation that aspired to the status of true knowledge, was the common thread relating cosmography, architecture, and geometric projective constructions. In part 1 of *Divina proportione,* after reconciling the Platonic cosmogony from *Timaeus* with Christian theology through the wondrous attributes of the Golden Section (a symbol of the uniqueness of God, the Trinity, etc.), and demonstrating the priority of this proportion in the nesting of the Platonic solids within the dodecahedron (Plato's quintessence, the sphere of the heavens), Pacioli named the 26- and 72-faced solids as particularly relevant for architecture. He devotes, for example, a whole chapter of his treatise to the architectural usefulness of the 72-faced solid, citing examples such as the *antico templo pantheon* in which half of this solid, resembling a hemisphere, is used literally in an architectural context.[111]

The representation of Platonic solids was an all-pervasive theme throughout the Renaissance, and it soon became a standard part of perspective and architectural treatises.

Title page from Jean Cousin's *Livre de
Perspective* (1560), showing the five
Platonic solids.

In *Livre de perspective* (1560), Jean Cousin included a title page
with a dodecahedron, icosahedron, tetrahedron, hexahedron
(or cube), and octahedron, together with an armillary sphere of
the universe. The perspective construction of the composition
is far from homogeneous, and gravity appears to operate in
different directions for every fragment. The space contained by
the structure represents an enigmatic "coincidence of opposites," in which the plurality of the elements symbolized by the
Platonic solids is resolved into the unity of the *prima materia,*
simultaneously the primordial space of Creation.[112] The construction of the five regular bodies is demonstrated in the last
part of the book, first by explaining their planar composition
(for example, the twelve pentagons of the dodecahedron), then
drawing them in orthographic plan, and finally raising the

2.47

Perspective projection of a cube, from Cousin's treatise.

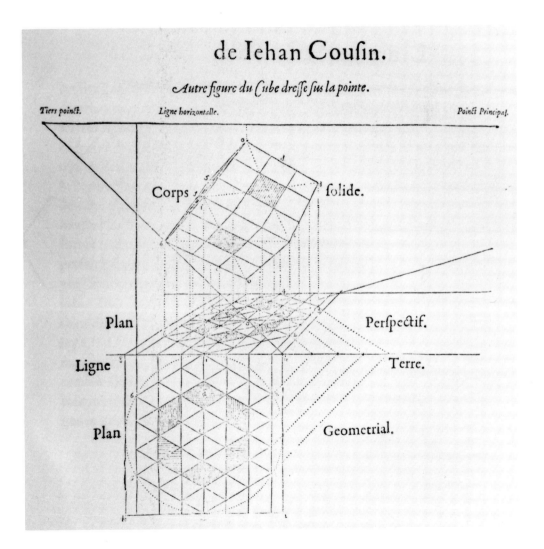

de Iehan Cousin.

Autre figure du Cube dreſſe ſus la pointe.

Tiers poinct.　　　　Ligne horizontalle.　　　　　　　　Poinct Principal.

Corps　　　　　　　　　　　ſolide.

Plan　　　　　　　　　　　Perſpectif.

Ligne　　　　　　　　　　　Terre.

Plan　　　　　　　　　　　Geometrial.

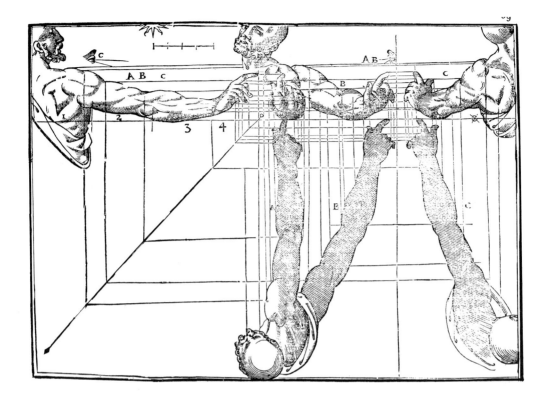

| 2.48 |

Cousin's orthogonal projections still positioned the sun and the eye of the observer in relation to the subject being depicted. From Cousin's *L'Art de dessiner* (1521).

three-dimensional solids from their perspective plan. Cousin's projections again are quite ambiguous, because even though the projection of orthographic plans are foreshortened toward a "principal point," the resulting solids seem to resist perspectival forshortening. Cousin's projections, even those that are expressly perspectival, do not reduce the tactile world to the infinite extension that excludes the participation of the viewer, since both the eye and the Sun still are included explicitly in the image, in distinction to the objectified space of descriptive geometry that his drawings seem to prefigure.

Also devoted entirely to the representation of the space-filling bodies, the *Perspectiva Corporum Regularum* (1568) by the Viennese goldsmith Wenzel Jamnitzer (1508–1585) features over 150 geometric figures derived from the five fundamental Platonic volumes. In fact, the entire treatise is organized around these five primary solids. Following a brief discussion of Plato's *Timaeus,* the book is divided into five parts, each devoted to one of the regular solids and preceded by a title page portraying the attributes, instruments, and creatures of fire; the creatures and musical instruments related to air; the abundance of the Earth; the attributes of the sea; and finally, the attributes of the heavenly spheres, framed by the Sun and the Moon. Each section comprises four plates, each with six illustrations of a geometric solid transmuted into progressively more complex related composites. Because of the impressive variety of geometric solids and the quality of the engravings, his work has rightly been considered a "virtuoso performance," in the tradition initiated by Piero della Francesca. Unlike his predecessors, however, Jamnitzer provides no instructions for constructing these exceedingly complex figures, nor any discussion of their proportional nature. His stated intention was to "explain the art of perspective to everyone in so concise and enjoyable a manner that all superfluity will be avoided and—as was the case with old-fashioned ways of teaching—no line or point will be drawn

| 2.49 |

Irregular space-filling bodies, from Wenzel Jamnitzer's *Perspectiva corporum regularum* (1568). Etching by Jost Amman.

Montreal, Collection Centre Canadien d'Architecture / Canadian Centre for Architecture.

needlessly."[113] There are signs in the case of Jamnitzer that he did not "construct" the projection of his Platonic solids geometrically by using the current projective methods of the time.[114] The absence of construction lines, together with the extremely shallow perspective in which the receding parallels barely converge, suggest the use of some perspective instrument to portray existing three-dimensional solids. One thing is clear, however: these figures are so complex that it would be extremely difficult for even an experienced draftsman to visualize their geometry without using three-dimensional models.

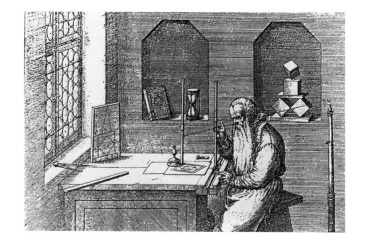

Amman, *Portrait of Jamnitzer in His Studio with a Perspective Machine* (ca. 1565).

London, copyright British Museum.

The measurement of regular and irregular bodies also became a standard part of perspective treatises. The accurate measurement of Euclidean solids was based on their fixed ratio with the sphere. Daniele Barbaro, in his unpublished manuscript *La Pratica della Prospettiva*,[115] claimed that the kind of *prospettiva* used to represent these volumes is useful to architects, and is distinct from the art of depicting that is useful to painters. While in his published treatise, *La Pratica della Perspettiva* (1569), detailed instructions for drawing polygons and polyhedra lead to painted representations of buildings and their architectural parts, and finally to the construction of theatrical scenery, in his unpublished manuscript Barbaro introduces the principles of perspective quite briefly. Assuming that the reader is not a beginner, he devotes the rest of his treatise to "the construction and perspectival rendering of geometrical bodies," based on the "physical" reality of the world that the artist must know first in order to do his work.[116] Influenced by Pacioli and Piero, Barbaro shared Plato's fascination for regular bodies, "which signified the elements of the world and heaven itself, and, by the secret intelligence of their forms, ascended to the highest speculation concerning the nature of things."[117] Barbaro therefore emphasized that perspective should do justice to the divine authority of mathematics, since perspective not only is based on natural science but also is an integral part of the geometric art and science that regulates the world and the cosmos.[118] He criti-

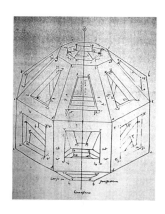

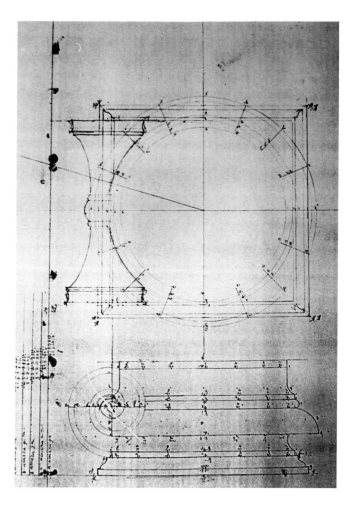

| 2.53 |

Above: Perspectival rendering of a geometric body, from Barbaro's *La Pratica della Prospettiva.*

| 2.54 |

Left: Architectural element, from Barbaro's *La Pratica della Prospettiva.*

Plan [2.55] and perspective projection [2.56] of a geometric body, from Barbaro's
La Pratica della Perspettiva (1569).

Montreal, Collection Centre Canadien d'Architecture / Canadian Centre for Architecture.

2.55

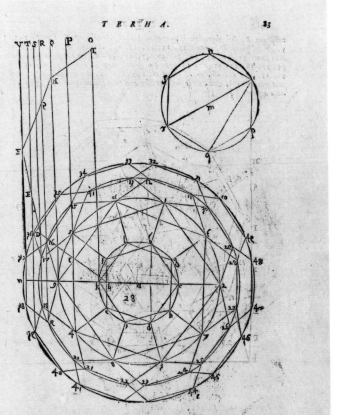

nel piano B, ferà digradato il pentagono bcdcf, & nel piano C, i punti 1, 2, 3, 4, G
5, & nel piano D, i punti 13, 14, 17, 18, 21, 22, 25, 26, 29, 30, & nel piano
E, i punti 31, 32, 35, 36, 39, 40, 43, 44, 47, 48, & nel piano F, i punti 33,
34, 37, 38, 41, 42, 45, 46, 49, 50, & nel piano G, i punti 11, 12, 15, 16, 19,
20, 23, 24, 27, 28, & nel piano H, i punti 6, 7, 8, 9, 10, & nel piano I, il
pentagono ghikl, & tirate le sue linee, hauerai tutti i piani, come nella figura 28, digra-
data appare.

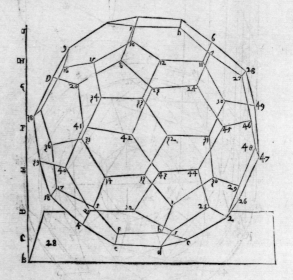

Ma se il detto corpo si poserà con la basa di sei lati, il perfetto si farà in questo modo, sia M
data altroue una linea tanto longa, quanto la bc, del sopra posto perfetto, laqual sia A B,
& per detta linea spacio, & centro a, sia dato il circulo, nelquale sia descritta una superficie
di sei lati eguali, bcdefg, nellaquale siano tratte le linee bc, & bd, sia poi appari della
linea A B, posta un'altra, di tanto spacio quanto è la linea bd, del peatagono del soprapo-
sto perfetto, & sia cD, & centro a, sia dato un'altro circulo di tanta circonferenza, che
la linea bc, dell'essagono predetto, & la linea C D, entri ciascuna sei fiate nella circonfe-
renza di quello terminando ne i punti h, i, k, l, m, n, o, p, q, r, s, t, sei fiate di-
co, perche tanto è hi, quanto qr, & kl, & così delle altre parti, che circondando la cir-
conferenza in tale modo, ogn'una di dette linee entra sei fiate nella circonferenza. & tanto
saria

| 2.57 |

Inlays from the Studiolo of Urbino depicting geometric bodies. Barbaro expressly connected the knowledge of space-filling bodies and the interests of architects. These bodies were perceived as representations of a classical cosmic order, stemming from Plato's and Pacioli's identification of the regular solids with the elements of nature. When these bodies are included in inlay wooden works, the thematic and formal connection between *perspectiva artificialis* and the traditional quadrivium is even more explicit. Unlike painting, where a story told is crucial, the *intarsia* constituted the stage for a new *orbis studiorum,* a new definition of knowledge distinct from medieval theology but not distant from its aspirations.

Photo by A. Perez-Gomez.

responding height and orientation of its sides. Like many of his predecessors, Barbaro projected the cosmological solids in a form of representation that resists perspective conventions. When parallel sides of a volume slightly converge toward the background, they do so in an almost accidental way. Moreover, their representation is created not through the window of *perspettiva,* but rather as a construction that accounts for the tactile perception of the "whole." As Barbaro stressed, the kind of projection used to represent space-filling bodies was particularly relevant for architecture. It represented the cosmological totality, that is, the visible and the invisible reality of the world. Like Pacioli, Barbaro also perceived these volumes as connected with architecture by the possibility of exploring musical or harmonic proportional variations of the five Platonic bodies, the very structure of the cosmos. We should note that while an interest in the orthogonal representation of volumes is indeed evident in many Renaissance treatises on perspective, orthographic projection prior to the seventeenth century was hardly systematized and should not be interpreted as geometric manipulation of a vantage point at infinity.

In other sixteenth-century works, parallel projections began to be used for more practical purposes. In Jacques Androuet du Cerceau's *Trois livres d'architecture* (1559–1582), while it is clear that his understanding of representation did not yet involve the notion of infinity, he freely alternated between foreshortened perspective and other kinds of frontal parallel projection to represent his architectural ideas. Between the first and the third book he tested modes of representation for his architectural projects, particularly the potential meaning and use of the Vitruvian *scenographia,* and his concern with precision is evident, since he was interested in providing a detailed cost estimate for every building included in the books. Du Cerceau's third book is devoted entirely to the building of villas in the country or in the fields.[119] His desire to represent the land, the gardens, and all the facilities surrounding every building, combined with his obsession with precision, led him to use a kind of frontal isometry, indeed one similar to that used in military architecture. In contrast, the second book includes strange, apparently irrational designs for wells, fireplaces, tombs, gates, and windows. Why, we may ask, are these elements included in a

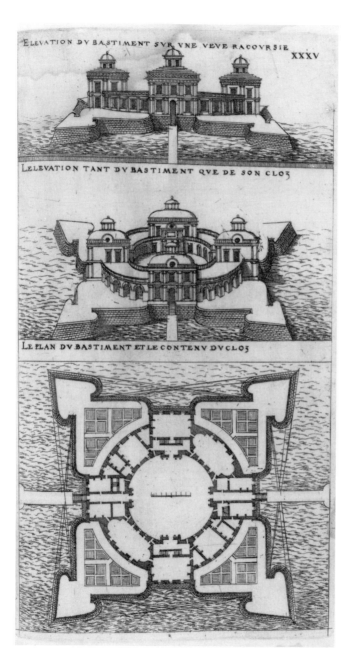

ELEVATION DV BASTIMENT SVR VNE VEVE RACOVRSIE
XXXV

L'ELEVATION TANT DV BASTIMENT QVE DE SON CLOS

LE PLAN DV BASTIMENT ET LE CONTENV DV CLOS

A fortified residence represented in three views, identified as the plan, the elevation of the building and the land, and a foreshortened elevation. From Jacques Androuet du Cerceau's *Livre d'architecture* (1582).

Montreal, Collection Centre Canadien d'Architecture / Canadian Centre for Architecture.

263

| 2.59 |

Frontal isometry of a villa, from du
Cerceau's *Livre d'architecture.*

Montreal, Collection Centre Canadien
d'Architecture / Canadian Centre for
Architecture.

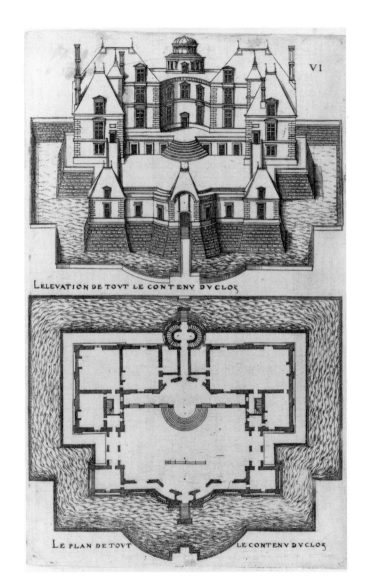

2.60

Fireplace with female centaur, from du Cerceau's *Second livre d'architecture* (1561).

Montreal, Collection Centre Canadien d'Architecture / Canadian Centre for Architecture.

265

seemingly pragmatic work, which is almost a catalogue of domestic buildings? The answer might be that these architectural elements explicitly celebrate water, fire, earth, and air, the four Platonic elements that were traditionally acknowledged as the very substance of architecture. In this light, the novel, mysterious depths disclosed in the fascinating "experimental" projective drawings that fill the book could indeed be related to a quest for the origin and quintessence of architecture, the enigmatic Platonic *chōra* (space/primordial matter) that we can grasp only in dreams.

Truth as Measurement: Fortifications and Isometry

Baroque architects, as we have seen, often were expressly concerned with revealing the divine order of the universe through their work. Villalpando, for example, despite his explicit interest in perspective as a way to visualize buildings, used orthographic projection to reveal this implicit order in his representation of the Temple of Jerusalem, for it reproduced the image drawn by the hand of God as if it were projected by His own light. After the seventeenth century, however, orthographic projection must be considered in light of Desargues's geometric perspective and his understanding of parallel projection as a specific case of his universal method of perspective. We should recall that Desargues's theory of parallel projection postulated the observer at an infinite distance from the object to be depicted. The embodied observer, traditionally an essential participant in the epiphanies of perspective and a crucial element for its constructions, became an abstract point that could be replaced by a scale or by other more convenient geometric coordinates. Desargues's entire perspective theory was explained in purely geometric terms and therefore aspired to become a neutral, objective tool. Perspective, including parallel projection, was thereafter destined to become a prescriptive tool of the engineer and the architect, devoid of metaphysical concerns.

Before Desargues, as we have suggested, there were some precocious applications of orthographic projection in military architecture. Most of these examples were frontal projections, which seem to have been concerned primarily with precise measurement. While there was usually a clear desire to present the symbolic order of the "whole" polygonal structure through its geometry, many treatises on the art of war in the second half of the sixteenth and in the seventeenth century attempted to develop particular kinds of projection that might combine a general view of the fortifications with the precision of a measurable drawing.[120] Fortifications and ballistics indeed were of great interest to perspectivists and geometricians, for they provided a field to test the practical and symbolic effectiveness of their theories. Consequently, it was not unusual for sixteenth- and seventeenth-century writers on perspective also to produce works on fortifications.

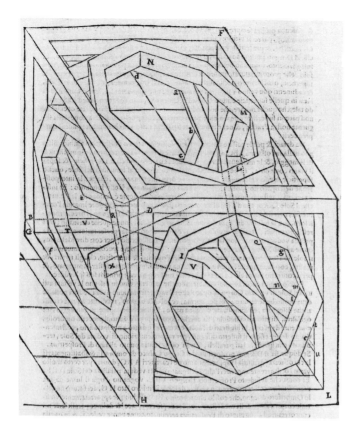

| 2.61 |

Parallel projection of a cube with an octagon inscribed in each of its sides, from Pietro Accolti's *Lo Inganno de gl'occhi* (1625).

Montreal, Collection Centre Canadien d'Architecture / Canadian Centre for Architecture.

267

Simon Stevin of Bruges (1548–1620)—known as the tutor of Maurice, count of Nassau, later prince of Orange and Stadholder of the United Provinces—was a clear example of this manifold interest in perspective theory and all its ramifications.[121] Pressed by the prince's desire to become familiar with the drawing of perspective, Stevin composed a work on the subject, *De Deursichtighe,* which literally means "On Optics" (although often translated as "On Perspective"). Since most current treatises on the subject had been written for painters and lacked mathematical rigor, Stevin decided to write his own theory.[122] In his treatise, he presented a mathematical method of perspective destined to enable Prince Maurice "to explain his views better in discussions concerning landscape, cities," and the art of fortification. The work was divided into two books.[123] The first book, *Van de Verschaeuwing* (a translation of the Latin word *scenographia*) was a general textbook that defined the basic terms and techniques of perspective construction. The second book of Stevin's treatise contains the theory and principles of reflection in mirrors, traditionally known as "catoptrics." The major innovations of this work consisted in Stevin's explanation of a perspective method in which the picture plane is not perpendicular to the ground plane and his solution to a problem that he called "the finding of the eye." Given an object and a perspective drawing of it, Stevin demonstrated how to determine the position of the observer's eye, using a method similar to that described in Del Monte's mathematical writings and later taken up by Lambert in the last section of his treatise on perspective.

In addition to his general interest in perspective, Stevin was also concerned with surveying and with the use of astronomy for navigation. He published a scientific treatise, the *Heaven-Finding Art* (1599), in which he applied existing quantitative data to explain his views on the magnetism of the Earth. He proposed a method of navigation, based on the observation of variations of the compass needle, which would enable seamen to navigate confidently without knowing either the longitude of the ship's destination or the longitude of its location at sea.[124] A few years earlier, Stevin had published another treatise, *The Art of Fortification* (1594), in which he maintained that "all fortresses must be designed . . . before the building is undertaken": that is why one needs to make drawings, so that one can "finally arrive at the best plan."[125] In fact, this was *not* common practice in his own time, and comprehensive planning hardly ever occurred before the late seventeenth century. According to Stevin, the design should be done in two steps: "first plain by a ground plan upon paper and afterwards bodily with potter's Earth, wax, wood or other matter."[126] After the Renaissance, warfare had become a more sophisticated discipline involving both mathematical and technical aspects of organization. Included in the sphere of the liberal arts, military architecture eventually sought to replace the simple wall construction of the Middle Ages with a polygonal structure that served as both a symbolic and a defensive boundary. Increasingly it was calculated to minimize the amount of fortress wall that could not be reached by defenders, while at the same time making an attack as difficult as possible for the enemy.[127] Unlike his Renaissance predecessors and most of his baroque successors, Stevin seemed to understand fortification as a purely strategic element in the art of war, devoid of symbolic values.

Stevin's inclination for scientific precision was also evident later in his book, when he discussed the question of scale. "Architects differ greatly in their opinions concerning the dimensions of the fortresses," he says, and the causes for these differences are numerous. "In the first place these measures' names sometimes deceive us: in many places they sound alike, but in one town they are much longer than in the other."[128] To make his point, Stevin compares the actual dimensions of various measures taken from French, Italian, and German prints. Again, for Stevin the importance of drawing fortifications ex-

| 2.62 |

Two pages from Stevin's *Art of Fortification* (1594), showing the relationship between perspective drawing and the desire to "arrive at the best plan for fortifications . . . before the building is undertaken." The perspective device on the right, presented as an improvement on Dürer's machines, connotes the possibility of precise surveying and planning.

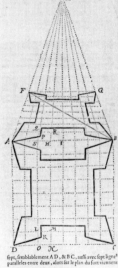

2.63

Examples of measuring units that vary for different authors and different cities, from Stevin's *Art of War*.

2.64

Opposite page: The debate between Mercury and Mars on the virtues of geometry for war and peace, from Johann Jakob Schübler's *Perspectiva Pes picturae* (1719–1720).

Montreal, Collection Centre Canadien d'Architecture / Canadian Centre for Architecture.

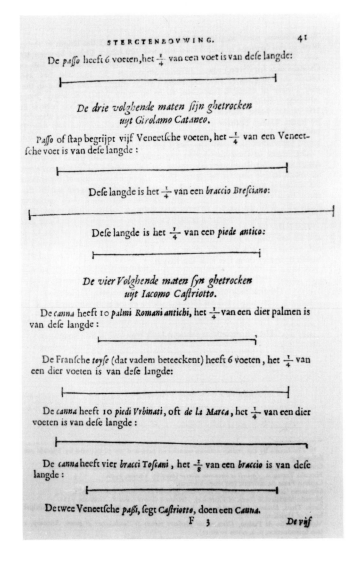

De *paſſo* heeft 6 voeten, het $\frac{1}{4}$ van een voet is van deſe langde:

De drie volghende maten ſijn ghetrocken
uyt *Girolamo Cataneo.*

Paſſo of ſtap begrijpt vijf Veneetſche voeten, het $\frac{1}{4}$ van een Veneetſche voet is van deſe langde :

Deſe langde is het $\frac{1}{4}$ van een *braccio Breſciano*:

Deſe langde is het $\frac{1}{4}$ van een *piede antico*:

De vier Volghende maten ſyn ghetrocken
uyt *Iacomo Caſtriotto.*

De *canna* heeft 10 *palmi Romani antichi*, het $\frac{1}{4}$ van een dier palmen is
van deſe langde :

De Franſche *teyſe* (dat vadem beteeckent) heeft 6 voeten , het $\frac{1}{4}$ van
een dier voeten is van deſe langde:

De *canna* heeft 10 *piedi Vrbinati*, oft *de la Marca*, het $\frac{1}{4}$ van een dier
voeten is van deſe langde :

De *canna* heeft vier *bracci Toſcani* , het $\frac{1}{8}$ van een *braccio* is van deſe
langde :

De twee Veneetſche *paſſi*, ſegt *Caſtriotto*, doen een *Canna.*
F 3   *De vijf*

plicitly was not simply to demonstrate geometric or proportional relationships, but to determine precise measurements. Stevin produced two other works on the "art of warfare." In *New Manner of Fortification by Means of Pivoted Sluice-Locks* (1617), he explained how to construct wet ditches for fortresses situated on the waterfront. In an unpublished manuscript, *On Besieging Towns and Fortresses,* Stevin included tactical directions for carrying out an attack.

| 2.65 |

Comparison of an axonometric and a
frontal perspective of a house, from
Christian Rieger's *Universae Architecturae Civilis Elementa* (1756).

Montreal, Collection Centre Canadien
d'Architecture / Canadian Centre for
Architecture.

Stevin's treatises on fortification are dominated by
practical concerns and are free from metaphysical speculation.
Yet he still maintained the connection between geometry and
music. In an unpublished fragment, *On the Theory of the Art of
Singing*—Stevin used the word "singing" instead of "music," as
he called the musical staff a "singing ladder"—he wrote an entire section titled "The Comparison of Geometrical Ratio with
Musical Ratio." "Just as all the ratios of two given rectilinear
plane figures or solids cannot be recognized by sight, but obey
geometrical rules teaching us how to find them," he says, "so
all the ratios of two given sounds cannot be judged by hearing,
but they are revealed by means of the musical rules governing
them." [129] Thus Stevin's concern with the geometric organization of fortifications was still based on a fundamental understanding of geometry as a *lingua universalis,* conceived as the true
order of the world during the seventeenth century.

Only later in the century did Sébastien Le Prestre de
Vauban (1633–1707), the marshal of France, bring the Galilean
scientific revolution to matters of fortification and military
practice. By combining modern science with his own experience as a soldier, he initiated modern military engineering. He
was concerned more with the technical aspects of building a
wall than with the overall geometric plan of the fortification,
and he used mathematics for planning and statistics. [130] In this
context, the traditional symbolic implications of drawing were
radically questioned. The maps of a country, a city, or a fortification began to be regarded as merely quantitative instruments
to further political or economic aims. This is key to understanding some of the muddled assumptions about the status of fortifications and their representation; mathematical artifacts,
instruments, and their products had revealed throughout the
seventeenth century an ontological continuity between a relative human condition and the absolute supralunary (divine)
world, acquiring a privileged status as symbols of a transcendental order.

Not surprisingly, the end of the seventeenth century
witnessed the introduction of new modes of representation that
sought to portray the complete view of a fortification and enable precise measurements to be taken from the drawing. Axonometry—which retains measurable angles in plan, unlike

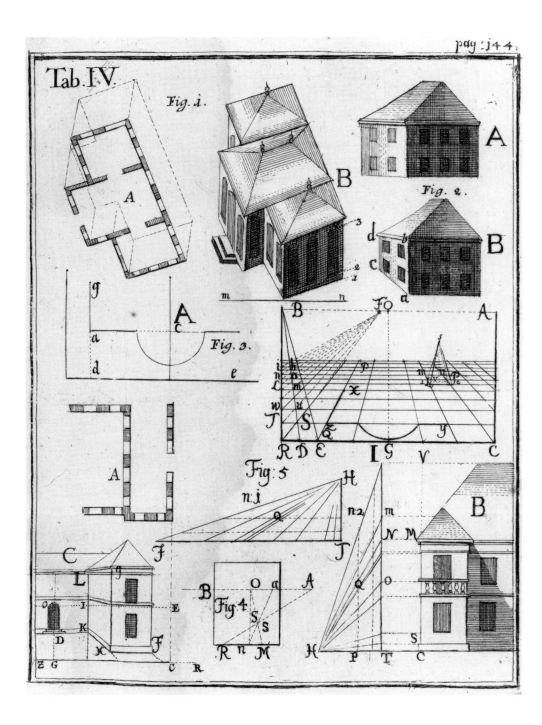

Tab. IV.

Fig. 1.

A

B

A

Fig. 2.

B

d   b
c
a

m   n

B   F O   A

g

a   A
                     C   Fig. 3.
d   e

A

Fig. 5.

n.1   H
        Q

n.2   m
                N M
J
        Q   O

C   F
L   g   B
                     Fig. 4.
o   i   E   B   O a   A
    K   S s
D   x   F   R n M
Z G   c R   H   P T   C

isometry—began to appear at that time in works on fortification and architectural representation. This kind of projection had appeared among other geometric experiments in mathematical tracts such as in T. Luders's treatise, *La première Partie de la Perspective Militaire* (1680). The earliest-known European example of architectural axonometry is a drawing by Leonhard Christoph Sturm (Amsterdam, 1699). The association of architecture and "military perspective" (another term for axonometry) was most explicit in the work of Christian Rieger, author of a treatise devoted specifically to military architecture, *Perspectiva militaris* (1758), and a previous work on civil architecture, *Universae Architecturae Civilis Elementa* (1756). In the latter, Rieger differentiated "common or regular perspective" from "military perspective," and postulated that while in a perspective drawing the height diminishes in proportion to the distance, the axonometric drawing is generated from the plan and the height coincides with the true dimension of the elevation. Rieger not only demonstrated the use of axonometry, he also insisted that its technique and application was appropriate for architects. He was interested in teaching architects how to project the image of their buildings from plan and elevations so that the "real" measurements were not distorted and did not result in "inelegant" representations. This goal was well fulfilled by axonometric drawings that precisely respect the measurements of the plan and the elevations while representing the building in space. Even though Rieger's axonometric projection implied that the eye of the spectator was geometrically "infinitely remote," no consideration was given to this notion of infinity. He did not describe how axonometry differs from "common perspective," nor did he use this type of projection elsewhere in his treatise—except to represent triangular prisms.

In the seventh section of his *Free Perspective,* Lambert discussed the mathematical and perceptual implications of isometric drawing, which he also identified with military or "soldier" perspective. By then the advantage of such a representation was clearly understood: it presents the spatial disposition of the whole and also provides scaled dimensions. From a practical point of view, Lambert's isometry was *specific* to military architecture, where the precision of measurements was important, and did not assume infinity in the world. As a mathematician, he was interested in the notion of *limits,* and even though he expressed some of his theories in terms of immense distances—as he did in his cosmology—he remained unwilling to turn real dimension into infinite extension. Lambert distinguished perspective from isometry, because while the former attempts to reproduce the visual appearances, only the latter gives precise measurements. He maintained that this form of orthographic projection, although useful for fortifications and mapping, was clearly distinct from the experience of a finite, perspectival universe. In the section of his treatise devoted to parallel projections, Lambert describes a case of "soldier perspective" (*perspective cavalière*) projected from the plan of a city or a fortification. When we use orthographic projections to draw large machines, cities, and fortresses, Lambert says, the primary objective cannot be to reproduce natural appearances, but must be to describe the dimensions of the object with clarity and precision. Consequently, shadows should be used not in a naturalistic manner, but to differentiate surfaces with different orientations. Lambert concludes this section on parallel projection by saying that these drawings also have their "phenomena" (i.e., their apparent pictorial quality and specific viewpoint), but it is unnecessary to consider these characteristics because visual appearance is not the primary objective. Moreover, we always contemplate them from a position outside their own viewpoint,

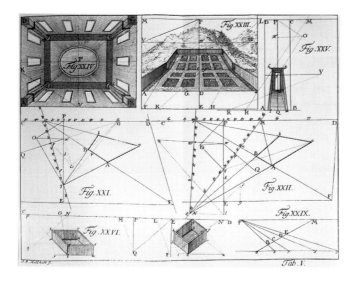

| 2.66 |

Two examples of parallel projection, also identified as military or "soldier" perspective, from Johann Heinrich Lambert's *La perspective affranchie* (1759).

which is inevitable, he says, if we are to understand anything from them.[131]

We saw that in order to deduce the laws of parallel projection, Lambert needed to redefine the problem in terms of a very small object located at a great distance from the observer, thus emphasizing the predominance of the finite world.[132] Once this condition was established, his rules of perspective also applied to parallel projection. However, since for parallel projection the position of the eye was assumed to be extremely remote, the distance between the object and the observer did not matter, and only the elevation of the eye above the horizon—expressed in terms of angles, as in astronomical observation—would affect the representation. This assimilation of parallel projection with perspective, first postulated by Desargues, implied that orthogonal projections ultimately are based on the same laws of optics, and for Lambert, they were variations of the same phenomena of vision. A few decades later, it became a matter of a simple syllogism for Monge to postulate that the homogeneous and infinite space of descriptive geometry is identical to that of perspective space, ultimately reducing qualitative spatial experience to quantitative data.[133]

In the second edition of his treatise on perspective (1774), Lambert included an appendix, "Comments and Addition," in which he elaborated further on the question of parallel projection. This annex includes fifteen specific problems of geometry that Lambert resolves by using principles originally developed for his perspective theory. The objective was to "examine how far one can go in perspective and then in geometry without using compasses but only a ruler, in order to render both perspective and geometry truly 'linear.'" The implicit result was a complete integration of perspective and geometry, as well as the assimilation of parallel and converging lines. "In graphic constructions using only a ruler," Lambert says, "perspective has an advantage over geometry, since in a perspective, parallel lines can be traced without difficulty."[134] Lambert meant that in a perspective construction, parallel lines do converge toward a point within the frame of the image and can therefore be traced with a single ruler. This seminal series of thoughts about projection and geometry has led his commentators to conclude that Lambert was the true founder of "projective geometry."[135] Lambert's insistent reference to "linear geometry" and his definition of *Lineal* or *Linearperspektive* (also known as "perspective of the ruler"), however, were related more to his interest in simplifying perspective and showing that it is much easier to use only a ruler and no compasses in constructing a perspective than to any form of abstract geometric projection. Like Desargues, Lambert's objective was to define a self-contained perspective method that did not require the use of points outside the picture frame. He indeed was conscious of many geometric conditions that eventually would lead to projective geometry. However, he always gave priority to the specificity of the problems at hand and never reduced them to a general theorem. Moreover, his assimilation of the concept of parallel lines to that of converging lines remained bounded by the Euclidean geometry that prevailed in the eighteenth century. Lambert qualified the converging sides of a parallelogram in perspective as being "perspectivally parallel."[136] He also concluded that we must accept Euclid's axiom of parallel lines even though it cannot be proven; he could never challenge the very basis of Euclidean geometry. Despite the mathematical sophistication of his geometric perspective, Lambert's theory was still concerned with retaining the tactile and finite dimension of the world, as opposed to Poncelet, whose geometry, as we will show, consciously abandons this concern.

   Lambert's perspective theory ultimately was based on optical laws in a *finite* world. He coined the word "phenomenology" in his *New Organon* (1764), which presents his theory of appearances. In that context, phenomenology was defined as the possibility of going beyond sensory appearances, since appearances themselves lead to the scientific understanding of the world—that is, to truth.[137] It would be naive to claim a direct filiation with twentieth-century phenomenology, itself defined in widely different ways by Edmund Husserl and his disciples, but the connection is suggestive. Lambert's conception of a finite cosmos, coupled with his emphasis on the priority of phenomena in his natural perspective, combined to avoid the pitfalls of relativism. Some of these concerns became indeed key questions for later Continental philosophy and hermeneutics. While there is no evidence that Lambert might have had a critical understanding of the limitations of a mechanistic psy-

"Physionotrace," invented by Gilles-Louis Chrétien (18th c.) for tracing profiles.

Paris, Bibliothèque Nationale.

chology of perception (*partes extra partes*) of the Descartes-Locke tradition, in which sensations are received one sense at a time and perception is reconstituted in the brain as a purely intellectual phenomenon, nevertheless in the epistemological landscape of the eighteenth century, his observer of perspectives was not the passive, autonomous subject of nineteenth-century democracy.

Lambert's natural perspective attempted to integrate the laws of visual perception—mechanistic optics—and the rationalization of representation—geometric perspective. It also

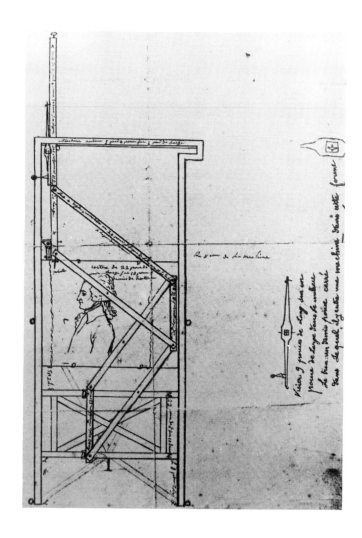

coincided with the renewed late-eighteenth-century interest in projection machines, but this time for truly "useful" purposes, with examples such as the "Physionotrace" by Gilles-Louis Chrétien (1786) for tracing profiles, and the development of "mechanical" portraiture. Truly effective machines for drawing, however, such as the camera lucida, which directly applies to tracing the rules of optics, had to wait until the nineteenth century. As we will discuss in our last Variation, the instrumentalizing of perspective became a reality when the natural perspective and constructed perspective were brought together in a long-desired union by synthesizing descriptive geometry with a new physiological optics that thoroughly objectified the subject.

Variation Three

The Image without an Observer
in a Scopophilic World

What a lot of time I wasted over that
camera lucida to be sure.

* * *

Samuel Butler, December 14, 1901

Up rather late this morning,
and lost time before breakfast over camera lucida;
drove to Argentière with my mother.

* * *

John Ruskin, diary entry, June 25, 1848

The growing eighteenth-century belief that perspective was a "natural" form of perception was related to increasing scientific interest in optical devices that were believed to emulate vision. One such device was the camera obscura, with which an external image, projected through a small orifice into a dark chamber, was created as in the eye. Although the principles of this device had been known since the sixteenth century, and the phenomenon probably had been observed even earlier,[1] the camera obscura, like other perspective machines, had been used mainly as an optical "demonstration" and not as an actual tool for drawing.

In 1569, Daniele Barbaro apparently was the first to describe the camera obscura, along with other "perspective instruments" such as solar clocks, Dürer's window, and a surveying quadrant invented by Baldassare Lanci—all were treated in short entries at the end of his treatise on perspective.[2] He speaks of "a very beautiful experience" taking place in a darkened room, noting that the images generated in this fashion demonstrated "naturally" the proportional diminution of objects, thereby adding to an understanding of the principles of perspective. In the same section, however, Barbaro insists that the effect requires very strong solar illumination and associates it with the plots of shadow tracers (solar clocks). Given the specific requirements for creating such images, Barbaro probably never believed that the image of the camera obscura could or should be imitated by artists.

Kepler's mechanistic theory of the eye was the first to suggest that an image "constitutes itself" within the eye's "dark chamber" without the volition of the observer, and without interference from the other senses. As opposed to the explanations of Euclidean and medieval optics, Kepler's definition of visual perception assumed the hegemony of sight itself and a phenomenal independence between the perceived image and the actual image of a thing, or *imago rerum*. Granting the autonomy of the image that forms itself in the eye, which he called "picturing," Kepler consequently acknowledged the potential of the eye to deceive the mind.[3] Similarly, he believed in the objectivity of the image that forms itself in the camera obscura

Plate from Athanasius Kircher's *Ars magna lucis et umbrae* (1649). Kircher believed that the camera obscura (a form of visual magic) revealed what was essential and enigmatic in nature — the primordial mathematical alphabet, hidden yet present like the figure in the anthropomorphic landscape.

Montreal, Collection Université de Montréal.

and used it for surveying, as reported by the English dilettante and architectural writer Henry Wotton.[4] Wotton apparently visited Kepler in Linz in 1622, and he described the scientist making a survey of the land from a series of pictures. The limited influence of a mechanistic theory of perception in a traditional world, however, should be considered carefully. As we have shown earlier, the potential disjunction between "presence" and "appearance" became a crucial problem for seventeenth-century scientists and philosophers such as Galileo and Descartes. Yet artists could never accept a mechanistic optics as an exclusive model for disclosing truth. The experiencing subject was not a passive observer. We need only recall the dilemmas implicit in anamorphosis and the oblique architecture of

the seventeenth century, where the prime objective was to relocate man as an active participant. Furthermore, the awareness of the distorting dangers of vision was well established in classical theory: its clearest expression was the discussion of the need for optical correction in most architectural treatises, corresponding to the traditional *perspectiva naturalis*. This is the sort of optics on which most seventeenth-century perspective treatises were based. Indeed, the camera obscura did not have a universal appeal for writers on perspective,[5] and it is hardly surprising that artists never found it obvious to relate their work to the appearances produced in the device. Up to the eighteenth century, their aim was to represent a meaningful dimensionality expressed in terms of a geometric depth constructed behind the picture plane, one that would account for the *whole* of experience in a traditional cosmological horizon.

Despite variations in size and form, the technical apparatus of the camera obscura did not change much for two hundred years. Like many mechanical devices, during the seventeenth century it remained an instrument of wonder rather than a practical tool. In the eighteenth century it seems to have undergone only minor improvements, such as better lenses and innovative lens-and-mirror combinations. Although "tent" cameras were used sporadically, the most popular were box cameras, which worked by transmitting an image through a sheet of translucent paper. In these devices the image would have been barely visible, although a hood was fitted around the drawing area to prevent extraneous light. Primitive lenses normally limited the angle of view to about 35 degrees.

Although there is no explicit proof that the camera obscura was used in painting, many authors have speculated on its importance, particularly to account for the striking originality of seventeenth-century Dutch painting and "descriptive" arts.[6] The affinity between Northern European painting and retinal images frequently has been pointed out, particularly regarding the work of Jan Vermeer. Kepler's new optics often has been invoked to explain different modes of "picturing" in the North, minimizing the importance of the frame and the section through the visual cone that artists in Renaissance Italy used to tell a dramatic story (Alberti's *storia*). Northern painting certainly demonstrates a descriptive, "scientific" attitude, espe-

Various examples of camera obscura, from Johannes Zahn, *Oculus artificialis teledioptricus* (1685). Technically, the camera changed little from its inception to the daguerreotype, but until the nineteenth century it was rarely used for surveying or artistic endeavors.

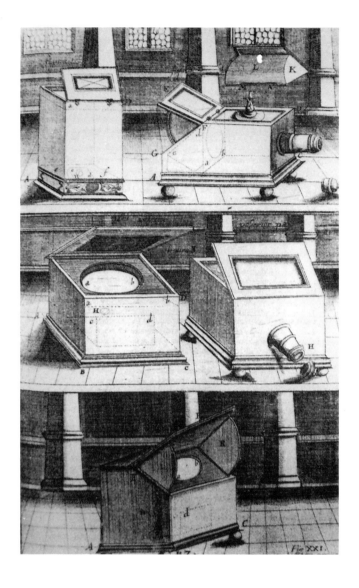

cially if compared with Southern "theatrical" space, with its emphasis on narratives. Unquestionably, Northern art and architectural representation have closer affinities to *perspectiva naturalis* and mapping. Perspective theory was influenced by Jean-Pelerin Viator's empirical "workshop method," while seventeenth-century Dutch writers often reiterated medieval optical notions such as extromission theories.[7] Yet for Northern painters, the issue also remained the disclosure of the meaningful depth of human experience *as* mathematical space.[8]

It is important to remember the overwhelming seventeenth-century faith in the possibility of a universal language, one whose origins were ultimately "pictorial" and whose nature is closely connected to the truth of the world of appearances, but one that is also conceived as a mathematical, syntactic, and logical structure.[9] In other words, the subjective mind and the objective world were named as the components of reality in modern philosophy, but only in the nineteenth century were they reified and emancipated. There was always a necessary co-presence of one to the other. Thus we must conclude that despite sporadic documented uses of the camera ob-

| 3.3 |

Samuel van Hoogstraten's peepshow box (ca. 1660). Seventeenth-century Dutch perspective boxes establish a specific viewpoint for the observer. The external geometry of the box disappears as soon as the spectator glances (with one eye) into the space as the shallow depth between the eye and the image deepens. Although the enclosed image recalls that of the camera obscura, the whole operation resembles baroque illusionist frescoes more than the autonomous constitution of an image in the camera obscura.

London, National Gallery.

Design for the upper part of a camera lucida [3.4] and a graphic telescope [3.5], from Cornelius Varley, *A Treatise on Optical Drawing Instruments* (1845); and a camera lucida [3.6] in the Science Museum, London. Synthesizing the optics of the camera obscura and the precise location of a subject (artist/observer) of the perspective machines, the nineteenth-century camera lucida and graphic telescope were useful and efficient means toward an end—unlike the camera obscura, which was a demonstration of "natural" optics. These new tools provided a simultaneous view of the tip of the drawing instrument and the reflected image, enabling an observer (now reduced to passive optical receptor) to make a systematic and precise reproduction of a visual image. The momentous epistemological transformation that underlies this synthesis of optics and geometric perspective would culminate in the photographic camera and other imaging techniques.

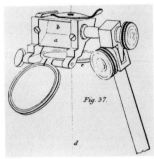

Fig. 37.

3.4

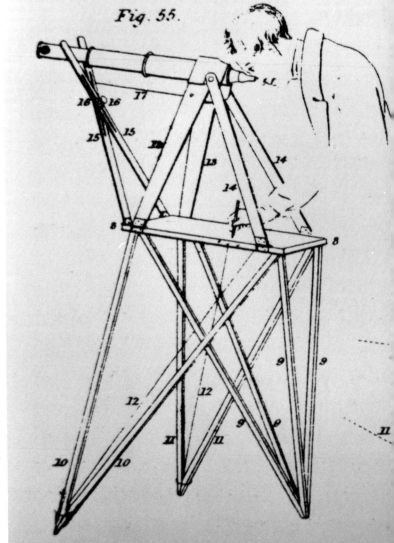

Fig. 55.

3.5

scura, seventeenth-century baroque images could not be reduced to a "copy" of visual reality (an objectified preexisting world), because reality was present only in the geometrical essence (of divine and human minds)—never fully explicit in the camera image. Even the most "descriptive" art seeks to reconcile itself with geometrical theories that "demonstrate" its ontological value. Thus we must qualify all forms of precise, geometric representation (architecture, cartography, fortifications) and the use of optical instruments during the seventeenth century. After 1650, perspectographs continued to be described in writings about perspective techniques, but there was less interest in perspective machines because it was no longer necessary to "demonstrate" the geometric construction of perspective through a mediating instrument. But during the eighteenth century, interest in the camera obscura did grow as a consequence of the naturalization of perspective previously described, as well as the popularization of British empiricism. The camera obscura increasingly was assumed to be a valid model of visual perception, capable of revealing the structural principles of Nature without imposing any inappropriate theories upon it.

3.6

In the wake of this tradition, the invention of the camera lucida at the beginning of the nineteenth century was significant as a culmination of the growing desire to depict the scientific, unmediated appearance of the world. Unlike the camera obscura, the camera lucida was created explicitly as an instrument for copying visual appearances. Although it remained relatively unknown and was never widely used by artists, different versions of this instrument were manufactured throughout the century. It embodied the first effective synthesis of scientific optics and *perspectiva artificialis,* possible only after important transformations in the epistemological assumptions of natural science and geometry had taken place. Patented by William H. Wollaston in 1806, the camera lucida provides a simultaneous view of the drawing instrument and a reflected image when the eye is positioned precisely.[10] The stated purpose of the device was to enable someone with no drawing skills— whether an artist, a scientist, or an engineer—to reproduce an image accurately. The device immediately was combined with telescopes and microscopes, creating an artificial control of the

The London Panorama, with a view of London by Thomas Hornor, from Rudolph Ackerman, *Graphic Illustrations of the Colosseum, Regent's Park* (1829). Popular panoramic views of cities and historical scenes, installed in specially constructed buildings in many European and North American cities, were meant to provide a truthful depiction of the subject matter, based on scientific optics.

angle of vision that made it possible to draw, for example, panoramic landscapes or "wild or savage animals without disturbing them"[11]—a true precursor of photography.

It is clear that these devices already manifested a different relationship between the observer and the world, one that has been defined as "voyeuristic." The objectification of external reality, so necessary for modern scientific documentation, was clearly a driving force behind these inventions, which aimed at "printing real sketches from nature, directly onto the (engraver's) stone."[12] Sir David Brewster, the inventor of the kaleidoscope and the refracting stereoscope, was fascinated by the camera lucida. He commended the graphic telescope (a variation of the camera lucida) for presenting scenes in "true perspective." Although the images may be "very steep or very flat," they are never distorted; thus when a background is mountainous, the graphic telescope reveals the "true proportions" of mountains, which are usually "exaggerated by artists." He believed the wish to gain credit for making sketches should be subordinated to the wish "to represent natural objects correctly."[13]

The instrumental uses of the camera lucida were also often related to the production of circular panoramas, those most popular attractions of the nineteenth century. The *Edinburgh Encyclopedia* (1830) set out a procedure for drawing such panoramas using a camera lucida on a telescope. The field view thus could be enlarged by diminishing the power of the telescope. The device was probably used by Thomas Hornor for his view of London from the top of St. Paul's Cathedral, one of the largest and most famous panoramas ever made.[14]

From Perspectivism to Pure Objectivity

Scientifically accurate representations, such as the cylindrical panoramas that were installed in every great city in Europe and North America, soon became the first stop on the itinerary of the new voyeuristic travelers of the nineteenth century. The basic principle of the camera lucida—using mirrors to project a ghostly image that would then be outlined with a drawing instrument—was also the basic principle for the immensely pop-

3.8

A stage magical trick performed with reflections in glass.

From Erik Barnouw, *The Magician and the Cinema* (New York: Oxford University Press, 1981).

ular stage magical tricks that fascinated nineteenth-century spectators, who were slowly being prepared for the magic of cinematography. The materialization of such phantasmagorias relied on the presence of a fully constituted and democratic "observer," the subject of the new dioramas and "dissolving frames" of Bouton and Daguerre that were deemed sensational in 1823: simultaneously a passive observer and political actor, emancipated from absolutist structures and from the "tyranny" of classical representation.[15] This complex condition can be summarized as arising from a deeply ingrained dichotomy between perspectivism (an acknowledgment of our necessarily relative point of view) and objectivity (the desire to find objective truth). This dichotomy splits the consciousness of contemporary men and women, often painfully, generating many well-documented pathologies, particularly the inability to "make sense" of one's life "here and now."[16]

The goal of "drawing" a cosmological picture like Lambert's, one that might vindicate a "true" way of representing our place in the world, became problematic in this context. Perspectivism, as an epistemological condition, had its origin in the eighteenth century. Lambert's work was perhaps one of its earliest formulations, although for him a personal perspective still could be reconciled with a theological (and scientific) conviction. Johann Martin Chladenius was the first to introduce the notion of "point of view" (*sehe-Punkt*) into hermeneutic considerations.[17] He associated the notion of perspective with the finite embodied nature of the interpreter and declared that the central problem of hermeneutics was the question of adjudication between perspectives, in order to arrive at the objective truth of a situation.[18] During the nineteenth century, differences of perspective were resolved by employing logical and systematic procedures in the hope that truth would be found either in the mind (intellectualism) or in the object (empiricism).

Art and architecture responded to this dualism, and the result was often solipsistic expression ("art for artists") or populist products ("commercial art"). In architecture, the most obvious polarization occurred between those who believed that architecture should adopt the "objective" values of engineering and applied science, mindful—in exceptional instances, at least—of sociological and behavioral "variables," and those who promoted the "artistic freedom" of the architect, a freedom that often led to irrelevant formalism, ranging from revivalism to "deconstruction." Yet, the same means of representation, when radicalized and imbued with ethical concerns, have produced works that manifestly transcend this dualism. The scopophilic subject, an optical receptor, may engage the mechanisms of reproduction and *mimēsis* in forms of renewed participation; the objective image, constructed as intentionally autonomous from a "natural" world of appearances, may be able to transcend its reductive and deadly stasis to become a tool of creativity and generator of enigmatic, embodied depth.

Philosophically, this transcendence corresponds to the realization that perspectives never yield completely to dialectical procedures and cannot be reduced by logical adjudication. The point is not to "find" truth but to "bring it into being," accepting the perspectival nature of perception while redefining reality beyond the objectified split of a *cogito* and its world in homogenized space and linear time. In the words of Paul Ricoeur, one can know one's perspective as perspective in the very act of perceiving only insofar as one can, somehow, escape it. According to Maurice Merleau-Ponty, since the Other's perspective exceeds one's own perspective, dialogue establishes both the limitation of perspective and the possibility of a lateral universality.[19] Nevertheless, language itself never escapes perspectivity. Unlike eighteenth-century works such as Chladenius's, the recent hermeneutics of ambiguity never claims to resolve completely, in an unambiguous way, the hermeneutic *aporia* concerning the possibility of truth. This formulation does not simply end in a despairing relativism but, as we shall see, corresponds to the unveiling of a "weak truth," as is present in the works of art of our tradition.

From Physics to Pataphysics

In the unified epistemological universe that survived until the late eighteenth century—one in which our common modes of specialization simply were not present—architects and theoreticians always acknowledged a relationship between their discipline and science. Indeed, in previous sections we have learned much about architectural representation by considering its relation to science.[20] Traditional and classical science, we should recall, always sought the "whole" and assumed that it was possible to reveal a meaningful order for man through a kind of discourse in which mathematical reason would not be at odds with narrative reason (the storytelling capacity that constitutes our basis for ethical action). Thus we were able to trace clear relationships between cosmology and the aspirations of architectural representation during the seventeenth and eighteenth centuries. Even Newtonian natural philosophy, despite its often explicit distinction between "true causes" and "laws," was grounded on an implicit metaphysics that included assumptions such as the identification of absolute space, the space of gravitation, with God. Newton's obsession with the Temple of Solomon represented his attempt to reconcile history and cosmology. Operating with a lived cosmology as an intersubjective point of departure, traditional science could reconcile truth-as-correspondence with the human experience of truth as a permanently shifting reality in everyday life. *Mythos* and *logos* could coexist in the same universe of discourse. The impact of Newtonian natural science on eighteenth-century architectural theory was greatly responsible for the delay in instrumentalizing theory. It also contributed to opening possibilities to develop alternative strategies to classical architecture: once the coincidence between history and cosmology was no longer self-evident, theoretical discourses associated architecture with language and the possibility of meaning with a hermeneutic approach to history through the notion of "character."[21]

After Laplace and Lagrange, in the early nineteenth century, science "purged" itself of speculation. Philosophy, we may remember, tried to follow suit. In his *Prolegomena to Any Future Metaphysics* (1783), Immanuel Kant sought to avoid discourse outside the strict parameters of mathematical logic; he particularly shunned metaphysical and theological speculation, recognizing that science could offer only partial truths, probabilities, or instrumental devices. Science stopped being concerned with either the whole "picture" or with essences, however much it would like to engage with such matters, especially when facing the enigma of the universe's creation. While it is impossible to generalize, this assumption has not changed since the nineteenth century, whether we examine the premises of fundamental physics, such as quantum electrodynamics, or of chaos theory.

For this reason, there is a basic aspect of Husserl's famous diagnosis of the crisis of European sciences that remains accurate.[22] Husserl believed that while increasing specialization and mathematization of all disciplines would result in a greater instrumentality and more effective control of practical tasks, the discourse and its products would be alienated from the expectations of lived experience. Human beings need language and artifacts to make sense of their world in the present, here and now. Husserl justly feared that specialized and positivistic scientific discourses would never be able to reconstitute the place for human dwelling, the poetic instant that may bring life and death to a single point of incandescent purpose. His diagnosis has direct consequences for architecture, concerned as it is with the life world.

Husserl was originally a mathematician. His obsession to make a rigorous science out of philosophy, continuing the philosophical vocation of the Western world, suggested to his disciples the possibility of developing a discourse for the *exceptional,* a *logos* to account for the thick vivid present of our everyday experience. Although Husserl himself fell short of grasping the full consequences of his insight, the philosophical understanding that stemmed from his thought was a recognition that experience, always mutable and changing, is "given" with a framework of categories. In the disorder of appearance there is order that makes meaning possible in the first place. Meaning is not simply a product of our mind, nor is it simply "out there": it appears literally in between. This is the fundamental character of our human reality. The world is neither chaos nor cosmos (in the sense of a dichotomy of order and disorder); rather, it is indeed *chaosmos,* the world revealed by James Joyce and Marcel Duchamp.

Some years later, speculative scientists arrived at analogous descriptions of reality. There are points of contact between chaos theory—in its questioning of classical physics, by examining concrete, ordinary phenomena—and phenomenology, just as there is a striking resemblance between some of Heidegger's and Heisenberg's philosophical concepts. It is impossible not to acknowledge a relationship between the space-time of Feynman's quantum electrodynamics—in which particles behave differently according to the experiment being performed, where time is reversible and light's essence must be proclaimed as utterly strange[23]—and the thick temporality of experience described by Merleau-Ponty as "the flesh of the world." For phenomenology, the elasticity of time and dimensionality are evident through the primary engagement of embodied being in the world; for example, vertical dimension is always greater than the identical horizontal measurement. Yet despite these interesting connections between science and philosophy, there are important differences, particularly when we consider the relationship between language and creative or productive action.

In recent years some architects have become fascinated by potential applications of chaos theory, especially fractal geometry, to questions of formal generation. Chaos theory is indeed different from classical physics in its expectation of finding complex behavior as a result of simple systems and in its understanding that complex systems give rise to simple behavior; it presumes that the laws of complexity hold universally, caring not at all for the details of a system's constituent parts.[24] In demonstrating self-similarity, chaos theory seems to recall Leibniz's seventeenth-century notion that "the world is in a drop of water," leading to the understanding that everything is connected. This is a formidable and exciting realization. Contemporary science is finally in a position to comprehend that the ancient analogical assumptions that drove traditional architecture and science were not merely foolish dreams. Scientific narratives about a living world and the life of minerals, about the body without organs, and about nature as a machine without parts are growing in popularity. Mandelbrot's fractals have demonstrated how the structures of the different orders of nature are analogous, despite scalar changes. Having conceived the reality of the world in a similar fashion, Leibniz had postulated a formal discipline, a "universal calculus," as the point of departure for action. In this baroque framework, formal (geometrical) manipulations were *also* substantial operations that revealed the meaning and purpose of creation. It is important to remember, however, that Leibniz could start from the mathematical realm and operate on his *clavis universalis* because of his theological a priori. God had ordered the world and chosen the best possible. God was at the end (and the beginning) of it all. Leibniz imagined our free will as a ferry boat in a river; we all, individual monads, go our own chosen ways, while we are still loosely guided by divine Providence. On this account, human action, however intelligently articulated, was still operating in a traditional world.[25]

The disjunction of form and content in aesthetics was indeed a baroque "invention," and anamorphosis most eloquently demonstrated this initial disjunction. But the splitting of art into form and content is also the result of our civilization being "thrown" into history. It could be argued that before the Enlightenment, particularly before the works of Vico and Rousseau, human actions were more or less irrelevant with respect to the explicit order of creation. Renaissance architecture, for example, turned its eyes toward the past, but only to confirm its actions of reconciliation with a cosmological order that was perceived as absolutely transhistorical, just as History was identified with the sacred narrative of the church. Modern history, on the other hand, assumes that human actions *truly* matter, that they can effectively change things (like the French Revolution), that there is potential *progress* (of course, the driving notion of modern science and technology), and that the present is qualitatively different from the past. This vector, which characterized modernity, was questioned first by Nietzsche and more recently by postmodern cultural critics.

In this regard, we share Gianni Vattimo's perception that while History as the Grand Narrative of progress and the quest for novelty may have ended, we must yet accept our historicity. We can never simply overcome modernity and leave it behind: instead, we can convalesce, heal ourselves of resentment, and reconcile our present with our past. In other words, it is time to embrace, rather than try to resolve, the *aporia*s associated with our human condition since the nineteenth century. We cannot act as if we lived in a cosmological epoch, in a perpetual present, where there would indeed be no distinction between architectural form and content and where we could thus abdicate responsibility for our actions, nor can we merely pretend to continue the project of modernity with its future orientation, its absurd disjunctions of form and content, and its deferral of responsibility. All we can do is modify the terms of our relationship to historicity, accepting the multiplicity of discourses and traditions, while assuming our personal responsibility for projecting a better future.

If we persevere in our obsessive search for a scientific theory of architecture, we may finally stumble upon a model that is truly appropriate for the architect's search for form: Alfred Jarry's "science" of pataphysics. As opposed to traditional science, pataphysics celebrates the sheer unlikeliness of pure theory, noting the remarkable improbability of the circumstance that we live on Earth *and* are able to see the stars. Indeed, pataphysics reminds us that the conditions necessary for life do not exclude those necessary for vision or vice versa, an exceptional point, often overlooked. Earth's unique atmosphere, transparent yet protective against cosmic rays and particles, allows a creature bent on self-preservation to lift its gaze beyond the realm of biological necessity to see the "star-dance of the heavens," the origin of all science and art. In order to memorialize this anthropological significance of vision, usually disregarded by contemporary science and philosophy, pataphysics literally casts cosmology into art. Thus it creates the possibility of a new understanding of our place in the universe, a "negative cosmology" of sorts. It brings together Anaxagoras's insight (fifth century B.C.E.) that a good reason to be born rather than not would be "for the sake of viewing the heavens and the whole order of the universe,"[26] with the realization, revealed to our vision by recent space probes and telescopes but incompatible with post-Copernican astronomy, that Earth may indeed be a unique oasis of life in a dead universe.[27]

Pataphysics is, of course, a paradoxical science. Although it dates from the early twentieth century, and its program often has been trivialized, the consequences of Jarry's "science" are still radical. Pataphysics is the science of the exceptional, a science of imaginary solutions, a celebration of mystery; indeed, it is analogous to art. Its master key is *irony:* what science clarifies is what remains obscure. Pataphysics enacts discovery through making; it celebrates technical processes and architecture as a verb. The artist's life is the paradigmatic work of art. In this sense the aim to deconstruct the distance between form and content is truly radicalized, in the only way possible for the twentieth century: Jarry became Ubu Roi, a process of self-transformation that takes precedence over formal products. Pataphysics demands a new relationship between thinking and making, where the thinking and values are crucial and the act "calculated," yet there is never a method or instrumental theory. In fact what Jarry described was the potential of art to embody a different kind of truth: the "unveiling" of Martin Heidegger, the blow of Walter Benjamin, the "weak truth" of Gianni Vattimo. Art and architecture communicate, but what they "say" cannot be transcribed. What they are cannot be reduced to information bits. The truth conveyed by art can be experienced only in its own medium, in the specificity of the work at hand.

As the ironic embodiment of the scientific project, we can understand pataphysics as the culmination of Western science and as a potential model for architecture. While the positive sciences demythified traditional natural science and philosophy, pataphysics demythifies positivism, revealing the potential richness of a technological world assumed to be prosaic, solid, and merely factual. This may be particularly relevant as we discover that architectural theory *is not* science, but that architecture as a mode of production *is* necessarily technology. The result is a theoretical discourse in the form of ontological hermeneutics (historical narratives) and a practice in the form of a poetics (fictional narratives) that emphasizes the *gap* between the two terms of a metaphor, revealing it as the place where meaning is present to experience, rather than expecting the particular analogy to disclose to our intellect *an* objectified meaning that could then be translated to other universes of discourse.

The Perspective Hinge

What is perspective?
A corpse with one eye closed.
The architect of the Middle Ages
could build because
he could not draw descriptive
geometry and perspective.

Bruno Taut,
Frühlicht 1920–1922

The desire for precise measurement and comprehensive representation of building projects became dominant in architectural theory at the turn of the nineteenth century. Durand's *mécanisme de la composition* supported his new rational and specialized theory, free from metaphysical speculation. Rather than relying on formal or stylistic traditions, his method for generating form placed the value of "architectural composition" in the syntactic relationship of parts. Although their intentions were fundamentally different, Durand's theory already prefigured the discourses of early-twentieth-century writers such as Lissitsky and Van Doesburg.[28] Indeed, one must fully understand that Durand's *mécanisme* operated in the new space of Monge's descriptive geometry,[29] an objectified matrix that would be identified eventually as the space of axonometric projection. In Durand's case, the *mécanisme* was clearly intended to be reductive. Emphasizing the affinity between architecture and engineering, he questioned the artistic pursuits of his immediate predecessors and teachers, such as Boullée and Ledoux, and criticized the architectural use of pictorial forms of representation. In his *Pré-*

cis, Durand expressed the notion that architects should be unconcerned with meaning; if the architectural problem was efficiently solved, meaning would follow. This led to an indictment of watercolor and any "artistic" means of representation in pursuit of "character."[30] His projects and examples invariably were pristine plans, sections, and elevations, drawn with fine ink lines guided by the modular grid of the *mécanisme.* The aim was to represent the project objectively; the subjective observer we associate with perspective's point of view was consistently ignored.

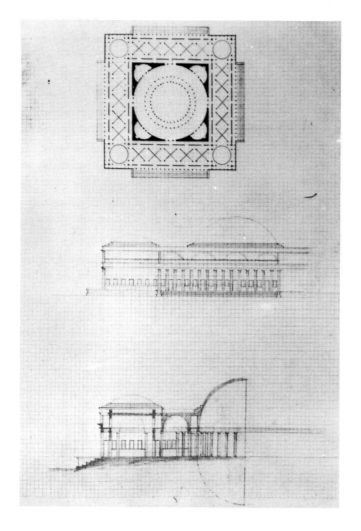

| 3.9 |

J.-N.-L. Durand's "mechanism of composition," the basic design tool in his *Précis des Leçons d'Architecture* (1819). The grid became an indispensable modular framework for architectural design in the student projects of the École Polytechnique and the École des Beaux-Arts.

Significantly, there is only one plate in Durand's work, added to the second edition of the *Précis,* in which two-point perspective was used to illustrate the volumetric "results of diverse horizontal and vertical combinations." For the first time since Perrault's indictment of proportions as a vehicle for "positive" beauty, Durand had articulated with great clarity the limitations that perspective imposes on architecture. It made the traditional concern for proportion in buildings irrelevant, given the unavoidable reality of constantly shifting and variable points of view. Indeed, while Durand reiterated Perrault's argument about the "absurdity" of optical correction, a new generation of writers used the same scientific understanding of optics to propose "better and more efficient" methods of perspectival representation. Despite the lack of interest in the subject during the eighteenth century, numerous works on perspective were published in the nineteenth century—at least thirty books between 1820 and 1860 in France alone. Johann Maria von

| 3.10 |

The only plate in Durand's *Précis* that uses perspective to illustrate the volumetric result of compositional combinations.

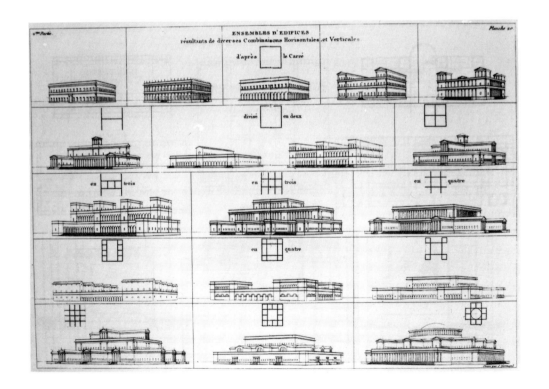

Quaglio, for example, who wrote *A Practical Guide to Perspective with Applications to Architecture* (1811), insisted that very few works seemed to have demonstrated clearly the subject of practical perspective as it applies to architecture. However strange it may seem to us, von Quaglio truly believed he was teaching a new form of architectural representation. He drew from the practical rules of sixteenth-century authors, consciously disregarding Pozzo and Bibiena, and insisted that "perspective shows us only the apparent and not the true forms of objects." Perspective drawing thus differs from geometric (orthographic) drawings "in that the latter represents the true position of objects with their real proportions, while the former represents the apparent form of those proportions when viewed from one single point."[31] For von Quaglio, as for most nineteenth-century writers on perspective, the aim was to produce "illusionistic" drawings—delusions, in fact—of a sort that had never been produced in architecture before. This tradition of "presentation" drawings still exists in contemporary architectural education around the world—drawings that always waver self-consciously between truth and deception.

The new nineteenth-century three-point and curvilinear perspective systems are extreme examples of this tradition. In 1836 Arthur Parsey announced his novel system that accounted for upward convergence. In *Perspective Rectified* (1836) and *The Science of Vision or Natural Perspective!* (1840), he claimed to have reached a synthesis of perspective and "natural

| 3.11 |

A three-point perspective, from Arthur Parsey's *Science of Vision* (1840).

Curvilinear perspective of an interior space, from William Herdmann's *Curvilinear Perspective* (1853).

vision" that, in his view, had never been accomplished in previous theories.[32] As with William Herdmann's *Treatise on the Curvilinear Perspective of Nature* (1853),[33] the issue can be summarized as a sort of inversion of the traditional argument for optical correction in architecture. The awareness of the autonomy of visual appearance, first articulated in Euclid's *Optics* and transformed by Kepler's mechanistic optics, modern physiology, and psychology, eventually resulted in an understanding of perception that construed meaning as the association of sensory data from autonomous senses. Thus Euclid's initial awareness could be transformed into an obsession to re-present an accurate retinal impression.

There were, of course, critical arguments and dissenting voices. John Ruskin, for example, recast Hoogstraten's argument by insisting that three-point perspective was inappropriate because the lines on the canvas are also subject to perspective distortion and therefore should not be painted as converging toward the top.[34] Regardless of the stated opinion of writers, architects, and artists, however, it is clear that during the nineteenth century perspective became "an object as experienced . . . , no longer a mathematical calculation."[35] In his influential *Handbook of Physiological Optics* (1856–1866), Hermann Ludwig Ferdinand von Helmholtz posited that a Kantian, a priori geometric space is the foundation for sensory intuition. If the direct perception of geometry and mathematics is made possible by such an a priori, we may assume that the space of our experience is precisely this homogeneous reality, enabling perspective to become the true image of the world—and thus anticipating documentary photography. The assumption that perspective is the "natural" way of seeing was also made in a popular book by Peter Schmid, *Das Naturzeichen,* published four times between 1828 and 1832, and in the influential pedagogical program of Johann Heinrich Pestalozzi, who believed that an important part of a proper education consisted in teaching children how to draw simple solids in perspective.

Not surprisingly, given this context, the Beaux-Arts architects of the nineteenth century could not immediately live up to the full, radical implications of Durand's theory. While the planning of buildings usually took place in a very short time, as stipulated by the school's competition regulations and the general desire for efficiency inherited from Durand's *Précis,* architects still felt the need to present their projects through grand perspectival representations and spent several months rendering them. These elaborate and often admired renderings made the projects comprehensible to the uninitiated, and they came to represent the "specificity" of the architect's *métier,* which had become problematic because of its threatened identification with the "mere" construction of efficient, well-engineered buildings. Nevertheless, the apparent objectivity of the project, dominated by precise scale and invariably judged in

| 3.13 |

Perspective by Viollet-le-Duc for his competition entry for the Opéra, Paris (1861).

Paris, Centre de recherche sur les monuments historiques, Palais de Chaillot.

terms of a *promenade* (a linear, voyeuristic "visit"), was always pervasive.[36]

Indeed, it is important to recognize that modern architecture's "objective space" originated with descriptive geometry, and that perspective theory was the *invisible hinge* systematizing its projections. Monge's late-eighteenth-century descriptive geometry was not merely an abstract mathematical formulation: it was driven by a desire to *describe* reality with absolute precision.[37] His often-expressed aim was to provide a truly efficient practical tool for technical and constructive operations. To fulfill this aim, however, Monge effectively had to functionalize Euclidean geometry, that is, to abstract this classical science by reducing it to algebraic functions. This he accomplished by systematizing the use of projections and bringing them into line with scientific optics. Clearly, an awareness of the properties of projective representation had been developing since the fifteenth or sixteenth centuries. However, the geometrical operations had never been constituted as a systematic method, as a series of coordinated steps *independent* of the objects being represented and independent of the ultimate purpose of the task at hand (with the significant exception of Desargues's *manière universelle*). Monge's *Géométrie descriptive* (1798) provided the first truly synthetic and systematized method that could be applied universally to all arts and crafts.

| 3.14 |

Drawing from Jules Pillet's *Shades and Shadows* (Philadelphia, 1896), showing how to construct shadows using the rigid system of descriptive geometry. Pillet's manual was used as a textbook by engineering students at the École Polytechnique and architecture students at the École des Beaux-Arts in the late nineteenth and early twentieth century.

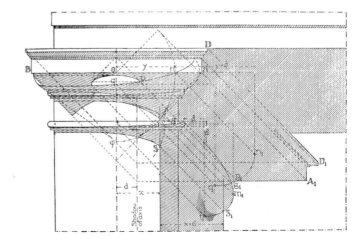

Some contemporary commentators such as J. B. Delambre stressed that while Euclidean geometry could measure only areas and volumes linearly, descriptive geometry could now consider "space itself" mathematically.[38] Monge understood that while the primary purpose of descriptive geometry was to represent three-dimensional objects for technological purposes, its origin in both geometry and algebra (associated with the notions of intuition and cognition) made it an epistemological model for the acquisition of truth. The success of descriptive geometry as a tool of representation was often acknowledged in the nineteenth century,[39] and this new discipline was instrumental in the development of industrial technologies and engineering. In mathematics, however, Monge's geometry was regarded as a crucial step toward more abstract and general methods. This aspect of his "general theory" motivated one of his most brilliant disciples, Jean-Victor Poncelet, to write his *Traité des propriétés projectives des figures* in 1822.

Monge finally had made it possible to "do algebra with geometry."[40] The "secret" of algebra is the "mechanism of transformations" that allows it to achieve a high degree of generality. Monge tacitly applied this mechanism to geometry, discovering a "principle of continuity" between the volume and the plane. It was Poncelet, however, who expressly discussed this principle of continuity, articulating the projective principles at work in the functionalization of reality. Poncelet had no need for Monge's orthogonal planes, for his transformational theory no longer gave priority to any direction, emphasizing continuity instead. For him, every geometric line and figure was merely a transformation, without intrinsic qualities; an infinite line was homologous to a circle, while no figure had true qualitative specificity. At the same time, Poncelet's geometry was an abstract discipline, constructed upon its own "internal" truths and ultimately *unconcerned* with representation. Poncelet's geometry had no need of images; its interest was to determine the relationships of position in geometric figures that remain constant before and after they are projected in perspective. Perhaps significantly, Poncelet's geometry was drafted while he was in prison in Russia during the Napoleonic campaign. He was obsessed with increasing the generality of theories in the mathematical sciences so that their realm of action could remain under the control of the intellect.[41] He clearly realized that Euclidean geometry relied on arithmetic and specific figures that diminished its generality and prevented a uniform method. In contrast, the universality of descriptive geometry, linking extension to algebra, "derived exclusively from the use of projections."[42] The projective properties—those that remain constant before and after a projection—constituted the true nature of figures. Their "essence," a complex of formal relations or transformations that remained independent of the visible world, therefore could be general, indeterminate, and independent of absolute dimensions. In Euclidean geometry every figure was qualitatively different; in each case properties and rules had to be deduced from sensuous appearance. For Poncelet, each form was examined not individually, but as part of a system to which it belonged and as an expression of the totality of forms into which it could be transformed through projection. Poncelet was the first to fully realize the consequences of Desargues's perspective geometry, establishing a clear and unambiguous homology between two-dimensional planes and three-dimensional space. All points projected to infinity on a plane could also be considered ideally as part of a straight line itself placed at infinity. Desargues's insights had been considered by other geometricians of the eighteenth century, but the apparently unacceptable implications of identifying lived space with infinity always kept this revolutionary systematization at bay.

Poncelet's projective geometry signaled the first effective assimilation of optics into geometric perspective, resulting in a comprehensive theoretical discipline. Whereas the optics of Monge's descriptive geometry was already that of the photographic camera, for Poncelet optics itself became irrelevant for truth. "Imaging" became potentially liberated from retinal hegemony, enabling its use in exploring other avenues conducive to a disclosure of truly scientific "internal" orders in the empirical world, such as those presented in functional diagrams and typologies in architecture.[43] Poncelet's formulation anticipated a multitude of abstract theoretical disciplines emancipated from intuition. The same epistemological transformation that made possible the Industrial Revolution, technological domination, and an often irresponsible exploitation of resources, however, was also instrumental for the invention of perspectival artifacts and machines (such as photography and cinematography, panoramas and dioramas),[44] capable of questioning, through human experience itself, the demystification underlying their own premises. These new devices revealed the mystery of depth through a critical "recovery" of the temporal dimension of lived experience, a dimension intentionally excluded or disregarded by technological forms of perspectival reduction and enframing, and they thus led to whole new possibilities for art and architecture.

Poncelet's theory also suggested the homology of the mind and the world, a notion that perhaps had always been present in traditional Eastern philosophies, but that in the European context resulted in the power to "substitute" the ideal for the real. This truly novel power is at the root of not only humanity's profound disorientation and Platonizing scientism but also the redemptive potential discovered by modern art since the early nineteenth century—and more particularly in the first two decades of the twentieth century after impressionism had taken the optic paradigms to their limit.[45] With Poncelet, geometry became an abstract, self-referential, syntactic system, capable of dispensing even with algebra, which pointed the way toward yet more conceptual non-Euclidean, multidimensional geometries. Its problems no longer needed to be placed in the lived world. It was ideal for technical applications based on pure logic and reduction since it did not rely on imagination. But this geometry that is both projective and turns its back on representation (as a mere copy of a prosaic sensual world) seems to encompass a saving power once the imagination is reactivated. That power is precisely the potential exploited by modern art and poetry to create new worlds, to express something worth saying by first speaking "of nothing" at all—the only option for art after the break with traditional cosmology.

From Measurement to Abstraction: Isometry and Axonometry

As objectified representations, isometry and axonometry occupy the ambivalent space opened up between the geometries of Monge and Poncelet, oscillating between the extremes of self-evident representation (accurate description) and self-referential formulation (freedom from representation).

The terms used to describe parallel projections in the European languages changed through time, and this has created some historiographic confusion. Axonometry sometimes was defined as a special case of isometry, and vice versa. Commentators have often confused them and have tended to disregard their implicit epistemological assumptions. Today, in the wake of Desargues and Lambert, we should recognize that isometry ("the equality of measures or dimensions") derives from a perspective construction in which the converging points are postulated at infinity, so that parallel lines can remain parallel. In the eighteenth century, it was usually conceived as a perspectival, "realistic" drawing by a very distant observer, or a drawing of a very small object (such as a scale model). We have argued that such a "tactile" concept was usually behind the use of isometric drawings and the very rare examples of axonometry prior to the nineteenth century. The desire for precision, which was also certainly present before the Industrial Revolution, appears to be related to isometric drawings mainly in the tradition of military architecture and surveying. The notion of infinity *in* the world, however, was impossible to reconcile with experience. Not even brilliant mathematicians such as Lambert and Saccheri

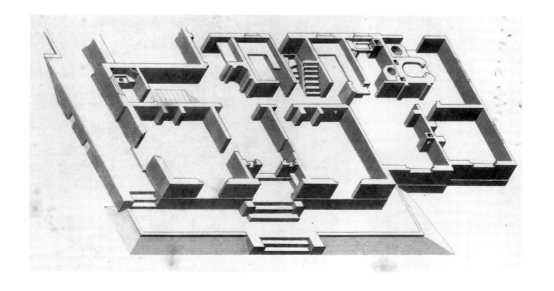

considered disproving Euclid's first postulate concerning the nonconvergence of parallel lines. Throughout the eighteenth century, the sublime infinity of nature preserved its inveterate sacred character; it was, in fact, *not* merely the space of everyday life, but the space revealed through representations such as Turner's paintings and Boullée's theoretical projects. In other words, parallel projection could not become a paradigmatic form of representation until the nineteenth century, when society could assume lived space, the space of the world and nature, to be infinite (and fully de-sacralized), both economically and physically. Paradoxically, parallel projection then became for the first time fully "perspectival": that is, generated by assuming its existence *in* the world of human experience, with its vanishing point at infinity. Furthermore, it should be remembered that the precise measurements needed for effective scaled representation demanded standard units. The project to develop a standardized system of measurement that superseded the local anthropometric units of measurement in prerevolutionary Europe was also an early nineteenth-century development.[46] Only after these developments could isometric drawing become fully autonomous from "deceptive" perspective drawings, and thus function as a truly efficient tool for technological representation.

It is in this sense that the importance of isometric drawing was celebrated by William Farrish in *Isometrical Perspective* (1820) and Joseph Jopling in *The Practice of Isometrical Perspective* (1835), the first complete treatises devoted exclusively to this topic. Farrish points out that this method is "preferable to the common perspective on many accounts[;] . . . it represents straight lines, which lie on the three principal directions, all on the same scale."[47] Jopling emphasizes that the success of this method is due to its applicability to cities, buildings and their details, bridges, canal locks, ornaments and furniture, mining, shipbuilding, machines, steam engines, models, scientific instruments, fortifications, land surveying, and the specification of patents.[48] "Isometrical perspective" was defined as a particular projection based on the representation of a cube. "The words imply that the measure of the representation of the lines forming the sides of each face are equal."[49] Isometry, therefore, started from a cubic space (existing as an a priori precondition)

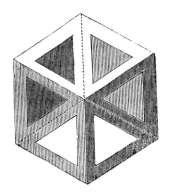

| 3.16 |

The cubic space of containment of isometric representation, from Jopling's treatise. Jopling labors to explain why the represented angles of the cube are not orthogonal, still emphasizing that appearance depends entirely upon the orientation of the image in relation to the observer.

Montreal, Collection Centre Canadien d'Architecture / Canadian Centre for Architecture.

that accepts "real" scaled measurements onto its faces. In Jopling's book, the procedure repeated in every exercise from the simple to the complex was always a "carving" of cubic space. Indeed, unlike all previous treatises in the Western tradition on the pictorial representation of volumes, the obsessive representation of Jopling's spatial matrix seems to take precedence over the objects it contains. All operations were based on a relationship between the three-dimensional cubic space, in which the orthogonal angles of the faces are represented by alternating angles of 60 degrees and 120 degrees, and the geometry of a two-dimensional hexagon. It is important to remember, however, that unlike axonometric drawings, isometric projections do not preserve any "real" angular dimensions. Furthermore, a "residual" observer is always present, as orientation seems to change the "nature" of the represented object. Jopling was fascinated by the fact that each of the objects in his treatise may be viewed in at least six different ways, so that the diagrams "may be considered equivalent to about *one thousand* representations of different objects." He emphasized that appearance "depends entirely upon the orientation of the image in relation to the observer" and the representation often flips from concave to convex, transforming the image from a space to a mass.[50]

Jopling's seemingly anachronistic and somewhat contradictory interest in the observer's position may be better understood in light of Hegel's interest in subjective vision and his definition of space. Hegel's concept of space was related to both isometric projection and the "perspectival" forms of representation that dominated nineteenth-century painting (romanticism, realism, symbolism, impressionism), literature (the authorial, subjective narratives of the romantic novel), and architecture (the academic work of the École des Beaux-Arts). On one hand, Hegel emphasized the importance of visual intuition as "the concrete awareness of actual things in surrounding space[,] . . . a space known to be present and real all around us[,] . . . the space we ourselves share." This notion could be interpreted as a precocious criticism of the "reflexive vision" associated with the perspectival observer and the mastering gaze.[51] On the other hand, however, he defined space as a homogeneous entity constituted by three dimensions that "are merely different, and quite devoid of determinations. . . . Consequently one cannot say how height, length and breadth (i.e., depth) differ from one another. . . . [I]t is a matter of indifference whether we call a certain direction height or depth; it is the same with length or breadth, which is also called depth, for nothing is determined in this way."[52] This absence of qualitative specificity in Hegel's definition of orientation makes clear that he is postulating space as an isotropic, geometric entity, contradicting the possibility of any vision "other" than the dominating gaze of perspective. In retrospect we can now understand that the presence of a "misunderstood" and well-intentioned subjectivity, extremely close to the Cartesian ego, tended to occlude the assumptions of modernity and thus postponed the possibility of radicalizing objectivity and abstraction in order to transcend modernity's negative, reductive aspects. The resulting reconciliatory formula, a sort of uncritical phenomenalism, which was embraced consciously or unconsciously by the most popular artistic disciplines during the nineteenth century, in effect perpetuated the delusions of an autonomous "aesthetic representation" (art for art's sake) and held back the necessary radicalization of subjective experience and of objective, abstract representation—both of which we may now recognize as our hope for retrieving a truly participatory artistic culture.

Jopling's interest in the relationship between objective representation and subjective appearance in isometry was generally not shared by authors interested in axonometric projec-

311

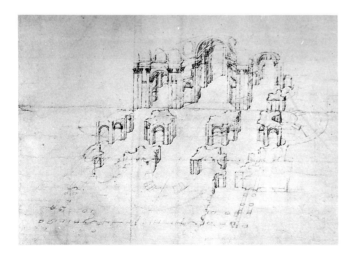

| 3.17 |

Baldassare Peruzzi's perspectival "section" of a centralized project for St. Peter's in Rome (between 1520 and 1535). In this exceptional drawing the architect clearly intended to visualize the "precise" internal configuration of space, although the cut through the pilasters recalls the materiality of a scale model.

Florence, Palazzo degli Uffizi.

A projective experiment from Jacques Androuet du Cerceau's *Livre d'architecture* (1582). Driven by a desire for precision, du Cerceau seems to abandon an earlier interest in aerial perspective (*scenographia*) to present a whole "idea" of his projects through composite "elevations in depth," producing a dimensionality not unlike frontal axonometrics.

Montreal, Collection Centre Canadien d'Architecture / Canadian Centre for Architecture.

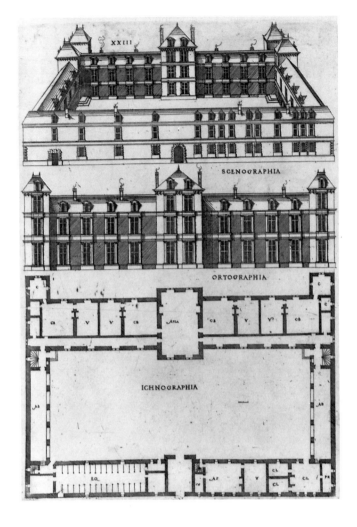

tion. One could argue that while isometry's origins may be traced back to the desire for precision that emerged after the Renaissance, axonometric projection is related strictly to nineteenth- and twentieth-century European epistemology. There were well-known examples of synthetic drawings in the European tradition, such as Peruzzi's famous perspective/section of St. Peter's Basilica in Rome and some of the experiments of du Cerceau, but these combinations of projections very rarely attained the universality, precision, and systematization required in axonometry. Axonometric projection could in fact be defined as a synthetic descriptive geometry. Its name also implies precise measurement, but this time along the three axes of homogenized space (x, y, and z), which are assumed to be qualitatively identical. Unlike the isometric "carving" of cubic space, axonometry is a constructive concept, usually generated from the plan, the paradigmatic modern generator of architectural form. Most significantly, of course, this objectified projection rids itself of a gravity-bound, embodied, and oriented subject. The perspective "hinge" becomes totally invisible and abstraction is taken a step further as the horizon is completely

| 3.19 |

An axonometric representation, from Auguste Choisy, *L'art de bâtir chez les romains* (1873), demonstrating the "determining" structural concept of a late Roman building.

Montreal, Collection Centre Canadien d'Architecture / Canadian Centre for Architecture.

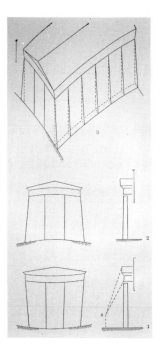

obliterated. The task is no longer to represent the *appearances* but the *objectivity* of precise measurements: the angles in plan as well as the vertical and horizontal dimensions.

Axonometric projection was first taught in engineering schools in the late nineteenth century for its usefulness as an accurate technical tool. In the architectural world, Auguste Choisy was the first author to use axonometric projections extensively. In his famous works on the history of architecture, published between 1873 and 1899, he used mostly worm's-eye-view axonometric projections and isometric projections to demonstrate what he assumed to be the deterministic principles according to which the great buildings of history were conceived.[53] His basic thesis already had been expressed earlier in the nineteenth century by Jean Rondelet: architectural form simply results from technical imperatives. This reductive view of architectural history as an unambiguous narrative of linear progress toward the technological ideals of efficiency was present throughout the century. Choisy's deliberate choice of axonometry as the appropriate form of representation for such a history, however, finally made explicit its previously hidden "objective truth." In a concise statement preceding the 1929 edition of his *Histoire de l'architecture,* he acknowledged that superfluous details have been suppressed from the "graphic documents" presented in axonometric projection, a system that possesses "the clarity of perspective while allowing for precise and immediate measurements." By using axonometry, Choisy claims that "one sole image, animated and in motion like the building itself, takes the place of abstract figuration" that fractures the whole building into plan, section, and elevation. It is important that "the reader has simultaneously under his eyes the plan, the exterior of the building, its section, and its internal disposition. All these figures are accompanied by a scale."[54]

Choisy also produced, late in his life, a translation of Vitruvius's *De architectura.* Not surprisingly, this is a very inaccurate and reduced version of the Latin text, emphasizing Vitruvius's progressive "discoveries" while criticizing his "excess of metaphysics" and "failed" inventions.[55] Choisy believed that for Vitruvius architecture was "synonymous to applied science," and he renders the text as a concise method for the "composition of buildings."[56] Translating the passage on architectural *ideae,* he repeats Perrault's misreading, taking for granted the inclusion of perspective, while assuming in addition that Vitruvius was referring to scaled drawings (*metriquement dessinés*) when defining the plan, or *ichnographia* (*tracé en plan*), and the elevation, or *orthographia* (*tracé en élévation*). One of Choisy's greatest innovations was to add a "graphic summary" of the treatise as a separate section. Here he illustrates with his characteristic drawings what he understood Vitruvius to be speaking about, freely improving on technical details, providing not only plans and elevations with precise, thin lines, but also axonometric drawings of buildings and machines. In two consecutive plates he summarizes all the different kinds of optical corrections that Vitruvius had named, including those addressing the thickening of the angle columns, the tapering of columns for verticality, the dimensions and projection of high elements like architraves, the fluting of columns on different planes, and the countercurvature of horizontal elements. The plates are particularly striking when one realizes, in light of the history of the problem as we have traced it, the absurdity of representing in the objective space of axonometry a practice that grew from a diametrically opposed understanding of the truth of reality.

Choisy's theory, implicit in his history, was indeed the culmination of the reductive dream. The architect could then regard himself as an absolute master-demiurge, in total control of the building operation from conception to execution, capable of a synthetic understanding that would ensure the act of design to be in agreement with the "Truth." For style, according to Choisy, "doesn't change according to fashion. . . . [I]ts variations are but changes in the process (of construction) and the logic of methods implies the chronology of styles."[57] All of the significant historical buildings that appear in his many books were represented in axonometric projection, suspended and freed from gravity, and presented as the result of a synthetic, all-powerful technical mentality that Choisy believed had operated indiscriminately throughout history.

It is nevertheless interesting that axonometric drawing in the nineteenth century could not rid itself of shadows. Jules de la Gournerie, Monge's disciple and the author of a treatise on descriptive geometry, insisted on the use of shadows in axo-

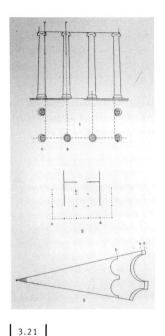

| 3.21 |

"Detail of optical corrections concerning the verticality and size of columns," from Choisy's translation of Vitruvius.

nometric drawing to avoid ambiguity.[58] Axonometry implicitly may question the perspectival subject, yet it is also a form of optical representation that flaunts its clarity and freedom from atmospheric distortions. This is the paradox that we must understand in order to engage it critically. We may remember that the "subject" of traditional perspective representation (and pre-revolutionary European architecture) was always an active, embodied observer, never totally disconnected from the world's passions and motions, willing to acknowledge and remain subordinate to the larger orders of nature and politics. Axonometry, on the other hand, addresses a disembodied observer in pursuit of individual prosperity, freedom, and pleasure—a passive observer for the first time capable of self-conscious disengagement from the limits granted by the body and the world. Thus axonometry could convey absolute objectivity, representing volume and tactility as no previous form of pictorial representation ever could. Not surprisingly, it would eventually become a privileged projection for decision making in computer-aided design.

In retrospect, axonometric projection seems to demonstrate an affinity with the geometry of Poncelet, for it operates by keeping a distance from the world of appearances. One might speculate that by using axonometry as a synthetic tool of representation, a tool in fact alien to the historical artifacts he wanted to depict, Choisy may have helped reveal its power to disclose spatial depths truly resonant with the modern age. Le Corbusier certainly was fascinated by Choisy's images, possibly for their abstract quality. He reproduced many of them in *L'Esprit nouveau*,[59] ushering in a new era in architectural ideation by recognizing the potential of axonometry as a constructive device and by realizing that its inherent, absolute clarity, once thoroughly devoid of shadows, was able to open up new options for embodied depth.

The Reversibility of Axonometry

Architecture is judged by eyes that see,
by the head that turns, and the
legs that walk. Architecture is not
a synchronic phenomenon but a successive one,
made up of pictures adding themselves
one to the other, following each other
in time and space, like music.
This is important, indeed it is capital and decisive:
the star-shapes of the Renaissance
gave an eclectic architecture,
intellectualized, a spectacle seen
only in fragments of intention. . . .
The cone of vision is in front,
concentrated upon a concrete field which is,
in reality, a limited one,
and limited still more by the mind . . .
[that] can interpret, appreciate and measure
only that which it has time to grasp.

Le Corbusier, The Modulor, 1

And this is a universal law:
a living thing can be
healthy, strong, and fruitful
only when bounded by a horizon.

Friedrich Nietzsche

Writers on modern architecture often have overemphasized a polarity between perspective and axonometry, stating that while perspective is about the subject (a specific observer), axonometry is about the object; axonometry is an objective tool rather than an illusionist representation of a building in its context or a means for presenting a project to a client.[60] Although axonometric drawing often has been perceived as hermetic (drawing by architects for architects),[61] and although it has served well the syntactic manipulations of many late-twentieth-century practitioners, it is crucial to keep in mind its wider historical roots (emerging from perspective) in order to perceive the possible alternatives that it offers for architectural representation. We have shown that there is no "subject" (if we mean by "subject" the political incarnation of the Cartesian *ego cogitans*) emancipated from external reality prior to the nineteenth century, and that at the same time architects believed that their projects were not complete unless they included perspective renderings. Also, we have witnessed perspective constituting itself "objectively" in the darkness of the camera obscura, a phenomenon observed and admired by many who considered it a model for the acquisition of knowledge during the eighteenth century. Only in the nineteenth century did the epistemological shift inherited from modern science and philosophy demand a reification of the subject and the object, as this articulation of reality came to permeate all aspects of everyday life. While it is a fact that axonometry is a form of representation particular to modernity,[62] we must not forget that it embodies the ultimate implementation of a perfectly systematic perspective theory.

By the 1920s, in the wake of cubism, futurism, and the metaphysical painting of Giorgio de Chirico, European artists clearly recognized that the revelation of a significant ("metaphysical") depth demanded a critique of the prosaic, naturalized, and homogeneous space of scientistic perspectivism, a critique of the new "common sense" that tended to identify reality and perspective. While this recognition had been manifested in earlier artistic work, it was after the First World War that the transformed social conditions finally seem to have incited architects to question the conventional Beaux-Arts presumption about architectural representation and to formulate a new definition of space.

At the 1923 De Stijl exhibition, axonometric drawing was presented as a privileged vehicle for conceiving architecture.[63] Its synthetic power was soon appreciated for its capacity simultaneously to address functional, constructive, and expressive concerns. As Theo van Doesburg put it, because "the new architecture has no form [and] it recognizes no fundamental or immutable types [and] it doesn't distinguish front from back, left from right and, if possible, neither up from down . . . , axonometry is the method most appropriate for designing the new spatial architecture."[64] Not surprisingly, emphasis was placed on

| 3.22 |

In Giorgio de Chirico's metaphysical paintings, such as *The Soothsayer's Recompense* (1913), the expectation of perspectival space is disrupted by the subtle variations of inserted elements that approximate isometry.

Philadelphia, Philadelphia Museum of Art: Louise and Walter Arensberg Collection.

319

the generation of architectural design—a truly seductive "methodological renewal," to paraphrase Hilberseimer—while the "product" and the aim of this operation became secondary. This emphasis on technique was rooted in the early-nineteenth-century theories of Durand. One hundred years later, however, the method of axonometric design was promoted as the very potential of a formalist syntax, expressing the "mental viewpoint of the architect-demiurge" and privileging a moment of "synthetic architectural gestation,"[65] when the technical virtuosity of the architect would be demonstrated as a comprehensive planning strategy. There were real dangers in this technical tool: its reductive power, ideally suited to describe all the assembly phases and operations of a rational and absolutely controlled construction process, and its tautological potential as an "artistic" tool for irrelevant formal manipulations. Because of its historical origins in perspective, however, axonometric space is also reversible and not necessarily hermetic; it can refer back to the world of experience to reveal significant depth.

El Lissitzky articulated most clearly the potential of the "new space" for art and architecture, while also criticizing the purely formalistic translations of surfaces into three dimensions by De Stijl architects. In his article "K. und Pangeometrie"

Theo van Doesburg, *Color Construction in the Fourth Dimension of Space-time* (1924). This axonometric of a private house designed by van Doesburg exemplifies the direct translation of color depth on a plane into inhabitable space that El Lissitzky criticized.

Amsterdam, Collection of Stedelijk Museum.

(1925), without mentioning axonometry by name, he makes some connections between mathematics and art.[66] After construing a relationship between arithmetic series and planimetric drawings, and between geometric series and perspective, he praises the destruction of "the rigid Euclidean space" by Lobachevsky, Gauss, and Riemann, as well as the shattering of "perspective space" by impressionism and cubism, the artistic movements responsible for bringing the horizon "to the surface of the painting." Futurism, according to Lissitzky, disengaged sight from the vertex of the optical pyramid in front of the work and transported it inside the work itself. His story culminates with Malevich's *White Square,* the first manifestation of "the amplification of art's numeric substance," which acknowledges zero as a number, the pure plane.

Lissitzky discusses, under separate subtitles, "irrational space" and "imaginary space."[67] "Irrational space," the space of the plane in suprematist painting, is the first truly infinite space; by expanding simultaneously forward from the plane and into its depth, it finally dispels the "illusion" of three-dimensional perspective space. Lissitzky obviously was fascinated by the properties of this space, by its homogeneity and reversibility. Nevertheless, he immediately noted the impossibility of "imagining" the mathematical abstractions of Gauss or Lobachevsky. He criticizes many of his contemporaries' simplistic attempts to extrapolate the physics of temporal relativity into art: "We can only change the form of our physical space, not its structure or three-dimensionality."[68] For Lissitzky, the reversibility of modern, axonometric space is closely associated with the possibility of making qualitative, differentiated places from the homogeneous and infinite space that is assumed by contemporary culture to be the space of everyday experience. This is tantamount to a redefinition of the horizon as a "limitless boundary," beyond the dichotomies of positivistic science.

Indeed, in his discussion of "imaginary space," Lissitzky tries to articulate how this new space could be realized in the world of embodied experience, as a construction for the body. He acknowledges that cinema is a first step in this direction, because of the way it engages time. For him, however, "film is only a flat, dematerialized projection that uses only one

321

| 3.24 |

Lissitzky, *Study to Proun 30 T* (1920).
New York, McCrory Corporation Collection (cat. no. 351).

aspect of visual possibilities." His objective is rather to imagine a "dematerialized materiality," the possibility of material objects creating wholly different and new spatial experiences when in motion, experiences that would last as long as the movement lasts. Lissitzky's version of "art into life" introduced temporality and emphasized the potential of synesthesia: "stereoscopic effects that motion produces when objects traverse colored media[;] . . . chromatic impressions produced by the polarization of light[;] . . . transformation of acoustic into optical phenomena." [69] His aim was to question old, classical notions of monumentality—that is, the reduction of the work of art or architecture to an aesthetic object—such as he observed in De Stijl projects and other works by his contemporaries. The new pictorial space, capable of expressing an inexpressible depth, had to be translated into a space of human habitation. Yet this was not a simple matter. The task could not be reduced to a question of methodology or form. Although his formulation ultimately remains vague, Lissitzky certainly realized that the temporality of embodied experience was crucial, that for architecture the ineffable meaning could appear only "in action," for the issue was "time" as much as "space."

The Collapse of the Image and the Represented Object

The scopic obsession of the nineteenth-century observer led to the extremes of impressionism and pointillism, as well as to all sorts of scientific imaging techniques such as Lumière's stereoscopic photography. It also prepared the ground for the arts' declaration of autonomy from the prosaic world of appearances. We may recall Mallarmé's definition of the poetic as the word that by definition does not "reflect" the world. In painting, this event generally has been associated with the "overcoming" of impressionism by cubism, futurism, and eventually abstract expressionism.

When the image and the represented object collapse they may indeed make visible what was there but hidden. We may immediately recall the possibilities that Walter Benjamin identified early on in photography, particularly in close-ups and other deliberately mediated mimetic products that could reveal a sort of visual unconscious.[70] While subsequent art critics often discussed the new temporality of cubism and futurism, architects became understandably enthusiastic about the "constructive" quality of the new artistic products. Le Corbusier, for example, declared that cubist painting had started after 1910 "toward its greatest revolution,"[71] following the new architectural aesthetic that had been brought about during the nineteenth century through the influence of iron and concrete on the art of building. For Le Corbusier this highly "constructive" painting, both "plastic and intellectual," was so different from impressionism that it signaled the way toward "an architectural synthesis," a transformation that he expected would affect sculpture in a similar way. Like Lissitzky, Le Corbusier understood that this synthesis was not merely a question of "applied arts." While he believed the "plastic epic" toward the synthesis of the arts had begun, he was well aware of the difficulties that "will be the subject of much study and will tend to group people around real tasks."[72]

Twentieth-century art pursued its quest toward autonomous, "nonobjective" (i.e., not imitative) constructions in many fascinating directions that obviously cannot be considered here even superficially. Perhaps one of the most intriguing results of this search, however, is the collapse of the projective distance represented by "indexic" forms of representation.[73] In photography and photograms, for example, a trace remains and bears witness to the presence of an object that was and is no more. These works are paradigmatic examples of the possibility that wholeness can be evoked through a fragment, actively engaging fundamental dualities such as light and shadow, or space and substance (solid and void), precisely in order to dissolve them into unity while simultaneously maintaining their specificity. They make appear plausible, in the realm of experience, a reality that conceptually remains contradictory, an "alchemical" unity that can never be conceptualized because it is of the order of embodied experience rather than pure thought.

Rachel Whiteread's *House* (1993) operates in this realm.[74] It is a nonoptical example of an index at building scale: a rather ordinary suburban house whose internal volume has been filled with concrete, rendering it impenetrable. As a construction, *House* is no mere reproduction of something preex-

France Morin, *Petit musée de taxonomie machinale* (1993) [3.25]; and Stephen Pack, *The Dark Interstice of Touch* (1993) [3.26]. The photogram collection and the trace of the hand were used as points of departure for design explorations.

Photos by F. Morin and S. Pack.

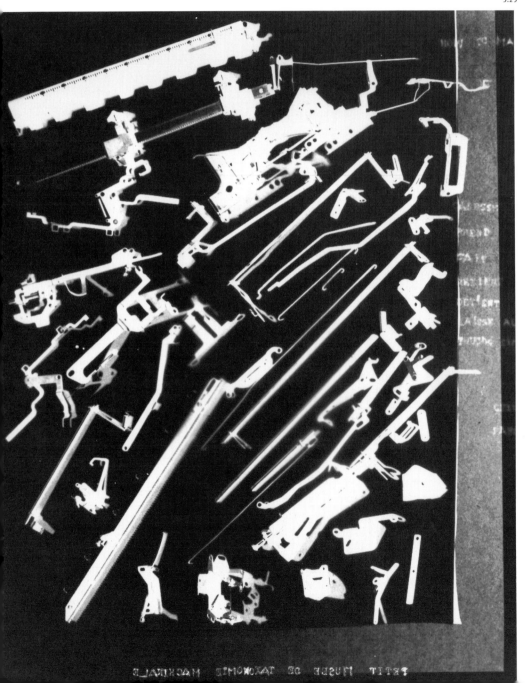

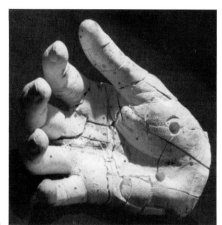

3.26a

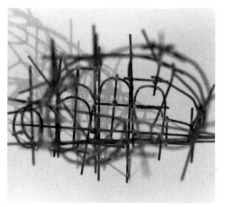

3.26b

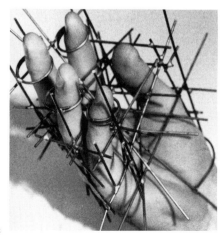

3.26c

isting. It fulfills the inveterate (Aristotelian) expectation of fiction: it brackets all prosaic reference to suggest unimagined future potentialities. Yet at the same time, it affirms the absurdity of arbitrary constructions and self-referential abstractions, explicitly referring back to a recognizable universe of discourse. The experience of works such as *House* eloquently reveals the fallacies of both a constructivist and a naturalist view of culture; without returning to a metaphysics of presence, it speaks about the impossibility of an absolute cultural relativism, defining the "ground" as our capacity to under-stand the co-incidence of presence and absence, space and substance, light and shadow. Meaning is on the surface, yet not every surface reveals poetic depth. The poetic and ethical intention of the maker is crucial, as is plainly demonstrated in Whiteread's work.

Thus, the physical trace itself becomes the most crucial challenge to a world that deliberately or unconsciously
seeks its dissolution in cyberspace. The trace is, furthermore,
the "open work" par excellence; it "forces" the participation of
the embodied observer for its completion, in opposition to the
"passivity" of the cybernetic subject. Not surprisingly, in
"Notes on the Index" Rosalind Krauss used Marcel Duchamp's
Tu m' (1918) as a seminal example of twentieth-century indexi-
cal representation. Not coincidentally, *Tu m'* also demonstrates
the reversibility of projection through its deliberate use of shadows and anamorphosis. Duchamp's last oil on canvas is indeed
a recapitulation of all the perspectivist deceits allowed by an
opaque surface. It is an explicit exploration of the paradigm
of projection, investigating the ambiguous dimension between
illusion and reality. In *Tu m'*, Duchamp questions the distinction between appearance and apparition, the delay between
presence and representation. He uses projection of shadows as
the trace of existing objects, yet he preserves a distance between
the imprint and the "shadow tracers," creating a variation on
the theme of anamorphosis. In contrast to traditional works of
this kind, in this modern anamorphosis the *truth* of the image is
no longer revealed to the beholder from a fixed position. The
painting calls for a new form of *participation* of the spectator, for
a dynamic involvement in the process of creation. As one walks
around it, certain elements of the composition become visible
while others vanish. When seen from the front, the shadows
cast by "ready-mades" are seen as anamorphic projections
stretched out on the surface; a bottle brush, which is the only
three-dimensional object piercing the surface of the canvas perpendicularly to its plane, is reduced to a dot. But seen from the
side, the shadows become progressively rectified—never coin-

| 3.28 |

Marcel Duchamp, *Tu m'* (1918).
New Haven, Yale University Art Gallery.

327

ciding perfectly with the objects from which they are projected—until they disappear again in the thickness of the
canvas. At this point, the brush releases itself from the canvas
and becomes the only visible reality of the hidden picture, in a
fashion similar to anamorphosis. The movement of the observer
is indispensable for the meaning of the image to appear, for
truth to disclose itself as a dialectic of revealing and concealing,
the Heideggerian *alētheia*. As he creates an allegory of ritual,
Duchamp reintroduces here the necessity for the spectator to
participate responsibly in the act of reception of the work of
art: that insight is fundamental to conceiving of a meaningful
architecture in a democratic social context.

If we now recollect our journey through the history
of architectural representation, the epic of footings and faces
larger than life, we may remember that the traditional understanding of architectural ideas was precisely as tactile traces
rather than visual projections. This was the meaning still present
in Vitruvius: *ichnographia* and *orthographia* as imprints, instants
taken out of the flow of becoming to signify an intention that
nevertheless had to be replayed to make it a reality that occupied the temporal space of human actions. Today our privileged
access to a historical perspective (Giambattista Vico would call
it a *ricorso*) has created the distance necessary for self-conscious
understanding. It is tempting to reflect on the consequences of
having come full circle, yet to a different place. The original
devices of architectural representation, which were tactile devices that reflected a physical relationship between dwelling and
the human body, having passed from technical tools to projective images, then transformed into efficient instruments of reduction to become, in the hands of twentieth-century artists,
the means for mounting a powerful challenge to the world of
prosaic images that our technological society uncritically identifies with reality.

This points to the hopeful possibility of plan, section,
and elevation being also reversible. Their capacity for activating
erotic space—a space of human participation, transcendent yet
cognizant of boundaries—is possibly undiminished. But their
common essence has been transformed by the perspectival
hinge. An uncritical use of these devices therefore will always
result in yet more reductive products: the question "how" can-

| 3.29 |

Gordon Matta-Clark's *Office Baroque* or *Walk through Panoramic Arabesque* (1977). The photograph—a literal section through the visual cone—destructures the reductive quality of section by presenting the actual "sectioning" of an existing building and revealing its otherwise hidden interiority. As opposed to the original anatomical dissection of cadavers that aimed at disclosing the objectified "order" of the human body, the sectioning of a "dead" building reveals the space of human habitation—real yet impenetrable, radiant yet obscure.

New York, private collection of Jane Crawford.

not be answered with a methodology. Can a recording of traces again be translated (rather than transcribed) in built architectural projects? Does the transition between sample and building necessitate a further representational mediation, and how can this mediation act as a generative process evolving from an existing sample? Possible answers are only examples and stories, and we shall provide one shortly. It is crucial, however, to formulate these questions clearly, placing them in the context of a philosophical conversation about vision and depth.

Vision and Depth

The mystery of the world is the visible,
not the invisible.

Oscar Wilde

The alternatives we contemplate for architectural making and representation hinge upon the very possibility of undoing the dualistic opposition between the visible and the invisible. While we all may be part of a world that increasingly identifies embodied and virtual realities, a world where vision is the organ of surveillance and pornography, we are not therefore unable to establish a critical distance through a phenomenology of ambiguity. It is given to us to see differently, and thus to act differently.

The ambivalence of the modern gaze seems to be already present in Renaissance extromission theories. Marsilio Ficino, for example, believed that in the act of seeing, "the internal fire" was externalized through the eyes and, mixed with the "pneumatic vapor, and even with thin blood," penetrated the Other's eyes and stroked the heart, often producing lesions. Conversely, when desire was too strong, this excessive "love" produced weakness in the subject until he or she wasted away.[75] In *De Vincoli in Genere,* Giordano Bruno articulated the power of the magician as the power of eros.[76] To exert magical powers, the operator had to seduce his target, while controlling his own desire and postponing fulfillment. In order for magic to be effective (and good—an inevitable connection in the Renaissance), the magician first had to fall in love himself. Vision as com-passion was therefore the true power of the benevolent magician, the power of white magic. The obvious danger, conversely, was the possibility of control without compassion: black magic, the "evil eye," a powerful pathology of envy that appears in practically every human culture and, significantly, is believed to affect both subjects and objects.

In the nineteenth century, Friedrich Nietzsche already understood that the question was not to valorize or devalorize modern vision as such, but rather to rethink it as a vision in the twilight.[77] While his well-known philosophical "suspicion" is highly visual, always staying close to the surface and distrusting any reality beyond appearances, Nietzsche was always motivated by an ethical quest for the Other who could share his vision. He believed that while the eye could be "evil," reductive, and domineering, it could also be "radiant," capable of receiving and honoring the spectacle. Just as we value learning to think, speak, and write, Nietzsche believed that it was important to learn to see: "habituating the eye to repose, to patience, to letting things come to it[;] . . . the essence of it is precisely *not* to 'will,' the ability to defer decision."[78] Of course this is a modality of seeing that is *neither* the objectifying vision of modern science and classical aesthetics *nor* the "distracted" vision of a self-less, animalized being, the blinking of Zarathustra's "last men," who desire not to look at anything too long or too attentively. Nietzsche's twilight vision, recalling the later formulation of Heidegger's *gelassenheit,* is "clear" because it is neither in pure light nor in pure darkness. "Is seeing itself not— seeing abysses?" he wrote in *Thus Spoke Zarathustra,* and in a moving passage of "Assorted Opinions and Maxims" he explicitly articulated the nature of the divine image in human artifacts as a "revealing/concealing": "No Greek ever truly beheld his Apollo as a wooden obelisk, his Eros as a lump of stone. . . . In the incompleteness . . . of these figures there lies a dreadful holiness which is supposed to *fend off* any association of them with anything human. It is not an embryonic stage of art at which such things are fashioned. . . . [O]ne thing was specifically avoided: direct statement. As the cella contains the holy of holies, the actual *numen* of divinity, and conceals it in mysterious semi-darkness, *but does not wholly conceal it;* as the peripteral temple in turn contains the cella and as though with a canopy and veil shelters it from prying eyes, *but does not wholly shelter it:* so the image is the divinity and at the same time the divinity's place of concealment."[79]

Walter Benjamin's dialectic of seeing reiterates Nietzsche's insight about the space of art as the space of metaphor. Particularly in his *Passagen-Werk,* at issue is the space of montage, the gap between words and images. Benjamin's overall program was driven by a rather unorthodox assimilation of Marxist and messianic aspirations. His "redemptive" aesthetics were predicated entirely on the power of the imaginary. As Susan Buck-Morss has pointed out, for Benjamin images constituted the realm of the real (from both the standpoint of materialism and metaphysics).[80] Thus he pointed to the possibility of engaging the nineteenth-century reproductive arts (photography, cinema) in the project to shock society out of its dream of commodification and to compel a collective, "revolutionary awakening." Benjamin's understanding of the mimetic faculty as a fundamental characteristic of human civilization, capable of revealing a "ground" beyond relativistic or scientistic views of nature and culture, enabled him to articulate with clarity the possible "reversal" of reductive optics. The dialectical images of cinema, for example, extending and contracting time and space, simultaneously include modernity and *poésie* (the modern equivalent of *mythos* in the sense of Aragon's surrealist *Paris Peasant*) and refute *both* modern rationality and archaic irrationality. Thus, they are capable of giving back to humanity, through technological reproduction, the very potentiality for experience that technological production threatens to take away.[81]

The danger with reproductive images, as we have often expressed, is their substitutive and objectifying power. Is the observer a participant or a voyeur? Not surprisingly, Jean Baudrillard sees himself as continuing Benjamin's project when he speaks about the capacity of "seduction," operating in a fully simulated realm (a world where "reality" is characterized as that which can be reproduced), to destructure production.[82] While the reversibility of the image must be well understood, for architecture it is crucial to recall that without "the body of experience," pure visuality is a fallacy. This gives rise to complex ethical questions for architectural practice, questions that hinge on a correct understanding of the question of "origins" of human reality, of its primary and secondary structures.

Georges Didi-Huberman adopts Benjamin's notion of the dialectic image as a framework to discuss not figurative art but minimalist sculpture. This work represents the extremes of reduction and abstraction in twentieth-century art, and through its "objective" and "constructive" character it has obvious affinities with architecture. Didi-Huberman discusses pure clarity and the absence of anything other than what is "visible" in Tony Smith's "black boxes," showing the pitfalls of assuming that "the empty tomb" is either nothing but emptiness or a manifestation of the absolute presence of an absent God. The discourse must be placed beyond the dualistic opposition between visible and invisible while remaining in the realm of visibility. The issue is that something would always be missing for the seeing subject to recover a certainty about what he or she is seeing. The gap opened in the realm of our visual certainty is precisely the place where "the image becomes truly our concern, where *it* also observes us."[83] Thus we may define the reciprocity between what we see and what regards or concerns us (*Ce que nous voyons, ce qui nous regarde*), this double distance between the viewer and the viewed, in terms both of Benjamin's "aura" and of Merleau-Ponty's late philosophy: "a remarkable intertwining of space and time."[84] This "spacing," becoming a forgotten trace, allows the works to "set their own distance," one that prevails between the viewer and the viewed, no matter how close they come in the universe of contemporary simulations. To acknowledge this distance is to accept that the work of art concerns us, that it is *not* self-referential—which is precisely the source of the "poetic," irrespective of artistic medium. Indeed, such an acknowledgement evokes a conception of architecture that requires neither a return to the notion of meaning as presence nor the concession that meaning is no more than momentary and arbitrary assignments of values to signifying variables.[85]

Maurice Merleau-Ponty's work was central to Didi-Huberman, and it remains crucial to understanding the possibility of a new ontology of sight. Unlike Jean-Paul Sartre, who believed that the "inhuman gaze" was necessarily objectifying, Merleau-Ponty argued that this mutual objectification exists only at the level of thought, not at the level of interactive presence. Perspective is therefore not a "subjective deformation of things"; on the contrary, "nontranscendental perspectivalism" reunites humanity with the objective, real world.[86] Merleau-Ponty was particularly critical of Descartes's *Dioptrics,* and he emphasized that sight was not simply a matter of the mind: "It is by means of the perceived world and its proper structures that one can explain the spatial values assigned to a point of the visual field in each particular case."[87] The next step for Merleau-Ponty was to demonstrate how sight is integrated with the other senses in order for us to "make sense" of our experience of the world. This is what he set out to do in dense, technical language in *Phenomenology of Perception.* "The senses translate each other without any need of an interpreter, they are mutually comprehensible without the intervention of any idea." Emphasizing the primordial status of temporality, he stated: "The lived perspective, that which we actually perceive, is not a geometric or photographic one."[88]

Perspective, therefore, is not "natural," but neither is it a "mere" cultural (linguistic) construction.[89] The "significant distance" in works of art belonging to our tradition has its roots in the "philosophical history" of Europe, burned into our collective memory. Merleau-Ponty seems to retrieve the wholeness of this tradition when he recognizes the primacy, though not the exclusivity, of the visual world in depth experience—along with the claims that depth itself is visible, that the body is "central" in this same experience, and that depth surrounds us and is directly perceivable—and, most important, when he rejects depth as a mere distance or interval, a barren "third dimension" equivalent to height or breadth. Depth is neither the prosaic interval between nearby and distant objects that one observes from above, nor the concealment of layered things that a perspectival drawing represents. "The riddle of depth," writes Merleau-Ponty, lies in the connection between these two views: "the fact that it is precisely because things disappear behind each other that I see them in place, [and] the fact that it is precisely because each is in its place that they are rivals for my gaze."[90] Depth is the dimension of perceptual cohesion and reversibility that allows for things to appear as mutually dependent through their autonomy and, reciprocally, to manifest their "objectivity" through mutual concealment. Depth is therefore not a "third dimension." If it were any dimension at all, writes Merleau-Ponty, it would be the first. "But a dimension which contains all others is not a dimension," at least not in the ordinary Cartesian sense of measurement. "Depth in the sense we are now discussing [is rather] our experiencing of the reversibility of dimensions, of an overall 'locality' in which everything exists at once and for which height and width and distance are abstractions."[91] In *Phenomenology of Perception,* he states: "This being simultaneously present in experiences which are nevertheless mutually exclusive, this implication of one in the other, this contraction into one perceptual act of a whole possible process, constitute the originality of depth. It is the dimension in which things . . . envelop each other, whereas breadth and height are the dimensions in which they are juxtaposed." [92]

In his later works, Merleau-Ponty adopted a more poetic language to discuss the questions of vision and reversibility. Without ever leaving behind his understanding of synesthetic perception as prior to sensory differentiation, he reexamined the importance of vision, no longer in relation to a potentially subjective perceiving body, but in relation to his notion of reality as "the flesh of the world." As Martin Jay points out, the implications of this "posthumanist" understanding of vision were anticipated in an essay entitled "Man and Adversity" (1951) in which Merleau-Ponty questioned the Cartesian *ego cogitans:* "if there is a humanism today, it rids itself of the illusion Valéry designated so well in speaking of 'that little man whom we always presuppose.' Philosophers have at times thought to account for our vision by the image or reflection things form upon our retina. This was because they presupposed a second man behind the retinal image who had different eyes and a different retinal image responsible for seeing the first." [93] For Merleau-Ponty "the map of the visible overlaps that of my intended motions," and this "extraordinary overlapping . . . makes it impossible to consider vision as an operation of the mind that erects in front of it a representation of the world." [94] This overlapping of vision and motion blurs the traditional oppositions of contemplation and action, vision and visibility, activity and passivity. As a result the body is at the same time decentered and centering. This has immense consequences both for legitimizing the role of the poetic (personal) imagination in architectural making and for considering the question of "reception" in a way that may go beyond the reduction of architecture to "text."

In Merleau-Ponty's late philosophy, the world's being appears inexhaustible, its "flesh" unsurveyable, whether this pertains to nature or to history. The "flesh of the world," as a hinge of the visible and the invisible, could never be observed from afar, as if in a picture. No representation therefore would be capable of "reducing" this reality, inhabited by a radiating, anonymous visibility. "Neither purely transparent nor completely opaque, the flesh is an interplay of dimensionalities, of light and shadow."[95] Working through and with temporality and spatiality, the fundamental challenge for art is precisely to manifest the very mystery of dimensionality. With the introduction of his concept of reality as the "flesh of the world," Merleau-Ponty could develop his earlier intuitions about reversibility, demonstrating that it is both spatial *and* temporal, or rather that such a distinction itself is undermined by reversibility. This is indeed a crucial realization if we are to grasp the nature of significant depth in architectural experience. "It is a question of finding in the present, the flesh of the world (and not in the past) an 'ever new' and an 'always the same'—a sort of time of sleep."[96] For Merleau-Ponty there is no present in time, no segment of a linear pattern, as we commonly imagine it. The reversibility of the flesh is the reversibility of past and present: "That is, that the things have us, and that it is not we who have the things. That the being which has been cannot stop having been. The 'Memory of the World.'" Every new present is itself transcendent, and one never coincides with it; "it is not a segment of time with defined contours that would come and set itself in place. It is a cycle defined by a central and dominant region and with indecisive contours."[97] Reversibility, we must emphasize, does not mean coincidence, in the sense of the old metaphysics of presence. Just as "my left hand is always on the verge of touching my right hand touching things, but I never reach coincidence." There is always a shifting gap, almost overcome at moments (in love's erotic fruition), but one that is not "an ontological void, a non-being; it is spanned by the total being of my body and by that of the world."[98]

In his late writings Merleau-Ponty also understood that language could emerge as potentially at odds with perception. Although his early and unexpected death prevented him from developing these insights, he significantly never conceived perception and language to be in opposition. "If perception is a mute version of language, needing it to come into full speech," summarizes Martin Jay, "so too language bears within it the residue of its silent predecessor, which inaugurated the drama of meaningfulness which is our destiny."[99] This capacity to embrace the space between experience and language as a noncontradictory chasm is consistent with Merleau-Ponty's critique of depth as an objective, stable geometric entity. It is interesting to recall here the striking analogy between Merleau-Ponty's depth, as the spatiotemporal setting of the "flesh," and the notion of *chōra* as articulated by Plato in his *Timaeus*.[100]

Plato's *chōra* is not only the primordial spatial matrix *and* undifferentiated substance (*prima materia*); it is also postulated as the *third* element of reality, responsible for an ontological continuum, a "ground" itself inexplicable through reason, yet undeniable to experience. It is the space, indeed, between Being and becoming, between words (stable and fixed) and the things of the world that bear the same name, yet are mutable and changing. We have already suggested the connection between Plato's *chōra* and the space that opened up between embodied consciousness and the cosmos after the "discovery" of philosophy and theory. That space is analogous to the distance between spectator and actor in the classical theater, and it brought about a privileging of contemplation (through vision and hearing) over ritual action as the medium for the spectator's participation in the order revealed by a work. The theater defined a liminal space that Vitruvius identified as precisely that of architecture (focused on the orchestra occupied by the choir, the paradigmatic space of exchange between divine will and human destiny), one where cosmic resonances definitely should be at work. This distance, we have also pointed out, is the erotic space that opened up with the inception of alphabetic writing, the "objectification" of speech that broke a previously existing continuum and took language out of lived time. Plato acknowledged that *chōra* was "very hard to grasp"—the substance of dreams, yet not immediately accessible to the senses. He seems to evoke the "blind spot" in human works that makes them significant, the space of metaphor and the space of collage, which is also the place where meaning is granted to human life, a space that "precedes" all linguistic models of signification. *Chōra* connotes a mysteriously dense space-time, the depth of art and architecture that has become transparent and seemingly irrelevant only after the hegemony of applied science began.

Today we live in the wake of this tradition. Thus we may understand our ambivalent relationship with "perspective."

One of the many versions of Paul Cézanne's *Le Mont Ste.-Victoire* (ca.
1906). In "Cézanne's Doubt" (1964),
Maurice Merleau-Ponty discusses
Cézanne's obsession with the Mont
Ste.-Victoire and demonstrates the
painter's desire to express a "constructive depth" different from Renaissance perspective, one more
resonant with our post-Cartesian understanding of reality.

Zurich, Bührle Collection.

Merleau-Ponty inadvertently unearthed the hidden potentiality
of our tradition in his articulation of depth, observing, "Four
centuries after the 'solutions' of the Renaissance and three centuries after Descartes, depth is still new, and it insists on being
sought, not 'once in a lifetime,' but all through life." Furthermore, this understanding of depth suggests the existence of a
polymorphism of being in the arts, a "system of equivalencies,
a *Logos* of the lines, of lights, of reliefs, of masses [and not a]
concept of universal Being,"[101] that accounts for the well-
known fact that good painters often turn into good sculptors,
and sometimes also into good architects, as history attests from
Brunelleschi and Michelangelo to Le Corbusier. This is why
architects during the last few centuries have been able to engage
in a strategy of resistance. Once geometric space had become
the locus of social and political life, these architects sought to
retrieve the mystery of depth, the transitional event of *chōra,* by
implementing strategies of destructuration and of recollection
of embodiment. Piranesi and Ingres were precocious members
of this group. Their quest was continued by members of various
artistic movements in the twentieth century, movements in-
tensely informed by Cézanne's obsession to abandon the external form of objects that preoccupied realism and impressionism
in order to retrieve a new depth; a true depth of experience
whose paradigm is *erotic,* a depth that traditional illusionism
could no longer convey. The artist's vision is no longer a view
of the outside, a mere "physical-optical" relation with the
world. As Merleau-Ponty has pointed out in regard to Cézanne, the world no longer stands before him through perspectival representation; rather it is the painter (and the observer) to
whom the things of the world give birth by means of a concen-
tration of the visible. These works proclaim a temporalization
of depth. The architectural and artistic works of resistance in
the last two hundred years have been, above all, "autofigura-
tive." They are a spectacle of something only by being a spectacle of nothing. Works in this tradition cut across conventional
art historical categories and find their expression in diverse media and styles, proposing widely differing personal visions, yet
they consistently break the skin of things in order to show "how
the things become things, how the world becomes a world."[102]

Axonometry as Collage: Le Corbusier's
Poème de l'angle droit

Truly the key to my artistic creation
is my pictorial work
begun in 1918 and pursued
regularly each day.
The foundation of my research
and intellectual production
has its secret in the uninterrupted
practice of my painting.
It is there that one
must find the source
of my spiritual freedom,
of my disinterestedness,
of the faithfulness and
integrity of my work.

Le Corbusier

Charles-Edouard Jeanneret (1887–1965) is perhaps the only major protagonist in this book who truly needs no introduction. His immense production, including paintings, sculptures, writings, architectural projects, and buildings, is certainly not free from contradictions. Recent critical theorists have spent much time demonstrating that his intentions were "encoded" at many levels, that his prose is not free from the temptations of self-promotion, and that he exhibits other even greater "evils" in the age of political correctness. Our interest, however, is to use some of his work as a model to demonstrate the potential of the tools of architectural representation, such as we have inherited them from our tradition. There is an immense wealth in his work that still begs to be recognized.[103]

Le Corbusier's fascination with axonometric projections has been emphasized by critics, historians, and architects alike.[104] He has been associated with Gropius, Sartoris, and Hilberseimer as one of the first to perceive the space of axonometry as the "homogeneous and transparent space of modernity[,] . . . recognizing it as part of our way of seeing things."[105] Some of his self-avowed North American disciples, particularly during the sixties, demonstrated through their own work the genealogy of axonometric projection in the work and artistic concerns of Le Corbusier, privileging this tool as the semantic instrument par excellence of twentieth-century architecture.[106]

As we have previously suggested, Le Corbusier admired Choisy's axonometric images so much that he appropriated them for his arguments in his early definition of *L'Esprit Nouveau*.[107] He obviously perceived the appropriateness of axonometry's objectified space and was also fascinated by the demonstration of technique as a determinant of form, a theme often reiterated in his writings. Unquestionably, he also understood quite early the relationship between axonometric space and the new space of painting. It is well known that Le Corbusier sought the integration of the arts. He painted all his life, seeking at first public exposure. After 1927, however, he decided to make his painting a private activity, to which he devoted every morning of the week. He believed profoundly that his painting was crucial for his understanding of architecture, not because of formal analogies but rather because of the activity of *making* itself—that is, an inquiry into the world of appearances coupled with the careful construction and realization of projects.[108] Critics and historians, incapable or unwilling to think beyond the Renaissance categories of the fine arts, have often underplayed Le Corbusier's painting as integral to his architectural quest, or have dismissed it as a propaganda ploy to have his architecture valorized as "art." On the contrary, Le Corbusier's rhetorical plea is crucial to understanding his legacy. As a reader of Friedrich Nietzsche's *Zarathustra* and admirer of Alfred Jarry, Le Corbusier struggled all his life to find ways to translate into architecture, into the pragmatic world of embodied experience, the new fascinating depth and temporality first fabricated in canvas and paint, or sketched for sculpture or tapestry. His quest echoes closely that suggested by Lissitzky in his "K. und Pangeometrie."

Le Corbusier sketched constantly. His work demonstrates a pervasive, sharp self-consciousness of the difficulties involved in art as will to power. Drawing for him was an act of reconciliation between the artist and the preexisting reality, that is, nature. *Pace* much critical misunderstanding, he was not naive about the polarities between nature and culture, geometry

Michael Graves, *Hanselmann House* (1967) [3.31]; John Hejduk, frontal axonometric of *Bernstein House* (1968) [3.32]; Daniel Libeskind, *Collage Rebus II* (1970) [3.33]; and Katsuhiko Muramoto, *Detached House, Separated Even* (1982) [3.34]. This series of images illustrates the potential "reversibility" of axonometry. From the homogeneous space of *Hanselmann House* to the disrupted "three-dimensionality" of *Detached House, Separated Even*, axonometry has the potential of opening up of a chasm in space, analogous to the unfamiliar gap between two familiar elements in a collage.

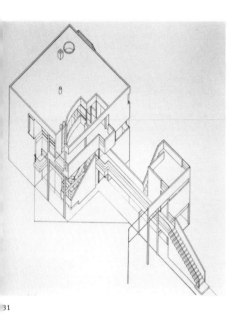

3.31

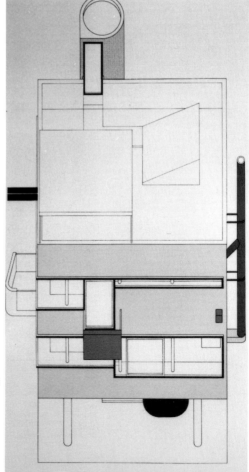

3.32

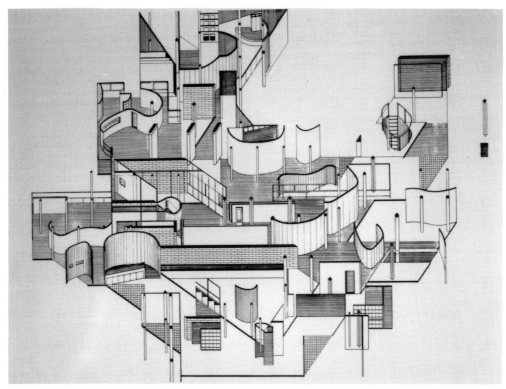

3.33

3.34

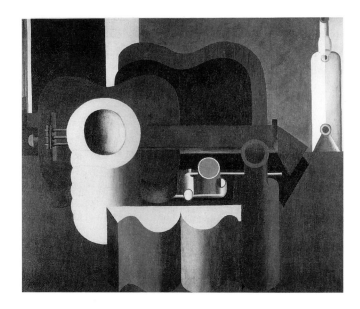

| 3.35 |

Le Corbusier, *Still Life* (1920).

Basel, Kunstmuseum.

and life, or the city and the country. It is true that early in his life, during his "purist" period, he stressed geometry, and possibly he never abandoned an uncritical, progressive view of history. His painting during the early 1920s paid attention to the intricate formal relationships between objects. Transformed into planes rather than merely "flattened," the superimposed objects seem to push out from the picture surface, "squeezing out" space, that is, common perspectival depth.[109] By the late 1920s he became friends with Fernand Léger. He had in his possession a catalogue of a major exhibition of Giorgio de Chirico's work (1928), and his own paintings focused on erotic themes. In the 1930s, Le Corbusier obviously came to the realization that the space of human significance had to be articulated as an erotic distance. He considered the potential polarity of humanity against nature no longer operative; hereafter the manufactured world and the natural one were to be accepted equally, without compromising either. Not surprisingly, his use of the golden section and *tracés regulateurs* practically disappeared from his art after 1929.[110]

A careful examination of Le Corbusier's sketchbooks from 1914 to 1964 reveals how he consistently used perspectival views to visualize his ideas.[111] There are often diagrammatic plans and elevations, but never objectified drawings. Never does one find an axonometric drawing as the initial idea for a building. There are, of course, some "air views," but these are always contextual and perspectival. The only generative "axonometric" spaces we find in the sketchbook are ideas for his paintings. We may recall here how Le Corbusier emphasized the importance of patience in creative work, expressing notions that echoed Filarete when it came to describing the process of an idea's gestation. After being entrusted a task, he would "place it in the interior of [his] memory." He would sketch no more and let the problem "float, simmer, ferment" until one day "out of the spontaneous initiative of the inner being" he takes a pencil, charcoal, color pencils, and "gives birth on the paper: the idea comes out—the child is delivered." [112]

The synthetic, comprehensive nature of architectural design generated in the matrix of axonometric space is incompatible with this conception. Indeed, this description is consistent with the total disappearance of axonometric representation

| 3.36 |

Axonometric drawing of Le Corbusier's *Maison Cook* (1926).

Paris, Fondation Le Corbusier #8309. © FLC/Adagp, Kinemage, 1997.

from Le Corbusier's mature work. In the *Oeuvre complète,* projects in their early or final stages are always presented in plans, sections, elevations, perspectives, and photographs. Sometimes aerial isometry was used to illustrate site ideas. Only in the period preceding 1929 (volume 1 of this work) was there a frequent use of axonometric drawing. It is notable that this type of projection first appeared in the Pessac project of standardized housing. Axonometry was used in this early period with a clear understanding of its potential to express reductive systematization. The first villa represented in axonometry, obviously the inspiration for the formalistic use of the system by later disciples, is the Villa Meyer of 1925. A colored interior axonometric of the Maison Cook (1926) clearly shows Le Corbusier's understanding of the potential analogy between pictorial and architectural space. Yet, with exception of Villa à Garches, the few other axonometric drawings of that period emphasize systematization: the Plan Voisin and the standardized *immeubles-villas* (1925), for example, are presented in axonometry. In the period between 1929 and 1934, we find only three axonometric drawings: a frontal sketch of the Cité du Refuge (1932) and two more for workers' housing in Barcelona and Zurich. Significantly, after the early 1930s and coinciding with his new realizations in painting, there are almost no axonometric drawings (see the remaining six volumes of the *Oeuvre complète*). A glaring exception is the virtuoso axonometric projection of Ronchamp's internal space, which is obviously an explanatory rather than a generative drawing.[113]

An examination of the vast *Le Corbusier Archives* yields a similar picture.[114] Isolated axonometric drawings appear around 1924 and became rare after 1935. Before 1924, three-dimensional representation was done primarily through interior and exterior perspectives in "box" frames. These gave way to isolated axonometric drawings, both as sketches and presentation tools, although perspectives were always abundant. In 1928, Le Corbusier used a "worm's-eye" axonometric in a drawing of the Villa Baizeau, and from 1929 to 1930 we find the majority of his "iconic" axonometrics, particularly those of the Villa Savoye, including "bird's-eye" and "worm's-eye" views. From 1935 to 1942, axonometry was used in sketches, but rarely in presentation drawings. After 1942, axonometrics

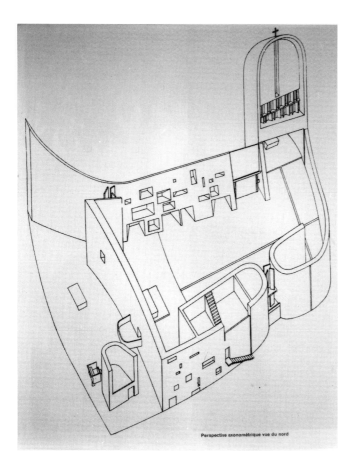

Perspective axonométrique vue du nord

| 3.37 |

The interior space of Ronchamp. It is one of the very few axonometric drawings to appear in the mature work of Le Corbusier.

Paris, Fondation Le Corbusier #7191. © FLC/Adagp, Kinemage, 1997.

347

ceases to be used, and in fact Le Corbusier tends to abandon three-dimensional representation altogether. By the 1960s his architectural drawings acquire a very flat, collage-like quality.

Le Corbusier's concern with this "modern space" in painting was, therefore, not simply transplanted to architecture. His work can hardly be reduced to the application of the matrix of axonometry as a place for modernist syntax, as the majority of his disciples have assumed. Relatively early in his career, his true struggle was to find equivalent modes of presencing in the visual/erotic space of architectural situations. His experimentation with projection in the space of representation reflected a lifelong passion that culminated in an awareness of artistic discovery—the unveiling of unexpected relationships between objects of the surrounding world, *rapports* emerging from the new contiguities construed in the work. In 1938 he wrote, in terms that recall a surrealist understanding of collage, that the difference between everyday, prosaic spoken language and painting consisted in their different ways of denoting things. While the former names things narrowly and specifically, the latter is concerned with the quality of things, bringing them together freely. Thus it is the unexpected relationships—that is, the space of metaphoric tension—that the artist discovers; this "is what the poet proclaims, that which the inspired being creates."[115] A decade later he wrote again about art in *New World of Space*.[116] He explained the genesis of his *Ubu* sculptures, deliberately named in honor of Alfred Jarry, the founder of pataphysics: "Stones and pieces of wood led me on involuntarily to draw beings who became a species of monster or god." Le Corbusier was aware of how the process offered much to his architecture precisely because it revealed "new things," "unex-

| 3.38 |

A study by Le Corbusier for abstract sculptural volumes (ca. 1940–1942).

Paris, Fondation Le Corbusier #464. © FLC/ Adagp, Kinemage, 1977.

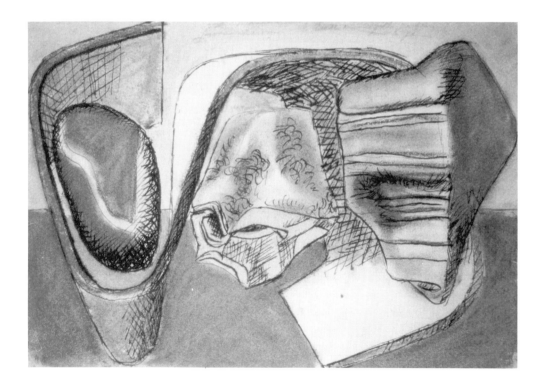

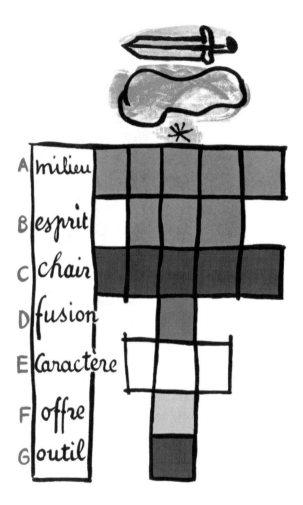

A milieu
B esprit
C chair
D fusion
E Caractère
F offre
G outil

| 3.39 |

Iconostase, the diagram for organizing the lithographs from Le Corbusier's *Poème de l'angle droit* (1955).

Montreal, Blackader-Lauterman Library Collection, McGill University.

349

pected" and "unknown." He concluded: "When the inexplicable appears in human work, that is, when our spirit is projected far from the narrow relation of cause and effect . . . to the cosmic phenomenon in time, in space, in the intangible[;] . . . then the inexplicable is the mystery of art."[117]

Articulating this experience in poetic language, Le Corbusier's *Poème de l'angle droit* (1955) remains his most comprehensive, albeit rather misunderstood theoretical statement about architecture.[118] Almost every important aspect of the architect's thought finds a place in the verses and images of the

Poème. The *Iconostase,* the prescribed arrangement for the color lithographs accompanying the text, is deployed between the tool of the architect (the right angle) at the center bottom and the realm of the "cosmos" at the top. The form of the work itself, in the wake of many other discursive writings, establishes a tension between words and images, demonstrating Le Corbusier's awareness of the importance of the poetic word and of the space of collage for fully expressing his thoughts. The relationship between image and words communicates the possibility of reconciling the ordering imagination of the architect and his tools, that is, the right angle, with the pregiven order that the architect encounters "already there."

This fundamental question for human making and for architecture since the origins of civilization is not resolved naively through some kind of theological formulation. Like Nietzsche, Le Corbusier looked at the unquestionably significant traces of human history, at the presence of genius, and at our ability to grasp the outlines of destiny, to fill the void left by God's demise. Echoing, perhaps unknowingly, the late writings of Nietzsche in *The Will to Power,* he seemed to identify the power of artistic creation with the erotic drive that characterizes the *Übermann,* leading the way for humanity to discover a new form of spirituality through a reconciliation of will to power and *amor fati.* Le Corbusier wrote: "A man who searches for harmony has a sense of the sacred, the secret which is in every being, a great limitless void where you may place your own notion of the sacred—individual, completely individual." [119] The issue then is to reconcile extreme individuality, the work of the creator's imagination, with a given world, *both* natural *and* constructed, in the absence of a positive theology or cosmology. Our contention is that the result is much more than a simple reiteration of the old romantic themes of transcendence through art, if by art we understand the production of "aesthetic objects" placed in the homogeneous space of a universal museum. While it is impossible to reduce the *Poème* to discursive language, we would like to examine some specific questions it raises before venturing a conclusion about its significance, at one with its modes of representation.

The uppermost level of the *Iconostase* refers to the milieu, a "cosmos" that is no longer merely fixed or "natural." In

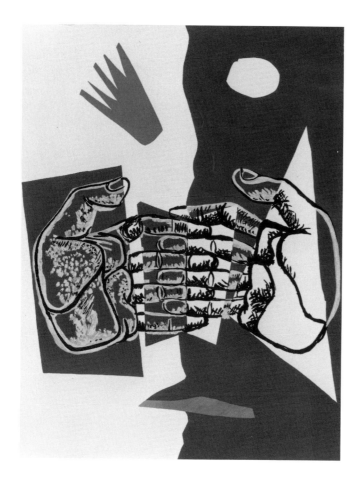

| 3.40 |

Third plate of *Milieu* (A.5), from *Poème de l'angle droit.*

Montreal, Blackader-Lauterman Library Collection, McGill University.

351

A.1, the uniqueness of our Earth is contrasted with the in-difference of the Sun, "master of our lives." Le Corbusier first reconciles the two times that rule our lives, the continuous time of night and day, with the breaks identified by dawn, sunset, and love. Time, logically inconceivable as both perpetually present and forever passing, is made understandable through the experience of *poésie*. In the same level (A.2) he invokes our experience of water (horizontality) and sunshine (verticality) as the "referent" of orthogonality; while we lie horizontally, face up, space appears incomprehensible, beyond grasp; as we stand upright, however, adopting a position that humanity alone is privileged to assume, we establish "a pact of solidarity" with

nature—the right angle (A.3); the meaning is at the crossing, in union through complementarity. The theme of the last two images in this level is the possibility of reconciliation between the "clairvoyant," with his geometric tools, and the meander, understood as the shape of rebirth, fertility, the feminine Earth (its streams and shores), and human thought.

The next level down refers to the mind (*esprit*). Fundamentally defined by its capacity to grasp the immutable *mathesis,* this level introduces the importance of proportion and measure, of rhythm and harmony in space and time. As is well known, Le Corbusier was obsessed by the possibility of establishing a universal proportional system, which he attempted in

The Modulor. This concern, which occupied him particularly between 1945 and 1950, has been interpreted as a desire to find absolute rules, instrumental mechanisms for architectural design. It is obvious that lacking roots in a shared, intersubjective cosmology, a proportional system posited as a vehicle to attain architectural meaning was doomed to failure. The criticism directed at *The Modulor* is therefore not totally unfair; there are long passages that clearly demonstrate Le Corbusier's practically exclusive concern with instrumentality. Other passages, however, when read in connection with his introduction of the Modulor man in the *Poème* (B.2), demand a different, far more subtle interpretation.

| 3.42 |

Title page of *Esprit* (B.3), from *Poème de l'angle droit.*

Montreal, Blackader-Lauterman Library Collection, McGill University.

Le Corbusier always emphasized the "miraculous" character of number, capable of freeing man from the constraints of the environment. He always insisted on the inevitability of proportions' connection to our embodied condition (not to the mind alone), ordering our relationship with the environment. In *The Modulor* he writes that harmony, regulating all things in our lives, "is the spontaneous, indefatigable and tenacious quest of man animated by a single force: the sense of the divine, and pursuing one aim: to make a paradise on earth."[120] This is, of course, the quest of Western technology in a secularized world. But Le Corbusier's vision was devoid of the guilt born of a nostalgia for "nature."[121] He adds: "Man can only think and act in terms of man (the measures which serve his body) and integrate himself in the universe (a rhythm or rhythms which are the breathing of the world)."[122]

Man must appropriate the universe because it is his destiny to be at home. Thus Le Corbusier justifies his quest to introduce the Modulor system of measurements. The tragedy of our time, he believes, is that measures have become "abstract or arbitrary: they should be *made flesh,* the living expression of our universe, *ours,* the universe of men, the only one conceivable to our intelligence."[123] If Le Corbusier embraced technology, he did so with a clear, critical mind, acknowledging the presence of a given ground impossible to articulate in traditional linguistic terms. With regard to the instrumental dimension of the Modulor, it is significant that Le Corbusier questioned the possibility of standard, universal measurements, such as the decimal system. In fact, he stated that the meter was responsible for "the dislocation and perversion of architecture," having become the unit of measurement for buildings that therefore had no relationship with the dwelling of humans.[124] The argument is not simply a rhetorical device to promote his own system; Le Corbusier understood very well the universalizing tendencies of human civilization, transformed by technological means of transportation and communication. He also clearly realized that the conclusion was the absolute interdependence of the modern world, which demanded an architecture whose meaning would transcend the specificities of language and cultural difference.[125]

When the issue of proportion is revisited in the *Poème* (B.2), accompanied by statements about architecture as the mistress of man—that is, harmony as erotic love, and architecture as a choreography of the Earth and the Sun—number appears more clearly as the trace of ontological continuity, as a "unique coincidence" in the spirit of pataphysics, rather than as a universal instrument of domination. The open question in *The Modulor* concerned the possibility of maintaining local measurements while postulating an effective system of dimensions for universal production. Le Corbusier maintained that the golden number unquestionably possessed very special mathematical properties and was the key to continuity and variety. This vision eventually transformed into the articulation of a general paradox, understood only through the experience of *poésie* in works of art, that only the imprecise is precise, and that the "scale . . . which is man" is not an anthropometric measure in the sense of dimension, yet remains "the invariable."

The next level of the *Iconostase* is devoted fully to incarnation: our ambiguous, mortal human condition, prone to dangers and delusions, yet our only vehicle for inhabiting and making a world. The emphasis Le Corbusier gives to the flesh should not be forgotten. This is crucial in the late twentieth century for our discussion of architectural meaning and appropriate architectural representation. The manifestation of human dimensionality, the space of architecture, is evident in love, in the erotic experience. Again, love is not proposed as a naturally given reality; rather it is a human creation, a task. Yet it is the place of boundaries, of joy and disclosure, even though this is not always recognized in the immediacy of our experience (C.2). In the place disclosed by sensuousness, where time, forms, and proportion appear beyond the comprehension of reason, we may acknowledge the embodiment of "the Creator" in the illusions of perception, "maybe" a disclosure of truth. Yet the "burden" of the body must be embraced (C.3). Perhaps unknowingly recasting Plato's well-known story to account for our incomplete nature, Le Corbusier declares that the work of creation is an erotic search for "the other half" (C.4).

The sole image and verse in the next level, entitled "Fusion" (D.4), is effectively a hinge between the lower part of the *Iconostase,* concerned with the tool and with the ethical questions that frame the architect's work, and the upper level, the flesh of the world. In "Fusion" we find the only explicit allusion to "the alchemist's metal," the ineffable unity. In this verse, extension is qualified as a great silence, the quality of the discovery of the new and unexpected in the work of art, before its rendition into language. "Fusion" also suggests that the self-transformation of the artist renders vision as a glance, a meditative and compassionate glance rather than a domineering gaze. This effectively opens us up to a "new time," a "delay," not unlike Marcel Duchamp's.

Levels E and F are concerned with the character and ethics necessary for appropriate work. The right angle becomes emblematic of rectitude (E.3), while the analogy of creation and procreation are also emphasized (E.4), together with the virtues necessary to build "modern cathedrals": constancy, uprightness, patience, vigilance, and a capacity for waiting and passionate desire. *Offre,* Le Corbusier's famous open hand, is the image at F.3. The fundamental virtue of compassion, made possible by the awareness that "sight is in the touch," the love of making, and the reciprocal virtues of giving and receiving are celebrated here.

The ultimate ground and foundation of the *Iconostase* (G.3) is the hand of the architect, drawing a right angle within a *bounded* space, the space of the human horizon. The *Poème* obviously fails if one attempts to read it in the traditional terms of theory as a logical, universally applicable structure for action, or if, following a semiotic model, one still expects the architecture it evokes to "signify." Le Corbusier sought the revelation of coincidences, bringing together a perceptual faith and the implementation of the architect's tools. While respecting the primacy of our technological world—we must emphasize that he never naively believed in an unchanging nature as the ground of meaning—he focused on the possible revelation of the poetic, the only kind of human "truth." This *poésie* could not be something imposed through a fabricated cosmology or imported from another time. It had to emerge from our world of experience, without resentment, embracing all its contradictions.

Given the opacity of the work, some commentators have put forward an alchemical interpretation of the text and

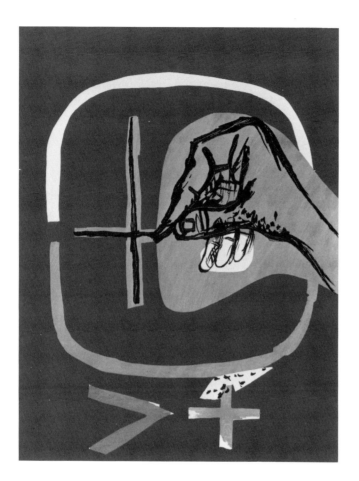

3.43

Title page of *Outil* (G.3), from *Poème de l'angle droit,* showing the architect inscribing the right angle inside the horizon. Architecture is presented as a discipline of boundaries and orientation, both physical and spiritual.

Montreal, Blackader-Lauterman Library Collection, McGill University.

357

images. The approach tends to rationalize the unresolved tensions in the work and has been used as an argument to demonstrate Le Corbusier's "symbolic" preoccupations, beyond the "formal" and "functional." [126] This argument backfires. True symbolization occurs only when the work is made "of" its own world, rather than construed through some alien construct. In fact, Le Corbusier never expressed himself in the language of alchemy or gnosticism. Obviously the alchemical interpretation of his pervasive concern with dualities and their engagement in the work of architecture might be adequate *after* an argument has been made that alchemy and mythology embody the traces of a collective unconscious. The work does disclose a "rare

Ubu Roi, the sublime and pathetic character created and drawn by Alfred Jarry (ca. 1896) [3.44], and reverse side of *Outil* (G.3), from *Poème de l'angle droit* [3.45]. The rule and the labyrinth, the archetypal instruments of architectural "projection," are transformed into a pataphysical emblem.

3.44 | Jarry, *Ubu Roi* (1900).
3.45 | Montreal, Blackader-Lauterman Library Collection, McGill University.

3.45

3.44

gold" in the gaps between fragments and words, in the spaces unveiled by bringing together disparate objects on the same "playing field" of the *Iconostase*. There is, of course, a significant affinity between the techniques of collage and the search for the ineffable unity in alchemy, and the issue of substantial transmutation (a self-transformation) through the opus is as present in the arcane science as it is desired by Le Corbusier from his work. Yet the focus is still on the specific disclosure of truth in the particular embodiments appropriate to our world, through its forms of representation.

For this reason we would like to suggest that the *Poème de l'angle droit* is rather a pataphysical text, where individuality and universality are reversed and reciprocal. It is concerned with self-transformation, which is accessible to us through Jarry's exemplary work. Indeed this is the fundamental question for the architect, as it is for the participants in (not mere observers of) his work. Truth must be sought in the unique coincidences disclosed in each artistic work, a wondrous truth that cannot be repeated or universalized. Like pataphysics, the *Poème* is a search for the exceptional, which is the universal, and architecture is therefore construed as a "science" of imaginary solutions. This discourse is posited as our only possible "cosmology," the "ground" for artistic action. The *Poème* now clearly appears as much more than a celebration of the *événement plastique*.[127] It is plain that Le Corbusier identified a sense of the sacred with a harmonious relationship (*accord*) with the cosmos, attainable through art and architecture. His work, however, is not simply a reiteration of the romantic program of man in a secular "nature"; his (our) nature is *also* art. It is our contention that Le Corbusier was conscious of this Nietzschean "paradox."

The lithographs of the *Poème* engage the homogeneous space of modernity through collage, while postulating its phenomenologic "grounding" in anthropomorphic directionality and motility. These new forms of "notation" were meant to do justice to the continuity of architectural experience, a problematic question that Le Corbusier had clearly identified in traditional forms of representation. In *The Modulor*, he quotes Henri Martin and states, "Music is not part of mathematics; on the contrary, it is the sciences which are part of music, for they are founded on proportion, and the resonance of the body of

359

sound engenders all proportion." After praising Pythagoras's accomplishment in relating human hearing to numbers, making it possible to write down and fix sound through notation, he declares: "The apotheosis of the machine age will demand a subtler tool, capable of setting down arrangements of sound hitherto neglected or unheard, not sensed or not liked."[128] Le Corbusier clearly related the temporality and spatiality of architecture and music. He suggested that the inherent continuum of the experience they convey was "destroyed" because of the artificial intervals created by man. While in *The Modulor* the new measure is posited as the arithmetic or geometric Fibonacci series, when he revisits the relationship between temporality and architecture in the *Poème* (B.4), stating that the "house" celebrates the dance of the Earth and the Sun, the question can no longer be reduced to one of aesthetic formalism or *tracés regulateurs*. Here the architect shows his grasp of the crucial issue of situation and experience, the "place" where the dark chasm of collage might find its translation in building. The dance of the Sun into human time demands a choreography and a new "notation" after the end of the "classical." The verse ends with the words: "*Et Vignole—enfin—est foutu! / Merci! Victoire!*" At stake is an awareness of the need for the architect to provide a script for life that may structure the rhythm of architectural experience, beyond aesthetic voyeurism. Thus the "depth" of collage in the *Poème* reveals the true validity of the tool. The truthfulness of the right angle is mediated; it is not about an unchanging, natural body image, yet it is not arbitrary. Le Corbusier's "patient search" from purism through surrealism led to an awareness that architecture could not be conceived or perceived in "aesthetic" terms, that its meaning had to be disclosed in a temporal medium, distinct from that of the "aesthetic objects" of the modernist tradition.

Time into Lived Space: Le Corbusier's La Tourette

To judge by oneself;
to understand relationships;
to have one's own feelings;
to tend to be *entirely disinterested;*
to force one's material self into the background —
is to conquer *reasoned conclusions* from life.
Rather than submit to the
constraints of a declining age,
one may as well sacrifice oneself[,] . . .
take risks, be sensitive to everything,
and open one's heart
more and more to others.

Le Corbusier, Precisions

The Monastery of Sainte-Marie de La Tourette in Eveux-sur-l'Arbresle, near Lyons (designed between 1953 and 1955), is one of those very rare twentieth-century buildings that are almost universally praised as masterpieces. It seems to possess the power to transform the inhabitant into a participant, to effectively "change one's life." Architects and critics from the most diverse persuasions have written eloquently about it, while the sensitive clients, the Dominican brothers, appreciate it as a most special place, "the most spiritual of all Dominican monasteries in France." [129] On his deathbed, Father Couturier, who was instrumental in ensuring that Le Corbusier proceed with the commission, called him "not only the greatest living architect" but also "the one in which the spontaneous sense of the sacred was most authentic and strong." [130]

If one compares the temporality in Le Corbusier's early projects—the well-known *promenades architecturales* along the ramps of the villas in the 1920s and 1930s, for example—with the experience of La Tourette, one must acknowledge an immense transformation. The clarity of transparent space threading the *objets-type* through a subjective, voyeuristic gaze is replaced by the experience of the labyrinth. In La Tourette there is *nothing* to thread. "The space is rigorous and demanding," emphasizes a young novice, "it is always discomforting in a way that vibrates with spirituality. . . . [N]othing fits, the furniture is always out of place[,] . . . yet it's the most appropriate . . ."[131] It is significant that among the preliminary proposals coming out of his own office, Le Corbusier rejected all that included rationalized ramps and circulations, in his own "style." Indeed, our experience of the building, despite its remarkably simple plan and the "familiarity" of all parts of the program, is one of utter and permanent disorientation. The internal space is always surprising, always new and mysterious. Time here is no longer linear; our participation with the build-

| 3.47 |

Axonometric drawing by Iannis Xenakis of a preliminary project for Sainte-Marie de La Tourette (1953–1954), rejected by Le Corbusier.

Paris, Fondation Le Corbusier #1244. © FLC/Adagp, Kinemage, 1997.

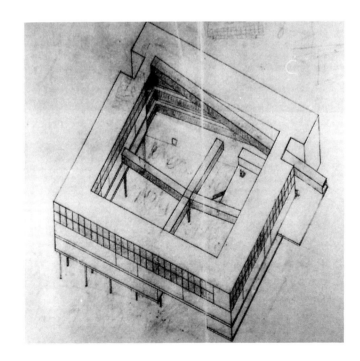

ing adds up into layers that both reveal and conceal, never resulting in a final clarification of the "idea" of the building.[132] The traditional paradigm of Daedalus, the archetypal architectural idea of our Western tradition, finally is transformed here into embodied experience.

La Tourette seems to embody the conviction that architecture must both reveal and constitute itself through *experience* as a de-idealized notion.[133] There *is* mystery in embodied perception: depth is not homologous to breadth and height, and the present is "thick" and reversible. In the monastery of La Tourette, architecture aims to manifest this mystery as such, through its own temporality and dimensionality.

The building appears as the crystallization of a sort of musical notation, ultimately made real through manifold levels of "interpretation" and "reenactment." The architect was conspicuously unconcerned by the errors that the often inexperienced craftsmen committed in the interpretation of the drawings. Le Corbusier always emphasized the difficulties imposed by the poverty of means in this project, turning this to his advantage to make a place that revealed the potential spirituality of the technological world, *our* world—an ecumenical spirituality predicated, as we know from the *Poème,* on the co-substantiality of light with darkness. La Tourette is a true "analogical" monastery, operating like a mirror that reflects something so that we can clearly see it, something slightly different that reveals what is already present but has never been truly seen.[134] The monastic "archetype" is always present and powerfully carried through. A monastic "type," a deceptively simple "index" of historical sedimentation, is the plan of the monastery, evidently recognizable as such, transformed and yet left intact in order to convey a more universal, contemporary meaning.

The work's intentions are fulfilled only *in* time. The building is emphatically not an aesthetic object; it must be *used.* Formal and programmatic decisions were never dissociated. Formalistic or aesthetic criteria, therefore, simply cannot account for the richness of this work. Its aim is a careful and thorough, if subversive, rewriting of the traditional programs and rituals. To name a few instances, we may recall the pervasive "inversions" that are present in the building: a residual cloister

Sketch by Le Corbusier of the plan of a "traditional" Dominican convent [3.48],
and the plan of the second level of La Tourette [3.49].

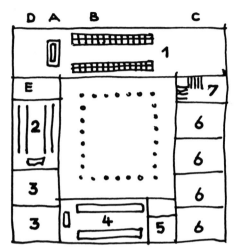

3.48

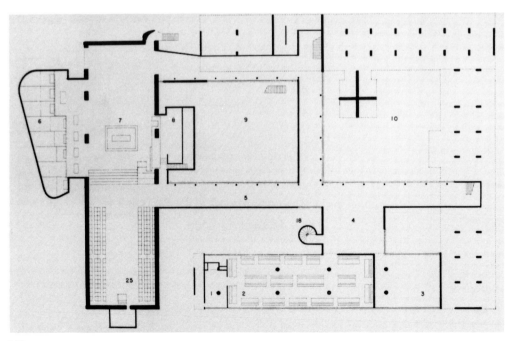

3.49

on the sloping ground that is hardly accessible and no longer reveals a natural relationship between the ground and the sky; a "sky cloister" on the roof that does not reveal the "infinity" of God in the landscape, but rather emphasizes the boundary, the (man-made) horizon, and does not allow a whole circum-ambulation; the small strip apertures throughout, in the process of closing us in and excluding all light; and the "musical walls," those large *ondulatoires* designed by means of the golden section that magically transform light into twilight, rather than simply letting it in. We may recall how Le Corbusier had praised the clarity of whitewashed walls in his earlier writings.[135] Dwelling stripped of all bourgeois "hangings" was for him a condition for self-mastery. In La Tourette the clarity no longer depends on finishes. His desire to show everything "as it is" is radical-ized, and space, embracing the darkness, becomes yet more lu-minous. As opposed to the shadows and dark corners that he deplored in the bourgeois home, the darkness in La Tourette can actually be "penetrated by one's eyes."[136] The light that Le Corbusier always considered "the fundamental basis of archi-tecture," the light in his famous definition of architecture as "the masterly, correct and magnificent play of masses brought together in light,"[137] became "contextual" in his later writings. In *New World of Space* he describes our perception of a flower, a mountain or a tree in a landscape as a deceptive objectifica-tion. "We pause, struck by such interrelation in nature, and we

Sainte-Marie de La Tourette, internal
view of the church.

Photo by A. Pérez-Gómez.

gaze, moved by this harmonious orchestration of space, and we
realize that we are looking at the reflection of light." This "just
consonance[,] . . . not simply the effect of the subject chosen,"
is for him the issue.[138] Then, he concludes, "A boundless depth
opens up, effaces the walls, drives away contingent presences,
accomplishes the miracle of ineffable space. I am not conscious of the
miracle of faith, but I often live that of ineffable space, the con-
summation of plastic emotion."[139] The space of the building, a
useful space, is also impenetrable; it is both bounded and infinite. "This is a difficult building to inhabit," state the clients
about La Tourette, "it is demanding during all hours and all
seasons of the year. . . . [D]uring the day it is dark, and at night
it is always alive[;] . . . but its hostility sings."[140]

While recognizing the necessary autonomy of
twentieth-century architectural syntax, these spaces bear witness to the power of the individual imagination to make works
that speak about something, and thus transcend self-referential
games. This building, as an experience, flaunts all logical contradictions; it is purposeful, yet it never yields to comfortable
use. In the austere church the rituals are always uneasy. The
confessional, traditionally placed in discrete locations along the
side aisles of seventeenth- and eighteenth-century churches, is
now displayed at the end of the long axis and painted red. The
slim steel cross, the only icon, stands by the side of the altar,
imbued by all the tension of its asymmetric location. And the

side altars for daily mass, which always "assume" a congregation in traditional church plans and are located also along the side aisles, are now truly private places for a personal conversation between the priest and the divine.

"The *only* time when the church has fit like a glove to a function," states one of the older brothers, "is when Le Corbusier's dead body spent the night here, on its way between the Mediterranean and Paris." Probably without knowing this, Arata Isozaki made a moving association between the "solid darkness" of La Tourette and the Mediterranean Sea—so loved by Le Corbusier—into which the architect walked to die. Isozaki also recognized the immense difference between the "Platonic" spaces of Le Corbusier's early work and the darkness and impenetrability of La Tourette.[141] Indeed, what is at stake here is the installation of darkness and interiority (as opposed to the light of classical metaphysics and theology).

The disclosure of depth in the building reappears as a primordial dimension *in time,* distinct from the "third dimension" of buildings reduced to aesthetic objects, reductive projections, or photographs. Bruno Reichlin similarly observed how the strip window destroys "traditional perspective space in architecture" by establishing a different relationship between what is near and what is far, obliterating the "frame" through the exaggerated distance between the vertical edges of the strip.[142] The building closes upon itself, physically stopping glances at the end of the corridors into the landscape; and when

367

| 3.52 |

Sainte-Marie de La Tourette, internal spaces.

Photo by A. Pérez-Gómez.

one does look out through the narrow strips, the far is brought near and is made subject to the same boundaries. Depth is here reinvested with a mysterious quality, a visual analogy to the interiority communicated by speech, poetry, and musical harmony.

This is architecture as a verb (ritual making), the ideation process that both is made by Le Corbusier and transforms him (his artistic practice), the enigmatic oral transmission of ideas between architect and craftsmen. Here the artist/maker accepts and embraces the distance that separates him from the craftsman, the break between conception and execution that Marcel Duchamp had made explicit through his "ready-mades" as a condition of our technological world. Only through the work can the irreconcilable be reconciled. The resulting architecture thus acquires the quality of a de-objectified production, a *caring* discipline beyond the dichotomies of substance/space and permanence/ephemerality, not merely a *seductive* practice. A discipline of love: to engage the senses without attachment, control or domination; to respect the solitude and integrity of the Other. This is perhaps the only possibility for architecture in the absence of tradition and "conventions."

Architectural meaning appears in *our* intersubjective space as in the space of a metaphor, as a recognition of that which cannot be reduced to words and yet begs to be named. La Tourette still proclaims the possibility of participatory, non-reductive representation in the world of electronic media and simulation; the possibility of a culturally significant architecture, facing the challenges posed by a privatized world and a perception of reality often identified with an objectified "picture." La Tourette's architecture, despite its spiritual theme, does not pretend to refer us back to absolute origins or foundations, and yet it is equally adamant against accepting a simplistic relativism and the expression of cultural "difference" as its only options. It proposes architecture as a discovery of order in making, which is also self-making, invoking a wholeness (and a holiness beyond all dogma) that may stand for all in our compressed planet, while yet remaining emphatically beyond tyranny and anarchy.

Coda

Machines for seeing modify perception.

* * *

Paul Virilio, Guerre et Cinéma

The early twentieth century witnessed a partial recovery of aspects of projection that had been abandoned by reductive forms of representation during the nineteenth century. Artists explicitly attempted to redefine a new relationship between their work and potential spectators/participants. In order to do so, they challenged the conventional limits of perspective and reconsidered the importance of temporality in the experience of their work. Marcel Duchamp's *The Large Glass,* also known as *The Bride Stripped Bare by Her Bachelors, Even* (1915–1923), is a good example of such a work, which seeks new modes of participation. Following from his earlier explorations in painting, this erotic "machine" embodies Duchamp's lifelong struggle to reveal an invisible dimension of projection beyond the conventional boundaries of Renaissance painting, sculpture, and architecture.[1] Yet what is most fascinating about Duchamp's work is that he uses the conventions of traditional perspective itself and subverts its instrumentality from within. As Wilfried Dörstel has written, Duchamp's work makes us look at the way we see, "at the generative power of the eye that lies at the origin of both *perspectiva naturalis* and *perspectiva artificialis,* forcing the spectator to act as a participant, witnessing a counterprojection of binocular vision."[2]

Indeed, *The Large Glass* became a literal window intersecting the cone of vision. The lower and upper parts are connected through a projective *hinge,* also identified with the horizon, again visible and finite. The lower part of the glass (the realm of the Bachelors) was conceived as a commentary on the rules of classical perspective. In it, the machine that distills desire (the chocolate grinder) is foreshortened toward the background—or the foreground, since the glass itself is reversible. The transparent screen lets the gaze venture through it without fixing the angle of vision. While in *Tu m'* the position of the observer transformed the *appearance* of the painting, in *The Large Glass* the support itself is affected by the changing background and the reflection of the spectator on the glass. The image cannot be perceived independently from the space in which it is placed. The multiplicity of angles of perception in *The Large Glass* is pushed beyond the opaque surface of a normal painting;

the support itself dissolves and becomes anamorphic. The impenetrable thickness of the glass, therefore, becomes the surface of projection for objects of the "fourth dimension."

This "transcendance" of perspective effectively takes place in the upper domain of *The Large Glass,* where the ambiguity between representation and the represented is used as a constructive projection to reveal something that we may recognize and yet have never before seen, as opposed to the more "figural" lower domain of the Bachelors. In the *White Box* Duchamp asserts that "all form is the projection of another form according to a certain vanishing point and a certain distance." By analogy with this notion of projected reality, all solid bodies could possibly represent the projection of an infinity of four-dimensional entities. The entire visible domain is for Duchamp an incessant flow of anamorphoses generated by those invisible entities. The Bride, a "four-dimensional" object is projected into a three-dimensional world.

Duchamp's Bride is also analogous to a shadow. As a projection of a three-dimensional entity, the shadow is determined by the object that casts it. It reveals the invisible side of the thing, outlining its hidden face as a *negative vision*. Removed from the projecting light, however, the shadow becomes an autonomous entity (as in a shadow play), an abstraction of the object projecting its absence. While traditional perspective aimed at closing the gap between the object and its representation, the manifestation of the invisible in Duchamp's work emerges from this gap—or delay—that distinguishes appearance and apparition, and the work becomes a quest for the missing object, the object of desire. Rather than perpetuating an objectified life world through a perspectival view, as an absolute truth outside of time, Duchamp's "hinge/window/hinged window" reveals our ephemerality, reciprocal to that of art—our existence as an in between, as an infra-thin yet purposeful moment of incandescence.

Working with time as "artistic material" is also essential for the expressive potential of film, the paradigmatic projective art of the twentieth century.[3] Indeed, the moving image in film opened up possibilities of introducing a whole new temporality into visual experience. Moreover, like the shadows in Duchamp's *Large Glass* and his painting *Tu m'*, the shadows of cinematographic projection work within the frame of perspective projection. Artists early recognized that this medium assumes the nonneutrality of its means of representation, as well as the explicit subjectivity of the phenomena of perception. Film offered a possibility of transcending the limitations of the technological, enframed vision through the juxtaposition of different realities. A previously invisible, uncharted aspect of experience found expression in this projective art.

Projecting a pyramid of light through the darkness of a cinema reversed the Renaissance visual pyramid and transformed it into an allegory of extromission, with its own window on the world. Cinematographic projection illustrates the reciprocity of light and shadow as an analogue of the complementarity of presence and absence, and it disrupts the fixed gaze of the perspective, which is the objectifying vision of Western science and philosophy. Western metaphysics emerged from a worldly vision that took the *gift* of daylight for granted and, unconscious of itself and its projections, assumed the permanent presence (*parousia*) of our source of illumination. In a poetic elaboration of this problem, David Michael Levin explains how this assumption made possible a condition of total unconcealment, a vision of total lucidity in perfect possession of its (transparent) object: "Western metaphysics reflects a worldly vision of truth which sees only sharp boundaries and divisions, the opposition permanently fixed in duality. . . . But this is a vision of truth which *occludes* our experience with shadows and shades [of meaning]; the enchantment of the sunset hour, the uncanny light of the twilight."[4]

During the cinematographic projection, we sit immobile between the light and the projected images, in the enduring present of a space-time of no fixed dimensions. The objectifying grasp of perspective seems to weaken and disappear as we witness the moving projection of "shadows" on an opaque screen, a paradoxical inversion of the perspectival transparent section through the cone of vision. These projections are shadows of a potential fourth dimension in Duchamp's sense, unveiling the possibility of truth in art, of work speaking about intersubjective otherness, and establishing a language that is *not* self-referential, despite its "conventionality" or intertextual character.

The tradition of the avant-garde, since its inception in nineteenth-century romanticism, was concerned with the irreducible dimension that exists between an evoked metaphoric space (the poetic space of montage) and the creative experience of the spectator through that space. The cinematographic montage of sequences follows a narrative form that opens up a gap between each juxtaposition and involves the audience at a spatial and temporal level. Sergei Eisenstein writes: "The power of montage resides in that it includes in the creative process the emotions and mind of the spectator. The spectator is compelled to proceed along that same creative road that the author traveled in creating the image. The spectator not only sees the represented element of the finished work, but also experiences the dynamic process of the emergence and assembly of the image just as it was experienced by the author."[5] The extreme terms of a metaphoric analogy open up a realm that invites inhabitation and activates the life of the imagination, the life of erotic engagement or *vita voluptuaria*. The spectator is not passive but rather creatively participates in the reconstruction of tactile space suggested by the montage, while giving up will to power and control. This metaphoric space of montage may constitute a potential model for appropriate architectural creation and reception.

Paradoxically, we may conclude that from its inception, particularly because of its inevitable relationship with light and optics, perspective has had a potential for unifying the relative time of our world with the absolute time of the image. The surrealists, and more specifically surrealist filmmakers, were

| 4.2 |

Still from Andrei Tarkovsky's *The Sacrifice* (1986). The horizon, which is never absent from Tarkovsky's films, engages the spectator in a constant "discovery" of the spiritual in the realm of the quotidian. In *The Sacrifice*, we witness the extreme terms of metaphoric analogies and recognize their complementarity. The reciprocity of action and thinking posits a different relationship between the spectator and the work, between human and the world, in which time is sculpted and space becomes again mimetic of the purposeful rhythms of everyday life.

Still from Peter Greenaway's film
Prospero's Books (1990), demonstrating a hybrid use of computers and
media.

Reproduced from Greenaway, *Prospero's
Books: A Film of Shakespeare's "The Tem-
pest"* (London: Chatto and Windus, 1991).

particularly aware of the need to redefine the distance between
the world and its representation: a distance that would allow
humanity to recognize its place in a new order. Today, in the
self-conscious work of a filmmaker such as Peter Greenaway,
the cinematographic montage, combined with spatial super-
positions generated through other media such as video and
computer imaging techniques, is capable of conveying a verita-
ble poetic disruption of the spatial and temporal perspective that
is considered "normal." Unlike the perspectival space and time
conveyed by conventional Hollywood films, which operate
within the basic parameters of the nineteenth-century novel,
the new synthetic narratives confound the linear structure of
filmic time and invite us to accept, through the undeniable evidence of our personal experience, the *aporia*s of time that seem
irreconcilable to reason. In the process, they deconstruct the
homogeneous, geometric space of technological enframing, the
"context" of the pathologies associated with life in the postindustrial city. By adding or subtracting a "fraction" of dimensionality to our experience, the projection of cinematographic

montage evokes the experience of an embodied, subjective spatiality, and it thus may be construed as the experience of architecture as it "could be."[6]

Digital Space

If you type any body's name,
no matter where they are,
the computer will scan the whole globe
until it finds that person
and you will see out of their eyes.

Ben Harris, age ten,
finalist in "The Coolest Computer,"
Microsoft competition (1995)

While cinematography is able to construe the experience of architecture as it "could be," the representation of architectural space through digital technologies, equally able to engage geometric solids and voids through temporal depiction, seems poised to offer immense opportunities. There is already evidence that complex detailing, as found in some projects by Frank Gehry and Norman Foster, would have been practically unrealizable without the help of the computer.[7] It seems able to facilitate the construction of complex buildings with considerably smaller tolerances, while more generally it is used as a powerful calculator to resolve more efficiently the many technical questions that pertain to the design process, which are particularly cumbersome in large projects. For the most part, however, computer graphic applications in architectural design, with their seductive manipulations of viewpoints and delusions of three-dimensionality, are still little more than an efficient "mechanism of composition." While they make the objectification of "another" reality appear more intense, their use has not improved the quality of our environment. Even for architects who believe in the significance of fragmentation and complex geometries, computers have contributed next to nothing toward destructuring the hegemony of panoptic space and proposing a more meaningful and participatory urban space.

The application of computers to architecture is, of course, one of the most hotly debated of unresolved contemporary issues. We shall not attempt to address all the implications raised by such a complex question. But for the purpose of our argument, it is important to emphasize that this instrument is *not* the equivalent of a pencil or a chisel, which could be easily manipulated. It is the culmination of the objectifying mentality of modernity and it is, therefore, inherently perspectival. Indeed, the invisible perspectival hinge operating in nineteenth-century axonometric space is internalized and made even more "natural" by computer technology, resulting in a powerful tool of reduction and control. The tyranny of computer-aided design and its graphic systems can be awesome: because its rigorous mathematical base is unshakable, it rigidly establishes a homogeneous space and is inherently unable to combine different structures of reference.

The issue in our posthistorical, postliterate culture is to avoid the pitfalls of further reductive, nonparticipatory representation, a threat constantly present in the electronic media and all forms of simulation. Artists and architects interested in the cultural consequences of cyberspace, however, emphasize the potential for computers to transcend their binary logic and become a tool for a poetic disclosure: they stress "random access" as opposed to "linear" memory. As a tool of representation, the computer seems to harbor a theoretical potential for heading toward either absolute fluidity or further fixation and reduction. In the wake of film and video, it is easy to conceive of cyberspace as a medium for theoretical projects that will continue a tradition of "critical practice" begun in the eighteenth century by Piranesi, Legeay, Boullée, and Ledoux. The ability to explore different, surprising dimensionalities, in a fluid medium where collage and monstrosity are almost natural, could hold great promise. Engaging time in visual experience, the ephemeral architecture constructed in cyberspace could conceivably function as a site for imagery and reverie.[8]

Nevertheless, there are great problems, even assuming this most optimistic scenario. The computer's own "architecture" is particularly resistant to destructuration; it tends to represent itself in its products with utter transparency, resulting in an often redundant self-referential formalism. Such gratuitous

| 4.4 |

Marcos Novak, *Liquid Architecture,*
composed algorithmically. Despite
Novak's conviction that the computer
can transform architecture through
time, the photograph reveals a dilemma. The formal composition of
his virtual architecture, not unlike De
Stijl explorations, is strictly controlled by 3-D (perspectival) space.

formalism is seldom poetic. Often the possibility of computers
"representing" *n*-dimensional spaces in the sciences is invoked
as a way that future architectural applications will overcome
their present, limiting "3-D" Cartesian space. Apart from the
philosophical fallacy involved in this argument (which we will
tackle later), it is curious that the model for this desire is the
intuitive work of artists such as Gris, de Chirico, and Magritte.[9]
While the creative potential of computers has been explored by
some contemporary artists, it should be remembered that these
works are usually openly subversive,[10] and thus not suited to
founding a new approach.

Cyberspace represents "the promise of control over
the world by the power of the will."[11] Poetic metaphors, by
contrast, are always an expression of reconciliation with destiny:
Nietzsche's *amor fati.* The poetic work is not merely the product
of personal will; true poetry speaks primarily of the world, pre-
serving for the reader/participant the freedom of interpretation
and orientation. Poetry, furthermore, results not from an excess
of reasoning or intellectual power, but rather from a lack
thereof;[12] it is, finally, an issue of making in order to know, not
of harboring information in order to make. The nature of the
poetic is to let us assume our true condition, which is not the
dilemma—life *or* death, in body *or* in soul, inside *or* outside
cyberspace—but a totality: life *and* death in the thickness of
the present, a single instant of incandescence.[13] Cyberspace and
simulation discourse assume rather uncritically a theory of per-

ception that comes directly from Descartes. While our culture seems to be in the process of questioning the seventeenth-century notion of a division between mind and body, cyberspace embodies precisely that division. Not surprisingly, even when a diagnosis of cyberspace tends to emphasize its character as a place for poetic and critical exploration, the discourse soon becomes blurred with imprecisions about what constitutes our given human spatiality.[14] Soon cyberspace is identified with space, and with cyberspace architecture.

To make sense of this problem it is crucial to remember the conditions and limitations of self-referentiality in art and thought. A major problem with the discourse on cyberspace as a medium for architecture seems to be a pervasive and radical gnosticism that forgets "prior" experience. Our reality is neither exclusively "natural" or "cultural." Although cultural "constructionism" is more fashionable these days, we would like to emphasize, with Walter Benjamin, that *mimēsis* is our true nature, a capacity that allows humans to transform inherited culture into second nature and thus under-stand our purpose. It is through *mimēsis* that images traditionally have acquired the power of their original. In this sense, sympathetic magic and cyberspace are not so far apart. However we must recognize that this mimetic condition of ours is a two-way street.[15]

Referring back to our discussion about vision and depth, we should reiterate what is taken for granted in the discourse about cyberspace. (1) When cyberspace is described in relation to a given space, the *existence* of space itself as a geometric entity constituted by three essentially homologous dimensions is simply assumed as something existing "out there," which is a priori the substance of the art of architecture. The problem of spatiality and temporality for an undivided human consciousness is infinitely more complex, always involving context, orientation, and a qualitative dimensionality where depth is primary. (2) Cyberspace is the space in a computer screen; thus regardless of how sophisticated the workstation may be, questions of perception are usually reduced to vision (or primarily to vision), and the origin of meaning in human experience is not questioned. It is usually assumed to be a purely intellectual process, which it is not. (3) The discourse on cyberspace usually assumes that the meaning of art and architecture can be effectively reduced to information. This is, of course, highly problematic. The form of expression, particularly in the arts, is at least as crucial to meaning as its content.

The ubiquitous character of electronic space also deserves some comment. Cyberspace's delusion of omnipresence tends to perpetuate the privatizing tendencies that have been at work in industrial and postindustrial cities for almost two hundred years. While it would be fair to argue that contemporary society seems to have no interest in traditional symbolic space—places where the individual may acknowledge a sense of belonging to cultural institutions, which are today often regarded as representative of old forms of repression and political control—many difficulties also arise from this radical homelessness. The alienation of the individual and its pathological consequences for the human psyche have been often discussed.[16] Rather than resulting in an ideal, transparent society, the space-time of telecommunications has encouraged an unexpected opacity, a reaction not unrelated to the late-twentieth-century obsession with ethnic and national differences.[17] It may be true that the accessibility of electronic "space" adds a new dimension to the old dialectic of public and private realms, suggesting possible new forms of human interaction. Nevertheless, we must remember that in this new space of communication, the expressive body, origin of all communicative action, is always left out. We should not be naive about the so-called public nature of cyberspace. True public space, the space of architecture, is the "space of appearance," where facing the Other and through his or her gaze, I encounter myself: I can know myself only through the eyes of the Other; self-knowledge is never the result of a specular or narcissistic operation. In this sense, appearance always implies embodiment. Bodies transformed into information are not phenomenal bodies. Although it could be argued that at the moment society's public forum is indeed the information highway, and that encounters in its nodes are fruitful, such a highway should not be construed as a substitute for the space of dialogue and erotic exchange, the space for an architecture of resistance.

Like surrealist collage, cyberspace constructions may reveal places for poetic dwelling, allowing us to visualize a temporalized architecture—ephemeral and changing like music, perhaps paradoxically facilitating our access to an archaic understanding of projection. Yet the crucial question of translation from digital space to the realm of full embodiment remains. Unlike the digital encoding of music on a disc, traditional musical notation, although it may be mathematical and inscribed on a page, demands the distance implied by *interpretation* in order for the music to actually exist. It is a historical misunderstanding to imagine the interpreter as a mechanical operator that always produces the same results. As late as the eighteenth century, composers understood and fully accepted the nature of this process. The music is made, by humans, in the vivid present, and it is always different; this is its quality, its *meaning,* rather than a defect. This is also the challenge to which architectural notation must respond, both as the origin of a process of making and as an open, participatory site for inhabitation. Ultimately, the question is not unlike that asked by Lissitzky. To build such magical places, both impenetrable and inviting, we cannot rely on a mere formal transcription. If we are disillusioned with the prosaic, passive, and static space of conventional building, and we yearn for a poetic, dynamic, and fictional architecture, then boundaries become a crucial matter. This is indeed at odds with the infinite malleability that characterizes cyberspace. The goal is hardly to pursue the dream (or nightmare) of our dissolution into networks of digitized information; it is rather to construe and build spaces that resist such collapse.

At this juncture, we may observe that promising computer applications in architectural design have less to do with dreams about a hypermalleable cyberspace, and more with a conscious intention to subvert the linear application process itself, deliberately embracing chance and computer "errors."[18] Using existing software programs as hybrid tools with other media, or interrupting the computer's processes at points where "it believes" it can provide a final answer, seems to yield interesting possibilities. If we accept the computer as a tool that demands care and patience in its use, one that should be mediated by language and a poetic (ethical) articulation of architectural programs—often using it "analogically" against its "original vocation," employing it perhaps in the initial stages of a project to generate a complex and difficult challenge for completion in other media—we may perhaps have better chances of success.

As we have pointed out, however, it is hardly surprising that the more common result of engaging this paradigmatic tool of instrumental representation is still to exacerbate the objectification and reduction of all building processes and to maintain the hegemony of standardization. Even the simple avoidance of using totally prespecified design components is difficult once the machine has become part of the office.[19] This is the deplorable outcome of the implementation of the technological will to power, of efficiency and rational control as the only unquestionable values for any practice lacking a real "theory," that is, lacking a philosophy and its concomitant historical grounding that may lead to ethical, critical, and subversive tactics.

Philosophical Corollary

Architecture addresses directly our whole embodied perception (rather than a "subjective" cybernetic receptor, an "objective" mechanism, or a composite organic body). Architecture is not an experience whose meaning may be fully translated into other media. Like a poem, its very presence is that which constitutes the means and end of the experience. Yet we must also acknowledge that human experience is always mediated linguistically. This understanding of architecture has been present throughout our long journey. While we hope to have clarified the most important questions concerning architectural representation, revealing the options available to us, we would nevertheless like to conclude by revisiting some fundamental issues in the general language of philosophy, if for no other reason than to emphasize the difficulty of the alternatives.

It is indeed hard to imagine how built architecture, a traditional instrument of political power and repression, may come to represent something other than male, egocentric will and ominous economic forces, regardless of its site in the world. We would like to reiterate, in terms that fully acknowledge our cultural reality, how despite its common origin with instrumental and technological forms of representation, architecture may yet allow for *participatory* human action and an affirmation of life-toward-death, enabling symbolization as "presencing" through the constructed work rather than manifesting the very denial of human capacity to recognize existential meaning in privileged artifacts such as works of art. In other words, we would like to suggest the terms by which architecture can embody values of a different order than those rooted in fashion, formal experimentation, or publicity, and can be cast in forms other than the seductive gloss characterizing all present mechanisms of cultural domination.

It is unlikely that architecture will somehow be miraculously saved by the acknowledgment of cultural or gender differences that recently have become more explicit in our epoch of incomplete nihilism. We should recall that the present cultural fragmentation, despite its complexity, is only the "other" side of the modern project and a consequence, like democracy, of epistemological *perspectivism*. In pondering potential alternatives for the architect—that is, generative theories for practice that may involve a more enlightened implementation of his or her projective tools—it is counterproductive to ignore or deny the common origin of our tradition that has resulted in a technological world. Although in different stages of accomplishment, the technological project is shared by all (or almost all) cultures of our planet. Indeed, it is crucial to remember our particular technopolitical context as we ask *what* and *how* architecture may *represent* as the stage of our late-twentieth-century everyday life.

The World as Technology

Technology is more than machines or neutral processes: it is our world, the historical reality that we have fabricated, qualitatively different from a world of traditional techniques. Ours is a world of artifacts that are no longer a *bridge* between our consciousness and the external realities which we have not created; our artifacts seem to have rather created a *wall,* impossible to escape, surrounding us with our own dreams of control, self-referentiality, and cyberspace. While seeking to answer the same old questions about the measure of man and place amid the immeasurable and alien, technology opted for control and domination, for arrogant and efficient action upon a reduced and objectified picture of the world. Success within this instrumental mode of action has reinforced humanity's ambition to exploit a universe reduced to "natural resources"—one that, we strongly suspect, may not have been created *only* for that purpose, but one whose final opacity, we may believe, gives us license to act in this fashion.

This all-encompassing technology has been bound up with the tools of architectural ideation, representation, and practice since the early nineteenth century. Architecture, the art of mediation par excellence, has tended to become a vehicle of political or economic domination, repression, and control. Technology problematizes architecture, itself a space-time of human situations whose meaning coexists with embodied consciousness. This realization is crucial if we are to engage critically our architectural tools of representation, finally overcoming the naive assumption of their neutrality.

It is important to emphasize, however, that technology cannot be simply dismissed from the point of view of the traditional fine arts, metaphysics, or humanism. The thrust behind its accomplishments (and failures) is indeed the human thirst for transcendence, in some contexts understood as the unending struggle for personal liberation. Once God and Man were removed from the center of the world, technology became a morally justifiable response to the inveterate human *lack* in the face of the cosmos—particularly in the Western tradition, with its focus on the transformation of the external (rather than the internal) conditions of human existence. Realities that traditionally had made us "whole" while belonging in the realm of the ideal and the imagination had to be made material: the Heavenly City had to be constructed. Obsessed by the accomplishments of instrumentality and its own assertive will to power, technology has led postmodern humanity into a gnostic trap in which the preexisting "world out there" is forgotten. Today we are often controlled by forces that we thought we were capable of mastering.

Within the wall we have built, it is difficult to understand that there is no human creation that is not also a *mimēsis*. In the process that makes it possible for the culture we inherit to become our nature, through works of art (and architecture), the nightmare of constructionism may be shattered. We cannot name the transhistorical ground, but we cannot do without it. However mutable and historically determined this world of primary experience may be, phenomenology discloses it as one where the universal and the specific are given *simultaneously* in the mystery of perception, in the space between Being and becoming. This ground gives us access to the inexhaustible meaning of historical artifacts and it must be presupposed by any narrative, the form language must take for a hermeneutics of ambiguity to articulate relevant truths.[20] Merleau-Ponty reminds us: "What consciousness does not see is what makes it see[,] . . . as the retina is blind where the fibers that will permit vision spread out into it."[21]

Despite all this evidence, it is still easier to believe that all reality is constructed and that we have little or no option but to embrace our "destiny": the *jouissance* of immaterial bodies in the cybernetic megalopolis. Under this assumption it is easy to affirm that architecture and design as technology are all-encompassing, that in this mode architecture offers a vision of life "yet to come" for a postromantic, decentered, and fully social-democratic self. Much critical theory emphasizes that we simply must have the courage to follow the project to its end. Can it really be that simple? What about our present contradictions and pathologies? Are television and the Internet truly our "reality"? How can one reconcile the claim that electronic space is a new, "more effective" form of public space in the face of the fragmenting postmodern world, torn by repression, genocide, random acts of terrorism, and war on a wholly new scale?

We must recognize that there are dangers present in the technological world that are more subtle, yet more serious, than humanity's potential for self-destruction and the threat of ecological disaster. The messianic denial of death as a positive limit and essential qualifier of life may end up jeopardizing the possibility that human existence can remain open to meaning and thus perpetuate civilization through its cultural institutions and symbols. A nihilism of despair may become a powerfully destructive force, overriding the balance that we must maintain when we engage, with Nietzsche, in an indispensable affirmative nihilism. While questioning the absolute truth of Western metaphysics as something outside *experience* (the Platonic truth–

as-correspondence), this form of affirmative nihilism enables humanity to remain open to the powerful silence of art and architecture and to the dark radiance of light, enhancing our sensitivity to the sound of an angel's flight, in case one might happen by . . . Therefore, rather than blindly embracing technology and the tools it offers, we must recognize its mysterious origin and its historical transformations. Diagnosing the enframing without resentment is a crucial step: technology itself is founded on "weak truths." Even in the absence of gods, our unique planet Earth and its sky are present as a ground for our full, embodied experience, one through which we may now be capable of questioning the hegemony of abstract constructs. In view of this realization, we are called to transform our own individual, often arrogant, relationship to the world and explore other options.

For architecture, the end of historical progress, itself bound up with technology and already resulting in a cultural disillusion about the future in the postindustrial world, places the hitherto unquestionable value of innovation in a different light. The point, however, is not merely to assume the collapse of differences between technological and aesthetic cultures, the often-expressed dream of the whole world becoming a work of art. This may express the desired end for an accomplished nihilistic epoch, were it ever to arrive. But our own time is hardly at that stage. We live in a time of incomplete nihilism, in which repressive economic, political or pseudo-religious values occupy the place of the strong values of the ancien régime. The identification of aesthetic and technological values could be dangerous. We should not readily give up the possibility of art and architecture destructuring technology and other hegemonic institutions. It is important to maintain the erotic distance that has constituted the effective human depth in our tradition, the space of presentation *and* representation, rather than accepting the collapse of desire into cyberspace, or the dissolution of function (or content) in the architectural form. Any sort of formalism, however sophisticated and despite its good intentions, could effectively exacerbate the barbaric aspects of our human nature: rather than designing a world for the *Übermann,* a democracy for creative and responsible individuals "beyond good and evil," we may end up with a society of violently territorial animals in a world of pseudo-events and make-believe participation, living in private, fenced-in suburban "communities" or "theme parks."

De architectura in Ten Notes

| B♯ |

The work of art's primary representative function, regardless of its medium or its nature as figurative or nonobjective, concerns the question of *recognition:* art's capacity to complete our everyday experience of existential lack and make us spiritually whole.[22] This possibility of completion, while acknowledging the irreducible reality of an opaque Beginning and unknown Beyond, has characterized art works since the inception of humanity and constitutes their primary symbolic function, their representative function. Architecture, a predominantly nonobjective art, is recognized through the rituals and actions it frames. By giving a human measure to time and space, by projecting a figure and rhythm, architecture has revealed the presence of the invisible in the world of the everyday. This recognition of the new in the familiar, a re-cognition that is also a self-cognition, is perhaps the only constant of true art and poetry through history. Partaking of this condition, the architectural works of the city allowed for existential orientation, cultural belonging, and the perpetuation of tradition. As an abstract order addressed primarily to the imagination, architecture was a form of knowledge that could be embodied at the scale of the reliquary, the garden, the ephemeral canvas and wood structure, or the *machina* for manifold celebrations and theatrical events.

This recognition, art's capacity to make us spiritually whole, is inherently difficult in a postmodern world where people are generally oblivious of their mortality and have grown accustomed to exploitation, simulations, and technological control. In our field, an understanding of the autonomy and polysemy of the symbols employed by the architect is an important first step in overcoming this predicament. One object, one model, or one drawing may, indeed, embody the full intentionality of a building. Embodied communication is irreducible to linguistic formulas. Legitimate forms of production that may lead to truly eloquent results are as manifold as there may be architects wishing to take up the challenge of self-transformation that results from a renewed hermeneutic relationship with history, such as we propose here. Using projections conceived as ephemeral traces or indexes rather than as reductive notation, engaging the building operation as an imaginative translation, may generate an architecture once more experienced as a flowing musical composition, as a temporal form in which the spectator/participant may catch a glimpse of his or her place in a "fragmented wholeness."

| C |

Artistic meaning rests upon an intricate interplay of showing and concealing. The work of architecture is no mere bearer of meaning, as if that meaning could be transferred to another bearer. Above all, emphasizes Hans-Georg Gadamer, this creation is not something that we can imagine being made deliberately by someone.[23] It is, first and foremost, of the world, and our experience of it overwhelms us. Rather than simply "meaning something," art and architecture allow meaning to present itself. We *recognize* the meaning as new and yet we cannot *name* it; we are invited to silence and yet must proclaim the utterly familiar. Thus art and architecture, as cultural forms of representation, present something that can exist only in specific, utterly concrete works. This "representative power"—which has nothing to do with replacement, substitution, or copy—distinguishes the work of art and architecture from other technological achievements. The "order" of architecture resists pure conceptualization. It is not an allegory in the sense that it says one thing and gives us to understand something else. What the work has to say can be found only within itself, grounded in language and yet beyond it. Experiencing and participating in a work of architecture have fundamental temporal dimensions. Acknowledging the ambivalent reality of its space constitutes a re-cognition that is, also, a creation of ourselves. Architecture as a meaning-for-embodied-consciousness demands an erotic projection from the maker and the participant, an abandonment of our selves for the Other that truly matters and may change our life, an act whose final objective is our realization as embodied, imagining selves.

E♭♭

In the context of our cities of shopping malls and traffic networks, the images of fashion, whether of old Europe or modern technology, are empty simulations. They carry no meaning except to reaffirm implicit repressive structures of power. A critical step toward our recovery of a lost historic richness is to escape the false hopes of perspectivism, understood as the "natural" space of cultural anthropology, television, or architectural practice. Democratic activism or Marxist or feminist critiques may indeed be capable of disclosing and deconstructing repressive structures. Yet although rational consensus, built on the perspectivism of the Enlightenment, may lead to more just political structures (democracy without the acceptance of personal responsibility will probably always be imperfect), it produces dreadful design; it is not a substitute for the poetic, thoughtful imagination.

In architecture, an uncritical acceptance of transparent communication as a dominant requirement (over potential meaning) has reinforced the use of projections to function as surrogates of buildings. When sets of drawings attempt to provide us with a "picture" of an architectural place or object, the buildings produced by such techniques necessarily reflect the predictive quality of their conception: the possibility of a revelatory dimension is abandoned. That this assumption of a literal relationship between the project and the building is basic to both the "correct" politics of rationality and industrial production in the modern city makes a critical reassessment all the more pressing.

E♭

The artistic paradigm of Renaissance illusionism became problematic once humanity started to "inhabit" homogeneous, geometric space during the eighteenth century. The "arts of resistance" adopted the traditional concerns of architecture. Indeed, during the last two centuries all art forms, including literature, music, sculpture, painting, and more recently film and other "hybrids," seem to be emphatically "about" space: space material and projective, yet qualitative and metaphoric.

The work of architecture as *projection* is *space-matter;* it demands a synthesis of the material and spatial imaginations (in the sense of Bachelard), obviously beyond any traditional typology of artistic products. Philosophers of art have generally avoided speaking about architecture because of its added complexities, its questions of utility and program. Yet it is our contention that architecture must be understood as the paradigmatic cultural product of *representation* after the demise of Renaissance illusionism. It is the fragmentary artifact par excellence that may allow us to identify our opaque nature under the linguistic "house of being," while embracing use-values in our secular society. Architecture is the technological artifact that may reveal the horizon of beings that we recognize (in our wholeness), while we acknowledge that this horizon is never fully present.

Once symbolic representation was replaced by instrumental representation, however, the aesthetic distance could be increased. The danger for art and architecture is, indeed, irrelevancy through potential solipsism, the closure to participation implicit in instrumental representation. It has been our contention, however, that it is possible to contemplate an opening through this paradox that may afford us a new opportunity to understand the *flesh* as the ground of being, but now in terms of a fully built culture. We are now in a better position to imagine a *ricorso* of history that starts by acknowledging that culture is our second nature, even as it respects the irreducible and silent presence of the body as our transhistorical ground.

| F |

While marking an intensification of being or embodying truth without objectifying it, architecture is "demanding" of the spectator or inhabitant. It requires from the architect and the inhabitant a different relationship with external reality.

This is the possibility that opens up once we understand Merleau-Ponty's definition of reality as "the flesh of the world" and grasp what Martin Heidegger has named *Gelassenheit,* an attitude standing beyond the dichotomy of ritual participation versus intellectual contemplation. Philosophy has now denounced its traditional claims to an absolute truth in the spirit of a rigorous science. We know from Heidegger's late philosophy that Being is no longer graspable through pure contemplation or pure instrumentality. Architecture rises up to the challenge of embodying a new "weak" truth. While accepting the technological language and body from which it issues, architecture seeks to destructure that language and body; it aims at love and recognition beyond optical seduction, demonstrating (often through monstrosity) the mysterious origin of technology itself.

| G |

In order to address the dangers of aestheticism, reductive functionalism, and either conventional or experimental formalism, architecture must consider seriously the potential of *narrative* as the structure of human life, a poetic vision realized in space-time. The architect, in a sense, now must also write the "script" for his or her dramas, regardless of whether this becomes an explicit or implicit transformation of the "official" building program. This is, indeed, a crucial part of the architect's design activity, and also the vehicle by which an ethical intention will inform the work. Only by accepting this responsibility will it be possible for that work to invite the radicalized "individual" of the late twentieth century to exercise, with his or her freedom, a reciprocal responsibility to "participate" in the re-creation of a work of art that is no longer the signifier of a shared cosmic order, nor the product of a romantic imagination attempting a construction ex nihilo. Architectural work is therefore articulated as a narrative, "metaphoric" projection grounded on recollection. On one hand, the spectator's perception must remain "distant," the work a representation of mysterious depth, a trace of cultural continuity. On the other hand, the rupture with the cosmological epoch is signaled by the inhabitant's intimate participation in re-creating the work through language so that it will yield its "sense" in the high-tension gap inherent in metaphor.

| A♭ |

The deconstruction of the Cartesian *ego cogitans,* rather than amounting to a denial of the creative self, goes hand in hand with a patient evocation of being through embodiment. The imagining self must prevail. Only the imagining self as creator and spectator, distinct from the fully transparent and coincidental Cartesian *ego,* can inhabit through architecture a world already beyond the future orientation of modernity, where the notion of infinite progress has collapsed and yet our human capacity to tell stories, the narrative function with its vectors of recollection and projection, remains the only means of articulating ethical action and construing an appropriate choreography for a postmodern world. The site of the *flesh,* an empty gap that is *not* nothingness, which common sense assumes to be the exclusive space of action, is the meaning of architecture. In works of architecture that transcend the reductions of functional "modernism" and the pastiches of "historicism," however, this site is never merely a comfortable and invisible geometric space functioning efficiently. Rather, it is always dense and ultimately impenetrable, challenging the spectator to experience the work (and the cultural situations it frames) in the "thick present"—the time and space of poetry and myth.

| A |

In order to deconstruct the logocentric metaphysical heritage of modernity as it appears in architecture, without obliterating the possibility of ethical creation, architects must recover a *perceptual faith* that affirms a capacity to perceive qualitative difference (and therefore purpose) in the works of our cultural and artistic heritage, very different indeed from the despair and homogenization of difference often exhibited in poststructuralist criticism. *Perceptual faith* alone allows for the discovery of exceptional coincidences we call order, discoveries through making of effective connections that then may be shared with the Other. This is the analogical conviction that allowed alchemists to perceive in their work the purpose of their individual life. As they partake of the rhythms of the world and understand the "weak" nature of human works in the context of intersubjective reality, the present perpetually returns. This is, as we have suggested, the "worldview" implicit in Alfred Jarry's pataphysics. A passionate involvement with the work at hand is required, as seductive images can be produced only by a heated lover. But such fabrications must be tempered by a sense of ethics informed by a historical understanding, that of a compassionate lover capable of releasing the object of desire. The realization that both lack and fulfillment are delusions when objectified, that life and death are always present and cannot be separated—and that the embodiment of these values in the work of architecture would amount to the possibility of caring profoundly about our making, and yet being truly detached from the products of our endeavor—amounts to a final acknowledgment of architecture's essence as a *verb*. To repeat: Architecture is not a noun, a text, objectified speech; it is rather a projection, a temporal form. Architecture as projection is antithetical to planning, both as an attitude to discover meaningful form and in the engagement of its narrative program.

A#

Lacking as we do a theological a priori, we must start from experience to construct a generative theory. The world of our experience includes the artifacts that make up our artistic tradition, the revelatory moments we call architecture, those moments of recognition in spatiotemporal forms that are completely new, yet strangely familiar. Understanding these forms of specific embodiment and articulating their lessons in view of our own tasks, we will have a better chance of construing an appropriate architecture, projecting imaginative alternatives going beyond stifling inherited institutions: we will find history as a discourse of the imagination aimed at discovering the inexhaustible hidden potential in the "traces" of our tradition, our true "memory" embedded in documents, buildings, drawings, and so forth, which will open up whole new worlds for us. We must ground architecture and its meanings through its relationship to language, understanding history (as stories) as the true normative discipline of humanity and therefore as the appropriate discourse of architectural theory.[24] It is by means of the ethical imagination, oriented historically yet not bound by History, that the architect must find effective connections between formal discoveries and new cultural situations.[25]

To reiterate, a radical revision of architectural ideation and its true potential—one that shows an understanding of the wisdom of the making hand and the power of a thoughtful and caring embodied consciousness—is urgently required. Thus, operating within the technological world, works can be produced that transcend self-referentiality and tautology, becoming privileged places of poetic epiphany. The place for architecture is the site where technology may be cracked open by the imagination. These may be marginal and liminal spaces in our postindustrial culture, places where humanity may become aware of its capacity for true understanding in the dark and silent space of metaphor, yet also spaces *within* technology, revealing the *actual presence* of mortality, the immanence of Being.

Notes

Prelude
Mapping the Question: The Perspective Hinge

1   Durand's legacy is perhaps better known as the objectification of style and technique in the establishment of apparently irreconcilable alternatives: *technological* construction (functional) versus *artistic* architecture (formal), and the false dichotomy of *necessary* structure and *contingent* ornament. Durand gave us the first architecture theory whose values were extrapolated directly from the aims of applied science and technology. Before Durand, the concern for meaning was never subordinated to the pursuit of efficiency and economy in the products of design. For our present discussion it is important to keep in mind the connection between this value system and its tools.

2   See Hubert Damisch, *L'origine de la perspective* (Paris: Flammarion, 1987), preface and part one. There is a recent English translation by John Goodman: *The Origin of Perspective* (Cambridge, Mass.: MIT Press, 1994).

3   Symbols afford us a glimpse of our transhistorical embodied reality (never fixed or reducible to a formulation such as the transparent Being of Western metaphysics) and thus make it possible for us to endure in the world as mortals, embodying a fleeting sense of purpose—bound to remain unresolved when subjected to rational scrutiny. Such understanding of symbolization as a reality immanent in the world of humans survives the critique of relativism, and as a goal of architectural design it seeks to overcome a trivial, self-referential formalism.

4   While making final revisions to this manuscript, we came across James Elkins's recent book *The Poetics of Perspective* (Ithaca: Cornell University Press, 1994), in which the author uses numerous historical examples from different fields to make this point. Elkins's main interest is to show the rifts that separate those who understand perspective as a pictorial device from those who see it as a linguistic or epistemological metaphor.

5   This is particularly important in a world where, for better or for worse, what individuals do *matters*—we can indeed self-destruct if we are not careful, or at least "disappear" into cyberspace . . . Furthermore, we must start from the realization that meaning in human experience is not something that merely vanishes with the "death of God." Meaning is firstly "given" in the prereflective engagement of each human—with his or her body—in the world. It has proven impossible to reduce meaning to a simple effect of associations, controllable by rational means. Human meaning remains, primordially, a mystery whereby we

recognize an order in the specificity of our perception. The objectified, *enframed* perception of objects that has dominated the last two centuries of Western civilization, however, makes it difficult for us to understand that this *perception with meaning* is indeed the very ground of our thoughts and actions, one that makes even "virtual reality" possible.

6   Such differences can be perceived only if the historical artifacts are understood hermeneutically, in the context of their respective cultural worlds and with particular regard to the concepts of space and time on which they are based. Paul Ricoeur thoroughly develops the notion of a hermeneutics of suspicion and the "world of the work" in several works, particularly *History and Truth,* trans. Charles A. Kelbley (Evanston, Ill.: Northwestern University Press, 1965) and *The Conflict of Interpretations: Essays in Hermeneutics,* ed. Don Ihde (Evanston, Ill.: Northwestern University Press, 1974).

7   The famous discussion surrounding the ideas and building of the Milan Cathedral is an excellent example of the complex process of architectural design in the Middle Ages. See particularly the writings of James Ackerman and Paul Frankl in *Art Bulletin,* March 1945 and June 1949: J. S. Ackerman, "'Ars Sine Scientia Nihil Est': Gothic Theory of Architecture at the Cathedral of Milan," *Art Bulletin* 31 (1949), pp. 84–111; P. Frankl, "The Secret of the Mediaeval Mason," *Art Bulletin* 27 (1945), pp. 46–60.

8   The connections between magic and architecture are clearest in Francesco Colonna's *Hypnerotomachia Poliphili* (1499); in the work of Juan de Herrera at the Escorial; in Heinrich C. Agrippa's famous *De occulta philosophia* (1533); and through the introduction of classical architecture into England by John Dee (in the preface to his edition of *Euclid*). The connection, however, runs deep and the list of works on this topic would be too long to cite. Some of the most insightful secondary sources are Frances Yates, *Giordano Bruno and the Hermetic Tradition* (London: Routledge and Kegan Paul, 1964), and her other related works; a cursory review of Marsilio Ficino's *Liber de Vita,* translated as *The Book of Life* (Dallas, Tex.: Spring Publications, 1980); George Hersey, *Pythagorean Palaces* (Ithaca: Cornell University Press, 1976); and René Taylor, "Architecture and Magic: Considerations on the *Idea* of the Escorial," in *Essays in the History of Architecture* (London: Phaidon, 1969), pp. 81–109.

9   See Marco Frascari and William Braham, "On the Mantic Paradigm in Architecture: The Projective Evocation of Future Edifices," paper given at ACSA 1994 Annual Meeting, Theory and Criticism Session, Montreal, March 12–15, 1994.

10 See Anne Carson, *Eros the Bittersweet* (Princeton: Princeton University Press, 1986), and particularly Longus, *Daphnis and Chloe* (second century C.E.).

11 It is in this sense that we can partially agree with Damisch, *L'origine de la perspective,* chap. 2, when he argues, against Panofsky, that perspective is more than a symbolic form belonging to the Renaissance or the Baroque.

12 Thomas Aquinas, *Summa theologiae* (1266–1273), cited by Wladyslaw Tatarkiewicz, *History of Aesthetics,* vol. 2, *Medieval Aesthetics,* ed. C. Barrett, trans. R. M. Montgomery (Warsaw: Polish Scientific Publishers, 1970), pp. 257–258, 262.

13 See Euclid, "The Optics of Euclid," trans. H. E. Burton, *Journal of the Optical Society of America* 35 (1945), pp. 357ff.

14 These categories are suggested by David C. Lindberg, *Theories of Vision from Al-Kindi to Kepler* (Chicago: Chicago University Press, 1976).

15 This is crucial for understanding the potential impact of Euclid's *Optics* on art and the representation of images in classical antiquity. In a recent article, "Ancient Perspective and Euclid's *Optics,*" *Journal of the Warburg and Courtauld Institutes* 53 (1990), pp. 14–41, Richard Tobin argues against Panofsky's interpretation of perspective in antiquity, emphasizing the distinction suggested by Euclid in Proposition 8 between what "is seen" or recorded and what actually appears to the observer. Tobin believes that this distinction does not rule out but rather "suggests" central-point perspective. While we will also take issue with Panofsky's conclusions, and we fully acknowledge the distinction Euclid is capable of naming, yet the epistemological reality of antiquity suggests that the curvilinear, mathematical understanding of optical distortion in Euclid's *Optics* led not to a "system" of central-point perspectival representation but rather to a concern for undistorted presence in the form of optical corrections in architecture. In Euclid, perception is never passive; "true" vision was not equated with a section though a visual pyramid, either spherical or flat. It is perhaps significant that in antique and medieval optics there is never a clear distinction between a "pyramid" and a "cone" of vision.

16 The story is from Gaius Julius Solinus, *Collectanea rerum memorabilium* (third century C.E.). Pliny recalls "Tiberius Caesar's ability . . . to see perfectly in darkness and the emission of light from the eyes of cats, wolves, and wild goats" (quoted by Lindberg, *Theories of Vision,* p. 88).

17 Plato's *Timaeus* was the basis for the cosmological presuppositions of architects and theoreticians from Vitruvius to the end of the Renaissance. See, for example, Rudolf Wittkower, *Architectural Principles in the Age of Humanism* (London: Alec Tiranti, 1952), and Alberto Pérez-Gómez, "Chora: The Space of Architectural Representation," in *Chora: Intervals in the Philosophy of Architecture,* ed. Alberto Pérez-Gómez and Stephen Parcell (Montreal: McGill-Queen's University Press, 1994), 1:1–34.

18 Plato, *Timaeus and Critias,* trans. by H. D. P. Lee (Harmondsworth: Penguin Books, 1965).

19 Alexander of Aphrodisias was part of the Stoic tradition. See Lindberg, *Theories of Vision*, p. 9.

20 Furthermore, Al-Hazen tried to provide a more comprehensive theory by accounting also for the physiology of vision. He asserted that beyond the eye, "the arrival of forms at the ultimate sentient power (in the brain) does not require extension in straight lines." See Al-Hazen (also known as Ibn al-Haytham), *Perspectiva,* in *Opticae Thesaurus* (New York: Johnson Reprint, 1972), p. 26.

21 As we shall see, intromission theories have a greater affinity with later Renaissance and particularly modern developments. Significantly, Leon Battista Alberti referred to the eye as a "living mirror" in *De Pictura* (Florence, 1435) and seemed very interested in Democritus's atomistic philosophy, as argued by Samuel Edgerton in *The Renaissance Rediscovery of Linear Perspective* (New York: Harper and Row, 1975), pp. 72–73. On the other hand, sophisticated seventeenth-century writers on linear perspective such as Samuel Marolois, *Opera Mathematica* (Amsterdam, 1614), and Dutch masters of perspective techniques, such as Samuel van Hoogstraten (ca. 1660s), still advocated extromission theories of sight. Reprinted nine times between 1616 and 1662, Marolois's treatise became the standard work for perspective representation in the Netherlands. He writes: "the artist should not naïvely represent what the eye receives" but should base its representation on the principles of projection that intersect a plane surface with the lines of light. As we will show, this long-lasting debate between theories of vision has important consequences for the problem of architectural representation.

22 Roger Bacon, *Opus maius,* chap. 2, trans. by Lindberg, *Theories of Vision,* pp. 114–115.

23 The writings in the *Corpus Dyonisiacum,* long ascribed to Dionysius the Areopagite (first century C.E.), were in fact written by an anonymous Christian from the Neoplatonic tradition who lived around the fifth century. Pseudo-Dionysius introduced into Christianity a concept of beauty based on the absolute perfection of God—and therefore His perfect beauty. He insisted that visible, earthly beauty contained something divine and therefore would provide access to invisible beauty. He made abundant references to beauty as light or brilliance—*lumen, claritas*—and was probably responsible for introducing this concept into medieval art.

24 Quoted by Lindberg, *Theories of Vision,* p. 96. In *De musica,* St. Augustine described beauty as harmony, order, and unity, pointing out that sight and hearing are the only senses capable of revealing beauty because only through them we can perceive mathematical relationships. He also praised music and architecture for their mathematical qualities and considered them superior to painting and sculpture, which were concerned mainly with the imitation of the sensible world. See Tatarkiewicz, *History of Aesthetics,* 2:49–57.

25 Robert Grosseteste, *Comm. in div. nom.*, quoted by Umberto Eco, *Art and Beauty in the Middle Ages,* trans. Hugh Bredin (New Haven: Yale University Press, 1986), pp. 48–49.

26 Grosseteste, *Comm. in hexameron,* quoted by Tatarkiewicz, *History of Aesthetics,* 2:226ff.

27 St. Bonaventure, *In II Sent.* 13.2.2, quoted by Eco, *Art and Beauty in the Middle Ages,* pp. 49–50. On his influence on church architecture, see Gregory Caicco, "Memory and Representation: St. Bonaventure's Itinerarium Mentis in Deum in the Franciscan High Middle Ages" (M. Phil. thesis, University of Cambridge, 1989).

28 Theodore Metochites in *Hypomnematismoi* (ca. 1328) describes musical harmony in this fashion. Gervase Mathew compares it to the multiplicity of colors in late Byzantine mosaics as "a re-enactment of the central problem of Medieval Byzantine philosophy, the relation of the multiple to the One" (*Byzantine Aesthetics* [London: John Murray, 1963], p. 160).

29 Damisch, *L'origine de la perspective,* p. 67.

30 We are referring more specifically to works such as Martin Kemp, *The Science of Art: Optical Themes in Western Art from Brunelleschi to Seurat,* 2d ed. (New Haven: Yale University Press, 1992), and Damisch, *L'origine de la perspective.*

31 Nicholas of Cusa, *The Vision of God* (New York: Frederick Ungar, 1928). This work is hereafter cited by chapter and page parenthetically in the text.

32 From the vantage point of the eighteenth century, Jean Etienne Montucla, who devoted a chapter to perspective in his *Histoire des mathematiques* (Paris, 1798–1802), wrote: "Strictly speaking, this branch of optics might have been considered solely as a geometrical problem; for its dependence on optics only applies to its basic principle, which, once assumed and understood abstractly, leaves the rest to pure geometry."

33 See Lorenzo Ghiberti, *I Commentarii* (Naples: R. Ricciardi; Editore, 1947), part 3.

34 Egnatio Danti deserves special mention in this regard. He was one of the most important writers on *perspectiva artificialis* during the sixteenth century and also the author of the first modern Italian translation of Euclid's *Optics, La Prospettiva di Euclide* (1573). For him, Euclid's book was important because it described in mathematical terms "all things perceived by straight rays, and those that appear in mirrors through reflected rays" (p. 3).

35 See Naomi Miller, "Euclides Redivivus: A Hypothesis on a Proposition," *Gazette des Beaux-Arts* 6 (May/June 1993), pp. 213–226.

36 See Werner Oechslin, "Architecture, Perspective, and the Helpful Gesture of Geometry," *Daidalos* 11 (1984), pp. 39–54.

37 See Thomas Frangenberg, "The Image and the Moving Eye: Jean Pelerin Viator to Guidobaldo del Monte," *Journal of the Warburg and Courtauld Institutes* 49 (1986), pp. 150–171. Frangenberg points out that the distinction made by Al-Hazen between "glance" and "scrutiny" sets the pattern for the literature on *perspectiva naturalis* from the thirteenth to the seventeenth century. Al-Hazen's distinction is present in the texts by Viator, Barbaro, and Danti, receiving its most coherent treatment in Guidobaldo (also known as Guido Ubaldo) del Monte's *Perspectivae Libri Sex* (Pesaro: Apud Hieronymum Concordiam, 1600).

38 As we will show in the following chapters, the desire to reconcile *perspectiva naturalis* and geometrical perspective under the guise of a baroque *mathesis universalis* coincides with the beginning of perspective actually becoming a tool for architectural ideation, as well as the inception of a new kind of optics predicated on modern science and philosophy.

39 Alberti, *On Painting and Sculpture,* ed. and trans. Cecil Grayson (London: Phaidon, 1972), pp. 40–41.

40 This assertion is made with full cognizance of Joseph Masheck's provocative revision of this assumption in "Alberti's Window," *Art Journal* 50 (Spring 1991), pp. 34–41. Masheck reminds us that Alberti actually wrote: "*If* you draw a rectangle [on the canvas], *then* you may treat it as an open window" (Masheck's emphasis). Art, indeed, is never a "mere" window, an "objective" product culminating in "realistic" representations or journalistic photography. The painter is always aware of "image structure"—what we today might call composition or syntax. Yet in view of the epistemological context of Alberti's statement (and *perspectiva artificialis* in general), it is important to emphasize that during the Renaissance the visual image of the painter acquired the status of mathematical truth. As a liberal art, perspective painting was intended to reveal the ontological truth of the world.

41 Hubert Damisch, while obviously familiar with Alberti's concept of the point of sight, insists that the constructive (geometric) nature of perspective implies a point at infinity. Focusing on Brunelleschi's experiences and early-sixteenth-century paintings of ideal cities, he suggests that infinity is "at work" or "appearing" in fifteenth-century perspective. Although late in his book he declares that Brunelleschi's *costruzione legittima* "prepared" but did not "anticipate" Desargues's infinite geometry, he often insists that a correspondence already existed between perspective representation and architectural practice (*L'origine de la perspective,* p. 439). Damisch is only the best known of many art historians and critics who have assumed the presence of this homology early in the history of the problem. Albert Flocon and René Taton in *La Prospettiva* (Milan: Franco Angeli, 1985), for example, write that the *costruzione legittima* "operates through the notions of plan and elevation" (p. 25). They add that while this procedure is "implicit" in Alberti and Brunelleschi, it is actually described by Piero della France-

sca in 1470. Artists, nevertheless, continued to use "simplified methods." Damisch understands that perspective, as it appears in the founding experience of Brunelleschi, is neither empirical nor purely theoretical or abstract, yet he nevertheless insists that it became a "code" or "language" for architects (p. 253). Ignoring much documentary evidence, Damisch concludes that *perspectiva artificialis* has always been related directly to the "interests" of architecture (the "correct" representation of objectifiable volumes), rather than to those of painting.

42 See Jehane R. Kuhn, "Measured Appearances: Documentation and Design in Early Perspective Drawing," *Journal of the Warburg and Courtauld Institutes* 53 (1990), pp. 114–132. The systematization that Kuhn sees in Brunelleschi's topographical practice became possible only in the eighteenth century and was, as we will show, a considerable accomplishment by the cartographer and mathematician Johann Heinrich Lambert.

43 See Francesco di Giorgio Martini, *Trattati di architettura ingegneria e arte militare* (Milan: Il Polifilo, 1967), 1:116ff. The manuscripts were written between the 1470s and the early 1490s.

44 We refer to the three panels, probably *spalliere* or sections of woodwork related to furniture or placed as inserts into the wainscotting of a room, now located in museums in Urbino, Baltimore, and Berlin. These panels have been the subject of many articles and discussions, most notably by Richard Krautheimer and Hubert Damisch. See Damisch, *L'origine de la perspective,* and Krautheimer, "The Panels in Urbino, Baltimore, and Berlin Reconsidered," in *The Renaissance from Brunelleschi to Michelangelo: The Representation of Architecture,* exhibition catalog, ed. Henry A. Millon and Vittorio Magnago Lampugnani (Venice: Bompiani, 1994), pp. 233ff.

45 Sebastiano Serlio, *The Five Bookes of Architecture* (1611; reprint, New York: Dover, 1982), second book, fol. 44ff. Serlio's opinion about the importance of perspective in architecture was considered controversial well into the seventeenth century.

46 For an examination of this question, see Werner Oechslin, "Geometry and Line: The Vitruvian 'Science' of Architectural Drawing," *Daidalos* 1 (1981) pp. 21ff.

47 Andrea Palladio, *I quattro libri dell'architettura* (Venice, 1570).

48 Robert Klein elaborates on the problem of transition between *perspectiva naturalis* and *perspectiva artificialis* in his article "Pomponius Gauricus on Perspective," *Art Bulletin* 43 (1961), pp. 211–213. Like Damisch, Klein draws conclusions opposite to ours about the constructive quality of Renaissance perspective, emphasizing the common reading of perspective as the origin of Renaissance architectural ideation.

49 Damisch, *L'origine de la perspective,* part 2, pp. 112ff.

50 Besides the small hole that Brunelleschi made in his panel and that, according to Manetti, was the viewing station for his first perspective construction, it has been speculated that he actually may have painted his image of the baptistery using a projected image through a perforated panel placed behind the doors of the darkened cathedral. Even if this highly speculative hypothesis were correct, which would imply a precocious application of the camera obscura to an artistic task, in the context of the early Renaissance this procedure cannot be construed as being at odds with the notion of perspective "window" as conceived by Alberti, or with the general interest in discovering (through "empirical" means such as surveying and the flattening effects of mirrors) the ontological "measure" of the world. It is true that Brunelleschi's constructions are presented to a privileged single eye, while the image takes place in an inaccessible space. Nevertheless, it is important to avoid simplistic misreadings. These Renaissance devices cannot be assumed to reveal a precocious "de-anthropomorphization" of vision, more or less equivalent to the disembodied eye of certain contemporary photography or video art.

51 Antonio Averlino detto il Filarete, *Trattato di architettura,* ed. F. L. Grassi (Milan: Il Poliphilo, 1972), book 23. Filarete discusses, in the form of a symposium, the construction of the city of Sforzinda. The manuscript has been dated ca. 1464. There is also an English translation by J. R. Spencer, *Filarete's Treatise on Architecture* (New Haven: Yale University Press, 1965).

52 Antonio Manetti, *Vita di Filippo Brunelleschi,* ed. by D. Robertis and G. Tanturli (Milan: Il Polifilo, 1976), pp. 57–59.

53 Models played different roles and took diverse forms during the Renaissance; they seem to range from study models to presentation pieces. In Brunelleschi's project for the dome and lantern of Florence Cathedral, the model was crucial for the discussion of issues among citizens and craftsmen. For a recent discussion of this issue see Henry A. Millon, "Models in Renaissance Architecture," and Massimo Scolari, "The Dome and Lantern of Florence Cathedral," in Millon and Magnago Lampugnani, *The Renaissance from Brunelleschi to Michelangelo,* pp. 19–74 and p. 583, respectively.

54 This is the sense in which we interpret Manetti's exclamation after looking through the orifice: "pareva che si vedessi 'l propio vero" (*Vita di Filippo Brunelleschi,* p. 59).

55 L. B. Alberti, *On Painting,* trans. J. Spencer (New Haven: Yale University Press, 1966), dedication.

56 Giorgio Vasari, *Lives of the Artists* (1568), trans. George Bull (London: Penguin Books, 1972), p. 136: "Filippo made a careful study of perspective, which because of all the errors of practice was in a deplorable state at that time. . . . He discovered for himself a technique by which to render it truthfully and accurately, namely, by tracing it with the ground-plan and profile and by using intersecting lines."

57 To grasp the difficulties involved in the argument it is interesting to compare the English translations of the text by James Leoni (1755; reprint, London: Alec Tiranti, 1965) and by Joseph Rykwert, Neil Leach, and Robert Tavernor (Cambridge, Mass.: MIT Press, 1988) with the Italian translation by Giovanni Orlandi (Milan: Il Polifilo, 1966) and the Latin original. The translation of *prominentia* as "projection from the ground plan" by Rykwert, Leach, and Tavernor could be problematic if left without qualification.

58 See Christoph Luitpold Frommel, "Reflections on the Early Architectural Drawings," in Millon and Magnago Lampugnani, *The Renaissance from Brunelleschi to Michelangelo,* pp. 101–122.

59 See Scolari, "The Dome and Lantern of Florence Cathedral." Scolari suggests that early elaborate models such as Brunelleschi's were "prescriptive" for a building operation in the absence of "precise drawings," such as were becoming available in Alberti's time. Thus, for Alberti, the model became "part of the process" of designing.

60 Filarete, *Trattato,* book 23. See also the English translation by Spencer, pp. 302ff.

61 Ibid., fol. 177r: "E cosi come è mestiere prima avere il sito per volere edificare e in esso cavare il fondamento, cosi ancora noi in prima faremo il sito a voler questo nostro disegno. In prima bisogna che questo sito ch'è piano si faccia con raggione."

62 Damisch believes that Filarete's comments on perspective undoubtedly reveal the homology implied in Brunelleschi's *costruzione legittima* (*L'origine de la perspective,* p. 87).

63 This hypothesis is clearly stated by Jacopo Barozzi da Vignola in the first part of his treatise, *Due Regole della Prospettiva Prattica* (Rome: Per Francesco Zannetti, 1583), p. 34.

64 Leonardo, quoted by Lindberg, *Theories of Vision,* p. 164.

65 Leonardo became well acquainted with Pecham's optics. By 1507–1508 he could claim that "it is true that every part of the pupil possesses the visual power, and that this power is not reduced to a point as the perspectivists wish" (MS, "On the Eye," quoted by Kemp, *The Science of Art,* p. 51).

66 See J. P. Richter, ed., *The Literary Works of Leonardo da Vinci* (Berkeley: University of California Press, 1977), vol. 1, par. 12, MS BN2038/23r.

67 Alberti, *On Painting,* pp. 36–37.

68 Martin Kemp bases his recently published, monumental history of perspective and painting on this problematic premise. For him, the artists' interest in "science" is demonstrated by the "progressive" systematization of pictorial representation toward an ideal "scientific perspective," a paradigm that culminates in color photography, "a mechanical method of imitating nature . . . capable of producing those illusionistic

effects for which the proponents of the science of art had striven for so long and with such intellectual effort." This misunderstanding, which Kemp qualifies as his "carefully considered hypothesis"—i.e., a belief in perspective as a natural way of seeing, beyond cultural and historical specificity—is particularly problematic when its consequences become the primary assumptions in architectural representation (*The Science of Art*, pp. 1, 131, 322).

69   The best examples of this mathematical treatment of perspective are to be found in Federigo Commandino's commentary on Ptolemy's work, particularly in his *Ptolomaei Planispherium* (Venice, 1558), in Egnazio Danti's commentary on J. B. Vignola's *Due Regole della Prospettiva Prattica* (Rome, 1583), and in Guidobaldo del Monte's *Montis Perspectivae libri sex*. A less known but significant tract in this tradition is Giovanni Battista Benedetti, *De rationibus operationum perspectivae* (Turin, ca. 1585).

70   This tendency, often difficult to detect as it is a primary assumption, is present in writings on perspective by both art historians and historians of mathematics, discussing "problems" that often are not real in the epistemological context of the Renaissance. Many of the otherwise excellent secondary sources from which we have profited simply assume, at one time or another, an instrumental relationship between perspective theory and practice. See for example, Kemp, *The Science of Art*, and J. V. Field, "Giovanni Battista Benedetti on the Mathematics of Linear Perspective," *Journal of the Warburg and Courtauld Institutes* 48 (1985), pp. 71–99.

71   See particularly Nicholas of Cusa, *The Vision of God*. Our gratitude goes to Stephen Pack, a former student in the Graduate Program in History and Theory of Architecture at McGill University, for stimulating conversations and suggestions about Dürer's work.

72   Vincenzo Scamozzi, *L'Idea della Architettura Universale* (Venice, 1615), 1:138.

73   See Alberto Pérez-Gómez, "The Myth of Dedalus," *AA Files* 10 (1985), pp. 49–52.

74   Today, while many architects remain fascinated by the revelatory power of cutting, this operation may have reached its limits in science. Further cutting in biology and particle smashing in physics do not seem able to reveal a greater interiority. We are always left on the outside by objectified vision. This awareness will be recalled in our conclusions, as we try to understand how the architect at the end of modernity may expect to transcend enframed vision.

75   See Condivi's *Life of Michelangelo*, quoted in David Summers, *Michelangelo and the Language of Art* (Princeton: Princeton University Press, 1981), p. 308; and Helmut W. Klassen, "Michelangelo: Architecture and the Vision of Anatomy" (M.Arch. thesis, McGill University, 1990, p. 83).

76 See Alberto Pérez-Gómez, *Polyphilo, or The Dark Forest Revisited* (Cambridge, Mass.: MIT Press, 1992), introduction.

77 Giovanni Pico della Mirandola, *De imaginatione* (1501), quoted in Summers, *Michelangelo and the Language of Art,* p. 113.

78 Klassen, *Michelangelo,* pp. 85–86.

79 It is well established that no complete drawings of his major works were produced before the execution of projects; the Campidoglio in Rome is a good example. For an extensive analysis of Michelangelo's work, see James S. Ackerman, *The Architecture of Michelangelo* (London: A. Zwemmer's, 1970).

80 See Paolo Rossi, *Philosophy, Technology, and the Arts in the Early Modern Era* (New York: Harper and Row, 1970).

81 Daniele Barbaro, *Vitruvius Pollio I dieci libri,* 2d ed. (Venice, 1567), p. 14. The first edition was published in 1556.

82 Ibid., p. 30.

83 Vitruvius, *The Ten Books on Architecture,* trans. Morris Hicky Morgan (1914; reprint, New York: Dover, 1960) I.2, pp. 13–14.

84 See for example "Sciagraphy," in the *Encyclopedia of Architecture* (London: Caxton Press, 1852), vol. 2.

85 We discuss this problem extensively below in "Variation One: *Scenographia* and Optical Correction."

86 Daniele Barbaro, *La Pratica della Perspettiva* (Venice: Appresso Camillo e Rutilio Borgominieri, 1569), p. 130.

87 See Pérez-Gómez, "Chora."

88 Witelo (late thirteenth century) was greatly influenced by Al-Hazen. See his *Perspectiva,* ed. F. Risner (New York: Johnson Reprint, 1972), and Tatarkiewicz, *History of Aesthetics,* 2:267–268. The first thorough application of modern associationist psychology to "explain" architectural meaning appears in the late-seventeenth-century theory of Claude Perrault. See Alberto Pérez-Gómez, introduction to the English translation of Perrault's treatise, *Ordonnance for the Five Kinds of Columns after the Method of the Ancients,* trans. Indra Kagis McEwen (Santa Monica, Calif.: Getty Center for the History of Art and the Humanities, 1993), pp. 1–44.

89 Felix Platter, *De corporis humani structura et usu libri III,* and Giovanni Battista Della Porta, *De refractione optices* and *Magia naturalis;* quoted by Lindberg, *Theories of Vision,* p. 176.

90 John Pecham, *Perspectiva communis,* cited in David C. Lindberg, "Laying the Foundations of Geometrical Optics," in *The Discourse of Light from the Middle Ages to the Enlightenment,* ed. David C. Lindberg and Geoffrey Cantor (Los Angeles: Castle Press, 1985), pp. 1–65; quotation, p. 27.

91 In his doctoral dissertation, Stephen Straker argues that Kepler, unlike his predecessors, initiated a mechanistic concept of light. Stephen Straker, *Kepler's Optics: A Study in the Development of Seventeenth-Century Natural Philosophy* (Ann Arbor: UMI Research Press, 1984), and Lindberg, "Laying the Foundations," p. 49.

92 Lindberg, *Theories of Vision,* p. 202.

93 See Alexandre Koyré, *Metaphysics and Measurement* (London: Chapman and Hall, 1968), and Hans Blumenberg, *The Genesis of the Copernican World* (Cambridge, Mass.: MIT Press, 1987).

94 Juan Bautista Villalpando, *In Ezechielem explanationes et apparatus urbi ac templi hierosolymitani* (Rome, 1596, 1604). We used the Spanish translation by José Luis Oliver Domingo, *El Templo de Salomón, Comentarios a la Profecía de Ezequiel,* ed. Juan Antonio Ramírez (Madrid: Ediciones Siruela, 1991), pp. 75–77.

95 See Lindberg, *Theories of Vision,* pp. 30, 38, 42.

96 Nicéron considered perspective as a tool that is partly magic, partly scientific. Rather than a technique of reduction, it was for him a vehicle by which to question, in the context of the Cartesian revolution, the ambiguity between the truth of perception and representation. Nicéron's *Perspective curieuse* (Paris: Chez Pierre Billaine, 1638) was translated into Latin as *Thaumaturgus Opticus* (Paris, 1646). For a detailed history of anamorphic art, see Jurgis Baltrusaitis, *Anamorphic Art,* trans. W. J. Strachan (New York: Harry N. Abrams, 1976).

97 We may suppose a diaphanous plain erected near the eye, perpendicular to the horizon, and divided into small squares. A straight line from the eye to the utmost limit of the horizon, passing through this diaphanous plain, as projected or represented in the perpendicular plain, would rise. The eye sees all the parts and objects in the horizontal plain through certain corresponding squares of the perpendicular diaphanous plain. . . . It is true this diaphanous plain, and the images supposed to be projected thereon, are altogether of a tangible nature: But then there are pictures relative to those images: and those pictures have an order among themselves" (Berkeley, *The Works of George Berkeley, Bishop of Cloyne* [London: T. Nelson, 1948–1957], 1:270–271).

98 Jonathan Crary, *Techniques of the Observer* (Cambridge, Mass.: MIT Press, 1991).

99 This hermeneutic approach is made possible by accepting as a premise the possibility of a de-idealized experience, presupposing (with Maurice Merleau-Ponty) nothing more than an encounter between "us" and "what is." As if in response to those poststructuralist philosophers who have declared the notion of experience to be part of a "metaphysics of presence," Merleau-Ponty writes, "Is it not the resolution to ask of experience itself its secret already an idealist commitment?" See G. B. Madison, "Did Merleau-Ponty Have a Theory of Perception?" in *Merleau-Ponty, Hermeneutics, and Postmodernism,* ed. Thomas Busch

and Shaun Gallagher (Binghampton: State University of New York Press, 1992), pp. 83–106; quotation, p. 106 n. 40.

100 See Guarino Guarini, *Architettura Civile* (Turin, 1737), and Alberto Pérez-Gómez, *Architecture and the Crisis of Modern Science* (Cambridge, Mass.: MIT Press, 1983), chap. 3.

101 It is important to remember that Dionysius the Areopagite, also known as Pseudo-Dionysius, author of *The Divine Names* and *The Mystical Theology,* had a strong impact upon medieval writers.

102 We would like to express our gratitude to Janine Debanné for stimulating conversation concerning the work of Guarini, as well as interesting insights from her master's thesis, "Guarino Guarini's SS. Sindone Chapel: Between Reliquary and Cenotaph" (M.Arch. thesis, McGill University, 1995).

103 We examine the work of Girard Desargues in detail in Variation One. For an extended analysis of his work and a complete biography, see René Taton, *L'oeuvre mathématique de G. Desargues* (Paris: Presses Universitaires de France, 1951). See also Pérez-Gómez, *Architecture and the Crisis of Modern Science,* chap. 5.

104 We acknowledge some mathematical precedents for Desargues's theory in Federigo Commandino, Giovanni Battista Benedetti, Guidobaldo del Monte, and Simon Stevin. These have been pointed out and discussed by authors such as Martin Kemp in "Geometrical Perspective from Brunelleschi to Desargues," extracted in *Proceedings of the Royal Academy,* vol. 70 (Oxford: Oxford University Press, 1984), and by Field in "Benedetti on Perspective." Often, however, a progressive understanding of the history of art and science, such as that implied by these authors, makes it difficult to appreciate differences that stem from changing epistemological frameworks. The sixteenth-century authors were indeed very close to Euclid. As good humanists, their task was mainly hermeneutical, rather than "scientific" in the sense of Francis Bacon or Descartes. Not surprisingly, Commandino could never fully grasp the principle of continuity in the conic sections despite his interest in the Ptolemaic projections and his understanding of their relationship with *perspectiva artificialis.* Similarly, Benedetti could resolve mathematically the "confusion" between *costruzione legittima* (Alberti) and distance point construction (Viator), providing a solution for a general point demonstrated in analogous two-dimensional and three-dimensional diagrams. He could therefore unintentionally "prove" Desargues's theorem of triangles in perspective, but without recognizing its generality and therefore, its far-reaching consequences for *technē,* particularly in the arts and architecture. As we have already suggested, parallel lines did not "truly" converge in Euclidean space, where tactile considerations, derived from bodily spatiality, still were more important than purely visual information.

105 Martin Heidegger emphasizes that the enframed "picture" implies a "standing-together, [a] system[,] . . . a unity that develops out of the projection of the objectivity of whatever is." This objectivity is comprehensible only in relation to the Cartesian subjectivity, taking place in the mathematical space of analytic geometry, yet its absolute universality was realized only in the nineteenth century, particularly after the scientific refutation of Euclidean geometry. See "The Age of the World Picture," in *The Question Concerning Technology and Other Essays,* trans. William Lovitt (New York: Harper and Row, 1977), pp. 115–154.

106 Andrea Pozzo, *Rules and Examples of Perspective Proper for Painters and Architects* (Rome, 1693; 1st English trans., London, 1700). From its first appearance in 1693 to the mid-eighteenth century, more than forty different editions and translations of Pozzo's treatise were published.

107 Denis Diderot, *De l'interprétation de la nature,* cited by Yvon Belaval, "La crise de la géométrisation de l'univers dans la philosophie des lumières," *Revue internationale de philosophie* 6 (1952), p. 348.

108 See Ferdinando Galli da Bibiena, *L'Architettura Civile* (Parma: Per Paolo Monti, 1711).

109 Karsten Harries examines this problem in his excellent study *The Bavarian Rococo Church* (New Haven: Yale University Press, 1983).

110 Here one may remember Sergei Eisenstein's interest in Piranesi's explosion of perspective, described in "Piranesi, or the Fluidity of Forms," *Oppositions* 2 (Winter 1977), pp. 83–110. Piranesi's *Carceri* etchings are characterized by the entanglement of beams, stairways, and bridges that emerge from the depth of the image and are projected beyond the limit of the frame. The contrast of shadows creates an ambiguity between interior and exterior space. The structure of Piranesi's etchings is projected forward and beyond the edge of the drawing, into the space of the observer. Similarly, Eisenstein's intellectual montage attempted to include the presence of the spectator in the creation of the dynamic image.

111 Despite often unstated assumptions, the boundaries among painting, sculpture, and architecture have been fluid throughout history and are closely connected to their respective "content." The arts, understood as the embodiment of truth, cannot be reduced to their material differentiation, scale, "function," etc. This dissolution of boundaries became more obvious after the Renaissance paradigms of art were exhausted in the nineteenth century, and the *constructed* character of culture (and the work of art) vis-à-vis nature was accepted. Is it still surprising, as stated by some critics, that in the 1990 Venice Biennale painters were consistently doing sculpture while sculptors were dealing mostly with flat surfaces?

112 This concept had been formulated by Michel de Fremin in his *Mémoires critiques* (Paris, 1702).

113 Legeay's lack of practical experience in building is discussed in Variation Two.

114 See Pérez-Gómez, *Architecture and the Crisis of Modern Science,* chaps. 3, 8, 9.

115 Ibid., chap. 8.

116 Even Kepler and Descartes shared this belief. The apparent exceptions are themselves never free of contradictions. A prime example is Roger Bacon's thirteenth-century *De multiplicatione specium.* In some passages Bacon feels the need to dissociate light from God, claiming that it is a "created thing," yet possessed of "infinite power" to be ubiquitous. This ambivalence is typical of his work. See David C. Lindberg, "Medieval Latin Theories of the Speed of Light," in *Romer et la vitesse de la lumière,* CNRS (Paris: Vrin, 1978), pp. 53–55.

117 This realization opened up a crucial philosophical problem of meaning for a cosmology that assumed "all natural processes to be temporal," i.e., the secularized Judeo-Christian cosmology of modern science and technology. See Francis Bacon, *Novum organum* II.46, in *Works* (London, 1857–1874; reprint, Stuttgard–Bad Cannstatt: Frommann-Holzboog, 1963), 1:326.

118 We have discussed the interest in this analogy during the Middle Ages. Athanasius Kircher in his *Ars magna lucis et umbrae* (Rome: Sumptibus Hermanni Scheus, 1646) reiterates the Aristotelian theory of color, suggesting also that color makes musical harmonies in the eye like a diapason in the ear (pp. 67ff).

119 Isaac Newton, *The Optical Papers of Isaac Newton,* vol. 1, *The Optical Lectures, 1670–1672,* ed. Alan E. Schapiro (Cambridge: Cambridge University Press, 1984), p. 50.

120 Gaspard Monge, *Géométrie Descriptive,* 2d ed. (Paris, 1798), p. 171.

121 We have in mind more specifically the writings of Charles-Francois Viel and Quatremère de Quincy.

122 Significantly, this is still the fallacy of "artistic" architecture such as "postmodern classical" styles, with their presumed references to a supposedly universal, ahistorical content or "myth." See also n. 123, below.

123 Philosophers and cultural historians have described the crisis of modern science and emphasized the necessity of transcending reductionist thinking in all disciplines. The need for a mythopoetic dimension of discourse, for narratives that acknowledge the transhistoric existential questions of our mortal human life, is much more widely accepted. A short list of philosophers following this path could start with Friedrich Nietzsche and include Edmund Husserl, Martin Heidegger, José Ortega y Gasset, and, more recently, Georges Gusdorf, David Michael

Levin, Gianni Vattimo, and Hans Blumenberg. The implications of myth are obviously complex and often contradictory in the work of these writers. Myth cannot simply be retrieved in its "prerational" form, i.e., like classical Greek myths, with the pretense that these stories contain some absolute truth applicable today. Myths are neither false stories aimed at perpetuating the abhorrent exploitative political structures of our history nor simple narratives that may be added to forms to make some kind of meaningful architecture. Blumenberg points out that myth is ultimately unavoidable in human culture and that it is our only means to articulate a *truth* grounded in our mortality and rationality. Even contemporary scientists now realize that narratives are crucial to the substantiation of specific theories.

It appears that the issue for human thought and action is to pursue actively the consequences of the demythicization of science to bring us to a novel understanding of myth in a profoundly Nietzschean sense: to fully participate in the dream while *knowing* that we are dreaming, recognizing the significance of that which we don't comprehend rationally and yet we *make* appear. In architecture, this openness to a mythopoetic articulation provides a point of departure for our fictive and historical narratives as we try to develop an ethical praxis. This postmodern philosophical understanding itself demands a theory of architecture that *is not* a methodology and therefore requires a critical examination of all reductive uses of projection-*cum*-prediction in design.

Variation One

Architectural Representation and the Distorted Image

1   Plato, *The Republic,* trans. P. Shorey, Loeb Classical Library (1935–1937; reprint, Cambridge, Mass.: Harvard University Press, 1982), X.601, 2:368–370.

2   Hugh of St. Victor (1096–1141) *Expositio in Hierarch. Coelest. II,* quoted by Wladyslaw Tatarkiewicz, *History of Aesthetics,* vol. 2, *Medieval Aesthetics,* ed. C. Barrett, trans. R. M. Montgomery (Warsaw: Polish Scientific Publishers, 1970), p. 197.

3   For more details about the artistic impact of the iconoclastic controversy between the Emperor Leo III and the Pope Gregory II that started around 725, see Tatarkiewicz, *History of Aesthetics,* 2:37–38.

4   See Marie-José Baudinet, "The Face of Christ, the Form of the Church," in *Fragments for a History of the Human Body,* ed. Michel Feher with Ramona Naddaff and Nadia Tazi, part 1 (New York: Zone Books, 1989), pp. 148–156. See also M. V. Alpatov, *Early Russian Icon Painting* (Moscow: Iskusstvo, 1978), introduction.

5   Fragment reprinted in Baudinet, "The Face of Christ," pp. 157ff; quotation, p. 150.

6   Pappus of Alexandria (early fourth century C.E.) introduced Euclid's *Optica* to the Byzantine world by including it in his *Little Astronomy.* It included the first four definitions, crucial to the Byzantine theory of vision. The Byzantines assumed the eyeball to be mobile and spherical, with a concave retina. Often they represented the horizon line as slightly curved. They were unable to imagine the visual world as a flat section of the visual cone. For more details see Gervase Mathew, *Byzantine Aesthetics* (London: John Murray, 1969), pp. 29–31.

7   See Jean Paris, *Painting and Linguistics* (Pittsburgh: Carnegie-Mellon University Press, 1975).

8   Ibid., pp. 37ff.

9   This premise underlies the otherwise learned and informative recent work by Martin Kemp, *The Science of Art: Optical Themes in Western Art from Brunelleschi to Seurat,* 2d ed. (New Haven: Yale University Press, 1992).

10   Leon Battista Alberti, *On Painting,* trans. J. Spencer (New Haven: Yale University Press, 1966), p. 52. On the use and misinterpretations of Euclid's theorems in the development of Renaissance *perspectiva artificialis,* see Erwin Panofsky, *Perspective as Symbolic Form,* trans. C. S. Wood (New York: Zone Books, 1991), pp. 34–36.

11   Samuel Y. Edgerton, *The Renaissance Rediscovery of Linear Perspective* (New York: Harper and Row, 1975), and *The Heritage of Giotto's Geometry: Art and Science on the Eve of the Scientific Revolution* (Ithaca: Cornell University Press, 1991). Edgerton's major points are as follows: (1) The belief that perspective is "natural." He writes: "all human beings, whatever their race, gender, or culture, are genetically predisposed" to perceive the world as a Renaissance *perspectiva artificialis* (*Giotto's Geometry,* p. 6). He fails to account for the fact that perception cannot be reduced to visuality alone. He assumes that Western perspective, from its inception in Euclidean science, is totally coherent with scientific optics, emphasizing that representations in this tradition are invariably "geometric replications to scale." This simplified view does not do justice to the tension between optics and *perspectiva artificialis,* always present in the European tradition during the early modern period. (2) Consequently, Edgerton sides with Gombrich, suggesting that perspective is *not* inherently culture bound, as opposed to writers such as Norman Bryson (and ourselves), who believe that it ultimately expresses the values of Western civilization, even as they recognize the problematic dimensions of a universalizing culture that has become our "nature" in the last century. (3) Edgerton constantly calls perspective "an Euclidean construct." Obviously perspective was based on Euclidean geometry and optics, but the distinctions between a fully developed "perspective geometry" (such as Desargues's in the seven-

teenth century) and "Euclidean geometry" are absolutely crucial to understand the "artificiality" of perspective and its consequences as a "hinge" in architectural representation.

12 Edgerton, *Renaissance Rediscovery of Linear Perspective,* pp. 70–71.

13 Federigo Commandino, *Ptolomaei Planisphaerium* (Venice, 1558). See Kemp, *The Science of Art,* p. 86.

14 Claudius Ptolemy, *The Geography,* trans. and ed. E. L. Stevenson (New York: Dover Publications, 1991), I.24, pp. 43–45. This version is an unabridged reprint of the work originally published by the New York Public Library in 1932, in a limited edition of 250 copies.

15 Edgerton, *Renaissance Rediscovery of Linear Perspective,* pp. 101–104. Diagrams VII–1 and VII–2 constitute a graphic misinterpretation of Ptolemy's text as an explicit form of conic section. Edgerton writes: "What Ptolemy now proceeded to explain is almost a clear-cut linear perspective projection based on geometric principles. . . . It was this third system, in fact, which fostered a special 'distance point method' for arriving at linear perspective which became popular among Italian theoreticians of the sixteenth and seventeenth centuries" (pp. 101–104).

16 Edgerton goes into a long—and indeed misleading—explanation of the shape of the map according to Ptolemy's last method. He claims that its general outline is comparable to an ellipse resulting from a disk projected in perspective (*Renaissance Rediscovery of Linear Perspective,* pp. 108–110). Concerning the controversy over the authorship of the maps accompanying Ptolemy's text, see Stevenson's commentary to *The Geography,* pp. 5–6.

17 Ptolemy, *The Geography,* VII.6, p. 162. We address the relationship between modern cartography and geography and architectural representation in Variation Two.

18 Lucia Nuti, "The Perspective Plan in the Sixteenth Century: The Invention of a Representational Language," *Art Bulletin* 76 (1994), p. 126 n. 71.

19 Ibid., p. 126.

20 Vitruvius, *The Ten Books on Architecture,* trans. Morris Hicky Morgan (1914; reprint, New York: Dover Publications, 1960), pp. 13–14.

21 In his translation of Vitruvius's treatise—the first truly modern rendition of the classical text, which he entitled *Les Dix Livres d'Architecture de Vitruve corrigés et traduits en 1684 par Claude Perrault* (reprint, Brussels: Pierre Mardaga éditeur, 1979)—Claude Perrault (1613–1688) gives to the Greek word *idea* the meaning of the Latin *species,* which he translates as "representation," insisting that Vitruvius's statement refers to three kinds of coordinated architectural drawings.

22 In Aristotelian philosophy, it is not possible to think without an image because to think is the same as to draw; but the image-making process

is exclusively imitative, for the imagination remains largely a "repro-ductive" rather than a "productive" activity. This, of course, means not that the image is concerned "merely" with appearances, but that consciousness is *of* the world (rather than the production of an emanci-pated *ego*). Concerning the question of image as *phantasia* in Aristotle's *De memoria* and the notion of imagination from Plato to Aristotle, see Richard Kearney, *The Wake of Imagination* (Minneapolis: University of Minnesota Press, 1988), chap. 2.

23 For Ptolemy, for example, *graphō* in *geographia* implied both picture and words; his primary aim was always *ekphrasis,* or description in words. Only in the Renaissance would geography become more akin to *pictura,* which describes the world.

24 We refer more specifically to Morgan's translation and to Frank Grang-er's translation for the Loeb Classical Library, 2 vols. (Cambridge, Mass.: Harvard University Press, 1934). The most recent French trans-lation (Paris: Les Belles Lettres, 1991) is equally problematic.

25 This is our translation of the famous passage "frontis et laterum ab-scedentium adumbratio ad circinique centrum omnium linearum re-sponsus" (Vitruvius, *De architectura,* ed. Granger, I.2.2). Both twentieth-century English translations of this passage are misleading. Granger translates, "Scenography (perspective) as in the shading of the front and the retreating sides, and the correspondence of all lines to the vanishing point [*sic*] which is the centre of the circle." Morgan's translation is also problematic: "Perspective is the method of sketching a front with sides withdrawing into the background, the lines all meet-ing in the centre of a circle."

26 Vitruvius, *The Ten Books on Architecture,* trans. Morgan, I.3, p. 16.

27 In his study of concepts of space in the western tradition, Max Jammer discusses the notion of space inherited by Aristotelian philosophy as a complex intertwining of form and matter, preceding any physical determination. See Max Jammer, *Concepts of Space: The History of Theo-ries of Space in Physics* (Cambridge, Mass.: Harvard University Press, 1954), p. 9.

28 Plato, *Timaeus and Critias,* trans. H. D. P. Lee (Harmondsworth: Pen-guin Books, 1965), 48–49, p. 67.

29 See for example Panofsky, *Perspective as Symbolic Form.*

30 *De architectura,* VII, pref. 2; based on Granger's translation (2:70–71) and modified by us according to Panofsky's interpretation, *Perspective as Symbolic Form,* pp. 38, 97–102, and to the Latin text: "uti de incerta re certae imagines aedificiorum in scenarum picturis redderent spe-ciem, et quae in directis planisque frontibus sint figurata, alia absceden-tia alio prominentia esse videantur." Morgan's translation reads as follows: "Given a centre in a definite place, the lines should naturally correspond with due regard to the point of sight and the divergence of the visual rays, so that by this deception a faithful representation of

the appearance of buildings might be given in painted scenery, and so that, though all is drawn on a vertical flat façade, some parts may seem to be withdrawing into the background, and others to be standing out in the front" (p. 198).

31 A recent thorough appraisal and critique of Panofsky's *Die Perspektive als symbolische Form* is offered by James Elkins, *The Poetics of Perspective* (Ithaca: Cornell University Press, 1994), especially chap. 5.

32 Panofsky, *Perspective as Symbolic Form*, p. 97.

33 Quoted by Mathew, *Byzantine Aesthetics*, p. 34.

34 Quoted by Morris R. Cohen and I. E. Drabkin, *A Source Book in Greek Science* (New York: McGraw-Hill, 1948), p. 257. Here Geminus uses the term "eurhythmics" to qualify the effect of *skēnographia*, a term also used by Vitruvius in connection with the three architectural ideas as the beauty of their assemblage. Moreover, "eurhythmics" usually was associated in Antiquity with the performing arts such as theater and poetry; in this case, *eurhythmics* is the coincidence of a specific time and space for undistorted perception, since the optically corrected image makes sense only from a specific position.

35 Ibid., p. 4.

36 Vitruvius, *De architectura*, III.3, trans. Granger, 1:179.

37 Panofsky, *Perspective as Symbolic Form*, p. 38.

38 See also ibid., p. 92 n. 13. The image of a pair of compasses rotating around its axis indeed recreates the shape of a cone (and thus the image of a visual cone) whose center, in our opinion, is not located on its base, but rather at its apex, the vantage point of *perspectiva naturalis*. In his *De Opticis Libri II* (Summary of theoretical optics), Damianus (fourth century C.E.) imagined the apex of the visual cone to be at the center of a sphere (analogous to the head) of which the pupil, and more precisely its projection onto the cornea, is a segment. This image enabled him to account for peripheral vision and for sizes of objects relative to angles of vision. See D. Gioseffi, "Optical Concepts," in *Encyclopedia of World Art* (London: McGraw-Hill, 1959), 10: col. 763.

39 See Alberto Pérez-Gómez's introduction to Claude Perrault, *Ordonnance for the Five Kinds of Columns after the Method of the Ancients,* trans. Indra Kagis McEwen (Santa Monica, Calif.: Getty Center for the History of Art and the Humanities, 1993), pp. 1–44.

40 "Les uns, comme Leon Baptiste Alberti & Serlio, croyent que cet Auteur a affecté l'obscurité à dessein & malicieusement, de peur que les architectes de son temps pour qui il avoit de la jalousie ne profitent de ses écrits." Vitruvius, *Les dix livres d'architecture,* trans. and comm. C. Perrault (Paris, 1684), preface.

41 He renders the famous passage on *scenographia* as follows: "La Scénographie fait voir l'élévation non seulement d'une des faces, mais aussi

le retour des costez par le concours de toutes les lignes qui aboutissent à un centre" (ibid., I.2, p. 10).

42 Panofsky's translation is even more explicit on this matter: "Scenography is the illusionistic reproduction . . . of the facade and the sides, and the correspondence of all lines with respect to the center of the circle (actually the 'compass point')" (*Perspective as Symbolic Form*, p. 100).

43 In this regard, see Pérez-Gómez's introduction to Perrault, *Ordonnance for the Five Kinds of Columns*, pp. 24–27.

44 This tendency in twentieth-century art history was reinforced recently by Hubert Damisch in *The Origin of Perspective*. See, for example, Bates Lowry, *Renaissance Architecture* (New York: Braziller, 1971), p. 14, and Quentin Hughes and Norbert Lynton, *Renaissance Architecture* (New York: David McKay, 1965), p. 27.

45 Elkins in *The Poetics of Perspective* emphasizes the diversity of perspective methods prior to 1601. The techniques of perspective during the Renaissance, furthermore, have no secure genealogy and exhibit no unified theory. See pp. 78–89.

46 Scamozzi writes:

I desegni che gli antichi chiamarono Graphidi cioè descritione di lineamenti; come dice Vitruvio, sono quelli, per mezo de' quali esplicamo ad altri la volontà nostra, e secondo noi non vegono ad esser più, che di tre sorti; cioè la pianta, ò superficie; l'impiedi, ò faccia; & il profilo; & ambedue questi servono allo elevato del corpo dell'edificio; e questa è una via infallibile per conoscer tutte le cose naturali, como artificiali, & anco in parte le sopranaturali: essendoche per mezo del disegno si reduce in picciolissima forma il Mondo terrestre, & anco il celestre: intanto, che e l'uno, e l'altro dimostra chiaramente sotto al senso, quasi tutte le cose nella sua vera somiglianza, e manca solo di corporeità, laquale si aspetta al Modello. Di modo che per via del disegno si esprime molto facilmente tutto quello, che non puo far la moltiplicità delle parole espresse, ò descrite in carta; e perciò à ragione si può dire, che il disegno sia più tosto dono celeste di Dio, che cosa ritrovata dall'ingegno humano.

(*L'Idea della Architettura Universale* [1615; reprint, Sala Bolognese: Arnaldo Forni Editore, 1982], vol. 1, part 1, book 1, chap. 14, p. 47.) We have respected Scamozzi's spelling in the notes and text.

47 "Scenographia cioè il diseyno del più, e meno rilievo della fronte, e parimonte de' lati di esso edificio, il quale noi chiamiamo profillo, ò sia in semplice disegno, ò tirato in prospettiva, overo anco in modello: dalquale si vede la corrispondenza, che fanno tutte le linee naturali all'occhio nostro" (ibid., p. 46).

48 Giorgio Vasari, *Lives of the Artists*, trans. George Bull (London: Penguin Books, 1972), pp. 90–91.

49 For references to architecture, compare the latest *Dizionario della Lingua Italiana*, 3:646, entry 20, with C. Battisti and G. Alessio, *Dizionario Etimologico Italiano* (Firenze: G. Barberi, 1954), p. 2484, and J. Coro-

minas, *Breve Diccionario Etimológico de la Lengua Castellana* (Madrid: Ed. Gredos, 1976), p. 399.

50 A substantial collection of *modani* was part of the recent exhibition about Renaissance architectural representation that took place in Venice's Palazo Grassi, 1994.

51 See the excellent article by Tracy A. Cooper, "*I Modani:* Template Drawings," in *The Renaissance from Brunelleschi to Michelangelo: The Representation of Architecture,* ed. Henry A. Millon and Vittorio Magnago Lampugnani, exhibition catalog (Venice: Bompiani, 1994), pp. 494–500. Cooper is quoting Howard Saalman.

52 Ibid., p. 494. *Hypographē* are visible in Didyma, Priene, and Pergamon, among other places.

53 Ibid., p. 495.

54 See, for example, M. C. F. Roland Le Virloys, *Dictionnaire d'Architecture, Civile, Militaire et Navale* (Paris: Chez les Librairies Associées, 1770), s.v. "modèle."

55 Ibid.

56 In fact, over 260 codices on many different subjects have been attributed to him. After browsing through Caramuel's manuscripts for a whole evening, King Fernando III is reported to have exclaimed, "I do not wish to judge whether the manuscripts I saw were good or bad. . . . I can only say that if I hadn't seen it, I could have never believed that a single hand with a single pen could have written so much on so many different subjects." Some of his titles include *Rationalis et realis philosophia* (1642), *Theologia moralis* (1643), *Mathesis audax* (1644), *Metalogica* (1654), and *Grammatica audax* (1651). Caramuel traveled extensively, and as a philosopher and scientist, he maintained international relations. While in Prague, he occupied various military positions as well as the important post of Vicario General de Bohemia. He fortified and defended the city with such success that he was awarded the highest military decoration. In 1673, he became bishop of Vigevano, Lombardy, where he stayed until his death in 1682. For more detailed biographical notes, see José Luis Abellán, *Historia crítica del pensamiento español* (Madrid: Espasa-Calpe, 1981), 3:333–338. Abellán, however, tends to overemphasize Caramuel's occasional opposition to Aristotle's doctrine as the sign of a thoroughly modern mind.

57 Caramuel, *Architectura Civil Recta y Oblicua* (1678; reprint, Madrid: Ediciones Turner, 1984).

58 Ibid., vol. II, p. 142.

59 Desargues was born in Lyon into a family of eight children. Very little else is known about him before the publication of his first treatise on perspective in 1636. At that time, however, Desargues seems to have

been already well acquainted with a group of important scientists and philosophers including Descartes and Mersenne, as well as Fermat, Roberval, and Étienne and his son Blaise Pascal. For more information about Desargues's life, see René Taton, *L'Oeuvre mathématique de G. Desargues* (Paris: Presses Universitaires de France, 1951), and Noël Germinal Poudra, *Oeuvre de Desargues . . . précédée d'une nouvelle biographie de Desargues suivie de l'analyse des ouvrages de Bosse,* 2 vols. (Paris: Leiber, 1864).

60   Daniele Barbaro, *La Pratica della Perspettiva* (1569; reprint, Bologna: Arnaldo Forni, 1980), part 4, chap. 1, p. 130; our translation.

61   "Io intendo il profilo essere una delle idee della dispositione detta da Vitruvio, ilquale conviene con le altre specie della dispositione, & porta molta cognitione delle qualità, & misure delle fabriche, & giova a fare il conto della spesa, & all'ordinare le grossezze dei muri" (Barbaro, *La Practica della Perspettiva,* p. 130). *Profilo* is described as a kind of section that provides rich information about the quality and dimensions of a construction, and helps determine its cost and the size of walls.

62   Alberti, *On Painting,* p. 47.

63   Vitruvius, *The Ten Books on Architecture,* trans. Morgan, I.10, p. 10.

64   Michel Serres discusses the gnomon in "L'axe du cadran solaire," *Études françaises* 24.2 (1988), pp. 35–52. Serres also describes the gnomon as an instrument that enables a model of the world to appear through the projected shadows it draws on the earth. He insists on the meaning of the word "gnomon": "that which understands, judges, decides, interprets or distinguishes . . . a rule that enables understanding . . . an instrument of knowledge" (p. 35). Geometry, he concludes, was either sleeping beneath the earth or dreaming in the shining sun; the gnomon and all other architectural tools such as the compass and the plumb line serve to wake it up.

65   See Thomas da Costa Kaufmann, "The Perspective of Shadows: The History of the Theory of Shadow Projection," *Journal of the Warburg and Cortauld Institutes* 38 (1975), pp. 258–287. Kaufmann also discusses the few instances in which shadows are discussed in relation to classical optics, always connected to the proof that light proceeds along straight lines. An exception exists in the medieval Byzantine tradition. Nicephorus Gregoras, in his *Astrolabica,* seems to connect painting with Ptolemy's methods of stereographic projection. The analogy between celestial mapmaking and the "exact imitation of objects," however, must be understood in the context of the Byzantine world of representation, which is quite distinct from our own post-Renaissance assumptions (see p. 264 n. 25).

66   Biagio Pelacani da Parma, *Questiones de perspective* [*sic*], quoted by Federici Vescovini, "Le questioni di perspettiva di Biagio Pelacani," *Rinascimento* 1 (1961), pp. 242–243.

67 Kaufmann, "The Perspective of Shadows," pp. 267ff.

68 Dürer, *Unterweysung der Messung* (Nuremberg, 1525), fol. 81v.

69 See Samuel van Hoogstraten, *In leyding tot de Hooge Schoole der Schilderkonst* (1641), quoted by Kemp, *The Science of Art,* pp. 118–119.

70 Samuel Marolois, *Perspective contenant la Théorie Practique et Instruction Fondamentelle d'icelle* (Amsterdam: Jean Jannson, 1628), p. 7, and Salomon de Caus, *La Perspective avec la Raison des ombres et miroirs* (London, 1611), fols. 42–43.

71 D'Aguilon, quoted by Kaufmann, "The Perspective of Shadows," p. 280.

72 Barbaro, *La Practica della Perspettiva,* pp. 175ff.

73 "With good practice you can project every shadow, of whatever body and shape you like, without drawing so many lines; and you can also determine the shadow of objects hanging in the air cast upon distant planes, for which judgment and experience are needed" (ibid., p. 178; trans. by Kaufmann, "The Perspective of Shadows," p. 277).

74 Marco Frascari traces a revealing connection to the mnemonic tradition of Giordano Bruno and Giulio Camillo Delmino in his insightful article "A Secret Semiotic Skiagraphy: The Corporal Theatre of Meanings in Vincenzo Scamozzi's *Idea* of Architecture," in *Architecture and Shadow,* ed. David Murray, *Via* 11 (Philadelphia: Graduate School of Fine Arts, University of Pennsylvania; New York: Rizzoli, 1990), pp. 32–51. The author compares Scamozzi's villas to Lullian wheels of memory as passive machines where shadows make the images in our mind work (p. 43). The movement of shadows implicit in Scamozzi's drawing recalls the combinatory nature of Lullian wheels and establishes analogical relationships between the parts of the projected construction, thus combining *ideas* of architecture.

75 Ibid., p. 47.

76 Caramuel, *Architectura Civil,* vol. II, p. 97.

77 Juan Bautista Villalpando, *El Templo de Salomón, Comentarios a la Profecía de Ezequiel,* ed. Juan Antonio Ramírez trans. José Luis Oliver Domingo (Madrid: Ediciones Siruela, 1991), p. 58.

78 Ibid., pp. 75–77.

79 Ibid., p. 77; our translation.

80 "[L]a sombra avanza siempre dentro de unas lineas paralelas" (ibid., pp. 77–78). A similar (quite exceptional) observation is found in the late antique recension of Euclid's *Optics* by Theon of Alexandria. He says that shadows equal in breadth to the bodies that project them are also equal in dimension to the illuminating fires. Shadows larger than the bodies projecting them are caused by fires smaller than the bodies, and vice versa. See *Euclides Optica; Opticorum Recensio Theonis,* ed. J. L.

Heiberg (Leipzig, 1895), pp. 144–147, quoted by Kaufmann, "The Perspective of Shadows," p. 265.

81   Villalpando, *El Templo de Salomón,* p. 77.

82   Abraham Bosse, *La Manière universelle de M. Desargues lyonnois pour posser l'essieu & placer les heures & autres aux cadrans du soleil* (Paris, 1643).

83   Robin Evans has argued in "Architectural Projection," in Murray, *Architecture and Shadow,* pp. 134–140, that a rational projection of shadows (such as those common in drawings in the tradition of the École Polytechnique during the nineteenth century) enables the viewer to imagine more easily the structure of architectural elements such as columns. While it is obvious that modern architects sometimes have used projective tools in highly imaginative ways, Evans fails to acknowledge historical distinctions between Renaissance and later projective uses. His posthumous book, *The Projective Cast: Architecture and Its Three Geometries* (Cambridge, Mass.: MIT Press, 1995), addresses similar issues though historical examples. Evans postulates geometrical projection as a sort of transhistorical essence for architecture, a tool that plays an active role in the production of meaningful buildings since the Renaissance. While many of his analyses are illuminating, his deliberate reluctance to engage the complex relationship between projection and optics in the tradition of Western architectural representation prevents him from recognizing the reductive danger of instrumental projections and their effect on the mainstream practice of architecture after the Industrial Revolution.

84   Kirby, *Taylor's Method,* part 1, p. 57; quoted by Kaufmann, "The Perspective of Shadows," p. 286.

85   Caramuel describes the two movements of the sun, one natural and the other violent (*rapto*). The natural movement describes the yearly cycle, divided into four seasons (*tiempos*) and twelve months. This is the celestial movement determined by God. The violent movement (*el impulso arrebatado*) goes from east to west. These two movements are derived directly from Aristotle, for whom the orbits of the sun around the earth were circular.

86   Caramuel, *Architectura Civil,* vol. II, p. 248–249; vol. III, p. 49, plate 10. Care must be taken not to overemphasize the "modernity" of Caramuel's cosmology. See A. Bonet Correa's introduction to Caramuel's *Architectura Civil,* p. xv.

87   "El primer Architecto, que en el Cielo y la Tierra hecho lineas Obliquas, fue Dios. Porque yendo en el Cielo los dos Tropicos, y los Circulos Arctico y Antartico parallelos a la Equinocial, hizo que el Sol con su movimiento annuo describesse la Ecliptica, que es un *circulo,* que corta a la Equinocial obliquamente al Zodiaco" (Caramuel, *Architectura Civil,* vol. II, p. 95, our emphasis).

88   Fernand Hallyn, *The Poetic Structure of the World: Copernicus and Kepler,* trans. D. M. Leslie (New York: Zone Books, 1993), p. 209.

89 Kepler's earlier *Mysterium cosmographicum* (1596) reveals the sources of his later work. It was inspired by the Copernican preoccupation with "symmetry," understood as "the proper arrangement of proportions."

90 Hallyn parallels the law of the ellipse, which represents a "submission to facts far removed from a dreamed perfection," and the artists' belief in "the impossibility of basing a realist representation on codes presumed to be perfect" (*The Poetic Structure of the World*, p. 172). For more details on the importance of the ellipse for Kepler and its potential relation to the arts, see pp. 203–209.

91 Ibid., pp. 217, 232.

92 Because the polyhedrons had fulfilled a cosmogonic function in Plato's *Timaeus* and ever since the Pythagoreans, Hallyn describes Kepler's accomplishment as a transformation of "the cosmogonic function of the five solids by transferring it from the creation of matter to the construction of cosmic space" (ibid., pp. 184, 197).

93 Caramuel's understanding of the cabalistic sun and his theory of *esteganographia* were derived from the sixteenth-century magician and astronomer Trithemius, who observed the face of the Sun as it rose into the sky.

94 Caramuel's fascination with languages and universal knowledge led him to invent his own universal language *de caracter combinatorio de tipo matematico*. In 1636, he published *Steganographia o Arte de escribir en cifra* on the art of writing with numbers.

95 Some recent commentators of Caramuel have established direct parallels with Desargues. See Bonet Correa's introduction to the reprint of *Architectura Civil* and A. Guidoni Marino, "Il colonnato di piazza S. Pietro: dall'architettura obliqua di Caramuel al 'Classicismo' Berniniano," *Palladio* 23.1–4 (1973), pp. 81–120. Even though Caramuel knew about the modern mathematics of Desargues, it is not certain that he could understand it. He was obviously much closer to the hermetic tradition of Fludd and Kircher.

96 Even today we tend to assume that orthogonal projections and perspective projections belong to two separate systems of representation (the use of computers in design may be slowly changing this).

97 Ernest B. Gilman, *The Curious Perspective: Literary and Pictorial Wit in the Seventeenth Century* (New Haven: Yale University Press, 1978), p. 97.

98 Gottfried Wilhelm von Leibniz, *Monadology and Other Philosophical Essays,* trans. Paul Schrecker (Indianapolis: Bobbs-Merrill, 1965), p. 175.

99 According to René Taton in *L'oeuvre mathématique de G. Desargues* (p. 87), only fifty copies of Desargues's original *Rough Draft of an Essay (Brouillon projet) on the Results of Taking Plane Sections of a Cone* were printed for distribution among Mersenne's circle. The work remained lost until the early nineteenth century (in 1675, Leibniz unsuccessfully tried to find it). Only after the work of Gaspard Monge and Carnot

did geometricians such as Servois, Poncelet, and Chasles understand the importance of Desargues's contribution. And see Johann Kepler, *Les fondements de l'optique moderne: Paralipomènes à Vitellion* (1604), trans. Catherine Chevalley (Paris: Librairie philosophique J. Vrin, 1980), pp. 220–222. Kepler was the first to postulate the possibility "that a straight line extended in either direction until its ends met; that the ends met at infinity; that they met in just one point" (William M. Ivins Jr., *Art and Geometry: A Study in Space Intuitions* [1946; reprint, New York: Dover Publications, 1964], p. 85).

100 Taton argues that Desargues probably based his reasoning on geometric figures of space that his intuition enabled him to imagine. His objective, however, was to complement this initial intuition—extremely complex to achieve—by returning every demonstration to a planar geometry. In order to accomplish this, it was important not to consider space in its entirety but to concentrate on a planar figure and on its perspective transformation, easily related to the plane of the initial figure (Taton, *L'oeuvre mathématique de G. Desargues,* p. 96).

101 For more details on the general reaction toward Desargues's theory, see ibid., pp. 27–41, 185–194. It is also revealing that despite Desargues's explicit rejection of philosophical speculation (or perhaps indeed because of it), Descartes always had a high opinion of his work. In a letter to Mersenne, in which Descartes included a summary of his *Meditations,* he states that he would trust Desargues's opinion over that of three theologians (quoted in ibid., p. 41).

102 Hallyn, *The Poetic Structure of the World,* p. 229.

103 Kepler, *Les fondements de l'optique moderne,* pp. 220–221; our translation.

104 Quoted by Hallyn, *The Poetic Structure of the World,* p. 224.

105 It is worth remembering that the English term "vanishing point" was only introduced in the eighteenth century, in Brook Taylor's treatise on perspective (1715), to designate the point of convergence of parallel lines.

106 See P. Marin Mersenne, "De l'utilité de l'harmonie," in *Harmonie Universelle* (Paris: Éditions du CNRS, 1965), 3:21–22. We do not agree completely with Hallyn, who sees in this reversal the end of "participation." In seventeenth-century perspectival public spaces, forms of participation associated with traditional ritual continue to take place, never at odds with the geometrized vantage point of the theater, the *quadratura* fresco, or the anamorphic painting.

107 Desargues makes this point in his *Brouillon Projet* on the conics (1639); see Taton, *L'oeuvre mathématique de G. Desargues,* pp. 133–134. Desargues's geometric theory is discussed brilliantly by Mark Schneider in his unpublished dissertation, "Girard Desargues, the Architectural and Perspective Geometry: A Study in the Rationalization of Figures" (Ph.D. diss., Virginia Polytechnic Institute, 1983), chap. 3.

108 "It was one of the recognized disadvantages of Alberti's construction that one had to use an 'eye point' which lay beyond the edge of the picture, at a distance equal to [that] between the picture and the eye of the observer" (J. V. Fields and J. J. Gray, *The Geometrical Work of Girard Desargues* [New York: Springer-Verlag, 1987] p. 27).

109 He was criticized by Beaugrand and others for not respecting the theory of the conics by the Greek geometer Apollonius of Perga (ca. 262–180 B.C.E.), which was commonly used by geometers at that time. Apollonius had discussed the geometric properties of the circle, parabola, hyperbola, and ellipse as autonomous figures, without ever grasping the principle of projective continuity among the conic sections. Desargues had criticized Beaugrand's own work some years earlier.

110 See Taton, *L'oeuvre mathématique de G. Desargues,* pp. 36–40.

111 For a more detailed description of this controversy, see ibid., pp. 50–54.

112 This question is discussed in Alberto Pérez-Gómez, *Architecture and the Crisis of Modern Science* (Cambridge, Mass.: MIT Press, 1983), chaps. 8, 9.

113 Schneider, "Girard Desargues," p. 68.

114 J. V. Poncelet, *Traité des propriétés projectives des figures* (Paris, 1822).

115 The word "anamorphosis" comes from the Greek: *ana-* (back) indicating a return toward, and *morphē* (form). Our understanding of anamorphosis is greatly indebted to Jurgis Baltrusaitis's major work, *Anamorphic Art,* trans. W. J. Strachan (New York: Harry N. Abrams, 1976). See also Alberto Pérez-Gómez and Louise Pelletier, *Anamorphosis, an Annotated Bibliography with Special Reference to Architectural Representation,* Fontanus Monograph Series 6 (Montreal: McGill University Libraries, 1995).

116 This intertwining of two different dimensions reintroduces an unfolding temporal dimension to the frozen frame. The viewer is asked to experience the revelation of the enigmatic image by proceeding through different virtual spaces. In his article "Anamorphosis and Architecture," one of the few recent discussions of this topic, Friedrich Piel argues that anamorphoses depicted on a vault are not meant to be hidden; their vantage point is already located in relation to a primary architectural frame of reference. In this context, Andrea Pozzo's *quadraturas* and distorted architecture such as that of Caramuel de Lobkowitz would seem to address similar issues as a potential "anamorphic architecture." Piel, however, fails to distinguish between pictorial anamorphosis and the technique of *quadratura.* See *Festschrift Wolfgang Braunfels* (Tübingen: Wasmuth, 1977), pp. 289–296.

117 Barbaro emphasizes the importance of hiding the distorted image in a landscape:

The better to hide what he paints, in accordance with the practices indicated, the painter who is proposing to delineate the two heads or other portrayals must know how to shade and cover the image so that instead of two heads, it shows landscapes, water, hills, rocks and other things. . . . The painter can and, indeed, must deceive our eyes by interrupting and separating lines which ought to be straight and continuous because, except at the viewing-point indicated, they do not reveal what they reveal at the chosen place. . . . The figures can be broken up with some parts separated from others so that they appear to join together again when they are looked at obliquely: thus, the forehead of a face can be placed at one point, the nose at another and the chin somewhere else. . . . And then one would no longer recognize that the painting represents an ear, but the nose would seem one thing and the forehead another, and, for example, the painter can make the nose look like a rock and the forehead like a clod of earth if he wishes. (La Pratica della Perspettiva, p. 161; translated by Baltrusaitis, Anamorphic Art, p. 32)

118 Samuel van Hoogstraten, *In leyding tot de hooge schoole der schilderkonst* (Introduction to the advanced school of painting) (Rotterdam: François van Hoogstraeten, 1678; 1st ed. 1641), p. 34.

119 Compare, for example, the position of William Herdmann, *A Treatise on the Curvilinear Perspective of Nature* (London, 1853).

120 See, respectively, Giovanni Paolo Lomazzo, *Trattato dell'arte della pittura, scoltura, et architettura,* (Milan: Appresso Paolo Gottardo Pontio, 1585), VI.19, p. 335; Barbaro, *La Pratica della Perspettiva,* part 5, chap. 1.

121 "L'optique a donc autant d'avantages sur les autres sciences, comme la veüe sur les autres sens: C'est pourquoy Villalpand dit en ses Commentaires sur Ezechiel, que la science de la Perspective est la premiere en dignité, & la plus excellente en toutes, puisqu'elle s'occupe à considerer les effets de la lumiere qui donne la beauté à toutes les choses sensibles . . . & Desargues qui en a donné une méthode generale & fort expeditive, avec plusieurs autres beaux secrets pour la Perspective" (Nicéron, *La Perspective Curieuse* [Paris: Chez Pierre Billaine, 1638), p. 3). Nicéron apparently changed his mind about Desargues, for in the Latin version (Paris, 1646) he accuses Desargues of copying previous authors, reflecting the current controversy. In the second French edition (Paris, 1663), the acknowledgment was restored to that of the first edition, a change attributed to Mersenne. For more details on the controversy, see Taton, *L'oeuvre mathématique de G. Desargues,* p. 17.

122 According to Baltrusaitis, Salomon de Caus used Vignola's first rule of perspective to compose the framework of his anamorphoses, while Nicéron relied on Barbaro's method (*Anamorphic Art,* p. 41).

123 Nicéron, *La Perspective Curieuse,* book 2, proposition 1. Nicéron's layout for the anamorphic grid eventually was taken up by Jean Dubreuil in *La Perspective Pratique* (Paris, 1649) and later universally adopted.

124 The letter is dated June 26, 1612. Cigoli's twenty-nine surviving letters and Galileo's two remaining letters have been published and annotated by A. Matteoli in "Macchie di sole e pittura: Carteggio L. Cigoli—G. Galilei," *Bollettino della Accademia degli Euteleti* 32 (1959), pp. 52–53. See also Kemp, *The Science of Art*, p. 94. Galileo writes, "I do not possess . . . a perfect faculty of discrimination. I am more like the monkey who firmly believed that he saw another monkey in the mirror . . . and discovered his error only after running behind the glass several times" (quoted by Maurice Clavelin, *The Natural Philosophy of Galileo* [Cambridge, Mass.: MIT Press, 1974], p. 399).

125 Galileo, quoted by Kemp, *The Science of Art*, p. 95.

126 Discourse IV on the *Dioptrics*, quoted by Baltrusaitis, *Anamorphic Art*, p. 68.

127 See Dalia Judovitz, "Vision, Representation, and Technology in Descartes," in *Modernity and the Hegemony of Vision*, ed. D. M. Levin (Berkeley: University of California Press, 1993), pp. 63–86. Descartes was fascinated with optics and perspective illusions, as evident from his *Cogitationes privatae* (1619), where he describes how one can make trees appear in a garden by manipulating shadows, or make limbs of fire and spectral figures appear in rooms through the use of mirrors. Judovitz clearly demonstrates how, through his interest in optics as a physical science and in vision as a dominant sense, Descartes systematically undermines the role of natural vision and its perceptual domain to privilege conceptual (i.e., mathematical and geometric) constructs for the acquisition of truth.

128 De Caus, *La Perspective*, book 2; Athanasius Kircher, *Ars magna lucis et umbrae* (Rome: Sumptibus Hermanni Scheus, 1646); Barbaro, *La Practica della Perspettiva*.

129 Alberto Pérez-Gómez and Louise Pelletier, "Architectural Representation beyond Perspectivism," *Perspecta* 27 (1992), pp. 21–39.

130 Caramuel, *Architectura Civil*, vol. I, pp. 73–76.

131 Luca Pacioli and Philibert de L'Orme can be cited as precedent. The history of the interest in the temple and its reconstructions is traced in a collective work that accompanies the first Spanish edition of Villalpando's text, *Dios, Arquitecto, J. B. Villalpando y el Templo de Salomón,* ed. Juan Antonio Ramírez, with essays by André Corboz, René Taylor, Robert Jan van Pelt, and Antonio Martínez Ripol (Madrid: Ediciones Siruela, 1992). The authors compiled and commented on the most significant theoretical reconstructions of the Temple of Solomon from the Middle Ages to the early nineteenth century.

132 Villalpando assumed a fundamental identity between the temple described by Ezekiel and the Temple of Solomon. Perhaps more importantly for European architecture, he emphasized the coincidence between the temple and the Vitruvian classical tradition (*El Templo de Salomón*). See also J. A. Ramírez, "Caramuel: Probabilista, Ecléctico y

'Deconstructor,'" in Ramírez, *Dios, Arquitecto,* pp. 109–114; J. J. León (1603–1675), *Retrato del Templo de Solomon* (Middelburg, 1642), from the Latin edition (1665).

133 Incidentally, Claude Perrault's reconstruction, based on Maimonides' medieval drawing of the temple's plan, was the first "archaeological" reconstruction whose elevations are based on a Jewish "style," rather than simply referring back to current traditions of design. This is of course consistent with Perrault's scientifically motivated skepticism concerning the tradition of optical correction which we have previously discussed. For the implications of this reconstruction see Pérez-Gómez, introduction to Perrault, *Ordonnance for the Five Kinds of Columns.*

134 Caramuel also mentions the central disposition of Villalpando's model but without commenting on it (*Architectura Civil,* vol. I, p. 29).

135 Caramuel quotes Hebrew, Greek, and Latin texts that, according to him, all describe the windows as oblique; he also quotes Ezekiel: "Et fenestras obliquas in thalamis." He concludes: "Se vuelve a dexar llevar de su prejuicio, que las Ventanas han de ser mas anchas por la parte de afuera" (ibid., vol. II, p. 96).

136 Bonet Correa, introduction to Caramuel, *Architectura Civil,* p. xxvi.

137 Caramuel, *Architectura Civil,* vol. II, p. 9.

138 In many art theories of the Counter-Reformation, God was the first craftsman, as well as the first sculptor, painter, and architect (ibid., vol. II, p. 95).

139 Ibid., vol. II, p. 115.

140 Ibid., plate 7, fig. 26. In the caption Caramuel describes the shape that makes a tower stable, demonstrating why all buildings are wider on top than at their footing: "Junto a ella se dibuxa una Torre, en que se demuestra claramente, como todos los Edificios son mas anchos por la parte de arriba; porque sus muros por ser a plomo, no constan de lineas parallelas, si no de inclinadas, que hazen angulo, y se juntan en Q que viene a ser el centro deste Globo Terraqueo" (vol. II, p. 248). A curious precedent to this unorthodox view is the thirteenth-century work of Roger Bacon. In this *De multiplicatione specierum,* Bacon argues that the shadows cast by the sun are parallel only "as far as the sense can discern, . . . for the axes of shadows proceed to the center of the sun, as do the axes of luminous pyramids." He then extends his conclusions: "There are many things that sense judges to be parallel because it does not perceive their intersection; thus the walls of a house are sensibly parallel, but are not parallel [in fact], since they extend toward the center of the world as do all heavy bodies" (trans. D. C. Lindberg [New York: Oxford University Press, 1983], part 2, chap. 9, p. 163).

141 See Ramírez, "Probabilista, Ecléctico y 'Deconstructor.'"

142 In an article on the use of full-scale models in the baroque tradition, George C. Bauer points out that Bernini apparently developed seven full-scale models of the colonnade of St. Peter's Square before deciding in favor of the oval shape over the *forma quadrata*. While both Caramuel and Bernini advocated the primacy of visual perception and emphasized the necessity of optically correcting the proportions of the components of the square, it is revealing that Bernini gave priority to the direct experience of a full-scale model while Caramuel gave priority to the conceptual mathematical order. See Bauer, "From Architecture to Scenography: The Full-Scale Model in the Baroque Tradition," in *La Scenographia Barocca* (Bologna: Editrice C.L.U.E.B., 1979), pp. 141–150.

143 Caramuel, *Architectura Civil,* vol. II, p. 231. In section X, Caramuel explains what these mistakes are.

144 To our knowledge, Bonet Correa's introduction to the reprint of *Architectura Civil* is the most recent critical appraisal of Caramuel's work on architecture.

145 Ibid., p. XVI.

146 Caramuel, *Architectura Civil,* vol. II, p. 104.

147 Ibid., vol. I, pp. 142–143.

148 These distortions seem to relate to Piero della Francesca's distortions of the horizontal dimension. However, while Piero applies the distortion to a pictorial image traced from the section of the visual cone, Caramuel is aware that architecture cannot be reduced to an image.

149 For an extensive discussion on the Cartesian absence of shadows, see D. M. Levin, *The Opening of Vision* (New York: Routledge, 1988), pp. 101ff.

150 Kepler, quoted by Hallyn, *The Poetic Structure of the World,* p. 244.

151 Ibid.

152 Ibid., pp. 244–245. Astronomy (astrology) indeed had been perceived since antiquity as the point of departure for science and philosophy. The fascination with the regularity of the heavens opened the realm of visual experience to the contemplation and comprehension of the geometric and mathematical disciplines. The origin of true knowledge in astrology was postulated by Ptolemy and Aristotle, among others, and was taken up by Vitruvius, who believed it was a crucial part of architectural theory. He devotes a whole book (book 9) of *De architectura* to the zodiac and the planets.

153 Hallyn, *The Poetic Structure of the World,* pp. 218–219.

154 In his technical treatise on perspective, *Prospettiva de' Pittori e Architetti* (Rome, 1693), Pozzo uses a simplified version of previous methods for his step-by-step lesson in perspective drawing, before revealing the procedure for casting it onto a vaulted ceiling.

155 See Kemp, *The Science of Art,* pp. 73–74, 96 and 137.

156 Recently this dimension of baroque art has been the subject of much discussion, mainly due to the exploding interest in the work of Walter Benjamin. Benjamin's doctoral dissertation (1925), published in English as *Origin of German Tragic Drama,* trans. John Osborne (London: New Left Books, 1977), has been the point of departure of many commentaries. See, for example, Richard Wolin, *Walter Benjamin: An Aesthetic of Redemption,* 2d ed. (Berkeley: University of California Press, 1994) and Susan Buck-Morss, *The Dialectics of Seeing* (Cambridge, Mass.: MIT Press, 1989).

157 Gilman, *The Curious Perspective,* p. 40.

158 For more details on Tesauro's fascination with optical devices and his opposition to Port-Royal's *Logic,* see Fernand Hallyn, "Port-Royal versus Tesauro: Signe, Figure, Sujet," in *Baroque 9–10, Revue Internationale* (Montauban: C.I.S.B., 1980), pp. 76–86. While the Jansenists defended logic and grammar as the effective path toward truth, Tesauro proposed rhetoric as a cure against the boredom of everyday life. He claimed that it is not enough for a glass to allow one to drink from it, it should also please the eye; it is not enough to consider a thing for its functional dimension, it has to be considered for itself. Similarly, rhetoric adds another dimension to the representative function of language (p. 82).

159 Quoted by Taton, *L'oeuvre mathématique de G. Desargues,* p. 55; our translation.

160 This second book is generally assumed to be a more independent work, developed by Bosse with some advice from Desargues. Taton, however, argues that Bosse made extensive use of another treatise by Desargues, *Leçon des ténèbres,* now lost, in which the geometry of shadows illustrated the principle of projection on vaults and curved surfaces.

161 In his book on perspective, *Optique et Portraiture et peinture, en deux parties. . . . La première est la perspective pratique acomplie, . . . La deuxième partie contient la perspective speculative* (Paris, 1670), Huret criticizes the use of optical adjustments, that transform the proportions of figures such as those suggested by Dürer and Desargues. In section 206, he emphasizes the difference between optical adjustments and anamorphic distortions.

162 For more details on Desargues's life during his period of "scientific production," see Taton, *L'oeuvre mathématique de G. Desargues,* chap. 2.

163 For a comprehensive survey of Desargues's practical work, from 1644 to 1649 and from 1657 to 1661, see ibid., chap. 3.

164 Abraham Bosse, *Les Ordres de l'Architecture* (Paris, 1688).

165 In the *Reconnoissance* included at the beginning of Abraham Bosse's *Manière universelle de Mr. Desargues* (Paris: P. Des-Hayes, 1648), Des-

argues introduces his interest in theory as follows:

Je n'eus jamais de goust, à l'étude ou recherche, ny de la Phisique, ny de la Geometrie, sinon entant qu'elles peuvent servir à l'esprit, d'un moyen d'arriver à quelque sorte de connoissance, des causes prochaines des effets de choses qui se puissent reduire en acte effectif, au bien & commodité de la vie qui soit en usage pour l'entretien & conservation de la santé; soit en leur application pour la pratique de quelque art. . . . Je m'aperceut que ceux qui s'y adonnent, avoient à se charger la memoire, d'un grand nombre de leçons diverses, pour chacune d'elles. . . . Le desir & l'affection de les soulager si je pouvois aucunement de cette peine, si laborieuse, & souvent ingrate, me fit chercher, & publier des regles abrégées de chacun de ces arts. (p. 3)

166 If a stone was spoiled, the "dead" stone was first laid on a stretcher and carried by masons to a pit called the "charnel house." The guilty mason was required to follow behind the stretcher as "chief mourner"; all of his fellow masons joined the procession. After the "dead" stone was "laid to rest," the offending mason was given a mock beating as punishment for his "negligent homicide." This account is from Paul Frankl, *The Gothic: Literary Sources and Interpretations through Eight Centuries* (Princeton: Princeton University Press, 1960), p. 132. See also Schneider, "Girard Desargues," chap. 2, pp. 3–4.

167 Caramuel, *Architectura Civil,* vol. II, treatise VI. Unlike other, more practical, architectural treatises of his time, Caramuel's text is addressed explicitly to a "general reader." As might be expected, the rhetorical introduction nevertheless emphasizes the novelty of the work, hoping that it will enable the old defects and mistakes of craftsmen to be corrected. See Bonet Correa, introduction, p. xxii.

168 Guarino Guarini, *Architettura Civile* (Torino, 1737), pp. 169, 172, 178. Guarini qualifies the variation of the diameter of columns in the multi-layered oval colonnade as a joke rather than judicious teaching: "sia piuttosto uno scherzo a parlar modestamente, che un giudizioso insegnamento."

169 Ibid., p. 112.

170 See, for example, Marino, "Il colonnato di piazza S. Pietro."

171 On Guarini's criticism of Caramuel's oblique architecture, see Werner Oechslin, "Osservazioni su Guarino Guarini e Juan Caramuel de Lobkowitz," in *Guarino Guarini e l'Internazionalità del Barocco* (Turin: Accademia delle Scienze, 1970), 1:573–595. See also Ludvik Hlavacek, "'Architectura obliqua' Jana Caramuela z Lobkovic," *Umení* 22.1 (1974), pp. 50–53, in which the author sees Guarini's opposition to Caramuel's obsession with modifying the apparent size and shape of architectural elements according to a predetermined vantage point as evidence that while baroque architecture considered perspective in its composition, it does not immobilize the spectator in a fixed position and does not disregard the objective reality of form.

172 See Pérez-Gómez, *Architecture and the Crisis of Modern Science,* chap. 3, pp. 88–89.

173 Guarino Guarini, *Placita Philosophica* (Paris, 1665). In a section entitled "De Infinito" (pp. 267–273), Guarini emphasizes that infinity is a metaphysical notion that does not exist as a geometric point in the physical world.

174 Guarino Guarini, *Euclides Adauctus et Methodicus* (Turin, 1671), proposition II, conclusion ii, quoted by Janine Debanné, "Guarino Guarini's SS. Sindone Chapel: Between Reliquary and Cenotaph" (M.Arch. Thesis, McGill University, 1995), pp. 75–79. For a comprehensive discussion of this issue, see Corrado Maltese, "Guarini e la Prospettiva," in *Guarino Guarini e l'Internazionalità del Barocco,* 1:560–572.

175 Guarini, *Placita Philosophica,* p. 720.

176 Debanné, "Guarini's SS. Sindone Chapel," p. 79.

177 On the political and physical development of the Piazza Ducale in Vigevano, see Wolfgang Lotz, *Studies in Italian Renaissance Architecture* (Cambridge, Mass.: MIT Press, 1977), chap. 4.

178 Caramuel, *Architectura Civil,* vol. II, table 5.

179 We may recall how, in this connection, perspective was often perceived as a "weakness" of human sight, for example by Lomazzo in his *Trattato dell'arte della pittura.* A whole tradition of interest in different sorts of parallel projections, present among architects since the sixteenth century, is clearly related to this concern, which is not simply the result of some progressive desire to instrumentalize representation that culminates in modern axonometry.

Variation Two
Cosmological Perspectives

1 From Copernicus's preface to *De revolutionibus* (1543), quoted by R. M. Wallace in his introduction to Hans Blumenberg, *The Genesis of the Copernican World* (Cambridge, Mass.: MIT Press, 1987), p. xii.

2 Sir Thomas Heath, in his book *Aristarchus of Samos, the Ancient Copernicus: A History of Greek Astronomy to Aristarchus* (Oxford: Clarendon Press, 1913), claims that Aristarchus was the first to propose that Earth revolves around the sun. However, the only proof of such a statement seems to come from the acknowledgements of other authors such as Archimedes and Copernicus himself.

3 This is a fundamental argument for Blumenberg, *The Genesis of the Copernican World;* see introduction, pp. xxxv–xxxviii, and part 2, chap. 2.

4   "Discurso Mathematico de D. Ioseph Chafrion. Ayudante de In-
    geniero Mayor del Exercito, en el Estado de Milan. En alabanza del
    Autor, y estos Tres ingeniosos Tomos de Recta y Obliqua Archi-
    tectura," in Caramuel, *Architectura civil recta y oblicua considerada y Dibu-
    xada en el Templo de Ierusale[m]* (1678; reprint, Madrid: Ediciones
    Turner, 1984), vol. I, pp. 33–54.

5   In his introduction to the reprint of *Architectura Civil,* A. Bonet Correa
    asserts wrongly that Caramuel adopted Copernicus's theory (p. xv).

6   "Estas dos propositiones son absolutamente falsas y assi no tiene seguri-
    dad lo que en ellas se funda" (Caramuel, *Architectura Civil,* vol. I, p. 51).

7   Fernand Hallyn, *The Poetic Structure of the World: Copernicus and Kepler,*
    trans. D. M. Leslie (New York: Zone Books, 1993), pp. 106–108.

8   Ibid., p. 108.

9   Copernicus, quoted in ibid., p. 100.

10 Alexandre Koyré associates this basic assumption of the new science
    with Galileo. He characterizes the emergence of experimental science
    as a result of the new metaphysical approach to nature in two ways:
    "a) the destruction of the cosmos, and therefore the disappearance
    from science . . . of all considerations based on this concept, and b)
    the geometrization of space, that is, the substitution of the homoge-
    neous and abstract . . . dimension of space of Euclidean geometry for
    the concrete and differentiated place continuum of pre-Galilean phys-
    ics and astronomy" (*Newtonian Studies* [Chicago: University of Chi-
    cago Press, 1965], pp. 6–7).

11 Hallyn oversimplifies the problem by asserting that "this space is like
    the perspective space of Renaissance painting, which in principle is
    also continuous and homogeneous." The analogy between Coperni-
    cus's system of the world and Dürer's perspective device is more evi-
    dent. They were both interested in discovering "the principle
    informing Creation—Creation of the heavens as well as man, since
    the organic unity of both is based on numbers. When Copernicus sets
    up the earth's sphere as the 'common measure' that alone can deter-
    mine the proportions of size and length for all the other spheres, he is
    applying Dürer's rule for artists" (*The Poetic Structure of the World,* pp.
    116, 97).

12 For a comprehensive edition of Johann Heinrich Lambert's writings
    on perspective, as well as biographical references and a complete bibli-
    ography of writings from and about Lambert until the first decades of
    the twentieth century, see *Schriften zur Perspektive,* ed. and comm. Max
    Steck (Berlin: G. Lüttke Verlag, 1943).

13 This event was recalled by Jean L. S. Formey, perpetual secretary of
    the Academy of Sciences, in his eulogy to Lambert, presented in Janu-
    ary 1778 and reprinted at the beginning of the French translation of
    Lambert, *Lettres cosmologiques* (Amsterdam: Gerard Hulst van Keulen,

1801), p. 28. In the introduction to his translation, *Cosmological Letters on the Arrangement of the World-Edifice* (New York: Science History Publications, 1976), Stanley L. Jaki relates the whole event in detail. See also Blumenberg, *The Genesis of the Copernican World,* p. 528.

14 Both Formey's obituary and Bernouilli's *Précis* are reprinted at the beginning of Lambert, *Lettres cosmologiques,* pp. 11–35.

15 The eldest son of a poor tailor from Mulhouse (Mulhausen), Lambert left school at the age of twelve to assist his father in the shop. At school he learned some geometry, and enough Latin and French to continue his own education through books. He continued to teach himself with remarkable assiduousness. Eager to master various disciplines, he would read at night by the light of the Moon—because his parents could not afford oil for the evening lamp—or by the light of candles that he would acquire by selling his drawings. Soon recognized as a child prodigy, he was given the means to pursue his studies, but he was never comfortable with his professors. He preferred the teachings of books on widely different subjects, from philosophy, astronomy, metaphysics, and rhetoric to mathematics, physics, meteorology, and mechanics. For more information on Lambert's life, see G. Chr. Lichtenberg, *Leben der berühmtesten vier Gelehrten unsers Philosophischen Jahrhunderts Rousseau's, Lambert's, Haller's und Voltaire's* (Frankfurt and Leipzig, 1779), reprinted in Lambert, *Schriften zur Perspektive,* pp. 27–53; for additional biographical references, see also *Dictionary of Scientific Biographies* (New York: Scribner, 1981), s.v. "Lambert."

16 Lagrange, Quoted by René Taton in his "Inaugural Lecture" to the *Colloque international et interdisciplinaire Jean-Henri Lambert* (Paris: Editions Ophrys, 1979), pp. 14–15.

17 There is, however, important correspondence between Lambert and the St. Petersburg academy, as well as with Euler and his students, edited by the Berlin astronomer J. Bernoulli. For more details about Lambert's connection with the Academy of Sciences of St. Petersburg, see A. T. Grigorian and N. I. Nevskia, "J.-H. Lambert et l'academie des sciences de Pétersbourg," in *Colloque international et interdisciplinaire,* p. 103.

18 "Johann Heinrich Lambert—A Biography," by Haus Maurer, in Johann Heinrich Lambert, *Notes and Comments on the Composition of Terrestrial and Celestial Maps,* trans. W. R. Tobler (Ann Arbor: Department of Geography, University of Michigan, 1972), p. 97.

19 See, for example, Salomon Bochner, *The Role of Mathematics in the Rise of Science* (Princeton: Princeton University Press, 1966); L. Brunschvicg, *Les étapes de la philosophie mathématique* (Paris: Librairie scientifique et technique, 1972); and Georges Gusdorf, *Les principes de la pensée au siècle des Lumières* (Paris: Payot, 1971).

20 For more information concerning Lambert's scientific accomplishments, see René Taton, *The Beginnings of Modern Science, from 1450 to*

1800, trans. A. J. Pomerans (London: Thames and Hudson, 1964), p. 418, and Morris Kline, *Mathematical Thought from Ancient to Modern Times* (New York: Oxford University Press, 1972), pp. 460, 868–869.

21   A draft of the dedication to Lambert can be found in *Reflexionen Kants zur Kritik der reinen Vernunft* (Leipzig: Fues's Verlag, 1884), pp. 1–2; see also S. L. Jaki, introduction to *Cosmological Letters*, p. 6 n. 30. In his introduction to Lambert's *Cosmological Letters*, pp. 17–18, Jaki emphasizes the fundamental differences between the cosmologies of Lambert and Kant. For a comparison of Kant's and Lambert's notions of space, see also Claude Debru, *Analyse et representation, De la méthodologie à la théorie de l'espace: Kant et Lambert* (Paris: Librairie Philosophique J. Vrin, 1977).

22   These regents eventually were associated with the notion of black holes. See Jacques Merleau-Ponty, introduction to the reprint of the French translation, *Lettres cosmologiques sur l'organisation de l'Univers* (Paris: Editions Alain Brieux, 1977), pp. ix–xiv.

23   In the first partial French translation of Lambert's work, *Système du monde* (Paris, 1770), Johann Bernard Merian rewrote a condensed version of the *Cosmological Letters* and was less than faithful to the original text. Merian overlooks the fact that Lambert always assigned boundaries to the universe and emphasized its finiteness. Merian uses the word "infini" in a rather imprecise manner, assuming an infinity of stars in the Milky Way. For more details about the translations of Lambert's *Cosmological Letters*, see Stanley L. Jaki "The Cosmological Letters of Lambert and His Cosmology," in *Colloque international et interdisciplinaire*, pp. 291–292.

24   For a discussion of the cultural context in which Lambert's *Cosmological Letters* appeared, see J. Merleau-Ponty, introduction to *Lettres cosmologiques* (1977), pp. vi–vii.

25   Isaac Newton, *Principia* (London, 1687), book III, proposition XIV, corollary 2; analyzed by Michael Hoskin, "Newton and Lambert," in *Colloque international et interdisciplinaire*, p. 363. This article provides a very interesting analysis of the relationship between Newton and Lambert, as well as a concise survey of the major figures that contributed to define the image of the cosmos in the eighteenth century (see pp. 363–370).

26   Hoskin, "Newton and Lambert," p. 366.

27   Lambert, *Cosmological Letters*, pp. 17–18.

28   Thomas Wright, *An Original Theory or New Hypothesis of the Universe, Founded upon the Laws of Nature* (London: H. Chapele, 1750); facsimile reprint, ed. M. A. Hoskin (London: Macdonald, 1971). Kant read a summary of Wright's work and acknowledged him in his *Allgemeine Naturgeschichte und Theorie des Himmels* (Königsberg and Leipzig, 1755).

29 This work was originally written in German, *Cosmologische Briefe über die Einrichtung des Weltbaus* (Augsburg, 1761).

30 This letter to Kant is translated by Stanley L. Jaki in *The Milky Way* (New York: Neale Watson Academic Publications, 1972), pp. 199–200.

31 Lambert, *Cosmological Letters,* pp. 57, 62.

32 Hermann Samuel Reimarus, *Abhandlungen von den vornehmsten Wahrheiten der naturlichen Religion* (1754), quoted by Blumenberg, *The Genesis of the Copernican World,* p. 550.

33 Lambert, *Cosmological Letters,* p. 73.

34 Ibid.

35 Later we will come back to Lambert's perspective theory in greater detail. Lambert himself acknowledged the continuity between his cosmological studies and his perspective theory in his *Monatsbuch* of November 1756, where he defines his work as "the problem of the art of perspective inverted" (quoted by Blumenberg, *The Genesis of the Copernican World,* p. 534).

36 Wright, *An Original Theory,* p. 63.

37 Lambert, *Cosmological Letters,* pp. 92–93.

38 Blumenberg, *The Genesis of the Copernican World,* pp. 525–526.

39 Ibid., pp. 127–132.

40 Lambert, *Cosmological Letters,* p. 45.

41 Ibid., p. 175.

42 Immanuel Kant, *Critique of Pure Reason,* trans. J. M. D. Meicklejohn (London: Dent and Sons; New York: E. P. Dutton, 1934) p. 19 n; quoted by Hallyn, *The Poetic Structure of the World,* p. 72.

43 This important text remained in manuscript form for almost two hundred years, until its transcription in *Schriften zur Perspektive,* pp. 157ff.

44 The transcription of Lambert's writings on perspective, including the text of 1752, his major work of 1759, and the late annex of 1774, can be found in *Schriften zur Perspektive,* pp. 157–328.

45 Johann Heinrich Lambert, *La Perspective affranchie de l'embaras du plan géométral* (Zurich, 1759; reprint, Alburgh: Archival Facsimiles, 1987), p. 2.

46 Roger Laurent discusses the technical aspects of Lambert's perspectograph in *La place de J.-H. Lambert (1728–1777) dans l'histoire de la perspective* (Paris: Cedic, 1987), pp. 50, 110–113. For a general history of the pantograph, with special reference to problems of representation, see Manlio Brusatin, "Arte pantografica, Osservazioni sugli organi riproduttivi delle forme," *Rassegna* 9 (1982), pp. 39–50.

47 In 1665, Pozzo "became a lay brother of the Society of Jesus in Milan, in which his task was to be *cook and dishwasher*." Interestingly, after being summoned to Rome in 1682 by the Jesuit general Padre Oliva, and while commissioned to decorate a corridor and to correct the proportions of the apse of the church of Sant'Ignazio using his perspective skills, Pozzo continued to be the cook in the Jesuit Casa Professa. For more information concerning Pozzo's life and education, as well as a list of the projects mentioned, see Fernanda de' Maffei, "Pozzo," in *Encyclopedia of World Art* (London: McGraw-Hill, 1959), 9:561, and Nino Carboneri, *Andrea Pozzo, Architetto (1642–1709)* (Trento: Collana Artisti Trenti, 1961), pp. 7–15.

48 We are aware of the controversy surrounding the reception of Pozzo's frescoes but shall not enter the debate. For an instructive discussion on the cultural context and the divergence of opinions among Pozzo's contemporaries, see Francis Haskell, "The Role of Patrons: Baroque Style Changes," in *Baroque Art: The Jesuit Contribution,* ed. R. Wittkower and I. B. Jaffe (New York: Fordham University Press, 1972), p. 56.

49 Quoted by Carboneri, *Andrea Pozzo,* p. 8.

50 Per Bjurström, "Baroque Theatre and the Jesuits," in Wittkower and Jaffe, *Baroque Art,* p. 104.

51 For a detailed description of Pozzo's theatrical stages for the Gesù, see ibid., pp. 103–104.

52 Ibid., p. 103.

53 As early as 1600, Guidobaldo del Monte had determined the vantage point as a mathematical coordinate of his geometric demonstration in *Perspectivæ libri sex* (Pesaro: Apud Hieronymum Concordiam, 1600).

54 Pozzo's treatise was originally published in two parts in an Italian and Latin edition, *Prospettiva de' Pittori e Architetti d'Andrea Pozzo, della Companis di Giesù/Perspectiva Pictorum Et Architectorum* (Rome, 1693–1700), and was later translated in an English and Latin edition (London, 1707). There are also French, German, Dutch, and even Chinese translations of the book.

55 It might be worth recalling that the determination of the observer's position in the *quadratura* was not identical to the Renaissance peephole, as has been suggested by Hubert Damisch in *L'origine de la perspective* (Paris: Flammarion, 1987). There is an obvious difference between the monocular construction, by which Brunelleschi's painting was seen through a hole from the back, and the binocular vision implied by the *quadratura* fresco. The position of the observer was precisely determined in both cases. Yet it is important to emphasize that the baroque *quadratura* fresco implied the geometrization of the three-dimensional space between the painting and the observer.

56 Andrea Pozzo, *Rules and Examples of Perspective* (London, 1707), preface.

57 Pierre Simon de Laplace, *Traité de mécanique céleste* (1799). On that subject, see Gusdorf, *Les principes de la pensée,* p. 156, and Koyré, *Newtonian Studies,* pp. 20–24.

58 Karl Schwarzschild, *Nachrichten der Königlichen Gesellschaft der Wissenschaft zu Göttingen* (Berlin, 1907), pp. 88–102, quoted by Blumenberg, *The Genesis of the Copernican World,* p. 566.

59 Blumenberg, *The Genesis of the Copernican World,* p. 565.

60 For more information concerning Karl Schwarzschild and his understanding of Lambert's theories, see ibid., pp. 565–572.

61 A. Hyatt Mayor, *The Bibiena Family* (New York: H. Bittner, 1945), pp. 21–22.

62 Ibid., p. 23.

63 Lambert, *La Perspective affranchie,* p. 120.

64 Ibid.

65 Ibid., p. 17.

66 We will save this discussion concerning Lambert's affiliation with Desargues and his followers for a later section, since it relates to considerations about parallel projections and non-Euclidean geometry that deserve special attention.

67 Jacques Alleume, *La Perspective speculative et Practique* (Paris: Chez Melchior Tavernier & Francois Langlois, 1643). We are grateful to Gerald Beasley, rare book bibliographer at the Canadian Centre for Architecture, for pointing out to us the existence of a copy of this treatise in the library of the Canadian Centre for Architecture, Montreal.

68 René Taton briefly mentions Alleaume's treatise in relation to this debate (*L'oeuvre mathématique de G. Desargues* [Paris: Presses Universitaires de France, 1951], p. 52).

69 Lambert, *La Perspective affranchie,* pp. 13–14.

70 Blumenberg, *The Genesis of the Copernican World,* p. 534.

71 *Correspondence des Directeurs de l'Académie de France à Rome,* ed. Montaiglon (1900); quoted by John Harris, "Le Geay, Piranesi, and International Neo-classicism in Rome 1740–1750," in *Essays in the History of Architecture Presented to Rudolf Wittkower,* ed. Douglas Fraser, Howard Hibbard, and Milton J. Lewine, (New York: Phaidon, 1967), p. 190.

72 Emil Kaufmann claims that Legeay had a greater influence on Piranesi's style, since only after Legeay's arrival in Rome in 1740 did Piranesi's etchings change radically, "passing from the composed representation of his *Prima parte di architettura* to the dramatic manner of the *Carceri* and *Caprici*" ("Three Revolutionary Architects: Boullée, Ledoux, and Lequeu," *Transactions of the American Philosophical Society*

42 [1952], p. 452). This opinion is shared by John Harris, *Sir William Chambers, Knight of the Polar Star* (London: A. Zwemmer, 1970), pp. 26–27; and by Gilbert Erouart, *L'architecture au pinceau* (Paris: Electa Moniteur, 1982) and "Jean-Laurent Legeay: Recherches," in *Piranèse et les Français,* ed. G. Brunel (Rome: Edizioni dell'Elefante, 1976), pp. 203–205. Others, such as Richard P. Wunder, support the hypothesis of a mutual influence at different moments in their career, favoring a more important general influence from Piranesi to Legeay ("The Spread of 'Piranesisme' in France through Legeay and Challes," in Brunel, *Piranèse et les Français,* p. 556).

73 Legeay taught in Paris from 1742 to 1748, according to Jean-Marie Pérouse de Montclos, *Étienne-Louis Boullée (1728–1799), de l'architecture classique à l'architecture révolutionnaire* (Paris: Arts et Métiers Graphiques, 1969). The École préparatoire de Blondel, founded in 1739, was a private school where aspiring architects were taught the rudiments of their art and of drawing. For more information on this subject, see René Taton, *Enseignement et diffusion des sciences en France au XVIIIe siècle* (Paris: Herman, 1964), pp. 345–351, 356–357. See also Louis Hautecoeur, *Histoire de l'Architecture classique en France* (Paris: Editions A. & J. Picard, 1950), 3:466–468, 470–471.

74 Charles-Nicolas Cochin, *Mémoires inédits sur le Comte de Caylus, Bouchardon, les Slodtz,* ed. M. C. Henry (Paris: Charavay Frères, Éditeurs, 1880), p. 142.

75 Pérouse de Montclos, *Boullée,* p. 45. Philippe Madec sees in Boullée's internal perspectives a direct influence from his master Legeay: "Before them, the visualization of architecture was done a posteriori by painters instead of a priori by architects. Legeay introduced in the project the general representation of the exterior of a building: Boullée adopted it to his need to represent the interior space" (*Boullée* [Paris: Fernand Hazan, 1986], p. 75).

76 Joseph Lavellée, "Nécrologie de Devailly," *Journal de Paris,* An VII [1798–1799], p. 261, and *Notice historique sur Charles De Wailly* (Paris, An VII [1798–1799]), p. 7; quoted by Erouart, "Jean-Laurent Legeay," p. 205.

77 "Vous qui voulez devenir Architecte, commencez par être peintre." From Claude-Nicolas Ledoux, *L'Architecture considérée sous le Rapport de l'Art, des Moeurs et de la Législation* (Paris: Chez l'auteur, 1804; reprint, Nördlingen: UHL Verlag, 1981).

78 Erouart, *L'architecture au pinceau,* p. 56.

79 Werner Oechslin diagnoses a separation between the academic and intellectual cultural architecture and the buildable architecture of the first half of the eighteenth century; see "Le groupe des 'Piranésiens' français (1740–1750): Un renouveau artistique dans la culture romaine," in Brunel, *Piranèse et les Français,* p. 366.

80 Pérouse de Montclos, *Boullée*, p. 39.

81 *C'était un de plus beaux génies en architecture qu'il y ait eu; mais d'ailleurs, sans frein, et, pour ainsi dire, sans raison. Il ne pouvoit jamais se borner à la demande qu'on lui faisoit, et le grand Mogol n'auroit pas été assés riche pour élever les bâtiments qu'il projettoit.*

  Je me souviens qu'il fit douze desseins pour la décoration du théâtre de la Tragédie des Jésuites, tous ingénieux, mais dont pas un n'étoit propre à être exécuté décemment dans ce lieu, tant ses idées étoient éloignées de ce qu'on lui avoit demandé. L'un étoit un Parnasse avec des cavernes, et l'on auroit vu sortir César et Pompée de ces souterrains; un autre étoit deux grands escaliers comme ceux de l'Orangerie de Versailles et les acteurs seroient venus de dessous ces escaliers. Meissonier à qui l'on en avoit aussi demandé avoit aussi eu cette idée folle d'escaliers. (Cochin, *Memoires inédits*, pp. 141–142)

82 For a discussion on Legeay's influence, see Erouart, *L'architecture au pinceau*, pp. 40–42, 184.

83 There is an important difference between the eighteenth-century notion of infinity and the nineteenth-century assumption of a culturally infinite space, a homogeneous, universal space assumed to be the context of everyday life—a space of technological control and social or economic exploitation, as well as the perspectival space of "difference" and political democracy.

84 Concerning Legeay's stay in Mecklenburg, see Erouart, *L'architecture au pinceau*, pp. 56–60.

85 For more details on the cultural context and the political situation in Berlin at the time of Legeay's arrival, see ibid., pp. 12, 52–53. On Legeay's architectural projects, including the New Sanssouci and the earlier Catholic church of St-Hedwige, see also Pierre du Colombier, *L'architecture française en Allemagne au XVIIIe siècle* (Paris: Presses universitaires de France, 1956), pp. 60–63, and Wunder, "The Spread of 'Piranesism,'" p. 557.

86 Charles-François Viel de Saint-Maux, *Lettres sur l'architecture* (Paris, 1787), Lettre 7, n. 29.

87 Kaufmann, "Three Revolutionary Architects," p. 452.

88 Lambert defines photometry as the discipline concerned with "l'éclat de la lumière, de sa densité, de sa force illuminante, de ses modifications dans les couleurs & dans l'ombre, de ses degrés, de ses accroissements & diminutions qu'elle souffre dans tous les cas" (*Les propriétés remarquables de la route de la lumière* [The Hague: N. van Daalen, 1759], p. 4).

89 "La luminosité décroit en proportion inverse du carré de la distance, proportionnellement au sinus de l'angle d'incidence, elle est d'autant plus forte que la surface tournée vers l'objet illuminé est grande et proportionnelle à l'intensité de la source lumineuse" (Johann Heinrich Lambert, *La Photometria sive de Mensura et Gradibus Lumina, colorum et umbrae* [Augsburg, 1760], §70; quoted by D. Speiser, "L'oeuvre de

Lambert dans le domaine de l'optique," in *Colloque international et inter-disciplinaire,* p. 320).

90 A. Kastler, "Allocution du Professeur Kastler," in *Colloque international et interdisciplinaire,* p. 22.

91 Lambert, *Terrestrial and Celestial Maps,* p. 98.

92 Johann Heinrich Lambert, *Beschreibung einer mit dem Calauschen Wachse ausgemalten Farbenpyramide* (Berlin: bey Haude und Spener, 1772).

93 "[U]n cinquième cas, celui, où un objet peint d'après vie, doit être comparé à l'original ou au plan géométral, & où l'on veut trouver l'endroit que le peintre a choisi, pour faire le dessin; comme p. ex., quand on veut comparer la vue d'une ville avec la ville même, ou avec le plan géométrique, qu'on a levé" (Lambert, *La Perspective affranchie,* p. 170).

94 Kirsti Andersen explains how Lambert freed his perspective method from the coordinates of the ground plan by developing "a series of constructions which enabled him to transfer information from the space (for instance the angle between two plans) into the picture plane" ("Some Observations Concerning Mathematicians' Treatment of Perspective Construction in the 17th and 18th Centuries," in *Mathemata Festschrift für Helmuth Gericke* [Stuttgart: Franz Steiner Verlag Weisbaden GMBH, 1985], pp. 420–421).

95 W. R. Tobler, introduction to Lambert's *Terrestrial and Celestial Maps,* p. vii; Kline, *Mathematical Thought,* p. 570.

96 Johann Heinrich Lambert, "Teorie der Parallellinien," written in 1766 and published posthumously by J. Bernouilli in *Magazin für die reine und angewandte Mathematik* (Leipzig, 1786), pp. 137–164. On this subject, see, for example, A. P. Youschkevitch, "Lambert et Léonard Euler," in *Colloque international et interdisciplinaire,* pp. 222–223, and Kastler, "Allocution," pp. 21–22.

97 Taton, *The Beginnings of Modern Science,* p. 418.

98 Hermann Weyl, *Raum, Zeit, Materie* (1918), quoted by Kastler, "Allocution," p. 22.

99 Lambert, *Terrestrial and Celestial Maps,* section 5, p. 3. For a concise description of the differences among Lambert's methods of mapmaking, see pp. 99–104.

100 Lloyd A. Brown, *The Story of Maps* (New York: Dover Publications, 1977), p. 69.

101 Claudius Ptolemy, *The Geography,* trans. and ed. E. L. Stevenson (1932; reprint, New York: Dover Publications, 1991), p. 43.

102 J. V. Field, "Giovanni Battista Benedetti on the Mathematics of Linear Perspective," *Journal of the Warburg and Courtauld Institutes* 49 (1985), pp. 75–78. Field defines these arbitrary points as having no specific

439

relation to the picture plane or the ground line, and he calls them "general points."

103 Lucia Nuti, "The Perspective Plan in the Sixteenth Century: The Invention of a Representational Language," *Art Bulletin* 76 (1994), p. 121 n. 53, includes a list of the major treatises on surveying in the sixteenth century, revealing their relationship with military concerns.

104 Cosimo Bartoli, *Del Modo di Misurare le distantie, le superficie, i corpi, le piante, le provincie, le prospettive, & tutte le altre cose terrene, che possono occorrere a gli huomini, Secondo le vere regole d'Euclide, de gli altri piu lodati scrittori* (Venice: Francesco Franceschi Sanese, 1564).

105 Lambert, *Terrestrial and Celestial Maps,* p. 6.

106 Lambert, *Schriften zur Perspektive,* p. 65.

107 Lambert, *La Perspective affranchie,* p. 148.

108 In "Elements for a History of Axonometry," *Architectural Design* 55 (May/June 1985), pp. 73–78, Massimo Scolari examines two instances in the past two thousand years when "parallel projection has alternated with central projection."

109 Margaret Daly Davis, *Piero della Francesca's Mathematical Treatises* (Ravenna: Longo Editore, 1977), pp. 41–43.

110 Luca Pacioli, *Divine proportion* (Paris: Librairie du Compagnonnage, 1980), part 2.

111 Luca Pacioli, *Divina proportione,* part 1, chap. 54, is entitled "Del corpo de 72 basis piano, solido, e vacuo." For more details on the explicit association between architecture and space-filling volumes in Pacioli's treatise, see Davis, *Piero della Francesca,* p. 58.

112 The inscription in the center reads "En ceste presente figure nous sont demonstrez les cinq Corps Reguliers de Geometrie, (lesquels sont deduits et declarez de poinct en poinct en la fin de ce present livre) ensemble certains personnages racourciz selõ cest Art, desquels Dieu aydant, espere au second livre vous les deduire plus amplement." Title page of Jean Cousin, *Livre de perspective* (Paris, 1560; reprint, Unterschneidheim: W. Uhl, 1974).

113 Wenzel Jamnitzer, *Perspectiva Corporum Regularum* (Nuremberg, 1568), introduction; trans. by Pierre Descargues in *Perspective: History, Evolution, Techniques,* trans. I.M. Paris (New York: Van Nostrand Reinhold, 1982), p. 58.

114 Martin Kemp emphasizes that Jamnitzer was well known for his inventions (*The Science of Art: Optical Themes in Western Art from Brunelleschi to Seurat,* 2d ed. [New Haven: Yale University Press, 1992], p. 64).

115 This text is available only in manuscript form: Venice: Biblioteca Marciana, MS. It. IV, 39 (=5446).

116 Davis, *Piero della Francesca,* p. 94.

117 Daniele Barbaro, *La Pratica della Perspettiva* (1569; reprint, Bologna: Arnaldo Forni, 1980), p. 37.

118 Ibid., p. 7.

119 Du Cerceau's volume is titled *Livre d'architecture de Iaques Androuet, du Cerceau. Auquel sont contenues diverses ordonnances de plants et élévations de bastiments pour Seigneurs, Gentilshommes, & autre qui voudront bastir aux champs: mesmes en aucuns d'iceux sont desseignez les bassez courts, avec leurs commoditez particulieres: aussi les iardinages & vergiers* (Paris, 1582).

120 For a brief survey of such treatises, see Scolari, "Elements for a History of Axonometry," pp. 74–77. For a more complete bibliography, see Martha D. Pollak, *Military Architecture, Cartography and Representation of the Early Modern European City* (Chicago: Newberry Library, 1991).

121 For a general introduction to Stevin's life and accomplishments, see *The Principal Works of Simon Stevin* (Amsterdam: C. V. Swets & Zeitlinger, 1955), 1:3–14.

122 Stevin's perspective theory has been compared to Guidobaldo del Monte's *Perspectivae libri sex* (1600) for its mathematical clarity. Stevin apparently was acquainted with Marolois, who published Jans Vredeman de Vries's works on architecture and perspective, and who also wrote his own treatise on perspective and fortification. Unlike the work of his compatriots, his work was highly mathematical and remained less accessible to painters and architects.

123 For a general introduction to Stevin's writings on perspective and an English translation of the texts, see *The Principal Works,* 2B: 783ff. The books were published in French as *Traité d'Optique* in *Oeuvre Mathématique* (Leiden, 1634). The French version includes a third book on refraction. Quotation: *The Principal Works,* 1:17.

124 Stevin, *The Principal Works,* 3:365.

125 Like his perspective work, Stevin's treatise on fortifications was regarded as a textbook. The first chapter is devoted to definitions of fortification terms (*The Principal Works,* 4:65).

126 Ibid.

127 Dirk J. Struik, *The Land of Stevin and Huygens: A Sketch of Science and Technology in the Dutch Republic during the Golden Century* (London: D. Reidel, 1981), p. 57.

128 Stevin, *The Principal Works,* 4:127–129.

129 Ibid., 5:429.

130 See Alberto Pérez-Gómez, *Architecture and the Crisis of Modern Science* (Cambridge, Mass.: MIT Press, 1983), pp. 203ff.

131 Lambert, *La Perspective affranchie,* pp. 156–166.

132 Ibid., p. 155.

133 A work by an Englishman, Brook Taylor, *New Principles of Linear Perspective* (London, 1719), also postulates the homology of architectural drawings and perspective for the presentation of architectural projects, in a way similar to Pozzo's postulating the homology between planar representation and spatial reality. While Taylor's treatise was less accessible to artists, a number of eighteenth-century English writers took it upon themselves to popularize his theories. Even though, as a mathematician, Taylor was also interested in the conic sections, in his understanding of limits he seems closer to his Continental contemporaries than to Desargues or Poncelet.

134 Our translation, from Jean-Henri Lambert, *Notes et additions à la perspective affranchie de l'embaras du plan géométral*, trans. J. Peiffer, notes by R. Laurent (Paris: Cedic, 1987), p. 262.

135 See, for example, Lambert, *Schriften zur Perspektive*, p. 70; Kemp, *The Science of Art*, p. 222; Laurent, *La place de J.-H. Lambert*, pp. 182–190.

136 Lambert, *Notes et additions*, p. 263.

137 H. W. Arndt, "J.-H. Lambert et l'esthétique du XVIIIe siècle," in *Colloque international et interdisciplinaire*, p. 206.

Variation Three

The Image without an Observer in a Scopophilic World

1 Some historians of perspective point to a passage in Al-Hazen as the earliest known description of the phenomenon. See Albert Flocon and René Taton, *La Prospettiva: Collana di architettura diretta da Massimo Scolari* (Milan: Angeli, 1985), p. 64.

2 Daniele Barbaro, *La Pratica della Perspettiva* (1569; reprint, Bologna: Arnaldo Forni, 1980), pp. 192–193.

3 See Svetlana Alpers, *The Art of Describing: Dutch Art in the Seventeenth Century* (Chicago: University of Chicago Press, 1983).

4 Wotton reported this fact in a letter to Francis Bacon (ibid., pp. 50ff.).

5 Egnatio Danti, for example, clearly aware of all treatises on perspective since the fifteenth century, and one of the sixteenth-century authors capable of translating mathematical speculations into practical principles, was always very critical of perspectival devices. See Jacopo Barozzi da Vignola and Ignazio Danti, *Le due regole della prospettiva pratica* (Rome: Per Francesco Zannetti, 1583).

6 Alpers, *The Art of Describing*, especially chaps. 1 and 2. For a more balanced view of the problem, see Arthur K. Wheelock Jr., *Perspective, Optics, and Delft Artists around 1650* (New York: Garland, 1977). Wheelock believes that Dutch artists were influenced by Kepler and the camera obscura but also used many diverse perspective systems.

More recently, this interest in both "natural" vision and geometric systems has been corroborated in a study on Saenredam by Rob Ruurs. Saenredam always made two preparatory sketches of his famous internal views of buildings, one empirical and the other constructed from measurements. His constructions combine Alberti's and Viator's methods. See Rob Ruurs, *Saenredam: The Art of Perspective* (Philadelphia: Benjamins/Forsten Publishers, 1987).

7   Alpers (*The Art of Describing*) polarizes the distinctions between Northern and Italian "perspective," claiming a special status for Viator's "workshop method."

8   We have demonstrated in Variation Two how in Italy and France there was a strong theoretical tradition of trying to understand perspective depth as it applied to surveying, cosmography, fortifications, and architecture. The clearest definition was given by Barbaro as he tried to differentiate *perspettiva* from *prospettiva*. The history of the problem, as a mathematical question, also starts in Italy with the work of Federigo Commandino and is continued by Benedetti, Guidobaldo del Monte, and eventually Simon Stevin in the Netherlands.

9   The works of the Jesuit Athanasius Kircher, the educator Jan Amos Comenius, the linguist John Wilkins, and the philosopher Gottfried Wilhelm Leibniz are instances of this, as is the theory of Juan Caramuel de Lobkowitz.

10 There were two kinds of camera lucida: "see through" and "split pupil." The first used glass and mirror to create the reflection, while the second employed a four-sided prism. See John H. Hammond and Jill Austin, *The Camera Lucida in Art and Science* (Bristol: Adam Hilger, 1987).

11 Cornelius Varley was credited with the invention of the "graphic telescope" in 1811. He also invented the "graphic microscope" (ibid., p. 65).

12 Ibid.

13 Ibid., pp. 84–85.

14 Robert Barker patented the idea of a succession of perspective frames with softened junctions in 1787. On the implications of the panorama for architecture and artistic representation, see Stephen Parcell, "The Momentary Modern Magic of the Panorama," in *Chora: Intervals in the Philosophy of Architecture,* ed. Alberto Pérez-Gómez and Stephen Parcell (Montreal: McGill-Queen's University Press, 1994), 1:167–188.

15 In this particular context we use the term "representation" in a Foucauldian sense.

16 Our democratic, pluralistic societies are constituted by individuals endowed with a subjective consciousness that demands respect for their differences. This is a popular, genuine point of departure for postmodern discourses. Epistemological perspectivism, however, often leads to

a despairing relativism, countered by the fanaticism of new cults based on cosmological or pseudo-scientific formulations. The residual hegemonic values inherited from the fallacious grand narratives of historical progress are still at the root of distorting discourses based on ethnicity, gender, or nationality and, at worst, remain the reason for much war, violence, and self-destruction around the world.

17   See Johann Martin Chladenius, *Einleitung zur richtigen Auslegung vernüftiger Reden und Schriften* (Leipzig, 1742), chap. 8.

18   See Shaun Gallagher, "The Hermeneutics of Ambiguity," in *Merleau-Ponty, Hermeneutics, and Postmodernism,* ed. Thomas Busch and Shaun Gallagher (Binghampton: State University of New York Press, 1992), p. 4.

19   Ibid., p. 6.

20   Searching for similar parallels, recent critical theories have explored the potential relationship between pure science (like chaos theory) and contemporary modes of architectural ideation. Similarly, the most provocative discourses on computer applications for architecture and on the consequences of cyberspace often insist that poetry must be restored to science if the new technologies are to be possible. See Marcos Novak, "Liquid Architectures in Cyberspace," in *Cyberspace: First Steps,* ed. Michael Benedikt (Cambridge, Mass.: MIT Press, 1991), pp. 225–254.

21   The discourse on character and custom as the basis for architectural meaning (originating in culture rather than in nature) can be traced back to Claude Perrault's theory at the end of the seventeenth century. It was recast in different forms throughout the eighteenth century by writers such as Germain Boffrand, Jacques-François Blondel, Etienne-Louis Boullée, and Claude-Nicolas Ledoux.

22   Edmund Husserl, *Phenomenology and the Crisis of Philosophy,* trans. Quentin Lauer (New York: Harper and Row, 1965).

23   Richard P. Feynman, *QED* (Princeton: Princeton University Press, 1985).

24   See James Gleick, *Chaos: Making a New Science* (New York: Penguin, 1987), p. 304.

25   It is nevertheless understandable that this potential reconciliation of form and content should be of great interest to contemporary architects. The generation of new form could then be immediately justified as an ethical practice. If it could be demonstrated that as we make forms we also make "content," that all must remain on the surface because depth is an illusion, then the architect could indulge indiscriminately in all manner of formal games because, supposedly, there is no alternative. Architecture would therefore be circumscribed to a quest for original form engaging all instrumental means at its disposal, like the computer and its axonometric matrix, producing formal cre-

ations intelligible for the initiates, supposedly thundering with mystical reverberations.

It is perhaps symptomatic that Mandelbrot himself expressed some opinions about architecture. He criticized the Bauhaus and especially the Seagram Building, qualifying their architecture as "inhuman" because of their simple geometry, while complex fractal geometries were supposed to "resonate with the way nature organizes itself." Curiously, Mandelbrot argued that the plurality of scales in a Beaux-Arts building therefore was much more appealing (ibid., pp. 116–117). This conservative "postmodern" view is obviously at odds with the recent fascination with fractals in architecture, often cited as a justification for a complex aesthetic of fragmented or "deconstructed" forms. Even though we may appreciate the unexpected formal consequences of these relations, now manipulable through computer-assisted design programs, it is important to recognize that the relationship between geometry and architecture imagined by Mandelbrot and his followers is thoroughly "classical," simply mimetic in the traditional sense.

26 We have drawn some of these remarks from observations by Hans Blumenberg, who is merely criticizing the forgetfulness of contemporary science. See *The Genesis of the Copernican World* (Cambridge, Mass.: MIT Press, 1987), p. xxxv.

27 In addition to realizing Earth's possible uniqueness in the universe, ecologists today have a renewed awareness of the limitations of the Earth's natural resources, while a handful of economists warn of the inevitable limit of growth and material progress in a finite world. These opinions, however, remain at odds with the still dominant discourse about constant economic growth and the desires of "developing" nations. In the popular imagination, the immensity of an expanding universe (that makes its own space as it grows!) and the necessary supposition of an infinite number of planets bear closely on the assumption that technological exploitation and scientific progress still offer endless possibilities for our future. It is clear that this obsession, perhaps driven by a secularized desire for liberation from given human constraints such as mortality, may end with our decimating the planet before we have time to modify our attitudes.

28 See, for example, Bruno Reichlin's introduction to *Alberto Sartoris,* exhibition catalog (Lausanne: École polytechnique fédérale de Lausanne, 1978).

29 Gaspard Monge's *Géométrie descriptive* (1795) was a crucial textbook for the students of Durand at the École Polytechnique.

30 Jacques-Nicolas-Louis Durand, *Précis des leçons d'architecture* (Paris, 1819), 1:34.

31 Johann Maria von Quaglio, *Praktische Anleitung zur Perspektiv* (Munich, 1811), trans. and cited by Werner Oechslin, "Architecture, Perspec-

tive, and the Helpful Gesture of Geometry," _Daidalos_ 11 (1984), pp. 50–51.

32   Arthur Parsey, _Perspective Rectified_ (London, 1836), and _The Science of Vision_ (London, 1840), p. x.

33   William Herdmann, _A Treatise on the Curvilinear Perspective of Nature_ (London, 1853).

34   See Martin Kemp, _The Science of Art: Optical Themes in Western Art from Brunelleschi to Seurat,_ 2d ed. (New Haven: Yale University Press, 1992), p. 242.

35   From Ferdinand Dupuis, _Exposé succint du polyskematisme ou méthode concernant le dessin linéaire géométrique_ (1841), quoted in ibid., p. 240.

36   This is very clear in the records of the evaluations of competitions at the École des Beaux-Arts, particularly for the Prix de Rome. See _The Architecture of the École des Beaux-Arts,_ ed. Arthur Drexler (New York: Museum of Modern Art, 1977), most especially Richard Chafee, "The Teaching of Architecture at the École des Beaux-Arts," pp. 61–109.

37   For a more extensive discussion on descriptive geometry and its uses in architecture, see "The Functionalization of Euclidean Geometry," in Alberto Pérez-Gómez, _Architecture and the Crisis of Modern Science_ (Cambridge, Mass.: MIT Press, 1983), pp. 279ff.

38   Ibid., pp. 276–277.

39   See, for example, Michel Chasles, _Aperçu historique sur l'origine et développement des méthodes en géométrie_ (Paris, 1837).

40   Ibid., pp. 208–210.

41   Jean-Victor Poncelet, _Traité des propriétés projectives des figures_ (Paris, 1822), title page.

42   Ibid., p. xxviii.

43   This abstraction of the image-making process anticipated twentieth-century images produced by electronic scanning devices, X rays, and eventually, twisting the paradigm, "virtual" animation, computer-generated "photography," and the like.

44   See in this regard Stephen Parcell's two articles on the panorama ("The Magic of the Panorama") and the diorama ("The Metaphoric Architecture of the Diorama"), in _Chora: Intervals in the Philosophy of Architecture,_ 1:167–216 and vol. 2 (Montreal: McGill-Queen's University Press, 1996), pp. 179–216.

45   The impressionists attempted to paint the color of light, rather than the color of things. Prior to the nineteenth century this split had remained practically incomprehensible. The consideration of the physiology of the eye had also been absent from color theory. Only during the nineteenth century was it truly possible to conceive the separation of thinking from seeing, to imagine the "physical" distinction between

the color of light and the color of pigments. By pursuing, in the scientific spirit of Helmholtz, the possibility of objective representation for a subjective observer, based on the knowledge of how the eye sees and on the scientific nature of color, Georges Seurat in his late works radically reversed empirical naturalism to become "constructions," intentionally akin to musical structure. Thus those following the tradition of "realistic" painting became aware of the need to resist reductive or referential attitudes regarding a prosaic, perspectival depth, and joined, through Cézanne, the new artistic paradigms of the twentieth-century avant-garde.

46 Elsewhere we have described the role played by Jean Rondelet, the author of the first modern book on building technology, in the project for the establishment of a decimal system of standard measurements in France. Rondelet, *Traité théorique et pratique de l'art de bâtir* (Paris, 1802); see Pérez-Gómez, *Architecture and the Crisis of Modern Science,* pp. 285ff.

47 William Farrish, *Isometrical Perspective* (Cambridge, 1820), introduction.

48 Joseph Jopling, *The Practice of Isometrical Perspective* (London: M. Taylor, 1835), p. 13.

49 Ibid., p. 1.

50 Ibid., pp. v, 9–11.

51 This has been postulated by some recent commentators. See Stephen Houlgate, "Vision, Reflection, and Openness," in David Michael Levin, ed., *Modernity and the Hegemony of Vision* (Berkeley: University of California Press, 1993), pp. 87–123; quotation, p. 114.

52 G. W. F. Hegel, *Philosophy of Nature,* trans. M. J. Petrey (London: Allen and Unwin, 1970), pp. 255–256.

53 See Auguste Choisy, *L'art de bâtir chez les romains* (Paris: Ducher, 1873), *L'art de bâtir chez les byzantines* (Paris: Société anonyme de publications périodiques, 1883), and *Histoire de l'architecture* (Paris: Gauthier-Villars, 1899).

54 Auguste Choisy, *Histoire de l'architecture* (Paris: Librarie Georges Baranger, 1929), "Avant propos."

55 Auguste Choisy, *Vitruve* (Paris: Imprimerie-Librairie Lahure, 1909). The work includes four "volumes" bound together: an analysis (book 1), the translation proper (books 2 and 3), and a graphic summary (book 4); quotations are from pp. vi, ix.

56 Ibid., book 1, p. 1. In his "analysis," Choisy systematizes the positive information provided by Vitruvius, including "scientific" explanations of the materials, construction techniques, building types, etc. mentioned in the Roman text.

57 Choisy, *Histoire de l'architecture,* quoted by Rayner Banham, *Theory and Design in the First Machine Age* (New York: Praeger, 1960), pp. 23–24.

58 Jules de la Gournerie, *Traité de géométrie descriptive* (Paris, 1860–1864). This issue is discussed by Yve-Alain Bois, "Metamorphosis of Axonometry," *Daidalos* 1 (1981), pp. 40–58.

59 Banham, *Theory and Design*, p. 25.

60 This is a point made by Bruno Reichlin in "Reflections—Interrelations between Concept, Representation, and Built Architecture," *Daidalos* 1 (1981), pp. 60–73, and in his introduction to *Alberto Sartoris*.

61 Reichlin, "Reflections," p. 72.

62 See Bois, "Metamorphosis of Axonometry," p. 42.

63 Ibid.

64 Quoted by Reichlin, introduction to *Alberto Sartoris*, p. 12.

65 Ibid., p. 12.

66 El Lissitzky, "K. und Pangeometrie," in *Europa-Almanach*, ed. Carl Einstein and Paul Westheim (Postdam: Gustav Kiepenheurer Verlag, 1925), pp. 103–113.

67 Ibid., pp. 108–13.

68 Ibid., pp. 110–111.

69 Ibid., p. 112.

70 We are grateful to Detlef Mertins for this suggestion, made in "Seeing the Closed Open: Walter Benjamin and the Architecture of the New Optics," paper given at Open and Closed Representation, a symposium at the Department of Architecture, University of Pennsylvania, March 24–26, 1995.

71 Le Corbusier, *Oeuvre complète, 1910–1965* (Zurich: Les Editions d'Architecture, 1946–1970), 4:152.

72 Ibid.

73 In her famous essay "Notes on the Index: Seventies Art in America," Rosalind Krauss writes: "As distinct from symbols, indexes establish their meanings along the axis of a physical relationship to their referents. They are the marks or traces of a particular cause" (in *October: The First Decade*, ed. A. Michelson et al. [Cambridge, Mass., MIT Press, 1987], p. 4).

74 Our gratitude to Joanna Merwood, a former student in the History and Theory of Architecture program at McGill University, for pointing out this work to us and for an engaging reflection about its consequences for architectural representation. See "Concrete Blonde: A Probe into Negative Space Where Mysteries Are Created," in *Chora: Intervals in the Philosophy of Architecture*, 2:135–148.

75 Marsilio Ficino, *Commentary on Plato's Symposium on Love* (Dallas: Spring Publications, 1985), translation of *De Amore*, speech 7, chap. 4, p. 159.

76 See I. P. Couliano, *Eros and Magic in the Renaissance* (Chicago: University of Chicago Press, 1987), pp. 87ff.

77 See the excellent essay by Gary Schapiro, "In the Shadows of Philosophy: Nietzsche and the Question of Vision," in Levin, *Modernity and the Hegemony of Vision,* pp. 124–142.

78 Friedrich Nietzsche, "What the Germans Lack," in *The Twilight of the Idols,* quoted by Schapiro, "In the Shadows of Philosophy," pp. 126–127.

79 Friedrich Nietzsche, "Assorted Opinions and Maxims," in *Human, All Too Human,* quoted by Schapiro, "In the Shadows of Philosophy," p. 131.

80 See Susan Buck-Morss, *The Dialectics of Seeing* (Cambridge: MIT Press, 1989), and "Dream World of Mass Culture," in Levin, *Modernity and the Hegemony of Vision,* pp. 309–338.

81 Buck-Morss, "Dream World of Mass Culture," p. 322.

82 Jean Baudrillard, *Seduction* (Montreal: New World Perspectives, 1990).

83 Georges Didi-Huberman, *Ce que nous voyons, Ce qui nous regarde* (Paris: Éditions de Minuit, 1992), pp. 75–76. Didi-Huberman writes: "l'image se rend capable de nous regarder." He constantly plays with the French usage of the verb *regarder,* meaning "to observe," but also "to concern [us]."

84 Ibid., p. 103. Didi-Huberman quotes Benjamin: "ein sonderbares Gespinst von Raum und Zeit."

85 We owe this formulation to Mary B. Wiseman reviewing Alberto Pérez-Gómez, *Polyphilo or The Dark Forest Revisited,* in *Journal of Aesthetics and Art Criticism* 52 (1994), pp. 263–264.

86 See Martin Jay, "Sartre, Merleau-Ponty, and the Search for a New Ontology of Sight," in Levin, *Modernity and the Hegemony of Vision,* pp. 143–185; quotation, p. 163. Jay is quoting from Merleau-Ponty's early work, *The Structure of Behavior,* trans. Alden L. Fisher, (Boston: Beacon Press, 1963), p. 186.

87 Ibid., p. 164.

88 Maurice Merleau-Ponty, *Phenomenology of Perception,* trans. Colin Smith (London: Routledge and Kegan Paul, 1962), p. 235; "Cézanne's Doubt," in *Sense and Non-Sense,* trans. Hubert L. Dreyfus and Patricia Allen Dreyfus (Evanston, Ill.: Northwestern University Press, 1964), p. 14.

89 As we have already shown, most art historians and critics interested in this problem tend to polarize the discussion in either of these directions. Kemp and Edgerton would generally argue that the representational techniques invented in the Renaissance are "correct" and universal, while disciples of Foucault, such as Jonathan Crary, tend to emphasize the radical historicity of all forms of representation.

449

90 Maurice Merleau-Ponty, "Eye and Mind," quoted by Edward S. Casey, "The Element of Voluminousness: Depth and Place Re-Examined," in *Merleau-Ponty Vivant*, ed. M. C. Dillon (Albany: State University of New York Press, 1991), p. 20. Casey is citing from a new, unpublished translation by Richard McCleary. (See Merleau-Ponty, *The Primacy of Perception*, ed. Richard C. McCleary [Evanston, Ill.: Northwestern University Press, 1964], pp. 159–190.)

91 Ibid., pp. 20–21.

92 Merleau-Ponty, *Phenomenology of Perception*, pp. 264–265.

93 Jay, "A New Ontology of Sight," p. 171.

94 Merleau-Ponty, "Eye and Mind," in *The Primacy of Perception*, p. 162; quoted by Jacques Taminiaux, "The Thinker and the Painter," in Dillon, *Merleau-Ponty Vivant*, p. 199.

95 Ibid., pp. 172, 173.

96 Maurice Merleau-Ponty, *The Visible and the Invisible*, ed. Claude Lefort, trans. Alphonso Lingis (Evanston, Ill.: Northwestern University Press, 1968), p. 267. See also Glen A. Mazis, "Merleau-Ponty and the Backward Flow of Time," in Busch and Gallagher, *Merleau-Ponty, Hermeneutics, and Postmodernism*, pp. 53–68.

97 Merleau-Ponty, *The Visible and the Invisible*, pp. 194, 184.

98 Ibid., pp. 147, 148.

99 Jay, "A New Ontology of Sight," p. 176.

100 See Alberto Pérez-Gómez, "Chora: The Space of Architectural Representation," in *Chora*, 1:1–34. This connection has also been noted by Casey, "The Element of Voluminousness," pp. 1ff.

101 Merleau-Ponty, "Eye and Mind," quoted by Casey, "The Element of Voluminousness," p. 1.

102 Merleau-Ponty, "Eye and Mind," p. 181.

103 By necessity we have been very selective. We have decided to ignore much fashionable criticism that is not directly pertinent, although our conclusions will be read as an implicit reaction to much of this writing. We would also like to express our gratitude to the students in the History and Theory Program at McGill University who over the years have examined Le Corbusier's work and challenged many of our assumptions. Deserving special mention are Torben Berns, Yvan Cazabon, Michael Splawn, and Claudio Venier.

104 See, for example, Gerard Monnier, "Perspective axonométrique et rapport au réel," *Techniques et architecture*, no. 358 (1985), pp. 120–123; Banham, *Theory and Design*, chap. 2; and the introduction to the work of Michael Graves by William La Riche in *Five Architects* (New York: Oxford University Press, 1975), pp. 39–41.

105 Monnier, "Perspective axonométrique," p. 121.

106 The popular success of Richard Meier's practice speaks for itself. The most significant theoretical developments, however, are in the work of Peter Eisenman and John Hejduk. Eisenman has explored the limits of self-referential syntax, deliberately cultivating the instrumentality of the tools of representation. Hejduk has grasped the significance of the reversibility of axonometric space in his work of the last twenty years, which was strikingly transformed through the use of narrative and a different understanding of temporality.

Although this is not the place to enter into a debate, we should recall the important role played by Colin Rowe's creative misreading of Le Corbusier's "formalism," which provided much of the theoretical framework for this discussion. See Rowe, *The Mathematics of the Ideal Villa and Other Essays* (Cambridge, Mass.: MIT Press, 1976); see also La Riche, *Five Architects.*

107 The magazine *L'Esprit Nouveau* was launched in 1920 and ceased publication in 1925. Le Corbusier was coeditor, with Amédée Ozenfant and Paul Dermée.

108 He described his work in these terms in a catalogue for an exhibition of his paintings at the Galerie Balay et Carré, Paris, 1938.

109 See Christopher Green, "The Architect as Artist," in *Le Corbusier, Architect of the Century,* ed. Susan Ferleger Raeburn with Muriel Walker (London: Arts Council of Great Britain, 1987), p. 113.

110 Ibid.

111 *Le Corbusier Sketchbooks,* 4 vols. (Cambridge, Mass.: MIT Press, 1981).

112 Quoted by Anthony Eardley, "Grandeur Is the Intention," in *Le Corbusier's Firminy Church,* ed. Kenneth Frampton and Sylvia Kolbowski, cat. no. 14, Institute for Architecture and Urban Studies (New York: Rizzoli, 1981), p. 13.

113 Le Corbusier, *Oeuvre complète,* 5:25.

114 Le Corbusier *Archives,* 15 vols. (New York: Garland Press, 1982–1985).

115 Le Corbusier, quoted by Green, "The Architect as Artist," p. 117.

116 Le Corbusier, *New World of Space* (New York: Reynal and Hitchcock, 1948).

117 Ibid.; cited in *Le Corbusier, Architect of the Century,* p. 246.

118 Le Corbusier, *Poème de l'angle droit* (Paris: Éditions Verve, 1955), hereafter cited parenthetically in the text.

119 Le Corbusier, *Oeuvre complète,* 4:170.

120 Le Corbusier, *The Modulor 1 and 2,* trans. Peter de Francia and Anna Bostock (Cambridge: Harvard University Press, 1980), 1:74. This work was first published in French in 1950.

121 This "guilt" is often present in the otherwise interesting diagnoses of the contemporary world by Christian writers such as Jacques Ellul, *The Technological Society,* trans. John Wilkinson (New York: Alfred A. Knopf, 1964).

122 Le Corbusier, *The Modulor,* 1:74.

123 Ibid., p. 160.

124 Ibid., p. 20.

125 Ibid., p. 18.

126 Richard Moore, "Alchemical and Mythical Themes in the 'Poème de l'Angle Droit,'" *Oppositions* 19 (1980), pp. 110–139.

127 We take issue with this crucial point made in the otherwise fascinating interpretation of the *Poème* by Peter Carl in "Le Corbusier's Penthouse in Paris, 24 Rue Nungesser-et-Coli," *Daidalos* 28 (1988), pp. 65–75.

128 Le Corbusier, *The Modulor,* 1:74, 15–16. His continuing fascination with music and sound are well known. We may recall in this connection his *Poème Electronique,* a multimedia light show for the Philips Pavilion in Expo 58 (Brussels). This was a collaborative work with Edgar Varèse and Iannis Xenakis meant to reveal the poetic by including all the noises of the universe "great and small."

129 Our reporting of the clients' commentary is based on notes taken by Alberto Pérez-Gómez during a three-day stay at the monastery in 1985. The occasion was an intimate symposium on architecture organized by Juhani Pallasmaa and attended by distinguished architects such as Henning Larsen, Christian Gullichsen, and Daniel Libeskind, among others—all witnesses to these remarkable revelations.

130 *L'Art sacrée* (1954); quoted in *Le Corbusier, Architect of the Century,* p. 252.

131 Interview conducted by A. Pérez-Gómez; see n. 129 above.

132 To turn to a literary analogy, La Tourette is particularly reminiscent of Alain Robbe-Grillet's *In the Labyrinth,* trans. Richard Howard (New York: Grove Press, 1960), which contrasts sharply with the linear narratives of nineteenth-century novelists.

133 While for Jacques Derrida and his followers the very notion of experience is still part of the metaphysics of presence, Le Corbusier's La Tourette clearly demonstrates the plausibility of a wholly other premise. The notion of experience traditionally has been interpreted idealistically, even by Derrida. Merleau-Ponty's goal in *The Visible and the Invisible* was precisely to de-idealize the notion of experience. The "denial" of experience is impossible, philosophical nonsense. Experience presupposes nothing more than an encounter between "us" and "what is." As if in response to Derrida, Merleau-Ponty writes: "Is it not the resolution to ask of experience itself its secret already an idealist commitment?" See G. B. Madison, "Did Merleau-Ponty Have a The-

ory of Perception?" in Busch and Gallagher, *Merleau-Ponty, Hermeneutics, and Postmodernism,* pp. 83–106.

134 We owe this formulation to Joanne Paul, who has been studying the origin of analogical thinking in modern architecture in the work of Carlo Lodoli.

135 We refer here to the fragment entitled "The Coat of Whitewash" in Le Corbusier, *The Decorative Art of Today,* trans. James I. Dunnett (Cambridge, Mass.: MIT Press, 1987), pp. 188ff. The text was originally published in French in 1925.

136 Ibid., p. 188.

137 Le Corbusier, *Precisions on the Present State of Architecture and City Planning,* trans. Edith Schreiber Aujame (Cambridge, Mass.: MIT Press, 1991), pp. 132–133 (the text was originally published in French in 1930); and *Towards a New Architecture* (London: Architectural Press, 1946), p. 37.

138 Le Corbusier, *New World of Space,* p. 7. He calls this "moment of limitless escape" the fourth dimension. His understanding has some resonance with Marcel Duchamp's in the *White Box.*

139 Ibid., pp. 7–8.

140 Interview by A. Pérez-Gómez, see n. 129 above.

141 Arata Isozaki, *Le Corbusier, Couvent Sainte Marie de La Tourette, Eveux-sur-l'Abresle, France,* ed. Yukio Futagawa, *Global Architecture* 11 (Tokyo: A.D.A. Edita, 1971). We are grateful to Robert Kelly for pointing out this work to us.

142 Bruno Reichlin, "'Une Petite Maison' on Lake Leman: The Perret-Corbusier Controversy," *Lotus* 60 (1988), pp. 59–84.

Coda

Projection Revisited: The Reversibility of Optics

1 The *Green Box* (limited ed., 1934), a diary of thoughts and diagrams for the fabrication of *The Large Glass,* shows Duchamp's interest in scientific developments in the field of non-Euclidean geometry. See M. Duchamp, *The Bride Stripped Bare by Her Bachelors, Even,* a typographic version by Richard Hamilton of Marcel Duchamp's Green Box (London: Lind, Humphries, 1960).

2 Wilfred Dörstel, "Perspectiva Rhetorica," *Daidalos* 11 (1984), pp. 67–68.

3 Maurice Merleau-Ponty praised film as the most important artistic development of the twentieth century. See *Signs,* trans. Richard C. McCleary (Evanston, Ill.: Northwestern University Press, 1968).

4   David Michael Levin, *The Opening of Vision* (New York: Routledge, 1988), pp. 350–351.

5   Sergei Eisenstein described his "Intellectual Cinema" as a structure of composition that defines the abstract and makes it appear. His method was based on analogy, a metaphor between the figurative image and human experience. See Eisenstein, *Film Sense* (New York: Harcourt Brace Jovanovich, 1942), p. 4.

6   In this connection see Maurice Merleau-Ponty, *Phenomenology of Perception,* trans. Colin Smith (London: Routledge and Kegan Paul, 1962), in which he establishes what embodied perception "could" be by disclosing its original reality. Merleau-Ponty's thesis, together with the posthumous notes published under the title *The Visible and the Invisible,* ed. Claude Lefort, trans. Alphonso Lingis (Evanston, Ill.: Northwestern University Press, 1968), are the cornerstones of our interpretation.

7   Heinrich Schnoedt, "Cultural Parametrics," a paper presented at the conference Terms of Engagement, Pratt Institute School of Architecture, Brooklyn, New York, April 24, 1995. Schnoedt alluded specifically to complex cut-stone details in Gehry's buildings and to the aluminum fireproofing of the main structural truss in Foster's Bank of Honk Kong, whose construction costs, nevertheless, were vastly over budget. Foster has often pointed out how the design of this building had to change in order to comply with geomantic concerns.

8   See Marcos Novak, "Liquid Architectures," a paper presented at the conference Terms of Engagement.

9   Ibid.

10   See Robert Reynolds and Thomas Zummer, eds., *Crash: Nostalgia for the Absence of Cyberspace* (New York: Thread Waxing Space, 1994). Alberto Pérez-Gómez, *Polyphilo, or the Dark Forest Revisited* (Cambridge, Mass.: MIT Press, 1992) examines issues associated with this question.

11   Reynolds and Zummer, *Crash,* p. 228.

12   This was poignantly demonstrated for the first time by Giambattista Vico in his eighteenth-century *The New Science.* See the introduction by T. G. Bergin and M. H. Fisch to the modern edition of *The New Science* (Ithaca: Cornell University Press, 1970). Vico's understanding of *poiēsis* as making and its relationship to myth is particularly relevant to this discussion.

13   We are paraphrasing Octavio Paz, *The Bow and the Lyre: The Poem, the Poetic Revelation, Poetry, and History,* trans. Ruth L. C. Simms (Austin: University of Texas Press, 1991), p. 139.

14   Marcos Novak, "Liquid Architectures in Cyberspace," in *Cyberspace: First Steps,* ed. Michael Benedikt (Cambridge, Mass.: MIT Press, 1991), pp. 225–254.

15 See Michael Taussig, *Mimesis and Alterity* (New York: Routledge, 1993), pp. xiii–xix.

16 See, for example, David Michael Levin, *The Body's Recollection of Being* (London: Routledge and Kegan Paul, 1985).

17 See Gianni Vattimo, *The Transparent Society,* trans. David Webb (Baltimore: John Hopkins University Press, 1992).

18 Schnoedt, "Cultural Parametrics."

19 Ibid.

20 This is what allows for the distance between historical artifacts and the interpreter to be not a hindrance but the very *condition* of interpretation and understanding. See, for example, the works of Paul Ricoeur and Hans-Georg Gadamer. For a good summary of hermeneutic philosophy see Joseph Bleicher, *Contemporary Hermeneutics* (London: Routledge and Kegan Paul, 1980).

21 Maurice Merleau-Ponty, "Eye and Mind," in *The Primacy of Perception,* ed. Richard C. McCleary (Evanston, Ill.: Northwestern University Press, 1964), 181.

22 Hans-Georg Gadamer has given one of the clearest elucidations of the question of representation in art in *The Relevance of the Beautiful and Other Essays,* trans. Nicholas Walker (Cambridge: Cambridge University Press, 1986). This notion is connected to the original Greek understanding of symbol as a token (*tessera*) that would enable an old friend to be recognized by members of the household (or any institution) as a member of the same group, a part of the whole, belonging to a cosmic place. In this connection, the word *agora* meant both a place and an assembly of citizens participating in the decision-making process concerning the future of their *polis.*

23 Ibid., pp. 31–39.

24 This is a tradition that develops from Vico's "New Science" to the hermeneutics of Hans-Georg Gadamer, Paul Ricoeur, and Gianni Vattimo.

25 This task was already beautifully stated by Nietzsche. In his seminal essay, "On the Uses and the Disadvantages of History for Life," he articulated both the dangers and the possibilities opened up by history for a new man, particularly for the creative and responsible individual in the postcosmological era. There are, of course, useless and problematic forms of history, particularly pseudo-objective progressive narratives, but this should not result in an unwillingness to pay attention to what we are—which is, indeed, what we have been. See Friedrich Nietzsche, *Untimely Meditations,* trans. E. J. Hollingdale (Cambridge: Cambridge University Press, 1983), pp. 57–123.

Selected Bibliography

This bibliography, which lists works consulted for the purpose of this book, is selective, not comprehensive.

Abellán, José Luis.
Historia crítica del pensamiento español. Madrid: Espasa-Calpe, 1981.

Accolti, Pietro.
Lo Inganno de gl'occhi, Prospettiva Pratica di Pietro Accolti gentilhvomo Fiorentino e della Toscana. Accademia del Disegno Trattato In Acconcio Della Pittura. Florence: Appresso Pietro Cecconcelli, 1625.

Ackerman, James S.
The Architecture of Michelangelo. London: A. Zwemmer's, 1970.

Agrippa, Heinrich Cornelius.
Three Books of Occult Philosophy. London, 1651. 1st Latin ed. is 1533.

Alberti, Leon Battista.
On Painting. Trans. J. Spencer. New Haven: Yale University Press, 1966.

Alberti, Leon Battista.
On Painting and Sculpture. Ed. and trans. Cecil Grayson. London: Phaidon, 1972.

Alberti, Leon Battista.
On the Art of Building in Ten Books. Trans. Joseph Rykwert, Neil Leach, and Robert Tavernor. Cambridge, Mass.: MIT Press, 1988.

Alberti, Leon Battista.
La pittura. Trans. L. Domenichi. Venice: Appresso Gabriel Giolito de Ferrari, 1547. 1st Latin ed. is 1435.

Alberti, Leon Battista.
Ten Books of Architecture. Trans. James Leoni. 1755. Reprint, London: Alec Tiranti, 1965.

Alberti, Leon Battista.
L'architettura. Trans. Giovanni Orlandi. Milan: Il Polifilo, 1966.

Alberto Sartoris.
Exhibition catalog. Intro. Bruno Reichlin. Lausanne: École polytechnique fédérale de Lausanne, 1978.

Al-Hazen.

Ibn al-Haytham's Completion of the Conics. Trans. J. P. Hogendijk. New York: Springer Verlag, 1985.

Al-Hazen.

Opticae Thesaurus. New York: Johnson Reprint, 1972.

Al-Hazen.

The Optics of Al-Haytham. Trans. A. I. Sabra. London: Warburg Institute, University of London, 1989.

Alleaume, Jacques.

La Perspective speculative et Pratique où sont demonstrez les fondemens de cet Art, & de tout ce qui en a esté enseigné jusqu'à present. Ensemble la maniere universelle de la pratiquer, non seulement sans Plan Geometral, & sans Tiers poinct, dedans ni dehors le champ du Tableau. Mais encores par le moyen de la Ligne, communément appellée Horizontale. Paris: Chez Melchior Tavernier & François Langlois, 1643.

Alpatov, M. V.

Early Russian Icon Painting. Moscow: Iskusstvo, 1978.

Alpers, Svetlana.

The Art of Describing: Dutch Art in the Seventeenth Century. Chicago: University of Chicago Press, 1983.

Apollonius of Perga.

Treatise on the Conic Sections. Cambridge: Cambridge University Press, 1896.

Aristarchus of Samos.

"On the Sizes and Distances of the Sun and the Moon." In *Aristarchus of Samos, the Ancient Copernicus: A History of Greek Astronomy to Aristarchus,* by Sir Thomas L. Heath. Oxford: Clarendon Press, 1913.

Aristotle.

Physics. Venice: Simonemide Luere, 1506.

Aristotle.

Poetics. Trans. S. H. Butcher. New York: Dover Publications, 1951.

Averroes.

Averroes' Three Short Commentaries on Aristotle's "Topics," "Rhetoric," and "Poetics." Ed. and trans. C. E. Butterworth. Albany: State University of New York Press, 1977.

Avicenna.

Avicenna's Commentary on the Poetics of Aristotle. Ed. and trans. I. M. Dahi-yat. Leiden: E. J. Brill, 1974.

Avicenna.

Le Livre de Science. 2 vols. Trans. M. Achena and H. Massé. Paris: Belles Lettres, 1955–1958.

Avicenna.

A Treatise on the Canon of Medicine of Avicenna, Incorporating a Translation of the First Book by O. Cameron Gruner. London: Luzac, 1930.

Bacon, Francis.

Works. 1857–1874. Reprint, Stuttgard–Bad Cannstatt: Frommann-Holzboog, 1963.

Bacon, Roger.

De Multiplicatione Specierum. Trans. D. C. Lindberg. New York: Oxford University Press, 1983.

Bacon, Roger.

De Speculis Comburentibus. Trans. D. C. Lindberg. New York: Oxford University Press, 1983.

Baltrusaitis, Jurgis.

Aberrations: An Essay on the Legend of Forms. Trans. Richard Miller. Cambridge, Mass.: MIT Press, 1989.

Baltrusaitis, Jurgis.

Anamorphic Art. Trans. W. J. Strachan. New York: Harry N. Abrams, 1976.

Banham, Rayner.

Theory and Design in the First Machine Age. New York: Praeger, 1960.

Barbaro, Daniele.

La Pratica della Perspettiva: Di Monsignor Daniel Barbaro Eletto Patriarca D'Aqvileia, Opera molto vtile a Pittori, a Scultori & ad Architetti. Con due tavole, una de' capitoli principali, l'altra delle cose piu notabili contenute nella presente opera. Venice: Appresso Camillo & Rutilio Borgominieri fratelli, al Segno di S. Giorgio, 1569. Reprint, Bologna: Arnaldo Forni, 1980.

Bartoli, Cosimo.

Del Modo di Misurare le distantie, le superficie, i corpi, le piante, le provincie, le prospettive, & tutte le altre cose terrene, che possono occorrere a gli huomini, Secondo le vere regole d'Euclide, de gli altri piu lodati scrittori. Venice: Francesco Franceschi Sanese, 1564.

Bassi, Martino.

Dispareri In Materia D'Architettvra, Et Perspettiva. Con Pareri Di Eccellenti, Et Famosi Architetti, che li risoluono. Di Martino Bassi Milanese. Brescia: Francesco, & Pie, María Marchetti Fratelli, 1572.

Baudinet, Marie-José.

"The Face of Christ, the Form of the Church." In *Fragments for a History of the Human Body.* Ed. Michel Feher with Ramma Naddaff and Nadia Tazi. Part 1. New York: Zone Books, 1989.

Baudrillard, Jean.

Seduction. Montreal: New World Perspectives, 1990.

Bauer, George C.

"From Architecture to Scenography: The Full-Scale Model in the Baroque Tradition." In *La Scenographia Barocca.* Bologna: Editrice C.L.U.E.B., 1979.

Belaval, Yvon.

"La crise de la géométrisation de l'univers dans la philosophie des lumières." *Revue internationale de philosophie* 6 (1952): 337–355.

Benedikt, Michael, ed.

Cyberspace: First Steps. Cambridge, Mass.: MIT Press, 1991.

Benjamin, Walter.

Gesammelte Schriften. 6 vols. Frankfurt: Suhrkamp Verlag, 1972.

Benjamin, Walter.

Origin of German Tragic Drama. Trans. John Osborne. London: New Left Books, 1977.

Benjamin, Walter.

Reflections: Aphorisms, Essays, and Autobiographical Writings. Trans. Peter Demetz. New York: Harcourt, Brace, Jovanovich, 1978.

Berkeley, George.

A New Theory of Vision and Other Select Philosophical Writings. London: J. M. Dent, 1910.

Berkeley, George.

The Works of George Berkeley, Bishop of Cloyne. 9 vols. London: T. Nelson, 1948–1957.

Bibiena, Ferdinando Galli da.

L'Architettura Civile Preparata sú la Geometria, e ridotta alle prospettive. Considerazioni Pratiche di Ferdinando Galli Bibiena Cittadino Bolognese architetto primario, capo mastro maggiore, e pittore di camera, e feste di teatro della maestra di

Carlo III. Il monarca delle Spagne dessegnate, e descritte in cinque parti. . . . Dedicata Alla Sacra Cattolica Real Maestà di Carlo III Re delle Spagne, d'Ungheria, Boemia &c. Parma: Per Paolo Monti, 1711. Reprint, New York: Benjamin Blom, 1971.

Bibiena, Ferdinando Galli da.
Direzioni a giovani studenti nel disegno dell'architettura civile: nell'Accademia clementina dell'Instituto delle scienze unite da Ferdinando Galli Bibiena. Bologna: Lelio dalla Volpe, 1725.

Bleicher, Joseph.
Contemporary Hermeneutics. London: Routledge and Kegan Paul, 1980.

Blumenberg, Hans.
The Genesis of the Copernican World. Cambridge, Mass.: MIT Press, 1987.

Bois, Yve-Alain.
"Metamorphosis of Axonometry." *Daidalos* 1 (1981): 40–58.

Bonaventure.
Meditations on the Life of Christ. Trans. I. Ragus. Princeton: Princeton University Press, 1961.

Bonaventure.
The Mind's Road to God. Trans. and intro. G. Boas. Indianapolis: Bobbs-Merrill, 1953.

Bosse, Abraham.
A. Bosse au lecteur, sur les causes qu'il croit avoir euës, de discontinuer le cours de ses leçons géométrales et perspectives, dedans l'Académie royale de la peinture et de la sculpture, & mesme de s'en retirer. Paris, 1666.

Bosse, Abraham.
Lettres écrites au Sr Bosse, graveur, avec ses réponses sur quelques nouveaux traittez concernans la perspective & la peinture. Paris: Chez le Sr Bosse, 1668.

Bosse, Abraham.
Manière universelle de Mr. Desargues, pour pratiquer la perspective: par petit-pied, comme le géométral. Ensemble les places et proportions des fortes & foibles touches, teintes ou couleurs Gerard Besargies, par A. Bosse. 2d ed. Paris: Impr. de P. Des-Hayes, 1648. Reprint, Alburgh: Archival Facsimiles, 1987. 1st ed. is 1643.

Bosse, Abraham.
La manière universelle de M. Desargues lyonnois pour posser l'essieu & placer les heures & autres aux cadrans du soleil. Paris, 1643.

Bosse, Abraham.
Moyen universel de pratiquer la perspective sur les tableaux ou surfaces irrégulières. Ensemble quelques particularitez concernant cet art, & celuy de la graueure en taille-douce. Paris: L'auteur, 1653.

Bosse, Abraham.
Les Ordres de l'Architecture. Paris, 1688.

Bosse, Abraham.
La Pratique du Trait a Preuve de Mr. Desargues Lyonnais, Pour la Coupe des Pierres en l'Architecture. Paris: Pierre Des Hayes, 1643.

Bosse, Abraham.
Sentimens sur la distinction des diverses manières de peinture, dessein & graveure, & des originaux d'avec leurs copies. Ensemble du choix des sujets, & des chemins pour arriver facilement & promptement à bien pourtraire. Paris: Chez l'auteur, Impr. de P. Des-Hayes, 1649.

Bosse, Abraham.
Traité des pratiques géométrales et perspectiues: enseignées dans l'Académie royale de la peinture et sculpture. Très utiles pour ceux qui désirent exceller en ces Arts, & autres, où il faut employer la Règle & le Compas. Paris: Chez l'auteur, 1665.

Bretez, Louis.
La perspective practique de l'architecture, contenant par leçons une manière nouvelle, courte et aisée pour représenter en perspective les ordinances d'architecture et les places fortifiées. Ouvrage très utile aux peintres, architectes, ingénieurs, et autres dessinateurs. Paris: L'auteur et Pierre Miquelin, 1706.

Brewster, David.
The Stereoscope: Its History, Theory, and Construction, with Its Application to the Fine and Useful Arts and to Education. London: J. Murray, 1856.

Brewster, David.
Treatise on Optics. London, 1853.

Brown, Lloyd.
The Story of Maps. New York: Dover Publications, 1977.

Bruno, Giordano.
Cena de la Ceneri. Trans. and intro. S. L. Jaki. The Hague: Mouton, 1975.

Buchwald, Jed Z.
The Rise of the Wave Theory of Light. Chicago: University of Chicago Press, 1989.

Buck-Morss, Susan.
The Dialectics of Seeing. Cambridge, Mass.: MIT Press, 1989.

Busch, Thomas, and Shaun Gallagher, eds.
Merleau-Ponty, Hermeneutics, and Postmodernism. Binghampton: State University of New York Press, 1992.

Caicco, Gregory.
"Memory and Representation: St. Bonaventure's Itinerarium Mentis in Deum in the Franciscan High Middle Ages." M.Phil. thesis, University of Cambridge, 1989.

Camper, Petrus.
Dissertatio optica de visu. Optical dissertation on vision. Nieuwkoop: de Graaf, 1962.

Cantor, Geoffrey N.
Optics after Newton: Theories of Light in Britain and Ireland, 1704–1840. Manchester: Manchester University Press, 1983.

Caramuel de Lobkowitz, Juan.
Architectura civil recta y obliqua considerada y Dibuxada en el Templo de Ierusale[m]. Intro. A. Bonet Correa. Madrid: Ediciones Turner, 1984. Reprint of Vigevano, 1678.

Carboneri, Nino.
Andrea Pozzo, Architetto (1642–1709). Trento: Collana Artisti Trenti, 1961.

Carl, Peter.
"Le Corbusier's Penthouse in Paris, 24 rue Nungesser-et-Coli." *Daidalos* 28 (1988): 65–75.

Carson, Anne.
Eros the Bittersweet. Princeton: Princeton University Press, 1986.

Cataneo, Pietro.
I quattro primi libri di architettura di Pietro Cataneo. Venice, 1554.

Cataneo, Pietro.
Le Pratiche Delle Due Prime Matemetiche Di Pietro Cantaneo Con La Aggionta, Libro D'Albaco E Geometria Con Il practico e uero modo di misurar la Terra, Non Piu Mostra Da Altri. Venice: Appresso Giovanni Griffio, 1559.

Caus, Salomon de.
La Perspective avec la Raison des ombres et miroirs, par Salomon de Caus Ingénieur du Serenissme Prince de Galles, Dedié à son Altesse. London: Chez Jan Norton Imprimeur du roy de la grande Bretaigne, aus langues estrangeres; Frankfurt: Ches la vesue de Hulsius, 1612. 1st ed. is London, 1611.

Chasles, Michel.

Aperçu historique sur l'origine et le développement des méthodes en géométrie: particulièrement de celles qui se rapportent à la géométrie moderne, suivi d'un mémoire de géométrie sur deux principes généraux de la science la dualité el l'homographi. Paris, 1837.

Chladenius, Johann Martin.

Einleitung zur richtigen Auslegung vernüftiger Reden und Schriften. Leipzig, 1742.

Choisy, Auguste.

L'art de bâtir chez les byzantins. Paris: Société anonyme de publications périodiques, 1883.

Choisy, Auguste.

L'art de bâtir chez les romains. Paris: Ducher, 1873.

Choisy, Auguste.

Histoire de l'architecture. Paris, 1899. Reprint, Paris: Librairie Georges Baranger, 1929.

Choisy, Auguste.

Vitruve. Paris: Imprimerie-Librairie Lahure, 1909.

Clagett, Marshall.

Greek Science in Antiquity. London: Abelard-Schuman, 1957.

Clavelin, Maurice.

The Natural Philosophy of Galileo. Cambridge, Mass.: MIT Press, 1974.

Cochin, Charles-Nicolas.

Mémoires inédits sur le Comte de Caylus, Bouchardon, les Slodtz. Ed. M. C. Henry. Paris: Charavay Frères, Éditeurs, 1880.

Cohen, Morris R., and I. E. Drabkin, eds.

A Source Book in Greek Science. New York: McGraw-Hill, 1948.

Colloque international et interdisciplinaire Jean-Henri Lambert.

Paris: Editions Ophrys, 1979.

Colombier, Pierre du.

L'architecture française en Allemagne au XVIIIe siècle. Paris: Presses universitaires de France, 1956.

Colonna, Francesco.

Hypnerotomachia Poliphili. Venice, 1499. Reprint, London: Methuen, 1904.

Condillac, Etienne Bonnot de.
Traité des Sensations. London, Paris: de Bure, 1754.

Coolidge, J. Lowell.
History of the Conic Sections. New York: Dover Publications, 1968.

Couliano, I. P.
Eros and Magic in the Renaissance. Chicago: University of Chicago Press, 1987.

Courtonne, Jean.
Traité de la perspective pratique, avec des remarques sur l'architecture. Suives de quelques édifices considérables mis en perspective, et de l'invention de l'auteur. Ouvrage très-utile aux amateurs de l'architecture & de la peinture. Par le Sieur Courtonne, Architecte. Dédié à Monseigneur Le Duc D'Antin. Paris: Chez Jacques Vincent, 1725.

Cousin, Jean.
Livre de perspective de Iehan Cousin, Senonois, maistre painctre à Paris. Paris: De l'imprimerie de Iehan le Royer Imprimeur du Roy és Mathematiques, 1560. Reprint, Unterschneidheim: W. Uhl, 1974.

Crary, Jonathan.
Techniques of the Observer. Cambridge, Mass.: MIT Press, 1991.

Cusanus.
See Nicholas of Cusa.

Daguerre, Louis Jacques Mandé.
Historique et description des procédés du daguerreotype et du diorama. Paris: A. Giroux, 1839.

Damisch, Hubert.
L'origine de la perspective. Paris: Flammarion, 1987.

Damisch, Hubert.
The Origin of Perspective. Trans. John Goodman. Cambridge, Mass.: MIT Press, 1994.

Danti, Ignazio.
See Vignola, Jacopo Barozzi da.

da Vinci, Leonardo.
The Notebooks of Leonardo da Vinci. Ed. J. P. Richter. New York: Dover Publications, 1970.

da Vinci, Leonardo.
Trattato della pittura di Leonardo da Vinci, nouamente dato in luce, con la vita dell'istesso autore, scritta da Rafaelle du Fresne. . . . Si Sonoggiunti i tre libré della pitture, & il trattato della statua di Leon Battista Alberti, con la vita del medesimo. Paris: Appresso Giacomo Langlois, 1651.

da Vinci, Leonardo.
Treatise on Painting = Codex urbinas latinus 1270. Trans. A. P. McManon. Intro. L. H. Heydenreich. 2 vols. Princeton: Princeton University Press, 1956.

Davis, Margaret Daly.
Piero della Francesca's Mathematical Treatises. Ravenna: Longo Editore, 1977.

Debanné, Janine.
"Guarino Guarini's SS. Sindone Chapel: Between Reliquary and Cenotaph." M.Arch. thesis, McGill University, 1995.

Debru, Claude.
Analyse et representation, De la méthodologie à la théorie de l'espace: Kant et Lambert. Paris: Librairie Philosophique J. Vrin, 1977.

Desargues, Girard.
Exemple de l'un des manières universelles du S.G.D.L. touchant la pratique de la perspective sans employer aucun tiers point de distance y d'autre nature qui soit hors du champ de l'ouvrage. Paris: A. Bosse, 1636.

Desargues, Girard.
"Example de l'une des manières universelles du S.G.D.L. touchant la pratique de la perspective sans employer aucun tiers point de distance ny d'autre nature qui soit hors du champ de l'ouvrage." In *The Geometrical Work of Girard Desargues.* Ed. J. V. Field and J. J. Gray. New York: Springer-Verlag, 1987. Facsimile reproduction of Paris, 1636.

Descargues, Pierre.
Perspective: History, Evolution, Techniques. Trans. I. M. Paris. Intro. and comm. P. Descargues. New York: Van Nostrand Reinhold, 1982.

Descargues, Pierre.
Traités de perspective choix des oeuvres et présentation par Pierre Descargues. Paris: Chêne, 1976.

Descartes, René.
Discourse on Method, Optics, Geometry, and Meteorology. Trans. and intro. Paul J. Olscamp. Indianapolis: Bobbs-Merrill, 1965.

Descartes, René.
Oeuvres. 11 vols. Paris: L. Cerf, 1897–1909.

Didi-Huberman, Georges.
Ce que nous voyons, Ce qui nous regarde. Paris: Éditions de minuit, 1992.

Dillon, M. C., ed.
Merleau-Ponty Vivant. Albany: State University of New York Press, 1991.

Diocles.
Diocles on Burning Mirrors: The Arabic Translation of the Lost Greek Original. Trans. G. J. Toomer. New York: Springer Verlag, 1976.

Ditton, Humphrey.
A treatise of perspective, demonstrative and practical: illustrated with copper cutts. London: Printed for B. Tooke . . . and D. Midwinter, 1712.

Drexler, Arthur, ed.
The Architecture of the École des Beaux-Arts. New York: Museum of Modern Art, 1977.

Dubreuil, Jean.
La perspective practique, nécessaire à tous peintres, graveurs, sculpteurs, architectes, orfevres, brodeurs, tapissiers, & autres se servans du dessein par un Parisien, religieux de la Compagnie de Iesus. 3 vols. Paris: Chez Melchior Tavernier . . . et Chez François L'Anglois, dit Chartres, 1642–1649.

Dubreuil, Jean.
La Perspective Pratique, . . . Reueuë corrigée & augmentées par l'Auteur en plusieurs endroits, et d'un Traité de la Perspective Militaire ou Méthode pour eslever sur des Plans Géométraux. Paris: François l'Anglois, 1647–1651.

Du Cerceau, Jacques Androuet.
Leçons de perspective positive par Iacques Androuet du Cerceau, Architecte. Paris: M. Patisson, Imprimeur, 1576.

Du Cerceau, Jacques Androuet.
Les plus excellents bastiments de France. Sous la direction de H. Destailleur. Graves en fac-simile par Faure Dujarric. 2 vols. Paris: A. Levy, 1868–1870.

Du Cerceau, Jacques Androuet.
Les trois livres d'architecture. 3 vols. Paris, 1559–1582.

Duclos, Albert.
Cours de perspective linéaire à l'usage des élèves de l'École des Beaux-Arts. Paris: Vincent, 1907.

Dupain de Montesson.
La science des ombres, par rapport des dessein: ouvrage nécessaire à ceux qui veulent dessiner l'architecture civile & militaire, ou qui destinent à la peinture: dans lequel ils trouveront des règles démontrées pour connoître l'espèce, la forme, la longueur &

la largeur des ombres que les différens corps portent, & qu'ils produisent tant sur des surfaces horizontales, verticales, ou inclinées, que sur des surfaces verticales, plates, convexes ou concaves. Paris: Chez C.-A. Jombert, 1760.

Durand, Jacques-Nicolas-Louis.
Précis des leçons d'architecture donneés à l'École Polytechnique. 2 vols. Paris, 1819. (Reprint, Munich: UHL Verlag, 1981.)

Dürer, Albrecht.
Vier Bücher von menschlichen Proportion. Latin Alberti Dureri clarissimi pictoris geometral de symmetria partium in rectis formis hu[m]anorum corporum: libri in latinum conversi. Nuremberg: In aedib. Vidual Durerianae, 1532.

Dürer, Albrecht.
Unterweysung der Messung. Nuremberg, 1525.

Eco, Umberto.
Art and Beauty in the Middle Ages. Trans. Hugh Bredin. New Haven: Yale University Press, 1986.

Edgerton, Samuel Y.
The Heritage of Giotto's Geometry: Art and Science on the Eve of the Scientific Revolution. Ithaca: Cornell University Press, 1991.

Edgerton, Samuel Y.
The Renaissance Rediscovery of Linear Perspective. New York: Harper and Row, 1975.

Eisenstein, Sergei.
Film Sense. New York: Harcourt Brace Jovanovich, 1942.

Elkins, James.
The Poetics of Perspective. Ithaca: Cornell University Press, 1994.

Ellul, Jacques.
The Technological Society. Trans. John Wilkinson. New York: Alfred A. Knopf, 1964.

Empedocles.
Works: Extant Fragments. Ed. M. R. Wright. New Haven: Yale University Press, 1981.

Encyclopedia of World Art.
15 vols. London: McGraw-Hill, 1959.

Encyclopédie ou dictionnaire raisonné des sciences, des arts et des métiers.
17 vols. Paris: Briasson et al., 1751–1780.

Erouart, Gilbert.
L'architecture au pinceau. Paris: Electa Moniteur, 1982.

Erouart, Gilbert.
"Jean-Laurent Legeay. Recherches." In *Piranèse et les Français.* Ed. G. Brunel. Rome: Edizioni dell'Elefante, 1976.

Euclid.
The elements of geometrie of the most auncient philosopher Euclide of Megara, faithfully (now first) translated into the English toung, by H. Billingsley. London: Iohn Daye, 1570.

Euclid.
Euclides Optica; Opticorum Recensio Theonis. Ed. J. L. Heiberg. Leipzig, 1895.

Euclid.
"The Optics of Euclid," trans. H. E. Burton. *Journal of the Optical Society of America* 35 (1945): 357–372.

Euclid.
La Perspective d'Euclide Traduite en françois sur le texte Grec, original de l'autheur, et demonstrée per Rol. Freart de Chantelou, Sieur de Chambray. Au Mans: De l'imprimerie de Iacques Ysambart, 1663.

Euclid.
The Thirteen Books of Euclid's Elements. Trans. T. L. Heath. New York: Dover Publications, 1956.

Euler, Leonhard.
Letters of Euler on Different Subjects in Physics and Philosophy, Addressed to a German Princess. Ed. and with a life of Euler by David Brewster. 2 vols. New York: J. and J. Harper, 1846.

Evans, Robin.
"Architectural Projection." In *Architecture and Shadow.* Ed. David Murray. Via 11. New York: Rizzoli, 1990.

Evans, Robin.
The Projective Cast: Architecture and Its Three Geometries. Cambridge, Mass.: MIT Press, 1995.

Farrish, William.
Isometrical Perspective. Cambridge, 1820.

Feo, Vittorio de.
"L'Architettura immaginata di Andrea Pozzo gesuita." *Rassegna di architettura e urbanistica* 16.46 (1980): 79–109.

Ficino, Marsilio.

The Book of Life. Dallas, Tex.: Spring Publications, 1980.

Ficino, Marsilio.

Commentary on Plato's Symposium on Love. Dallas, Tex.: Spring Publications, 1985.

Field, J. V.

"Giovanni Battista Benedetti on the Mathematics of Linear Perspective." *Journal of the Warburg and Courtauld Institutes* 48 (1985): 71–99.

Field, J. V., and J. J. Gray.

The Geometrical Work of Girard Desargues. New York: Springer-Verlag, 1987.

Filarete.

Trattato di architettura. Intro. and notes F. L. Grassi. 2 vols. Milan: Il Polifilo, 1972.

Filarete.

Treatise on Architecture. Trans., intro. and notes J. R. Spencer. New Haven: Yale University Press, 1965.

Flocon, Albert, and René Taton.

La prospettiva: collana di architettura diretta da Massimo Scolari. Milan: Franco Angeli, 1985.

Fournier, Daniel.

A treatise of the theory and practice of perspective: wherein the principles as laid down by Brook Taylor are explained by means of moveable schemes. London, 1746.

Frangenberg, Thomas.

"The Image and the Moving Eye: Jean Pelerin Viator to Guidobaldo del Monte." *Journal of the Warburg and Courtauld Institutes* 49 (1986): 150–171.

Frankl, Paul.

The Gothic: Literary Sources and Interpretations through Eight Centuries. Princeton: Princeton University Press, 1960.

Frascari, Marco.

"A Secret Semiotic Skiagraphy: The Corporal Theatre of Meanings in Vincenzo Scamozzi's *Idea* of Architecture." In *Architecture and Shadow,* edited by David Murray. *Via* 11. Philadelphia: Graduate School of Fine Arts, University of Pennsylvania: New York: Rizzoli, 1990.

Frascari, Marco, and William Braham.
"On the Mantic Paradigm in Architecture: The Projective Evocation of Future Edifices." Paper presented at ACSA 1994 Annual Meeting, Theory and Criticism Session, Montreal, 1994.

Fraser, Douglas, Howard Hibbard, and Milton J. Lewine, eds.
Essays in the History of Architecture Presented to Rudolf Wittkower. New York: Phaidon, 1967.

Fresnel, Augustin Jean.
Oeuvres complètes. 3 vols. Paris: Imprimerie impériale, 1866–1870.

Gadamer, Hans-Georg.
The Relevance of the Beautiful and Other Essays. Trans. Nicholas Walker. Cambridge: Cambridge University Press, 1986.

Galen.
Galen on the Natural Faculties. Trans. A. J. Brook. London: W. Heinemann; New York: G. P. Putnam's Sons, 1916.

Gaurico, Pomponio.
De Sculptura Pomponio Gaurico. Ed. A. Placidus. Florence: Printed by Filippo Giunta, 1504.

Geminus.
Introduction aux Phénomènes. Trans. G. Aujac. Paris: Belles Lettres, 1975.

Ghiberti, Lorenzo.
I Commentari del Ghiberti. Intro. O. Morisani. Naples: R. Ricciardi Editore, 1947.

Gilman, Ernest B.
The Curious Perspective: Literary and Pictorial Wit in the Seventeenth Century. New Haven: Yale University Press, 1978.

Gleick, James.
Chaos: Making a New Science. New York: Penguin, 1987.

Goethe, Johann Wolfgang von.
Theory of Colours. Trans. C. Eastlake. 1840. Reprint, London: Cass, 1967.

Goldstein, Leonard.
The Social and Cultural Roots of Linear Perspective. Minneapolis: MEP Publications, 1988.

Grant, Edward.
A Sourcebook in Medieval Science. Cambridge, Mass.: Harvard University Press, 1974.

Green, Judy, and Paul S. Green.
"Alberti's Perspective: A Mathematical Comment." *Art Bulletin* 69 (1987): 641–645.

Grignon, Marc.
"Pozzo, Blondel, and the Structure of the Supplement." *Assemblage* 2 (1987): 96–109.

Grimaldi, Francesco Maria.
Physico-mathesis de lumine coloribus et iride. Ferrara: Università degli studi di Ferrara, 1966.

Guarini, Guarino.
Architettura civile del padre D'Guarino Guarini opera postuma. Turin, 1737. Reprint, London: Gregg Press, 1964.

Guarini, Guarino.
Placita Philosophica. Paris, 1665.

Gusdorf, Georges.
Les principes de la pensée au siècle des Lumières. Paris: Payot, 1971.

Hallyn, Fernand.
The Poetic Structure of the World: Copernicus and Kepler. Trans. D. M. Leslie. New York: Zone Books, 1993.

Hallyn, Fernand.
"Port-Royal versus Tesauro: Signe, Figure, Sujet." In *Baroque 9–10, Revue Internationale.* Montauban: C.I.S.B., 1980.

Hammond, John H., and Jill Austin.
The Camera Lucida in Art and Science. Bristol: Adam Hilger, 1987.

Harries, Karsten.
The Bavarian Rococo Church. New Haven: Yale University Press, 1983.

Harris, John.
Sir William Chambers, Knight of the Polar Star. London: A. Zwemmer, 1970.

Hautecoeur, Louis.
Histoire de l'Architecture classique en France. 7 vols. Paris: Editions A. & J. Picard, 1950–1967.

Heath, Sir Thomas L.
Aristarchus of Samos, the Ancient Copernicus: A History of Greek Astronomy to Aristarchus. Oxford: Clarendon Press, 1913.

Heath, Sir Thomas L.
A History of Greek Mathematics. 1921. Reprint, New York: Dover Publications, 1981.

Hegel, G. W. Friedrich.
Philosophy of Nature. Trans. M. J. Petrey. London: Allen and Unwin, 1970.

Heidegger, Martin.
The Question Concerning Technology and Other Essays. Trans. William Lovitt. New York: Harper and Row, 1977.

Heidegger, Martin.
"The Origin of the Work of Art." In *Basic Writings.* Ed. David Farrell Krell. New York: Harper and Row, 1977.

Helmholtz, Hermann Ludwig Ferdinand von.
Handbook of Physiological Optics. Trans. J. P. S. Southall. 3 vols. 1924–1925. Reprint, New York: Dover Publications, 1962.

Herdmann, William.
A Treatise on the Curvilinear Perspective of Nature. London, 1853.

Hero of Alexandria.
The Pneumatics of Hero of Alexandria, from the original Greek. Ed. and trans. B. Woodcroft. 1851. Reprint, London: MacDonald, 1971.

Herschel, John Frederick William.
Light. London, 1827.

Hersey, George.
Pythagorean Palaces. Ithaca: Cornell University Press, 1976.

Highmore, Joseph.
The practice of perspective, on the principles of Dr. Brook Taylor: in a series of examples, from the most simple and easy, to the most complicated, and difficult cases, In the course of which, his method is compared with those of some of the most celebrated writers before him on the subject. . . . Written many years since, but now first pub., by Joseph Highmore. London: Printed for A. Millar and J. Nourse, 1763.

Hlavacek, Ludvik.
"'Architectura obliqua' Jana Caramuela z Lobkovic." *Umení* 32.1 (1974): 50–53.

Hondius, Hendrick.
Instruction en la science de Perspective par Hondius. The Hague, 1625. Reprint, Alburgh: Archival Facsimiles, 1987.

Hoogstraten, Samuel van.
In leyding tot de hooge schoole der schilderkonst: anders, de Zichtbaere Werelt. Verdeelt in negen Leerwinkles, yder bestiert door eene der zanggodinnen. Ten hoogsten noodzakelijk, tot onderwijs, voor alle die deeze edele, vrye, en hooge Konst oeffenen, of met yver zoeken to leeren, of anders eenigzins beminnen. Beschreven door Samuel van Hoogstraten. Rotterdam: François Van Hoogstraeten, 1678. Reprint, Ann Arbor: University of Michigan, 1972.

Hooke, Robert.
Micrographia, or some physiological descriptions of minute bodies made by magnifying glasses, with observations and inquiries thereupon. London: J. Martyn and J. Allestry, 1665. Reprint, New York: Dover Publications, 1961.

Hooke, Robert.
"The Nature, Motion, and Effects of Light." In *The Posthumous Works.* Ed. Richard Waller. Intro. Richard S. Westfall. New York: Johnson Reprint, 1969.

Huret, Grégoire.
Optique et Portraiture et Peinture, en deux parties. . . . La première est la perspective pratique acomplie, pour representer les somptueuses Architectures des plus superbes bâtimens en Perspective par deux manières. . . . La deuxième partie contient la perspective speculative, . . . Par Gregoire Huret, Desseignateur & Graveur ordinaire de la Maison du Roy, & de l'Académie Royale de Peinture & Sculpture. Paris: Chez l'Auteur, près la Boucherie de la Porte-Paris, 1672.

Husserl, Edmund.
Phenomenology and the Crisis of Philosophy. Trans. Quentin Lauer. New York: Harper and Row, 1965.

Huygens, Christian.
Treatise on Light. Trans. Silvanus P. Thompson. 1945. Reprint, New York: Dover Publications, 1962.

Hyatt Mayor, A.
The Bibiena Family. New York: H. Bittner, 1945.

Isozaki, Arata.
Le Corbusier, Couvent Sainte Marie de La Tourette Eveux-sur-l'Abresle, France. Ed. Yukio Futagawa. *Global Architecture* 11. Tokyo: A.D.A. Edita, 1971.

Ivins, William Mills, Jr.
Art and Geometry: A Study in Space Intuitions. 1946. Reprint, New York: Dover Publications, 1964.

Jaki, Stanley L.
The Milky Way. New York: Neale Watson Academic Publications, 1972.

Jammer, Max.
Concepts of Space: The History of Theories of Space in Physics. Cambridge, Mass.: Harvard University Press, 1954.

Jamnitzer, Wenzel.
Perspectiva corporum regularum. Das ist, Ein fleyssige Fürweysung, wie die fünff regulirten Cörper, daruon Plato inn Timaeo, Und Euclides inn sein Elementis schreibt, &c. Durch einen sonderlichen, newen, behenden und gerechten Weg der vor nie im Gebrauch ist gesehen worden, gar Künstlich inn die Perspectiua gebracht, Und darzu ein schöne Anleytung, wie aus denselbigen fünff Cörpern one Endt, gar viel andere Cörper, mancherley Art und Gestalt, gemacht unnd gefunden werden mügen. Nuremberg, 1568.

Jaucourt, Le Chevalier de.
"Perspective." *Encyclopédie ou, Dictionnaire raisonné des sciences, des arts et des métiers par une Société de gens de lettres: mis en odre & publii par M. Diderot . . . ; quanta la partie mathématique par M. D'Alembert.* Vol. 19. Paris: Briasson, 1751–1780.

Jeurat, Edmé-Sebastien.
Traité De Perspective A L'Usage Des Artistes. Où l'on démontre Géométriquement toutes les pratiques de cette Science, & où l'on enseigne. Selon la Méthode de M. Le Clerc, à mettre toutes sortes d'objects en perspective, leur réverbération dans l'eau, & leurs ombres, tant au Soleil qu'au flambeau. Paris: Chez Charles-Antoine Jombert, Libraire du Roi pour l'Artillerie & le Génie, 1750.

Jopling, Joseph.
The Practice of Isometrical Perspective. London: M. Taylor, 1835.

Kaufmann, Emil.
"Three Revolutionary Architects, Boullée, Ledoux, and Lequeu." *Transactions of the American Philosophical Society* 42 (1952): 433–564.

Kaufmann, Thomas da Costa.
"The Perspective of Shadows: The History of the Theory of Shadow Projection." *Journal of the Warburg and Cortauld Institutes* 38 (1975): 258–287.

Kearney, Richard.
The Wake of Imagination. Minneapolis: University of Minnesota Press, 1988.

Kemp, Martin.
Geometrical Perspective from Brunelleschi to Desargues: A Pictorial Means or an Intellectual End? London: British Academy, 1985.

Kemp, Martin.
The Science of Art: Optical Themes in Western Art from Brunelleschi to Seurat. 2d ed. New Haven: Yale University Press, 1992.

Kemp, Martin.
"Simon Stevin and Pieter Saenredam: A Study of Mathematics and Vision in Dutch Science and Art." *Art Bulletin* 68 (1986): 237–252.

Kepler, Johannes.
Ad Vitellionem paralipomena, quibus astronomiae pars optica traditur: potissimum de artificosa observatione et aestimatione diametrorum deliquiorumque, solis & lunae. Cum exemplis insignium eclipsium. Habes hoc libro, lector, inter alia multa nova, tractaum luculentum de modo visionis, et humorum oculi usu, contra opticos et anatomicos. Frankfurt: Apud Claudium Marnium & Haeredes Ionnis Aubrii, 1604.

Kepler, Johannes.
Dissertatio cum Nuncio Sidereo. Kepler's conversation with Galileo's Sidereal Messenger. Trans., intro., and notes by Edward Rosen. New York: Johnson Reprint, 1965.

Kepler, Johannes.
Epitome of Copernican Astronomy and *The Harmonies of the World.* Trans. Charles Glenn Wallis. Chicago: Encyclopaedia Brittanica, [1952].

Kepler, Johannes.
Les fondements de l'optique moderne: Paralipomènes à Vitellion (1604). Trans., intro., and notes Catherine Chevalley. Intro. René Taton and Pierre Costabel. Paris: J. Vrin, 1980.

Kepler, Johannes.
Mysterium Cosmographicum: The Secret of the Universe. Trans. A. M. Duncan. Intro. and comm. E. J. Aiton. Intro. I. Bernard Cohen. New York: Abaris Books, 1981.

Kepler, Johannes.
Somnium: The Dream, or Posthumous Work on Lunar Astronomy. Trans. and comm. Edward Rosen. Madison: University of Wisconsin Press, 1967.

Kepler, Johannes.
Strena, seu, de nive sexangula: The six-cornered snowflake. Ed. and trans. Colin Hardie, with essays by L. L. Whyte and B. F. J. Mason. Oxford: Clarendon Press, 1966. 1st Latin ed. is Frankfurt-am-Main, 1611.

Kirby, John Joshua.
Dr. Brook Taylor's method of perspective, compared with the examples lately publish'd on this subject as Sirigatti's, Being a Parallel between those two Methods of Perspective. In which the superior Excellence of Taylor's is shown by self evident Principles, or simple inspection. London, 1757.

Kirby, John Joshua.
Dr. Brook Taylor's method of perspective made easy, both in theory and practice. In two books . . . By Joshua Kirby, painter. Illustrated with fifty copper plates; most of which are engrav'd by the author. Ipswich: Printed by W. Craighton, for the author, 1755.

Kirby, John Joshua.
The perspective of architecture: in two parts: a work entirely new; deduced from the principles of Dr. Brook Taylor: and performed by two rules only of universal application. 2 vols. London: Printed for the Author . . . by R. Francklin, 1761.

Kircher, Athanasius.
Ars magna lucis et umbræ in decem Libros digesta Quibus Admirandæ in mundo, atque adèo universa natura, vires effectusq. uti nova, ita varia novorum recorditiorumq. Speciminum exhibitione, ad varios mortalium usus, panduntur. Rome: Sumptibus Hermanni Scheus, 1646.

Kircher, Athanasius.
Physiologia Kircheriana experimentalis, qua summa argumentorum multitudine & varietate naturalium rerum per experimenta physica, mathematica, medica . . . comprobatur atque stabilitur. Amsterdam: Ex officina Janssonio-Waesbergiana, 1680.

Klassen, Helmut W.
"Michelangelo: Architecture and the Vision of Anatomy." M.Arch. thesis, McGill University, 1990.

Klein, Robert.
"Pomponius Gauricus on Perspective." *Art Bulletin* 43 (1961): 211–213.

Kline, Morris.
Mathematical Thought from Ancient to Modern Times. New York: Oxford University Press, 1972.

Koyré, Alexandre.
Metaphysics and Measurement. London: Chapman and Hall, 1968.

Koyré, Alexandre.
Newtonian Studies. Chicago: University of Chicago Press, 1965.

Krauss, Rosalind.
"Notes on the Index: Seventies Art in America." In *October: The First Decade.* Ed. A. Michelson et al. Cambridge, Mass.: MIT Press, 1987.

Kruft, Hanno-Walter.
A History of Architectural Theory from Vitruvius to the Present. Trans. R. Taylor, E. Callander, and A. Wood. New York: Princeton Architectural Press, 1994.

Kubovy, Michael.
The Psychology of Perspective and Renaissance Art. New York: Cambridge University Press, 1986.

Kuhn, Jehane R.
"Measured Appearances: Documentation and Design in Early Perspective Drawing." In *Journal of the Warburg and Courtauld Institutes* 53 (1990): 114–132.

Lambert, Johann Heinrich [Jean-Henri Lambert].
Cosmological Letters on the Arrangement of the World-Edifice. Trans. Stanley L. Jaki. New York: Science History Publications, 1976.

Lambert, Johann Heinrich.
Lettres cosmologiques. Amsterdam: Gerard Hulst van Keulen, 1801.

Lambert, Johann Heinrich.
Lettres cosmologiques sur l'organisation de l'Univers. Intro. Jacques Merleau-Ponty. Paris: Editions Alain Brieux, 1977.

Lambert, Johann Heinrich.
Notes and Comments on the Composition of Terrestrial and Celestial Maps. Trans. W. R. Tobler. Ann Arbor: Department of Geography, University of Michigan, 1972.

Lambert, Johann Heinrich.
La Perspective affranchie de l'embaras [sic] du plan géométral. Zurich, 1759. Reprint, Alburgh: Archival Fascimiles, 1987.

Lambert, Johann Heinrich.
Les propriétés remarquables de la route de la lumière, par les airs et en général par plusieurs milieux refringens spheriques et concentriques, avec la solution des problèmes, qui ont du rapport, comme sont les refractions astronomiques et terrestres, et ce qui en dépend. The Hague: N. van Daalen, 1759.

Lambert, Johann Heinrich.
Schriften zur Perspektive. Ed. and comm. Max Steck. Berlin: G. Lüttke Verlag, 1943.

Lambert, Johann Heinrich.
Système du monde. Trans. Johann Bernard Merian. Paris, 1770.

Laplace, Pierre Simon de.
Oeuvres complètes, publiées sous les auspices de l'Académie des sciences. 13 vols. Paris, 1878–1904.

La Riche, William.
Five Architects. New York: Oxford University Press, 1975.

Laurent, Roger.
La place de J.-H. Lambert (1728–1777) dans l'histoire de la perspective: suivie de Notes et Additions (1774) à la perspective affranchie de l'embarras du plan géométral (1759). Trans. Jeanne Peiffer. Paris: Cedic, 1987.

Le Corbusier.
The Decorative Art of Today. Trans. James I. Dunnett. Cambridge, Mass.: MIT Press, 1987.

Le Corbusier.
The Modulor 1 and 2. Trans. Peter de Francia and Anna Bostock. Cambridge, Mass.: Harvard University Press, 1980.

Le Corbusier.
New World of Space. New York: Reynal and Hitchcock, 1948.

Le Corbusier.
Oeuvre complète, 1910–1965. 8 vols. Zurich: Les Éditions d'Architecture, 1946–1970.

Le Corbusier.
Poème de l'angle droit. Paris: Éditions Verve, 1955.

Le Corbusier.
Precisions on the Present State of Architecture and City Planning. Trans. Edith Schreiber. Cambridge, Mass.: MIT Press, 1991.

Le Corbusier.
Towards a New Architecture. Trans. Frederick Etchells. London: Architectural Press, 1946.

Le Corbusier.
Vers une architecture. Paris: G. Crès, 1923.

Le Corbusier, Architect of the Century.
Ed. Susan Ferleger Raeburn with Muriel Walker. London: Arts Council of Great Britain, 1987.

Le Corbusier Archives.
15 vols. New York: Garland, 1982–1985.

Le Corbusier's Firminy Church.
Ed. Kenneth Frampton and Sylvia Kolbowski. Catalog no. 14, Institute for Architecture and Urban Studies. New York: Rizzoli, 1981.

Le Corbusier Sketchbooks.
4 vols. Cambridge, Mass.: MIT Press, 1981.

Leibniz, Gottfried Wilhelm von.
Monadology and Other Philosophical Essays. Trans. Paul Schrecker. Indianapolis: Bobbs-Merrill, 1965.

Leibniz, Gottfried Wilhelm von.
New Essays on Human Understanding. Ed. and trans. Peter Remnant and Jonathan Bennett. Cambridge: Cambridge University Press, 1981.

Leibniz, Gottfried Wilhelm von.
"Unicum opticae, catoptricae, and dioptricae principium." In *Acta eruditorum.* Leipzig, 1682.

León, J. J.
Retrato del Templo de Solomón. Middelburg, 1642.

Leroy, Charles François Antoine.
Traité de stéréotomie, comprenant les applications de la géométrie descriptive, la théorie des ombres, la perspective linéaire, la gnomonique, la coup des pierres et la charpente. 2 vols. Paris: Gauthiers-Villars, 1870.

Levin, David Michael.
The Body's Recollection of Being. London: Routledge and Kegan Paul, 1985.

Levin, David Michael.
The Opening of Vision. New York: Routledge, 1988.

Levin, David Michael, ed.
Modernity and the Hegemony of Vision. Berkeley: University of California Press, 1993.

Lindberg, David C.
The Beginnings of Western Science. Chicago: University of Chicago Press, 1992.

Lindberg, David C.
"Medieval Latin Theories of the Speed of Light." In *Romer et la vitesse de la lumière.* CNRS. Paris: Vrin, 1978.

Lindberg, David C.
"The Science of Optics." In *Science in the Middle Ages.* Ed. D. C. Lindberg. Chicago: University of Chicago Press, 1978.

Lindberg, David C.
Theories of Vision from Al-Kindi to Kepler. Chicago: University of Chicago Press, 1976.

Lindberg, David C., and Geoffrey Cantor.
The Discourse of Light from the Middle Ages to the Enlightenment. Intro. Robert S. Westman. Los Angeles: Castle Press, 1985.

Lissitzky, El.
"K. und Pangeometrie." In *Europa-Almanach*. Ed. Carl Einstein and Paul Westheim. Potsdam: Gustav Kiepenheurer Verlag, 1925.

Lomazzo, Giovanni Paolo.
Idea del tempio della pittura di Gio. Paolo Lomazzo pittore. Nella quale egli discorre dell'origine, & fondamento delle cose contenute nel suo trattato dell'arte della pittura. Milan: Per Paolo Gottardo Pontio, 1590.

Lomazzo, Giovanni Paolo.
A Tracte containing the artes of curious paintinge carvinge and buildinge. Trans. R. Haydoke. Oxford: Joseph Barnes, 1598. Reprint, Franbourgh: Gregg Press, 1970.

Lomazzo, Giovanni Paolo.
Trattato dell'arte della pittura, scoltura, et architettura di Gio. Paolo Lomazzo Milanese Pittore diviso in sette libri. 2d ed. Milan: Appresso Paolo Gottardo Pontio, 1585. 1st ed. is 1584.

Lotz, Wolfgang.
Studies in Italian Renaissance Architecture. Cambridge, Mass.: MIT Press, 1977.

Lowry, Bates.
Renaissance Architecture. New York: Braziller, 1971.

Lucretius.
On the Nature of Things. Trans. J. H. Martinband. New York: Ungar, 1965.

Madec, Philippe.
Boullée. Paris: Fernand Hazan, 1986.

Malebranche, Nicolas de.
De la recherche de la Vérité. Paris: Michel David, 1721.

Malebranche, Nicolas de.
Entretiens sur la métaphysique. 2 vols. Paris: Michel David, 1711.

Malebranche, Nicolas de.
Réflexions sur la prémotion physique. Paris: Michel David, 1715.

Malton, Thomas.
An Appendix or Second Part, to the Compleat Treatise on Perspective, containing a brief history of Perspective, from the earliest and most Authentic accounts of it, down to the eighteenth century, when it first began to flourish in England. In which, the methods of Practice, used by the ancients, are exemplified and compared with those in use now. Military Perspective, Bird's Eye Views &. . . . The applications

of Perspective to Scenery, also to a Ship, and in Landscape. Projection of Curved surfaces, with other distortions, or anamorphoses. Inverse Perspective; also, the Doctrine or reflection, on plane Mirrors. London: printed for the Author, 1783.

Malton, Thomas.
A compleat treatise on perspective, in theory and practice: on the true principles of Dr. Brook Taylor: made clear, in theory, by various moveable schemes, and diagrams; and reduced to practice shewing how to delineate all kinds of regular objects, by rule. The theory and projection of shadows, by sun-shine, and by candle-light. The effects of reflected Light, on objects; Their reflected images, on the surface of water, and on Polished, Plane surfaces, in all positions. Keeping, aireal Perspective, &c. . . . Containing diagrams, views, and original designs, in architecture, &c. . . . all originals invented, delineated, and, great part, engraved by the author, Thomas Malton. London: Printed for the author, and sold by Messrs. Robson et al., 1776.

Manetti, Antonio.
Vita di Filippo Brunelleschi. Ed. D. Robertis and G. Tanturli. Milan: Il Polifilo, 1976.

Marino, Angela Guidoni.
"Il colonnato di piazza S. Pietro: dall'architettura obliqua di Caramuel al 'Classicismo' Berniniano." *Palladio* 23.1–4 (1973): 81–120.

Marolois, Samuel.
Opera Mathematica: ou Oeuvres mathématiques traictons de géométrie, perspective, architecture et fortifications. Amsterdam: I. Ianssen, 1614.

Marolois, Samuel.
Perspective contenant la Théorie Pratique et Instruction Fondamentelle d'icelle par Samuel Marolois. Amsterdam: Jean Jansson, 1628. 1st ed. is The Hague, 1614.

Martini, Francesco di Giorgio.
Trattati de architettura ingegneria e arte militare. 2 vols. Milan: Il Polifilo, 1967.

Matteoli, A., ed.
"Macchie di sole e pittura: Carteggio L. Cigoli–G. Galilei." *Bollettino della Accademia degli Euteleti* 32 (1959): 52–53.

Mathew, Gervase.
Byzantine Aesthetics. London: John Murray, 1963.

Merleau-Ponty, Maurice.
Phenomenology of Perception. Trans. Colin Smith. London: Routledge and Kegan Paul, 1962.

Merleau-Ponty, Maurice.
The Primacy of Perception, and Other Essays on Phenomenological Psychology, the Philosophy of Art, History, and Politics. Ed. Richard C. McCleary. Evanston, Ill.: Northwestern University Press, 1964.

Merleau-Ponty, Maurice.
Sense and Non-Sense. Trans. Hubert L. Dreyfus and Patricia Allen Dreyfus. Evanston, Ill.: Northwestern University Press, 1964.

Merleau-Ponty, Maurice.
Signs. Trans. Richard C. McCleary. Evanston, Ill.: Northwestern University Press, 1964.

Merleau-Ponty, Maurice.
The Structure of Behavior. Trans. Alden L. Fisher. Boston: Beacon Press, 1963.

Merleau-Ponty, Maurice.
The Visible and the Invisible. Ed. Claude Lefort. Trans. Alphonso Linghis. Evanston, Ill.: Northwestern University Press, 1968.

Mersenne, P. Marin.
Correspondance. 17 vols. Ed. Cornelis de Waard with René-Pintard. Paris: Beauchesne, 1932–1988.

Mersenne, P. Marin.
Harmonie Universelle. 3 vols. Paris: Éditions du Centre national de la recherche scientifique, 1965. 1st ed. is Paris, 1636.

Mersenne, Marin.
L'Optique et la Catoptrique du Reverend Père Mersenne. Nouvellement mise en Lumière après la mort de l'Autheur. Paris: Chez la veufe F. Langlois, dit Chartres, 1651.

Merwood, Joanna.
"Concrete Blonde: A Probe into Negative Space Where Mysteries Are Created." In *Chora: Intervals in the Philosophy of Architecture.* Ed. Alberto Pérez-Gómez and Stephen Parcell. Vol. 2. Montreal: McGill-Queen's University Press, 1996.

Miller, Naomi.
"Euclides redivivus: A Hypothesis on a Proposition." *Gazette des Beaux-Arts* 6 (May/June 1993): 213–226.

Millon, Henry A., and Vittorio Magnago Lampugnani, eds.
The Renaissance from Brunelleschi to Michelangelo—The Representation of Architecture. Exhibition catalog. Venice: Bompiani, 1994.

Monge, Gaspar.
Géométrie descriptive. 2d ed. Paris, 1798. 1st ed. is 1795.

Monte, Guidobaldo del.
Perspectivæ libri sex. Pesaro: Apud Hieronymum Concordiam, 1600.

Montucla, Jean Etienne.
Histoire des mathématiques: dans laquelle on ren compte de leurs progres depuis leur origine jusqu'à nos jours, ou l'on expose le tableau et le développement des principales découvertes dans toutes les parties des mathématiques, les contestations qui se sont élevées entre les mathématiciens, et les principaux traits de la vie des plus célèbres par J. F. [sic] Montucla. 4 vols. 2d ed. Paris: Chez Henri Agasse, an VII [1798 or 1799]–an X [1801–1802].

Moore, Richard.
"Alchemical and Mythical Themes in the 'Poème de l'angle droit.'" *Oppositions* 19 (1980): 110–139.

Moxon, Joseph.
Practical Perspective; Or Perspective made easie. Teaching By the Opticks, How to Delineate all Bodies, Buildings, or Landskips, &c. By the Catoptricks, How to Delineate confused Appearences, so as when seen in a Mirror or Pollisht Body of any intended shape, the reflection shall shew a Designe. By the Dioptricks, How to draw parts of many Figures into one, when seen through a Glass or Christal cut into many Faces. Usefull for all Painters, Engravers Architects, &c. and all others that are any waies inclined to Speculatory Ingenuity. London: Printed by Joseph Moxom, at the Signe of Atlas, 1670.

Müller, Claudia.
"Ferdinando Galli Bibienas "Scene di nuova invenzione." *Zeitschrift für Kunstgeschichte* 49 (1986): 356–375.

Newton, Isaac.
Correspondence. 7 vols. Cambridge: Published for the Royal Society at the University Press, 1959–1977.

Newton, Isaac.
The Optical Papers of Isaac Newton. Vol. 1, *The Optical Lectures, 1670–1672.* Ed. Alan E. Shapiro. Cambridge: Cambridge University Press, 1984.

Newton, Isaac.
Opticks, or a Treatise of the Reflections, Refractions, Inflections and Colours of Light. 4th ed. London, 1730. Reprint, New York: Dover Publications, 1952.

Newton, Isaac.

Philosophiae naturalis principia mathematica: Mathematical Principles of Natural Philosophy. Motte's trans. of 1729 revised and supplied with an historical appendix by Florian Cajori. *Sir Isaac Newton's Mathematical Principles of Natural Philosophy and His System of the World.* Berkeley: University of California Press, 1934. 1st ed. is London, 1687. Also 3d ed., [first title above], ed. Alexandre Koyré and I. Bernard Cohen, 2 vols. Cambridge, Mass.: Harvard University Press, 1972.

Nicholas of Cusa.

The Vision of God. New York: Frederick Ungar Publishing, 1928.

Nicéron, Jean-François.

La Perspective Curieuse ou Magie Artificiele des Effets Merveilleux. De L'Optique, par la vision directe. La Catoptrique, par la réflexion des miroirs plats, cylindriques & coniques. La Dioptrique, par la réfraction des Crystaux. Dans laquelle, outre un abbregé & méthode générale de la perspective commune, réduite en pratique sur les cinq corps réguliers, est encore enseignée la façon de faire & construire toute sortes de figures difformes, qui estant veuës de leur poinct paroissent dans une juste proportion: le tout par des pratiques si familières, que le moins versez en la Géométrie s'en pourront servir avec le seul compas & la règle. Oeuvre très-utile aux Peintres, Architectes, Graveurs, Sculpteurs, & à tous autres qui se servent du dessin en leurs ouvrages. Par le Père F. Iean François Nicéron Parisien de l'Ordre des Minimes. Paris: Chez Pierre Billaine, 1638.

Nicéron, Jean-François.

Thaumaturgus Opticus (Latin trans. of *La Perspective Curieuse*). Paris, 1646.

Nietzsche, Friedrich.

Human, All Too Human: A Book for Free Spirits. Trans. R. J. Hollingdale. Cambridge: Cambridge University Press, 1986.

Nietzsche, Friedrich.

Untimely Meditations. Trans. R. J. Hollingdale. Cambridge: Cambridge University Press, 1983.

Nuti, Lucia.

"The Perspective Plan in the Sixteenth Century: The Invention of a Representational Language." *Art Bulletin* 76 (1994): 105–128.

Oechslin, Werner.

"Le group des 'Piranèsiens' français (1740–1750): Un renouveau artistique dans la culture romaine." In *Piranèse et les français.* Ed. G. Brunel. Rome: Edizioni dell'Elefante, 1976.

Oechslin, Werner.
"Osservazioni su Guarino Guarini e Juan Caramuel de Lobkowitz." In *Guarino Guarini e l'Internazionalità del Barocco*. Vol. 1. Turin: Accademia delle Scienze, 1970.

Oresme, Nicolas.
Nicolas Oresme and the Marvels of Nature: De Causis Mirabilium. Ed. and trans. B. Hansen. Toronto: Pontifical Institute of Medieval Studies, 1985.

Oresme, Nicolas.
Nicolas Oresme and the Medieval Geometry of Qualities and Motions. Trans. and comm. M. Clagett. Madison: University of Wisconsin Press, 1968.

Ozanam, M. (Jacques).
La perspective théorique et practique: où l'on enseigne la manière de mettre toutes sortes d'objets en perspective, & d'en représenter les ombres causées par le soleil ou par une petite lumière [tirée du cours de mathématique de M. Ozanam]. Paris: Chez Claude-Antoine Jombert, 1769.

Ozanam, Jacques.
Récréations mathématiques et physiques qui contiennent les problèmes & les questions les plus remarquables. 4 vols. Paris: Jombert, 1778.

Pacioli, Luca.
Divine proportion: Œuvre nécessaire à tous les esprits perspicaces et curieux, où chacun de ceux qui aiment à étudier la Philosophie, la Perspective, la Peinture, la Sculpture, l'Architecture, la Musique et les autres disciplines Mathématiques, trouvera une très délicate, subtile et admirable doctrine, et se délectera des diverses questions touchant une très secrète science. Trans. G. Duchesne and M. Giraud with M. T. Sarrade. Paris: Librarie du Compagnonnage, 1980. 1st Latin ed. is Venice, 1509.

Palladio, Andrea.
I quattro libri dell'architettura. Venice, 1570.

Panofsky, Erwin.
Albrecht Dürer. Princeton: Princeton University Press, 1945.

Panofsky, Erwin.
Perspective as Symbolic Form (1927). Trans. C. S. Wood. New York: Zone Books, 1991.

Pappus of Alexandria.
The Commentary of Pappus on Book X of Euclid's Elements. Trans. and ed. W. Thomson and G. Junge. Cambridge, Mass.: Harvard University Press, 1930.

Parcell, Stephen.
"The Metaphoric Architecture of the Diorama." In *Chora: Intervals in the Philosophy of Architecture.* Ed. Alberto Pérez-Gómez and Stephen Parcell. Vol. 2. Montreal: McGill-Queen's University Press, 1996.

Parcell, Stephen.
"The Momentary Modern Magic of the Panorama." In *Chora: Intervals in the Philosophy of Architecture.* Ed. Alberto Pérez-Gómez and Stephen Parcell. Vol. 1. Montreal: McGill-Queen's University Press, 1994.

Paris, Jean.
Painting and Linguistics. Pittsburgh: Carnegie-Mellon University Press, 1975.

Parsey, Arthur.
Perspective Rectified. London, 1836.

Parsey, Arthur.
The Science of Vision or Natural Perspective! London, 1840.

Pavlovitch Zoubov, Vassili.
"Vitruve et ses commentateurs du XVIe siècles." In *La science au seizième siècle.* Paris: Herman, 1960.

Paz, Octavio.
The Bow and the Lyre: The Poem, the Poetic Revelation, Poetry, and History. Trans. Ruth L. C. Simms. Austin: University of Texas Press, 1991.

Peckham, John.
John Peckham and the Science of Optics: Perspecta communis. Ed. and trans. D. C. Lindberg. Madison: University of Wisconsin Press, 1970.

Pèlerin, Jean (Viator).
"De artificiali perspectiva." In *On the Rationalization of Sight, with an Examination of Three Renaissance Texts on Perspective,* by W. M. Ivins Jr. New York: Da Capo Press, 1973. Both the 1st ed. (Toul, 1505) and the 2d ed. (Toul, 1509) are included.

Pérez-Gómez, Alberto.
"Abstraction in Modern Architecture." In *Re-presentation.* Ed. Charles Hay.Via 9 (New York: Rizzoli, 1988).

Pérez-Gómez, Alberto.
Architecture and the Crisis of Modern Science. Cambridge, Mass.: MIT Press, 1983.

Pérez-Gómez, Alberto.
"Chora: The Space of Architectural Representation." In *Chora: Intervals in the Philosophy of Architecture.* Ed. Alberto Pérez-Gómez and Stephen Parcell. Vol. 1. Montreal: McGill-Queen's University Press, 1994.

Pérez-Gómez, Alberto.
"The Myth of Dedalus." *AA Files* 10 (1985): 49–52.

Pérez-Gómez, Alberto.
Polyphilo, or The Dark Forest Revisited. Cambridge, Mass.: MIT Press, 1992.

Pérez-Gómez, Alberto, and Louise Pelletier.
Anamorphosis, an Annotated Bibliography with Special Reference to Architectural Representation. Fontanus Monograph Series. Montreal: McGill University Libraries, 1995.

Pérez-Gómez, Alberto, and Louise Pelletier.
"Architectural Representation beyond Perspectivism." *Perspecta* 27 (1992): 21–39.

Perouse de Montclos, Jean-Marie.
Étienne-Louis Boullée (1728–1799), de l'architecture classique à l'architecture révolutionnaire. Paris: Arts et Métiers Graphiques, 1969.

Perrault, Claude.
Ordonnance des cinq espèces de colonnes selon la méthode des anciens. Paris: Coignard, 1683.

Perrault, Claude.
Ordonnance for the Five Kinds of Columns after the Method of the Ancients. Trans. Indra Kagis McEwen. Intro. Alberto Pérez-Gómez. Santa Monica: Getty Center for the History of Art and the Humanities, 1993.

Perret, Jacques.
Des Fortifications et artifices, architecture et perspective de Iaques Perret. Paris, 1601.

Piel, Friedrich.
"Anamorphosis and Architecture." In *Festschrift Wolfgang Braunfels.* Tübingen: Wasmuth, 1977.

Piero della Francesca.
De prospectiva pingendi Piero della Francesca. Florence: Casa Editrice le lettere, 1984.

Pillet, Jules Jean.
Traité de géométrie descriptive. Paris: C. Delagrave, 1887.

Pillet, Jules Jean.
Traité de perspective Lineare précédé du tracé des ombres usuelles (rayon a 45 degres) et suivi du rendu dans le dessin d'architecture et dans le dessin de machines. Texte et dessins par Jules Pillet, Cours de sciences appliquées aux arts. Paris: C. Delagrave, 1885.

Plato.
The Republic. Trans. P. Shorey. 2 vols. Loeb Classical Library. 1935–1937. Reprint, London: W. Heinemann; Cambridge, Mass.: Harvard University Press, 1982.

Plato.
The Sophist. Trans. H. N. Fowler. Loeb Classical Library. Cambridge, Mass.: Harvard University Press, 1921.

Plato.
Timaeus and Critias. Trans. H. D. P. Lee. Harmondsworth: Penguin Books, 1965.

Plotinus.
Essay on the Beautiful. Trans. T. Taylor. Edmonds, Wash.: Alexandrian Press, 1985.

Pollak, Martha.
Military Architecture, Cartography, and Representation of the Early Modern European City. Chicago: Newberry Library, 1991.

Pomodoro, Giovanni.
Geometria Prattica Tratta dagl'Elementi d'Euclide et altri Auttori da Giovanni Pomo doro Venetiano Mathematico eccellentissimo descritta et Dichiarata da Giovanni Scala Matematico. . . . Opera non meno Uttile che necessaria a Misuratori di terreni, di fabriche, et altri simmili ma in' oltre ancora a, Geografhi, Cosmografi, Architetti Civili, et Militari a' Bombardiere, Soldati priuati, a Capitani, Mastri di Campo, a qual si Voglia altra persona Virtuosa. Rome: Apresso Stefano de Paulin, 1599.

Poncelet, Jean-Victor.
Traité des propriétés projectives des figures; ouvrage utile a ceux qui s'occupent des applications de la géométrie descriptive et d'opérations géométriques sur le terrain. 2d ed. Paris: Gauthier-Villars, 1865–1866. 1st ed. is 1822.

Porta, Giambattista della.
De refractione optices parte: libri novem. Naples: Ex Officina Horatii Saluiani, Apud Io. Jacobum Carlimum, & Antonium Pacem, 1593.

Porta, Giambattista della.
Natural Magick. Trans. T. Young and S. Speed. London, 1658. Reprint, New York: Basic Books, 1957. 1st Latin ed. is Naples, 1558.

Porterfield, William.

A treatise on the eye, the manner and phenomena of vision. 2 vols. Edinburgh: A. Miller, 1759.

Poudra, Noël Germinal.

Oeuvre de Desargues . . . précédée d'une nouvelle biographie de Desargues suivie de l'analyse des ouvrages de Bosse. 2 vols. Paris: Leiber, 1864.

Pozzo, Andrea.

Rules and Examples of Perspective Proper for Painters and Architects, etc. In English and Latin: Containing a most easie and expeditious Method to Delineate in Perspective All Designs relating to Architecture, After a New Manner, Wholly free from the Confusion of Occult Lines. By That Great Master Thereof, Andrea Pozzo, Soc. Jef . . . Sturt. London: Printed by Benj. Motte, 1707. 1st ed. is Rome, 1693; 1st English trans. is London, 1700.

489

Proclus.

A Commentary on the First Book of Euclid's Elements. Trans. G. R. Norrow. Princeton: Princeton University Press, 1970.

Proclus.

The Elements of Theology: a Revised Text with Translation. Ed. and trans. E. R. Dodds. Oxford: Clarendon Press, 1963.

Ptolemy, Claudius.

Almagest. Trans. G. J. Toomer. London: Duckworth, 1984.

Ptolemy, Claudius.

Cosmographia: Roma, 1478. Trans. R. A. Skelton. Amsterdam: Theatrum Orbis Terrarum, 1966. Text in English and Latin.

Ptolemy, Claudius.

Geographia: Basle, 1540. Ed. S. Munster. Intro. R. A. Skelton. Amsterdam: Theatrum Orbis Terrarum, 1966. Text in English and Latin.

Ptolemy, Claudius.

The Geography. Ed. and trans. E. L. Stevenson. Intro. J. Fischer. 1932. Reprint, New York: Dover Publications, 1991.

Quaglio, Johann Maria von.

Praktische Anleitung zur Perspektiv: mit Anwendung auf die Baukunst. Munich: In der lithographischen Kunst-Anstalt, 1811.

Ramírez, Juan Antonio, ed.

Dios, Arquitecto, J. B. Villalpando y el Templo de Salomón. Madrid: Ediciones Siruela, 1992.

Reichlin, Bruno.
"'Une Petite Maison' on Lake Leman: The Perret-Corbusier Controversy." In *Lotus* 4 (1988).

Reynolds, Robert, and Thomas Zummer, eds.
Crash: Nostalgia for the Absence of Cyberspace. New York: Thread Waxing Space, 1994.

Ricci, Corrado.
Bibiena, Architetti Teatrali. Milan: Alfieri & Lacroix, 1915.

Richter, Jean-Paul.
The Literary Works of Leonardo da Vinci. 2 vols. Berkeley: University of California Press, 1977.

Ricoeur, Paul.
The Conflict of Interpretations: Essays in Hermeneutics. Ed. Don Ihde. Evanston, Ill.: Northwestern University Press, 1974.

Ricoeur, Paul.
History and Truth. Trans. Charles A. Kelbley. Evanston, Ill.: Northwestern University Press, 1965.

Rieger, Christian.
Universae architecturae civilis elementa brevibus recentiorum observationibus illustrata. Vienna, Prague, and Trieste: Typis Ioannis Tomae Trattner, 1756.

Rieger, Christian.
Universae architecturae militaris elementa brevibus recentiorum observationibus illustrata. Vienna, Prague, and Trieste: Typis Ioannis Tomae Trattner, 1758.

Rodler, Hieronymus.
Eyn schön nützlich büchlin und underweisung der kunst des Messens, mit dem Zirckel, Richtscheidt oder Linial. Zu nutz allen kunstliebhabern, fürnemlich den Malern, Bildhawern, Goldschmiden . . . auch allen andern, so sich der kunst des Messens (Perspectiva zu latin gnant) zugebrauchen lust haben. Pfalz-Simmern: Getruckt unnd volnendet [sic] in[n] verlegu[n]g Hieronimi Rodlers, 1531.

Romano, Bartolomeo.
Proteo Militare di Bartolomeo Romano Diviso in tre Libri. Naples: Gio Iacomo Carlino & Antonio Pace, 1595.

Ronchi, Vasco.
The Nature of Light: An Historical Survey. Trans. V. Barocas. London: Heinemann, 1970.

Ronchi, Vasco.
Scritti di ottica. Contains an intro. by Ronchi and essential tracts in the history of optics by Lucretius, Leonardo, G. Rucellai, G. Cardano, D. Barbaro, G. Fracastoro, F. Maurolico, G. B. della Porta, Galileo, F. Sizi, E. Torricelli, F. M. Grimaldi, and G. B. Amici. Milan: Edizioni Il Polifilo, 1968.

Rondelet, Jean Baptiste.
Traité théorique et pratique de l'art de bâtir. Paris, 1802.

Rossi, Paolo.
Philosophy, Technology, and the Arts in the Early Modern Era. New York: Harper and Row, 1970.

Ruskin, John.
The Elements of Perspective: Arranged for the Use of Schools and Intended to Be Read in Connexion with the First Three Books of Euclid. London: Smith, Elder, 1859.

Sarkis, Hashim, and Pegor Papazian.
"Perspective, Its Epistemic Grounding, and the Sky: An Outline for a Research Project." *Harvard Architecture Review* 9 (1993): 28–41.

Sarton, George.
Ancient Science and Modern Civilization. New York: Harper, 1959.

Sassi, Maria Michela.
Le Teorie della Percezione in Democrito. Florence: La Nuova Italia, 1978.

Scamozzi, Vincenzo.
L'Idea della Architettura Universale. 2 vols. Venice, 1615. Reprint, Bologna: Arnaldo Forni editore, 1982.

Schneider, Mark.
"Girard Desargues, the Architectural and Perspective Geometry: A Study in the Rationalization of Figures." Ph.D. diss., Virginia Polytechnic Institute, 1983.

Schott, Gaspar.
Magia Universalis naturæ et artis, Sive Recondita Naturalium & Artificialium rerum Scientia, cujus Ope per variam Applicationem . . . Opus Quadripartitum. Continet Pars. I. Optica II. Acoustica. III. Mathematica. IV. Physica. Bamberg: sumpt. Joh. Martini Schönwetteri, 1659, 1674–1677.

Schott, Gaspar.
Physica curiosa; sive, Mirabilia naturae et artis libris XII. 2d ed. Wurzburg: Sumptibus Johannis Andreae Endteri & Wolfgangi Jun. Haeredum, excudebat Jobus Hertz typ., 1667.

Schübler, Johann Jakob.
Perspectiva Pes picturae. Das ist: Kurtze und leichte Verfassung der practicabelsten Regul, zur perspectivischen Zeichnungs-Kunst . . . *inventirt, gezeichnet und heraus gegeben: von Johann Jacob Schübler.* Nürnberg: [Jn] Verlag Johann Christoph Weigels, [Kunsthändlers], 1719–1720.

Scolari, Massimo.
"Elements for a History of Axonometry." *Architectural Design* 55.5–6 (1985): 73–78.

Serlio, Sebastiano.
The Five Bookes of Architecture. London, 1611. Reprint, New York: Dover Publications, 1982.

Serlio, Sebastiano.
Tutte l'opere d'architettura. [Libro 1–6] Il primo [–sexto] libro d'architettura di M. Sabastiano Serlio Bolognese. Venice: Per Cornelio de Nicolini da Sabbio a instantia de Marchio Sessa, 1551.

Serres, Michel.
"L'axe du cadran solaire." *Études françaises* 24.2 (1988): 35–52.

Siguret, Françoise.
L'oeil surpris: perception et représentation dans la première moitié du XVIIe siècle. Paris: Papers on French Seventeenth Century Literature, 1985.

Sirigatti, Lorenzo.
La pratica di prospettiva del cavaliere Lorenzo Sirigatti. Al Ferdinando Medici, granduca di Toscana. Venice: Per Girolamo Franceschi, 1596.

Sjöström, Ingrid.
Quadratura: Studies in Italian Ceiling Painting. Stockholm: University of Stockholm; distributed by Almqvist and Wiksell International, 1978.

Slakey, Thomas J.
"Aristotle on Sense Perception." *Philosophical Review* 70 (1961): 470–499.

Spilamberto, Giulio Troili da.
Paradossi per pratticare la prospettiva senza saperla: fiori, per facilitare l'intelligenza, frutti, per non operare alla cieca. Cognitioni necessarie à pittori, scultori, architetti, ed à qualunque si diletta di disegno dat' in luce da Givlio Troili da Spinlamberto, detto Paradosso. Bologna: Per G. Longhi, 1683.

Stevin, Simon.
Oeuvre Mathématique de Simon Stevin de Bruges. Où sont insérées les Mémoires Mathématiques, esquelles s'est exercé le Très-haut & Très-illustré Prince Maurice de Nassau. . . . Le tout revue, corrigé & augmenté par Albert Girard. Leiden: Bonaventure & Abraham Elsevier, 1634.

Stevin, Simon.
The Principal Works of Simon Stevin. 5 vols. Amsterdam: C. V. Swets & Zeitlinger, 1955.

Strabo.
The Geography of Strabo. Trans. H. L. Jones. 8 vols. London: W. Heinemann, 1917–1933.

Straker, Stephen.
Kepler's Optics: A Study in the Development of Seventeenth-Century Natural Philosophy. Ann Arbor: U.M.I. Research Press, 1984.

Struik, Dirk J.
The Land of Stevin and Huygens: A Sketch of Science and Technology in the Dutch Republic during the Golden Century. London: D. Reidel, 1981.

Summers, David.
Michelangelo and the Language of Art. Princeton: Princeton University Press, 1981.

Tachau, Katherine.
Vision and Certitude in the Age of Ockham. New York: E. J. Brill, 1988.

Tatarkiewicz, Wladyslaw.
History of Aesthetics. Ed. C. Barrett. Trans. R. M. Montgomery. 3 vols. Warsaw: Polish Scientific Publishers, 1970.

Taton, René.
The Beginnings of Modern Science, from 1450 to 1800. Trans. A. J. Pomerans. London: Thames and Hudson, 1964.

Taton, René.
Enseignement et diffusion des sciences en France au XVIIIe siècle. Paris: Herman, 1964.

Taton, René.
L'oeuvre mathématique de G. Desargues. Paris: Presses Universitaires de France, 1951.

Taussig, Michael.
Mimesis and Alterity. New York: Routledge, 1993.

Taylor, René.
"Architecture and Magic: Considerations on the *Idea* of the Escorial." In *Essays in the History of Architecture.* London: Phaidon, 1969.

Tesauro, Emanuele (1591–1675).
Il cannocchiale aristotelico. Turin, 1670. Reprint, Berlin: Gehlen, 1968.

Tobin, Richard.
"Ancient Perspective and Euclid's *Optics* (with appendices)." *Journal of the Warburg and Courtauld Institutes* 53 (1990): 14–41.

Tosca, Thomas, Vicente.
Compendio mathematico: en que se contienen todas las materias mas principales de las ciencias, que tratan de la cantidad que compuso el doctor Thomas Vicente Tosca. Madrid: Impr. de A. Marin, 1727.

Troili, Giulio.
See Spilamberto, Giulio Troili da.

Tsjui, Shigeru.
"Brunelleschi and the Camera Obscura: The Discovery of Pictorial Perspective." *Art History* 13 (1990): 276–292.

Vallée, Louis Léger.
Traité de la science du dessin: contenant la théorie générale des ombres, la perspective linéaire, la théorie générale des images d'optique, et la perspective aérienne appliquée au lavis: pour faire suite à la géométrie descriptive. 2 vols. Paris: Madame Courcier, Librairie pour les sciences, 1821.

Van Helden, Albert.
Measuring the Universe: Cosmic Dimensions from Aristarchus to Halley. Chicago: University of Chicago Press, 1985.

Vasari, Giorgio.
Lives of the Artists (1568). Trans. George Bull. London: Penguin Books, 1972. First ed. 1550.

Vasari, Giorgio.
"Vita di Filippo de Ser Brunellesco." In *Le Vite de' più eccellenti pittori, scultori et architettori cor. da molti errori.* Florence: Appresso i Giunti, 1568.

Vattimo, Gianni.
The End of Modernity: Nihilism and Hermeneutics in Post-modern Culture. Trans. Jon R. Snyder. Baltimore: John Hopkins University Press, 1988.

Vattimo, Gianni.
The Transparent Society. Trans. David Webb. Baltimore: John Hopkins University Press, 1992.

Veltman, Kim H., with Kenneth D. Keele.
Studies on Leonardo Da Vinci. Munich: Deutscher Kunstverlag, 1986.

Vescovini, Federici.
"Le questioni di perspettiva di Biagio Pelacani." *Rinascimento* 1 (1961): 242–243.

Vescovini, Federici.
Studi sulla prospettiva medievale. Turin: Stamperia Editoriale Rattero, 1965.

Vesely, Dalibor.
"Architecture and the conflict of representation." *AA Files* 8 (Spring 1985): 21–39.

Vico, Giambattista.
The New Science. Trans. T. G. Bergin and M. H. Fisch. Ithaca: Cornell University Press, 1970.

Viel, Charles-François.
Décadence de l'Architecture à la Fin du 18ème Siècle. Paris, 1800.

Viel de Saint-Maux, Charles-François.
Lettres sur l'architecture. Paris, 1787.

Vignola, Jacopo Barozzi da, and Ignazio Danti.
Le due regole della prospettiva pratica di M. Iacomo Barozzi da Vignola; con i comentarij del r.p.m. Egnatio Danti. Rome: Per Francesco Zannetti, 1583.

Vignola, Jacopo Barozzi da, and Ignazio Danti.
Regole della Prospettiva Pratica di M. Iacomo Barozzi da Vignola con i comentari del Rev. Padre M Egnatio Danti dell'ordine de' Predicatori Professore di Mathematica nell'Università di Bologna. Ora in questa quarta Edizione diligentemente migliorata. Venice, 1743. Reprint, Bologna: Arnaldo Forni Editore, 1978.

Villalpando, Juan Bautista.
El Templo de Salomón, Comentarios a la Profecía de Ezequiel. Ed. Juan Antonio Ramírez. Trans. José Luis Oliver Domingo. Madrid: Ediciones Siruela, 1991.

Virilio, Paul.
Guerre et Cinéma: Logistique de la perception. Paris: Éditions de l'étoile, 1984.

Virloys, M. C. F. Roland Le.
Dictionnaire d'Architecture, Civile, Militaire et Navale. Paris: Chez les Libraires Associées, 1770.

Vitruvius [Marcus Vitruvius Pollio].
De architectura. Trans. Cesare di Lorenzo Cesariano. Como, 1521. Reprint, New York: B. Blom, 1968.

Vitruvius.
De architectura (On architecture). Ed. and trans. Frank Granger. 2 vols. Loeb Classical Library. London: W. Heinemann; Cambridge, Mass.: Harvard University Press, 1934.

Vitruvius.
I dieci libri dell'architettura di M. Vitruvio; tradotti et commentati da Monsig. Daniel Barbaro. Venice: Appresso Francesco de'Franceschi Senese, 1584.

Vitruvius.
Les dix livres d'architecture de Vitruve: corrigez et traduits nouvellement en françois, avec des notes & des figures. Seconde edition reveuë, corrigé, & augmentée par M. Perrault. Paris: Chez Jean Baptiste Coignard, 1684. Reprint, Brussels: Pierre Mardaga éditeur, 1979.

Vitruvius.
Les dix livres d'architecture. Traduction intégrale de Claude Perrault, 1673, revue et corrigée sur les textes latins et présentée par André Dalmas. Paris: Editions Errance, 1986.

Vitruvius.
Les dix livres d'architecture. Paris: Les Belles Lettres, 1991.

Vitruvius.
The Ten Books on Architecture. Trans. Morris Hicky Morgan. 1914. Reprint, New York: Dover Publications, 1960.

Vredemann de Vries, Jan.
Perspective: c'est à dire, Le très renommé art du poinct oculaire d'une veuë dedans où travers regardante . . . inventé par Ioan Vredeman Frison; Henric. Hondius sculpsit. Lyon: H. Hondius, 1604–1605.

Wade, Nicholas J.
Visual Perception. New York: Routledge, 1991.

Wade, Nicholas J., ed.
Brewster and Wheatstone on Vision. London: Academic Press, 1983.

Wheelock, Arthur K., Jr.
Perspective, Optics, and Delft Artists around 1650. New York: Garland, 1977.

White, John.
The Birth and Rebirth of Pictorial Space. New York: Yoseloff, 1958.

Witelo.
"Perspectiva." In *Opticae Thesaurus Alhazeni Arabis libri septem.* Intro. D. C. Lindberg, ed. F. Risner. Reprint, New York: Johnson Reprint, 1972. 1st ed. is Basel, 1572.

Witelo.
Perspectiva XXVIII Books Two and Three. Trans. Sabetai Unguru. Wroclaw: Ossdineum, 1991.

Witelo.

Perspectiva XXIII Book Five. Trans. A. M. Smith. Wroclaw: Ossdineum; Warsaw: Polish Academy of Sciences Press, 1983.

Witelo.

Witelonis Perspectiva liber primus = Book I of Witelo's Perspectiva. Trans. Sabetai Unguru. Wroclaw: Polish Academy of Sciences Press, 1977.

Wittkower, Rudolf.

Architectural Principles in the Age of Humanism. London: Alec Tiranti, 1952.

Wittkower, Rudolf, and I. B. Jaffe, eds.

Baroque Art: The Jesuit Contribution. New York: Fordham University Press, 1972.

Wolin, Richard.

Walter Benjamin: An Aesthetic of Redemption. 2d ed. Berkeley: University of California Press, 1994.

Wright, Thomas.

An Original Theory or New Hypothesis of the Universe, Founded upon the Laws of Nature, and Solving by Mathematical Principles The General Phænomena of the Visible Creation; and Particularly The Via Lactea. London: H. Chapele, 1750. Facsimile reprint. Ed. M. A. Hoskin. London: Macdonald, 1971.

Yates, Frances.

Giordono Bruno and the Hermetic Tradition. London: Routledge and Kegan Paul, 1964.

Zajonc, Arthur.

Catching the Light: The Entwined History of Light and Mind. New York: Bantam, 1993.

Zanotti, Eustachio (1709–1782).

Trattato teorico-pratico di prospettiva di Eustachio Zanotti. Bologna: Nella Stamperia di Lelio dalla Volpe, 1766.

Index of Names

Page numbers in italics indicate illustrations.

| N |

| P |